New C

CHARLES TOMLINSON was b
studied at Cambridge with
University of Bristol from
published many collections of
and translation, and has edited the *Oxford Book of Verse in Translation* (1980). His poetry has won international recognition and has received many prizes in Europe and the United States, including the 1993 Bennett Award from the *Hudson Review*; the New Criterion Poetry Prize, 2002; the Premio Internazionale di Poesia Ennio Flaiano, 2001; and the Premio Internazionale di Poesia Attilio Bertolucci, 2004. He is an Honorary Fellow of the American Academy of the Arts and Sciences and of the Modern Language Association. Charles Tomlinson was made a CBE in 2001 for his contribution to literature.

Also by Charles Tomlinson from Carcanet / Oxford Poets

Poetry
Annunciations
The Door in the Wall
Selected Poems
The Vineyard Above the Sea
Skywriting
Cracks in the Universe

Prose
American Essays
Metamorphoses: Poetry and Translation

CHARLES TOMLINSON

New Collected Poems

Oxford*Poets*

CARCANET

First published in Great Britain in 2009 by
Carcanet Press Limited
Alliance House
Cross Street
Manchester M2 7AQ

A CIP catalogue record for this book is available from the British Library
ISBN 978 1 903039 94 6

The publisher acknowledges financial assistance from Arts Council England

Typeset by XL Publishing Services, Tiverton
Printed and bound in England by SRP Ltd, Exeter

to Brenda

to Brenda

Contents

A Peopled Landscape (1963)

The Way of a World (1969)

Written on Water (1972)

The Way In and Other Poems (1974)

The Shaft (1978)

The Flood (1981)

Notes from New York and Other Poems (1984)

The Return (1987)

Annunciations (1989)

The Door in the Wall (1992)

Jubilation (1995)

The Vineyard Above the Sea (1999)

Skywriting (2003)

Cracks in the Universe (2006)

RELATIONS AND CONTRARIES

1951

Poem

Wakening with the window over fields
To the coin-clear harness-jingle as a float
Clips by, and each succeeding hoof fall, now remote,
Breaks clean and frost-sharp on the unstopped ear.

The hooves describe an arabesque on space,
A dotted line in sound that falls and rises
As the cart goes by, recedes, turns to retrace
Its way back through the unawakened village.

And space vibrates, enlarges with the sound;
Though space is soundless, yet creates
From very soundlessness a ground
To counterstress the lilting hoof fall as it breaks.

THE NECKLACE

1955, 1966

The necklace is a carving not a kiss
Wallace Stevens

Aesthetic

Reality is to be sought, not in concrete,
But in space made articulate:
The shore, for instance,
Spreading between wall and wall;
The sea-voice
Tearing the silence from the silence.

Venice

Cut into by doors
The morning assumes night's burden,
The houses assemble in tight cubes.

From the palace flanking the waterfront
She is about to embark, but pauses.
Her dress is a veil of sound
Extended upon silence.

Under the bridge,
Contained by the reflected arc
A tunnel of light
Effaces walls, water, horizon.

Floating upon its own image
A cortège of boats idles through space.

Nine Variations in a Chinese Winter Setting

I
Warm flute on the cold snow
Lays amber in sound.

II

Against brushed cymbal
Grounds yellow on green,
Amber on tinkling ice.

III

The sage beneath the waterfall
Numbers the blessing of a flute;
Water lets down
Exploding silk.

IV

The hiss of raffia,
The thin string scraped with the back of the bow
Are not more bat-like
Than the gusty bamboos
Against a flute.

V

Pine-scent
In snow-clearness
Is not more exactly counterpointed
Than the creak of trodden snow
Against a flute.

VI

The outline of the water-dragon
Is not embroidered with so intricate a thread
As that with which the flute
Defines the tangible borders of a mood.

VII

The flute in summer makes streams of ice:
In winter it grows hospitable.

VIII

In mist, also, a flute is cold
Beside a flute in snow.

IX

Degrees of comparison
Go with differing conditions:
Sunlight mellows lichens,
Whereas snow mellows the flute.

Eight Observations on the Nature of Eternity

I

You would not think the room
(Grown small as a honey pot
And filled with a slow yellow light)
Could so burden itself with the afternoon.

II

It is neither between three and four
Nor is it time for the lamps:
It is afternoon – interminably.

III

Elsewhere there is sky, movement or a view,
Here there is light, stillness and no dimension.

IV

The afternoon violet
Is not so unthinkably itself,
Nor does that imperceptibly greening light
Freeze so remotely in its own essence
As this yellow.

V

Red flowers
Detonate and go out
At the curtain fringe.

VI

Objects regard us for the last time,
The window, that enemy of solitude,
Looks inward.

VII

Jaws of unhurried shade
Yawn on the masonry.

VIII

We will light no candles:
What is to be will be.
The room is merging
Into a moonless landscape.

Suggestions for the Improvement of a Sunset

Darkening the edges of the land,
Imperceptibly it must drain out colours
Drawing all light into its centre.

Six points of vantage provide us with six sunsets.

The sea partakes of the sky. It is less
Itself than the least pool which, if threatened,
Prizes lucidity.

The pond is lime-green, an enemy
Of gold, bearing no change but shadow.

Seen from above, the house would resemble
A violin, abandoned, and lost in its own darkness;

Diminished, through the wrong end of a glass,
A dice ambushed by lowering greens;

Accorded its true proportions,
The stone would give back the light
Which, all day, it has absorbed.

The after-glow, broken by leaves and windows,
Confirms green's triumph against yellow.

Sea Change

To define the sea –
We change our opinions
With the changing light.

Light struggles with colour:
A quincunx
Of five stones, a white
Opal threatened by emeralds.

The sea is uneasy marble.

The sea is green silk.

The sea is blue mud, churned
By the insistence of wind.

Beneath dawn a sardonyx may be cut from it
In white layers laced with a carnelian orange,
A leek- or apple-green chalcedony
Hewn in the cold light.

Illustration is white wine
Floating in a saucer of ground glass
On a pedestal of cut glass:

A static instance, therefore untrue.

Through Binoculars

In their congealed light
We discover that what we had taken for a face
Has neither eyes nor mouth,
But only the impersonality of anatomy.

Silencing movement,
They withdraw life.

Definition grows clear-cut, but bodiless,
Withering by a dimension.

To see thus
Is to ignore the revenge of light on shadow,
To confound both in a brittle and false union.

This fictive extension into madness
Has a kind of bracing effect:
That normality is, after all, desirable
One can no longer doubt having experienced its opposite.

Binoculars are the last phase in a romanticism:
The starkly mad vision, not mortal,
But dangling one in a vicarious, momentary idiocy.

To dispense with them
Is to make audible the steady roar of evening,
Withdrawing in slow ripples of orange,
Like the retreat of water from sea-caves.

Montage

The cheval-glass is empty
The sky is a blank screen.

In the buried room
They look back upon themselves.

The comity of three objects
Builds stillness within stillness.

The scene terminates without words
A tower collapsing upon feathers.

Dialogue

She: It turns on its axis.

He: To say that it was round
       Would be to ignore what is within.
       The transparent framework of cells,
       The constellation of flashes.

She: It reveals the horizon.

He: It surrounds it,
       Transmits and refines it
       Through a frozen element:
       A taut line crossing a pure white.

She: It contains distance.

He: It distances what is near,
       Transforms the conversation piece
       Into a still life,
       Isolates, like the end of a corridor.

She: It is the world of contour:

He: The black outline separating brilliances
       That would otherwise fuse,
       A single flame.

She: If it held personages –

He: They would be minute,
       Their explicit movements
       The mosaic which dances.

Both: In unison, they would clarify
       The interior of the fruit,
       The heart of the cut stone.

Flute Music

There is a moment for speech and for silence.
Lost between possibilities
But deploring a forced harmony,
We elect the flute.

A season, defying gloss, may be the sum
Of blue water beneath green rain;
It may comprise comets, days, lakes
Yet still bear the exegesis of music.

Seeing and speaking we are two men:
The eye encloses as a window – a flute
Governs the land, its winter and its silence.

The flute is uncircumscribed by moonlight or irised mornings.
It moves with equal certainty
Through a register of palm-greens and flesh-rose.

The glare of brass over a restless bass
(Red glow across olive twilight)
Urges to a delighted excess,
A weeping among broken gods.

The flute speaks (reason's song
Riding the ungovernable wave)
The bound of passion
Out of the equitable core of peace.

The Bead

At the clear core, morning
Extinguishes everything save light.

Breaking the spectrum
Threads cross, flare, emerge
Like the glitter of dust before stained windows.

Turned in the shadow
It is a black diamond
Containing nothing but itself.

The idea dissolves in passion:
The light holds,
Circling the cold centre.

The Art of Poetry

At first, the mind feels bruised.
The light makes white holes through the black foliage
Or mist hides everything that is not itself.

But how shall one say so? —
The fact being, that when the truth is not good enough
We exaggerate. Proportions

Matter. It is difficult to get them right.
There must be nothing
Superfluous, nothing which is not elegant
And nothing which is if it is merely that.

This green twilight has violet borders.

Yellow butterflies
Nervously transferring themselves
From scarlet to bronze flowers
Disappear as the evening appears.

Observation of Facts

Facts have no eyes. One must
Surprise them, as one surprises a tree
By regarding its (shall I say?)
Facets of copiousness.

The tree stands.

The house encloses.

The room flowers.

These are fact stripped of imagination:
Their relation is mutual.

A dryad is a sort of chintz curtain
Between myself and a tree.
The tree stands: or does not stand:
As I draw, or remove the curtain.

The house encloses: or fails to signify
As being bodied over against one,
As something one has to do with.

The room flowers once one has introduced
Mental fibre beneath its elegance,
A rough pot or two, outweighing
The persistence of frippery
In lampshades or wallpaper.

Style speaks what was seen,
Or it conceals the observation
Behind the observer: a voice
Wearing a ruff.

Those facets of copiousness which I proposed
Exist, do so when we have silenced ourselves.

Fiascherino

Over an ash-fawn beach fronting a sea which keeps
    Rolling and unrolling, lifting
The green fringes from submerged rocks
    On its way in, and, on its way out
Dropping them again, the light

Squanders itself, a saffron morning
    Advances among foam and stones, sticks
Clotted with black naphtha
    And frayed to the newly carved
Fresh white of chicken flesh.

One leans from the cliff-top. Height
    Distances like an inverted glass; the shore
Is diminished but concentrated, jewelled
    With the clarity of warm colours
That, seen more nearly, would dissipate

Into masses. The map-like interplay
    Of sea-light against shadow
And the mottled close-up of wet rocks
    Drying themselves in the hot air
Are lost to us. Content with our portion,

Where, we ask ourselves, is the end of all this
    Variety that follows us? Glare
Pierces muslin; its broken rays
    Hovering in trembling filaments
Glance on the ceiling with no more substance

Than a bee's wing. Thickening, these
    Hang down over the pink walls
In green bars, and, flickering between them,
    A moving fan of two colours,
The sea unrolls and rolls itself into the low room.

SEEING IS BELIEVING

1958, 1960

to
Donald and Hugh
who saw and believed

The Atlantic

Launched into an opposing wind, hangs
    Grappled beneath the onrush,
And there, lifts, curling in spume,
    Unlocks, drops from that hold
Over and shoreward. The beach receives it,
    A whitening line, collapsing
Powdering-off down its broken length;
    Then, curded, shallow, heavy
With clustering bubbles, it nears
    In a slow sheet that must climb
Relinquishing its power, upward
    Across tilted sand. Unravelled now
And the shore, under its lucid pane,
    Clear to the sight, it is spent:
The sun rocks there, as the netted ripple
    Into whose skeins the motion threads it
Glances athwart a bed, honeycombed
    By heaving stones. Neither survives the instant
But is caught back, and leaves, like the after-image
    Released from the floor of a now different mind,
A quick gold, dyeing the uncovering beach
    With sunglaze. That which we were,
Confronted by all that we are not,
    Grasps in subservience its replenishment.

Winter Encounters

House and hollow; village and valley-side:
    The ceaseless pairings, the interchange
In which the properties are constant
    Resumes its winter starkness. The hedges' barbs
Are bared. Lengthened shadows
    Intersecting, the fields seem parcelled smaller
As if by hedgerow within hedgerow. Meshed
    Into neighbourhood by such shifting ties,

The house reposes, squarely upon its acre
    Yet with softened angles, the responsive stone
Changeful beneath the changing light:
    There is a riding-forth, a voyage impending
In this ruffled air, where all moves
    Towards encounter. Inanimate or human,
The distinction fails in these brisk exchanges –
    Say, merely, that the roof greets the cloud,
Or by the wall, sheltering its knot of talkers,
    Encounter enacts itself in the conversation
On customary subjects, where the mind
    May lean at ease, weighing the prospect
Of another's presence. Rain
    And the probability of rain, tares
And their progress through a field of wheat –
    These, though of moment in themselves,
Serve rather to articulate the sense
    That having met, one meets with more
Than the words can witness. One feels behind
    Into the intensity that bodies through them
Calmness within the wind, the warmth in cold.

Reflections

Like liquid shadows. The ice is thin
    Whose mirror smears them as it intercepts
Withdrawing colours; and where the crust,
    As if a skin livid with tautening scars,
Whitens, cracks, it steals from these deformations
    A style too tenuous for the image. A mirror lies, and
Flawed like this, may even lie with art,
    With reticence: 'I exaggerate nothing,
For the reflections – scarcely half you see –
    Tell nothing of what you feel.' Nature is blind
Like habit. Distrust them. We, since no mirrors,
    Are free both to question this deployment
And to arrange it – what we reflect
    Being what we choose. Though without deference,
We are grateful. When we perceive, as keen

As the bridge itself, a bridge inlaying the darkness
Of smooth water, our delight acknowledges our debt –
To nature, from whom we choose;
And, fencing that fullness back, to habit,
The unsheathed image piercing our winter sleep.

Oxen: Ploughing at Fiesole

The heads, impenetrable
And the slow bulk
Soundless and stooping,
A white darkness – burdened
Only by sun, and not
By the matchwood yoke –
They groove in ease
The meadow through which they pace
Tractable. It is as if
Fresh from the escape,
They consent to submission,
The debris of captivity
Still clinging there
Unnoticed behind those backs:
'But we submit' – the tenor
Unambiguous in that stride
Of even confidence –
'Giving and not conceding
Your premises. Work
Is necessary, therefore –'
(With an unsevered motion
Holding the pauses
Between stride and stride)
'We will be useful
But we will not be swift: now
Follow us for your improvement
And at our pace.' This calm
Bred from this strength, and the reality
Broaching no such discussion,
The man will follow, each
As the other's servant
Content to remain content.

The Mediterranean

I

In this country of grapes
Where the architecture
Plays musical interludes, flays
The emotions with the barest statement
Or, confusing the issue and the beholder,
Bewilders with an excessive formality,
There is also the sea.

II

The sea
Whether it is 'wrinkled' and 'crawls'
Or pounds, plunders, rounding
On itself in thunderous showers, a
Broken, bellowing foam canopy
Rock-riven and driven wild
By its own formless griefs – the sea
Carries, midway, its burning stripe of light.

III

This country of grapes
Is a country, also, of trains, planes and gasworks.
'Tramway and palace' rankles. It is an idea
Neither the guidebook nor the imagination
Tolerates. The guidebook half lies
Of 'twenty minutes in a comfortable bus'
Of 'rows of cypresses, an
Uninterrupted series of matchless sights.'
The imagination cannot lie. It bites brick;
Says: 'This is steel – I will taste steel.

Bred on a lie, I am merely
Guidebooks, advertisements, politics.'

The sea laps by the railroad tracks.
To have admitted this also defines the sea.

Distinctions

The seascape shifts.

Between the minutest interstices of time
Blue is blue.

A pine-branch
Tugs at the eye: the eye
Returns to grey-blue, blue-black or indigo
Or it returns, simply,
To blue-after-the-pine-branch.

Here, there is no question of aberrations
Into pinks, golds or mauves:
This is the variation Pater indicated
But failed to prove.

Art exists at a remove.
Evocation, at two,
Discusses a blue that someone
Heard someone talking about.

Variant on a Scrap of Conversation

'There's nothing at all to be said for the day…'

Except that through the wet panes
Objects arrange themselves,
Blue tessellations, faintly irised
Dividing the room
Into an observed music.

As one approaches the windows
Fugues of colour
May be derived from a familiar interior,
A chair may be segmented and reassembled
In two steps.

To challenge the accepted vision
A further instance would be the wine-stopper,
Its head (cut into facets)
An eye for the cubist.

Icos

White, a shingled path
Climbs among dusted olives
To where at the hill-crest
Stare houses, whiter
Than either dust or shingle.
The view, held from this vantage
Unsoftened by distance, because
Scoured by a full light,
Draws lucid across its depth
The willing eye: a beach,
A surf-line, broken
Where reefs meet it, into the heaving
Blanched rims of bay-arcs;
Above, piercing the empty blue,
A gull would convey whiteness
Through the sole space which lacks it
But, there, scanning the shore,
Hangs only the eagle, depth
Measured within its level gaze.

How Still the Hawk

How still the hawk
Hangs innocent above
Its native wood:
Distance, that purifies the act
Of all intent, has graced
Intent with beauty.
Beauty must lie

As innocence must harm
Whose end (sited,
Held) is naked
Like the map it cowers on.
And the doom drops:
Plummet of peace
To him who does not share
The nearness and the need,
The shrivelled circle
Of magnetic fear.

Object in a Setting

I

From an empty sky
The morning deceives winter
With shadows and cold sapphire.

II

Astral, clear:
To wish it a more human image
Is to mistake its purpose.

Silent:
It is the marble city without trees.

Translucent, focal:
It is the city one may hold on the palm
Or lift, veined, against the sun.

Faceted, irised, burning:
It is the glass stair
To the hanging gardens.

III

The days turn to one their hard surfaces
Over which a glacial music
Pauses, renews, expands.

The Mausoleum

It is already six. From the steeple
  The even tones of a steady chime
Greet with their punctuality our lateness.
  The hall is shut. But one may
Visit the mausoleum in its now public grove
  Without cost or hindrance, and
With half as many steps as one would lose
  Were one to proceed. Here is the turning.

The trees thin and one sees its pyramid
  A steep roof tapering above stone steps.
Climb them. It is empty. The dead
  Have buried their dead and the living
Can approach it without fear and push open
  (As one may find it) the frayed door
To stand where a child might and where children do
  Play under the bare shelves of stone tiers.

We enter, the sunlight just about
  To fade on the wall and, from its glowing ground,
A blurred shadow detaches itself hovering
  And cannot decide whether a green or blue
Will the more grace its momentary existence
  Or whether a shot-red could invade
Decorously so impoverished a kingdom.

The light withdraws and the shadow softens
  Until it floats unnameably, gathered up
Into the colourless medium of early dusk:
  It is then that the eye, putting aside
Such distractions can move earnestly
  Past the slung swag, chipped where it hangs
Under a white tablet, and slowly
  Climb upwards with its burden of questions.

For the tablet-square, remotely white
  But yellowed as if an effect of ivory
That has aged and which age has cracked,
  Proffers, scarified like the swag beneath it,

Unhealed wounds; ivory fractures
But marble bruises, flakes, and these dark
Incursions, heavy with shade, are the work
Of hands, recording such meanings as you shall read.

Were I a guide you would vouchsafe my legend
Of how a race halted in tumult here
To exorcise in such a wavering light
The authority of death, and by left-hand magic
Practised not against that but procreation,
Signing each with his own name
Their composite work. But you must judge
As you will and as the light permits.

For to grant to such fears their myth
Is to distinguish them out of pity for a failing house.
Unleashed, it was no flickering colonnade
Debouched this horde. The elegant swag
With the trim incision of the epitaphs no less
Than the stone skull, mocked their impatience
And the blackened streets, the creeping architraves
Of their Pandemonium, a city of mean years.

Swarming the base of the narrow walls
As far as the raised arm can incise
Graffiti and beyond that as high as stone
Can be aimed against stone in such a confine
The legend is complete however it is simple,
Is plain, though under this dimmed
Clerestory the darkness liquefies it,
And the work, however many the hands, one.

As surely as the air cooling and the scents
That burn on the chillness at our exit,
The gravel rasping its trodden canon
Under the weave of thought, usher us
Into that world to which this silence
Scarred by so many hands is prologue,
You will concede that they have gained it whole
Whatever they have lost in its possession.

Glass Grain

The glare goes down. The metal of a molten pane
Cast on the wall with red light burning through,
Holds in its firm, disordered square, the shifting strands
The glass conceals, till (splitting sun) it dances
Lanterns in lanes of light its own streaked image.
Like combed-down hair. Like weathered wood, where
Line, running with, crowds on line and swaying
Rounding each knot, yet still keeps keen
The perfect parallel. Like... in likes, what do we look for?
Distinctions? That, but not that in sum. Think of the fugue's theme:
After inversions and divisions, doors
That no keys can open, cornered conceits
Apprehensions, all ways of knowledge past,
Eden comes round again, the motive dips
Back to its shapely self, its naked nature
Clothed by comparison alone – related. We ask
No less, watching suggestions that a beam selects
From wood, from water, from a muslin-weave,
Swerving across our window, on our wall
(Transparency teased out) the grain of glass.

Gli Scafari

Rock reproduces rock
In miniature
On rock; and where
The sheerness fails
Particularity resumes:
Layers, in flakes;
Piled shale; or
Minutest slates
Not slatted – packed and pitted
Against each
Barbarous element,
For all four
Climb with this sea
Save fire (and fire

Galls from above)
To will a corrosion
In so much silent decision among
Toy fortresses
Which can resist.

Tramontana at Lerici

Today, should you let fall a glass it would
    Disintegrate, played off with such keenness
Against the cold's resonance (the sounds
    Hard, separate and distinct, dropping away
In a diminishing cadence) that you might swear
    This was the imitation of glass falling.

Leaf-dapples sharpen. Emboldened by this clarity
    The minds of artificers would turn prismatic,
Running on lace perforated in crisp wafers
    That could cut like steel. Constitutions,
Drafted under this fecund chill, would be annulled
    For the strictness of their equity, the moderation of their pity.

At evening, one is alarmed by such definition
    In as many lost greens as one will give glances to recover,
As many again which the landscape
    Absorbing into the steady dusk, condenses
From aquamarine to that slow indigo-pitch
    Where the light and twilight abandon themselves.

And the chill grows. In this air
    Unfit for politicians and romantics
Dark hardens from blue, effacing the windows:
    A tangible block, it will be no accessory
To that which does not concern it. One is ignored
    By so much cold suspended in so much night.

Northern Spring

Nor is this the setting for extravagance. Trees
    Fight with the wind, the wind eludes them
Streaking its cross-lanes over the uneasy water
    Whose bronze whitens. To emulate such confusion
One must impoverish the resources of folly,
    But to taste it is medicinal. Consider

How through that broken calm, as the sun emerges,
    The sky flushes its blue, dyeing the grass
In the promise of a more stable tone:
    Less swift however than the cloud is wide –
Its shadow (already) quenching the verdure
    As its bulk muffles the sun – the blue drains
And the assault renews in colourless ripples.

Then, lit, the scene deepens. Where should one look
    In the profusion of possibilities? One conceives
Placing before them a square house
    Washed in the coolness of lime, a hub
For the scattered deployment, to define
    In pure white from its verdant ground
The variegated excess which threatens it.

Spring lours. Neither will the summer achieve
    That Roman season of an equable province
Where the sun is its own witness and the shadow
    Measures its ardour with the impartiality
Of the just. Evening, debauching this sky, asks
    To be appraised and to be withstood.

The Gorge

Wind in the fleece of ivy
As, from above, the pilot
Sees water, moved by its currents.

But we are closer: he would miss
Such evident ripples
Like a conflagration
Climbing the rockface.

Light, swept perpendicular
Into the leaf-mass
Flickers out, only to reappear momentarily
Stippling remoter clumps.

The movement deceives, a surface
For silence, inaccessible
Inactivity. Even the sea
Shifts to its centre.

On a Landscape by Li Ch'eng

Look down. There is snow.
Where the snow ends
Sea, and where the sea enters
Grey among capes
Like an unvaried sky, lapping
From finger to finger
Of a raised hand, travellers
Skirt between snow and sea.
Minute, furtive and exposed,
Their solitude is unchosen and will end
In comity, in talk
So seasoned by these extremes
It will recall stored fruits
Bitten by a winter fire.
The title, without disapprobation,
Says, 'Merchants'.

The Crane

That insect, without antennae, over its
Cotton-spool lip, letting
An almost invisible tenuity
Of steel cable, drop
Some seventy feet, with the
Grappling hook hidden also
Behind a dense foreground
Among which it is fumbling, and
Over which, mantis-like
It is begging or threatening, gracile
From a clear sky – that paternal
Constructive insect, without antennae,
Would seem to assure us that
'The future is safe, because
It is in my hands.' And we do not
Doubt this veracity, we can only
Fear it – as many of us
As pause here to remark
Such silent solicitude
For lifting intangible weights
Into real walls.

Paring the Apple

There are portraits and still-lifes.

And there is paring the apple.

And then? Paring it slowly,
From under cool-yellow
Cold-white emerging. And ...?

The spring of concentric peel
Unwinding off white,
The blade hidden, dividing.

There are portraits and still-lifes
And the first, because 'human'
Does not excel the second, and
Neither is less weighted
With a human gesture, than paring the apple
With a human stillness.

The cool blade
Severs between coolness, apple-rind
Compelling a recognition.

Rose-hips

Weather the frost, stir
At the cold's passing
Where white alone (were it not
For such drops of fire)
Would dominate, as the incessant
Massing of mist on mist
Draws-to over distance, leaving
Only a white of frost
On a white of fog, but
Deepened in dye by such
Candid obscurity, they stare
Sharper than summer berries
From this unlit air.

More Foreign Cities

Nobody wants any more poems about foreign cities...
(From a recent disquisition on poetics)

Not forgetting Ko-jen, that
Musical city (it has
Few buildings and annexes
Space by combating silence),

There is Fiordiligi, its sun-changes
Against walls of transparent stone
Unsettling all preconception – a city
For architects (they are taught
By casting their nets
Into those moving shoals); and there is
Kairouan, whose lit space
So slides into and fits
The stone masses, one would doubt
Which was the more solid
Unless, folding back
Gold segments out of the white
Pith globe of a quartered orange,
One may learn perhaps
To read such perspectives. At Luna
There is a city of bridges, where
Even the inhabitants are mindful
Of a shared privilege: a bridge
Does not exist for its own sake.
It commands vacancy.

At Delft

Johannes Vermeer, 1632–75

The clocks begin, civicly simultaneous,
    And the day's admitted. It shines to show
How promptness is poverty, unless
    Poetry be the result of it. The chimes
Stumble asunder, intricate and dense,
    Then mass at the hour, their stroke
In turn a reminder: for if one dances
    One does so to a measure. And this
Is a staid but dancing town, each street
    Its neighbour's parallel, each house
A displacement in that mathematic, yet
    Built of a common brick. Within

NEW COLLECTED POEMS

The key is changed: the variant recurs
  In the invariable tessellation of washed floors,
As cool as the stuffs are warm, as ordered
  As they are opulent. White earthenware,
A salver, stippled at its lip by light,
  The light itself, diffused and indiscriminate
On face and floor, usher us in,
  The guests of objects: as in a landscape,
All that is human here stands clarified
  By all that accompanies and bounds. The clocks
Chime muted underneath domestic calm.

The Jam Trap

Wings filmed, the threads of knowledge thicken
Corded with mire. Bodies immerse
Slackly in sweetness. Sweetness is not satisfaction
Nor was the elation of the pursuit
The measure of its end. Aromas and inclinations
Delectable essences, and now
The inextricable gesture, sounds
Which communicate nothing, their sole speech
A scurrying murmur, each to himself his own
Monotone burden of discouragement. Preferring
The fed flock that, scattered, re-forms
Massed into echelon above copious fields,
The sky, their chosen element, has abandoned them.

Poem

Upended, it crouches on broken limbs
About to run forward. No longer threatened
But surprised into this vigilance
It gapes enmity from its hollowed core.

Moist woodflesh, softened to a paste
Of marl and white splinter, dangles
Where overhead the torn root
Casts up its wounds in a ragged orchis.

The seasons strip, but do not tame you.
I grant you become more smooth
As you are emptied and where the heart shreds
The gap mouths a more practised silence.

You would impress, but merely startle. Your accomplice
Twilight is dragging its shadows here
Deliberate and unsocial: I leave you
To your one meaning, yourself alone.

A Meditation on John Constable

*Painting is a science, and should be pursued as an inquiry into the laws of
nature. Why, then, may not landscape painting be considered as a branch of
natural philosophy, of which pictures are but the experiments?*
    John Constable, *The History of Landscape Painting*

He replied to his own question, and with the unmannered
    Exactness of art; enriched his premises
By confirming his practice: the labour of observation
    In face of meteorological fact. Clouds
Followed by others, temper the sun in passing
    Over and off it. Massed darks
Blotting it back, scattered and mellowed shafts
    Break damply out of them, until the source
Unmasks, floods its retreating bank
    With raw fire. One perceives (though scarcely)
The remnant clouds trailing across it
    In rags, and thinned to a gauze.
But the next will dam it. They loom past
    And narrow its blaze. It shrinks to a crescent
Crushed out, a still lengthening ooze
    As the mass thickens, though cannot exclude

Its silvered-yellow. The eclipse is sudden,
  Seen first on the darkening grass, then complete
In a covered sky.
                          Facts. And what are they?
He admired accidents, because governed by laws,
  Representing them (since the illusion was not his end)
As governed by feeling. The end is our approval
  Freely accorded, the illusion persuading us
That it exists as a human image. Caught
  By a wavering sun, or under a wind
Which moistening among the outlines of banked foliage
  Prepares to dissolve them, it must grow constant;
Though there, ruffling and parted, the disturbed
  Trees let through the distance, like white fog
Into their broken ranks. It must persuade
  And with a constancy, not to be swept back
To reveal what it half-conceals. Art is itself
  Once we accept it. The day veers. He would have judged
Exactly in such a light, that strides down
  Over the quick stains of cloud-shadows
Expunged now, by its conflagration of colour.
  A descriptive painter? If delight
Describes, which wrings from the brush
  The errors of a mind, so tempered,
It can forgo all pathos; for what he saw
  Discovered what he was, and the hand – unswayed
By the dictation of a single sense –
  Bodied the accurate and total knowledge
In a calligraphy of present pleasure. Art
  Is complete when it is human. It is human
Once the looped pigments, the pin-heads of light
  Securing space under their deft restrictions
Convince, as the index of a possible passion,
  As the adequate gauge, both of the passion
And its object. The artist lies
  For the improvement of truth. Believe him.

Frondes Agrestes

on re-reading Ruskin

A leaf, catching the sun, transmits it:
'First a torch, then an emerald.'

'Compact, like one of its own cones':
The round tree with the pyramid shadow.

First the felicities, then
The feelings to appraise them:

Light, being in its untempered state,
A rarity, we are (says the sage) meant
To enjoy 'most probably' the effects of mist.

Nature's difficulties, her thought
Over dints and bosses, her attempts
To beautify with a leopard-skin of moss
The rocks she has already sculpted,
All disclose her purposes – the thrush's bill,
The shark's teeth, are not his story.

Sublimity is. One awaits its passing,
Organ voice dissolving among cloud wrack.
The climber returns. He brings
Sword-shaped, its narrowing strip
Fluted and green, the single grass-blade, or
Gathered up into its own translucence
Where there is no shade save colour, the unsymbolic rose.

Geneva Restored

The secreted city…
F.T. Prince

Limestone, faulted with marble; the lengthening swell
Under the terraces, the farms in miniature, until
With its sheer, last leap, the Salève becomes
The Salève, juts naked, the cliff which nobody sees
Because it pretends to be nothing, and has shaken off
Its seashore litter of house-dots. Beneath that,
This – compact, as the other is sudden, and with an inaccessible
Family dignity: close roofs on a gravel height,
Building knit into rock; the bird's nest of a place
Rich in protestant pieties, in heroic half-truths
That was Ruskin's. Guard and rebuild it. We are in the time
(The eternity rather) before the esplanades, New York
Bear-ridden and the casino unbuilt, Paris and London
Remain at Paris and London, and four miles square
A canton of resined air that will not be six
Refreshes a sociality that will not be pent
In the actual. Round this inconceivable
Point of patience, men travel on foot.

Farewell to Van Gogh

The quiet deepens. You will not persuade
    One leaf of the accomplished, steady, darkening
Chestnut-tower to displace itself
    With more of violence than the air supplies
When, gathering dusk, the pond brims evenly
    And we must be content with stillness.

Unhastening, daylight withdraws from us its shapes
    Into their central calm. Stone by stone
Your rhetoric is dispersed until the earth
    Becomes once more the earth, the leaves
A sharp partition against cooling blue.

Farewell, and for your instructive frenzy
    Gratitude. The world does not end tonight
And the fruit that we shall pick tomorrow
    Await us, weighing the unstripped bough.

Cézanne at Aix

And the mountain: each day
Immobile like fruit. Unlike, also
– Because irreducible, because
Neither a component of the delicious
And therefore questionable,
Nor distracted (as the sitter)
By his own pose and, therefore,
Doubly to be questioned: it is not
Posed. It is. Untaught
Unalterable, a stone bridgehead
To that which is tangible
Because unfelt before. There
In its weathered weight
Its silence silences, a presence
Which does not present itself.

In Defence of Metaphysics

Place is the focus. What is the language
Of stones? I do not mean
As emblems of patience, philosophers' hopes
Or as the astrological tangents
One may assemble, draw out subjectively
From a lapidary inertia. Only we
Are inert. Stones act, like pictures, by remaining
Always the same, unmoving, waiting on presence
Unpredictable in absence, inhuman
In a human dependence, a physical

Point of contact, for a movement not physical
And on a track of force, the milestone
Between two infinities. Stones are like deaths.
They uncover limits.

Reeds

The blades sway. They ride
Unbleached, tugged in their full sap
By the slow current. Hindering
From thought, they think us back
To that first green, which the mind
Tender-skinned, since grazed to the pain of sight,
Shrank at, lapping us in a half-green content
And, there, left us. By nature
Trenchant, blue double-whets them,
Burned through the water from a sky
That has long looked at it
Untempered by any mist. In this
There is of theme or apophthegm
No more than meets the eye. The blades sway.

The Shell

A white spire,
Its peak encircled
By a stair, a second
Stair corkscrewed inside it:
Gradually
You absorb all thought
Into that twisted matrix
From which nothing is born;
And like the speaker
Who hesitates to offend
And offends by hesitation

You propose your question
In silence, your hesitancy
The appearance only
Of a fragility whose centre
Is hard. You offend
Because you are there
Like the mountain
Which the too–civil fancy
Cannot appropriate to itself.
Your opalescence
Has seemed beautiful,
But a surface is as beautiful
As that which hides beneath it.
The irony of your finitude
Mirroring our own, we halt
Here where the shadow stains
At its white threshold
Your concealed stair.

Night-Piece: The Near and the Far

Declivities, striations, ledge over ledge of mounting
Cloud. A solid smoke, unsifted before the wind,
But shaped against it, crowded and blown together
From the horizon upwards. It goes on drifting, piling,
Rags into rock-ranks, mist to masses
Caught endlessly through the alien current, held
Riding the stream which buoys, then bloats, drags it
Into a further dark. Fissured, lit by the moon behind
Prizing from black an ore of undertones,
Over the houseless space, a hearth spills down.

At Holwell Farm

It is a quality of air, a temperate sharpness
    Causes an autumn fire to burn compact,
To cast from a shapely and unrifted core
    Its steady brightness. A kindred flame
Gathers within the stone, and such a season
    Fosters, then frees it in a single glow:
Pears by the wall and stone as ripe as pears
    Under the shell-hood's cornice; the door's
Bright oak, the windows' slim-cut frames
    Are of an equal whiteness. Crude stone
By a canopy of shell, each complements
    In opposition, each is bound
Into a pattern of utilities – this farm
    Also a house, this house a dwelling.
Rooted in more than earth, to dwell
    Is to discern the Eden image, to grasp
In a given place and guard it well
    Shielded in stone. Whether piety
Be natural, is neither the poet's
    Nor the builder's story, but a quality of air,
Such as surrounds and shapes an autumn fire
    Bringing these sharp disparities to bear.

On the Hall at Stowey

Walking by map, I chose unwonted ground,
    A crooked, questionable path which led
Beyond the margin, then delivered me
    At a turn. Red marl
Had rutted the aimless track
    That firmly withheld the recompense it hid
Till now, close by its end, the day's discoveries
    Began with the dimming night:

A house. The wall-stones, brown.
    The doubtful light, more of a mist than light
Floating at hedge-height through the sodden fields
    Had yielded, or a final glare
Burst there, rather, to concentrate
    Sharp saffron, as the ebbing year –
Or so it seemed, for the dye deepened – poured
    All of its yellow strength through the way I went:

Over grass, garden-space, over the grange
    That jutted beyond, lengthening – down
The house line, tall as it was,
    By tying it to the earth, trying its pride
(Which submitted) under a nest of barns,
    A walled weight of lesser encumbrances –
Few of which worsened it, and none
    As the iron sheds, sealing my own approach.

All stone. I had passed these last, unwarrantable
    Symbols of – no; let me define, rather
The thing they were not, all that we cannot be,
    By the description, simply of that which merits it:
Stone. Why must (as it does at each turn)
    Each day, the mean rob us of patience, distract us
Before even its opposite? – before stone, which
    Cut, piled, mortared, is patience's presence.

The land farmed, the house was neglected: but
    Gashed panes (and there were many) still showed
Into the pride of that presence. I had reached
    Unchallenged, within feet of the door
Ill-painted, but at no distant date – the least
    Our prodigal time could grudge it; paused
To measure the love, to assess its object,
    That trusts for continuance to the mason's hand.

Five centuries – here were (at the least) five –
    In linked love, eager excrescence
Where the door, arched, crowned with acanthus,
    Aimed at a civil elegance, but hit

This sturdier compromise, neither Greek, Gothic
    Nor Strawberry, clumped from the arching-point
And swathing down, like a fist of wheat,
    The unconscious emblem for the house's worth.

Conclusion surrounded it, and the accumulation
    After Lammas growth. Still coming on
Hart's-tongue by maiden-hair
    Thickened beneath the hedges, the corn levelled
And carried, long-since; but the earth
    (Its tint glowed in the house wall)
Out of the reddish dark still thrust up foison
    Through the browning-back of the exhausted year:

Thrust through the unweeded yard, where earth and house
    Debated the terrain. My eye
Caught in those flags a gravestone's fragment
    Set by a careful century. The washed inscription
Still keen, showed only a fragile stem
    A stave, a broken circlet, as
(Unintelligibly clear, craft in the sharp decrepitude)
    A pothook grooved its firm memorial.

Within, wet from the failing roof,
    Walls greened. Each hearth refitted
For a suburban whim, each room
    Denied what it was, diminished thus
To a barbarous mean, had comforted (but for a time)
    Its latest tenant. Angered, I turned to my path
Through the inhuman light, light that a fish might swim
    Stained by the greyness of the smoking fields.

Five centuries. And we? What we had not
    Made ugly, we had laid waste –
Left (I should say) the office to nature
    Whose blind battery, best fitted to perform it
Outdoes us, completes by persistence
    All that our negligence fails in. Saddened,
Yet angered beyond sadness, where the road
    Doubled upon itself I halted, for a moment
Facing the empty house and its laden barns.

Stone Walls: At Chew Magna

In this unyielding, even
Afternoon glow
One by one
You could unfasten
Like the tendrils of ivy
The filaments of all these
Sagging networks
Where the shadowed space
Divides walls
Into friable pink blocks
And the glow would spread
More evenly over
Their resolved opacity,
But who would unmake
This dislocation where
Each is located?

Cradock Newton: From an Epitaph

'Gurney, Hampton, Cradock Newton, last
Held on the measure of that antient line
Of barons' blood…' Paused by whose tomb,
Ignorant of its bones I read the claim
(Lie, half-lie or three-quarters true): 'He lov'd
To feed the poor.' Tasting such phrases,
So I taste their plight, and pity them,
But seeing the angel with its scales of stone –
Who suffers (I ask in thought) the greater need
Now time has stripped them both – those nameless
Or these named? For pity is the most
That love dares plead from justice. And will the poor
Love Cradock Newton when he creeps unhoused,
Naked at last before the rich man's door?

The Castle

It is a real one – no more symbolic
Than you or I. There are no secrets
Concerning the castellan; in the afternoons
His hospitality labours for the satisfaction
Not of guests, but visitors; in the mornings
Directing his renovations, he sits alone;
A settled gloom is threaded by scavengers
Who, through the dust of galleries, down
Through those sadder reticulations from which the myths have
                                                            faded,
Resurrect for the present as much of the improbable past
As it can tolerate. Dust is their element
But they finger the mysteries, as they unlink
The pendants of chandeliers into their winking suds:
He is easeless watching this progress, they
Sullen among their swaying burdens, remain
Unmindful of the minuter jealousies he would haunt them with
But which (since his power is nominal)
He must mute into reprimands, or twist, unnoticed
Round the stem of a candle-sconce, to suffer in person
Those daily burnishings under a menial hand.
He looks away. Townwards, below him
Where the sidings smoke, his glance struggles
Then settles. He has risen by the scale of talent
Into the seat of blood. But justice is less than just
And he is bored. His own master and his prisoner,
He serves a public. The soot sifts through
In flocculent grains and the clouds he watches
He now tastes. Whom does a public serve?
The smoke unwinds from its mounting coils,
Falling apart, a wavering drift
As the wind takes it. This morning blur
Conceals no innuendoes. A statement in prose,
It reserves on its neighbouring hill
A last artifact which, dusted, is ready now
To receive the solemnity or the distraction
Of visitors. He rises to go down.
It is twelve, and conscience excuses him.

Sconset

I have never been
To Sconset, but the gleam
Of painted houses
Adding a snow-tone
To the sea-tone in the mind's
Folder of the principal views
With the courthouse
Seen from the harbour, the harbour
Obscured by the whiteness
Of the church, crouched
Behind a dark shrub
Whose serrated leaves
Hang mounted (as it were)
On the spine of a feather –
These have invaded
All I shall ever hear
To their contrary.

Civilities of Lamplight

Without excess (no galaxies
Gauds, illiterate exclamations)
It betokens haven,
An ordering, the darkness held
But not dismissed. One man
Alone with his single light
Wading obscurity refines the instance,
Hollows the hedge-bound track, a sealed
Furrow on dark, closing behind him.

Fire in a Dark Landscape

And where it falls, a quality
Not of the night, but of the mind
As when, on the moonlit roofs,
A counterfeit snow
Whitely deceives us. And yet...
It is the meeting, of light
With dark, challenges the memory
To reveal itself, in an unfamiliar form,
As here: red branches
Into a transparency
In liquid motion, the winds'
Chimera of silk, twisting
Thickened with amber shadows,
A quality, not of the mind
But of fire on darkness.

The Request

Look from your stillness as the light resumes.
   From underneath your brim that, shading,
Sags like a burdock leaf, review
   Once more the accretions of moss
Greying the stones at the level of your eye.

Recover, rising, the ease in which you came
   Spreading on the grass your scarf and then yourself
Laid on its crimson that would have challenged
   Till you offset it, leaning there
With the unconscious rectitude of grace
   A little stiffly upon the elbow. Recall

Gradually the supple line
   With which your hand, composing the calm
You and your solitary companion share,
   Dipped, reiterated the brim in undulation,
Then subsided as you removed your elbow
   To slide instantly into that present shade.

She looks. And a flawed perfection
   Disburses her riches. She is watched
And knows she is watched. The crimson reveals itself
   Recommending her posture and assured by it
Both of her charm and her complicity: the error
   And the request were mine, the conclusion is yours.

The Ruin

Dissolving, the coals shift. Rain swaddles us
   And the fire, driving its shadows through the room
Recalls us to our intention as the flames
   That, by turns, sink guttering or mount
To pour red light through every crater,
   Threaten the galleries of crumbling ash.

The ruins sag, then sift downwards,
   Their fall so soundless that, for the first time,
We distinguish the unbroken, muffled sibilance
   Rain has accompanied us with. Our talk
Recovers its theme – the ruin we should have visited
   Abandoned, now, in its own emptiness.

For the morning promised what, through the darkening air,
   Afternoon retracted, nor will the evening
Welcome us under its turmoil of wet leaves
   Where we have lost the keenness of such acridity
As a burnt ruin exhales long afterwards
   Into the coolness when rain has ceased.

It stands on the hill slope. Between green and green
   There is the boundary wall that circles
And now hides it. Within, one can see nothing
   Save the third, chequered indefinite green
Of treetops – until, skirting these limits
   One discovers, open upon the emptied confine, the gate.

For a week, the swift traffic of demolition
　　That mottled with oil their stagnant rain,
Advanced through the deepening ruts,
　　Converged on the house, disjointed, reassembled
And carted, flung (what had sprawled unhinged)
　　The door into the wreckage and burnt both.

The door which, though elegant, leaned from the true
　　A little to one side, was shamed
By the nearby, slender but rigid elm —
　　An unchanging comedy, varied
Only as the seasons thought fit and as the days
　　Under their shifting lights reviewed it.

The house was not ancient, but old: deserted,
　　The slewed door had focused its rotting style
And, as proportion tugged from decrepitude
　　A faint self-respect, it was the door
With the firmness of an aged but practised arbiter
　　Bestowed it back over the entire ruin.

Impartial with imperfections, it could accuse
　　By this scant presence its clustering neighbours
Gross with the poverty of utility. Thus challenging, it stayed,
　　A problem for the authorities, a retreat for urchins
Until the urchins burnt half and the authorities
　　Publicly accomplished what their ally had attempted by stealth.

There remains now the levelled parapet of earth,
　　The bleak diagram of a foundation, a hearth
Focusing nothing and, cast into it, the filigree ghost
　　Of an iron fanlight. Could we assemble
Beside its other fragments, that last grace
　　Under this meaner roof, they would accuse us still —

And accusing, speak from beyond their dereliction
　　Out of their life; as when a vase
Cracked into shards, would seem
　　Baldly to confess, 'Men were here',
The arabesque reproves it, tracing in faint lines:
　　'Ceremonies and order were here also.'

Nor could we answer: our houses
    Are no longer ourselves; they dare not
Enter our hopes as the guests of meditation
    To reanimate, warmed by this contact,
The laric world where the bowl glistens with presence
    Gracing the table on which it unfolds itself.

Thus fire, renewed at our hearth, consumes.
    Yet it cannot create from the squalor of moderation
A more than fortuitous glory, multiplying its image
    Over the projections of lacquered wood. Charged with their past,
Those relics smoulder before they are compounded
    And turned by the spade under a final neatness.

The window lightens. The shell parts
    Beyond between cloud and sky line.
Thunder-light, flushing the walls, yellows them
    Into a more ardent substance than their own
And can do no more. The effect is nature's
    Who ignores it, and in whose impoverishment we domicile.

Aqueduct

Let it stand
A stone guest
In an unhospitable land,
Its speech, the well's speech,
The unsealed source's,
Carrying thence
Its own sustenance. Its grace
Must be the match
Of the stream's strength,
And let the tone
Of the waters' flute
Brim with its gentle admonitions the conduit stone.

Encounter

Birdless, the bush yet shakes
With a bird's alighting. Fate
Is transmitting flight
That rootwards flows,
Each unstilled spray
Tense like a dense arrival of targeted arrows.

Antecedents

A Homage and Valediction

Oh! que ses yeux ne parlent plus d'Idéal
Mais simplement d'humains échanges!

After such knowledge, what forgiveness?

The scene
Chiefly the Paris of Jules Laforgue and Stéphane Mallarmé

I Nothing: A Divagation

Not the calm – the clarity
After the storm. There are
In lucidity itself
Its crystal abysses
Perspective within perspective:
The white mind holds
An insufficiency, a style
To contain a solitude
And nothing more. Thus,
The infirm alchemy
Of platonic fantasy –
Word, the idea,
Spacing the vacuum: snow-prints
Wanting a direction; perhaps
At the most, as a constellation

The cut stone
Reassembled on dark.

II *Praeludium*

Je ne puis quitter ce ton: que d'échos...
                                    Derniers Vers

The horn has sounded.

Sunsets! They are interminable. Too late, however
For his exclamations. Sunsets... A point
Of interrogation, perhaps? How long
Can a sun go on setting? The thin refrain
Dies in a dying light as
'The splendour falls.' And it continues
Falling flaking into the leaf-drift. First,
It was Byron; the laureate
Next remarked on the inveterate music
Microscopically, reserving his
Tintinnabulations (caught in the half-stopped ear)
For elegiacs between occasions, the slow sun
Maintaining its progress (downwards)
Chromatically lamented. 'He is a master
Of miniature,' said Nietzsche
Speaking from solitude
Into solitude – he was describing
The bayreuthian minotaur, lamenting the hecatombs,
Yet forced to concede
An undionysiac, unapollonian distinction
In that gamut of melancholias. 'Art is a keyboard
For transitions,' said Mallarmé: 'between something and nothing.'
The music persisted
'And when I heard it' (Charles Baudelaire, the
Slow horn pouring through dusk an orange twilight)
'I grew insatiate.' We had our laureates, they
Their full orchestra and its various music. To that
                                                        Enter
On an ice-drift
A white bear, the grand Chancellor

From Analyse, uncertain
Of whom he should bow to, or whether
No one is present. It started with Byron, and
Liszt, says Heine, bowed to the ladies. But Jules...
Outside,

De la musique avant toute chose
The thin horns gone glacial
And behind blinds, partitioning Paris
Into the rose-stained mist,
He bows to the looking-glass. Sunsets.

III *Lacunae*

Autumn! Leaves in symphonic tumult,
Fall of Antigones and Philomelas
That my grave-digger (alas, poor Yorick!)
Must shift with his spade; and from the window
In the wet, all my chimneys
On the factories...

Chaplin, as Hamlet. A role we have yet to see
For the most part. As also
That spoiled Lutheran, masked
As his Zarathustra. Our innate
Perspicacity for the moderate
Is a national armoury. 'I have not
Read him; I have read about him':
In usum delphini – for the use
Of the common man. After Nietzsche
(Downwards) Sartre, after whom
Anouilh, dauphin's delight. And thus
Rimbaud the incendiary,
Gamin contemporary
With Gosse, the gentleman
Arrived late. He was dressed
In the skin of a Welsh lion, or the lion
Wore his – for the light
Was dubious, the marsh softening
And the company, willing to be led

Back to the forsaken garden by a route
Unfamiliar – yet as it wound
Dimly among the fetishes, a bewilderment
Of reminiscence. The force
That through the green dark, drove them
Muffled dissatisfactions. Last light, low among tempests
Of restless brass. Last music
For the sable throne (She comes, she comes!)
As the horns, one by one
Extinguish under the wave
Rising into the level darkness.
                            And Chaplin,
As Hamlet? That would have been
A more instructive frenzy. Eye-level light
Disclosing the field's wrinkles
Closes.

IV *Milieux*

                    We lack nothing
But the milieu.
                            De la fumée avant toute chose
Weaving the smoke, subjective
Faun with a cigarette Stéphane assembled one:
The page (the horns gone glacial)
Discovered its landscapes
As arctic gardens,
A luminous aura, hinting the penetration
Of green skeins, a snow-light
Bruising the mind.
                        There were divagations (platonic)
There were departures (actual)
And the predilection
For a confirmed madness
Confused them, one with another. Thus Missolonghi
Was re-enacted at Harrar
At Papeete, Atouana – 'alone
And surrounded by verdure':
Preludes to Taos.
                        We lack nothing
But a significant sun.

V *The Bells: A Period Piece*

What a world of solemn thought...
                                                    Poe

Hygienic bells, pale
Galilean bells (O what a wealth
Of melody!) – the lingering
Aftertone of all that sullen, moneyed harmony
Drove, and will drive, before its tidal choir
The great departures and the soft refusals.

Expostulation with the deaf – impossible
'To modify this situation':
Rustle of lavender and thyme, clean collars
As the wind is gagged
Full of this crystalline confusion:

The sky, dressed in the sound of Sunday colours
The season (fall of Antigones and Philomelas!)
The trains (picturesque destinations!) missed
The girls (white as their prayer-books) are released,
Rustle in lavender and thyme
From incense back to houses where
Their white pianos cool each thirsty square.

Chimeric bells, provincial bells –
And from the rust within their throats (O what a world
Of solemn thought!) now silence breaks:
Secure no longer in their theme
Or violence of its repetitions,
The generations abdicate
To us the means to vacillate.

VI *Something: A Direction*

Out of the shut cell of that solitude there is
     One egress, past point of interrogation.
Sun is, because it is not you; you are

Since you are self, and self delimited
Regarding sun. It downs? I claim? Cannot
    Beyond such speech as this, gather conviction?
Judge, as you will, not what I say
    But what is, being said. It downs
Recovered, coverless, in a shriven light
    And you, returning, may to a shriven self
As from the scene, your self withdraws. You are downing
    Back from that autumn music of the light, which
Split by your need, to know the textures of your pain,
    Refuses them in your acceptance. You accept
An evening, washed of its overtones
    By strict seclusion, yet are not secluded
Withheld at your proper bounds. From there
    Your returns may enter, welcome strangers
Into a civil country (you were not the first
    To see it), but a country, natural and profuse
Unbroken by past incursions, as the theme
    Strung over stave, is rediscovered
After dismemberment in the canon, and over stave
    Can still proceed, unwound, unwinding
To its established presence, its territory
    Staked and sung; and the phrase descends
As a phase concluded. Released
    From knowing to acknowledgement, from prison
To powers, you are new-found
    Neighboured, having earned relation
With all that is other. Still you must wait,
    For evening's ashen, like the slow fire
Withdrawn through the whitened log
    Glinting through grain marks where the wood splits:
Let be its being: the scene extends
    Not hope, but the urgency that hopes for means.

Notes

III *Lacunae*
'The force/That through the green dark...' (Cf. Dylan Thomas, *Eighteen Poems*.)

IV *Milieux*
Rimbaud departed to Harrar; Gauguin to Papeete and Atouana. From

Atouana the latter wrote: 'You have no idea of the peace in which I live here, entirely alone, surrounded by verdure.' (Quoted by R.H. Wilenski, p. 177, *Modern French Painters*, Faber 1944.)

V   *The Bells*
'Impossible de modifier cette situation.' In rendering this from *Derniers Vers*, one cannot avoid the tone of (early) Eliot because Eliot himself has not avoided the tone of Laforgue.

The Churchyard Wall

Stone against stone, they are building back
    Round the steepled bulk, a wall
That enclosed from the neighbouring road
    The silent community of graves. James Bridle,
Jonathan Silk and Adam Bliss, you are well housed
    Dead, howsoever you lived – such headstones
Lettered and scrolled, and such a wall
    To repel the wind. The channel, first,
Dug to contain a base in solid earth
    And filled with the weightier fragments. The propped yews
Will scarcely outlast it; for, breached,
    It may be rebuilt. The graves weather
And the stone skulls, more ruinous
    Than art had made them, fade by their broken scrolls.
It protects the dead. The living regard it
    Once it is falling, and for the rest
Accept it. Again, the ivy
    Will clasp it down, save for the buried base
And that, where the frost has cracked,
    Must be trimmed, reset, and across its course
The barrier raised. Now they no longer
    Prepare: they build, judged by the dead.
The shales must fit, the skins of the wall-face
    Flush, but the rising stones
Sloped to the centre, balanced upon an incline.
    They work at ease, the shade drawn in
To the uncoped wall which casts it, unmindful
    For the moment, that they will be outlasted

By what they create, that their labour
    Must be undone. East and west
They cope it edgewise; to the south
    Where the talkers sit, taking its sun
When the sun has left it, they have lain
    The flat slabs that had fallen inwards
Mined by the ivy. They leave completed
    Their intent and useful labours to be ignored,
To pass into common life, a particle
    Of the unacknowledged sustenance of the eye,
Less serviceable than a house, but in a world of houses
    A merciful structure. The wall awaits decay.

Epitaph

Enamoured by
Brevity in method,
'The unlettered muse'
Now outdoes
Her favourite
Device of rhetoric –
Namely, the pretence
Of having none.
Wordsworth admired
The named and dated
Day-old child, of her
Who alike conceived
This dateless
And initialled grave.

A PEOPLED LANDSCAPE

1963

I want the cries of my geese to echo in space.
Jean-François Millet

A Prelude

I want the cries of my geese
To echo in space, and the land
They fly above to be astir beneath
The agreement of its forms, as if it were
A self one might inhabit: life
Under leaf, gulls going in
Behind the encroachment of the plough.
Futurity, now open-handedly
Leans to the present and the season
Re-establishes a reign of outwardness,
Begins to build the summer back in cries
Still haunted by the cold, as geese
Cross over skies where mid-March balances.

Return to Hinton

written on the author's return to Hinton Blewett from the United States

Ten years
            and will you be
                        a footnote, merely,
England
            of the Bible
                        open at Genesis
on the parlour table?
            'God
                        saw the light
that it was good.'
            It falls
                        athwart the book
through window-lace
            whose shadow
                        decorates the sheets
of 'The Bridal March' –
            a square of white
                        above the keyboard

and below
        a text which is a prayer.
                The television box
is one,
        the mullions and flagged floor
                of the kitchen
through an open door
        witness a second
                world in which
beside the hob
        the enormous kettles'
                blackened bellies ride –
as much the tokens of an order as
        the burnished brass.
                You live
between the two
        and, ballasted against
                the merely new, the tide
and shift of time
        you wear
                your widow's silk
your hair
        plaited, as it has been
                throughout those years
whose rime it bears.
        A tractor
                mounts the ramp of stones
into the yard:
        a son surveys
                the scenes
that occupied a father's days.
        Proud of his machine,
                will he transmit
that more than bread
        that leaves you undisquieted?
                This house
is poorer by a death
        than last I saw it
                yet
who may judge
        as poverty that
                sadness without bitterness

those sudden tears
        that your composure
                clears, admonishes?
Your qualities
        are like the land
                – inherited:
but you
        have earned
                your right to them
have given
        grief its due
                and, on despair,
have closed your door
        as the gravestones tell you to.
                Speak
your composure and you share
        the accent of their rhymes
                express
won readiness
        in a worn dress
                of chapel gospel.
Death's
        not the enemy
                of you nor of your kind:
a surer death
        creeps after me
                out of that generous
rich and nervous land
        where, buried by
                the soft oppression of prosperity
locality's mere grist
        to build
                the even bed
of roads that will not rest
        until they lead
                into a common future
rational
        and secure
                that we must speed
by means that are not either.
                Narrow
        your farm-bred certainties

I do not hold:
    I share
        your certain enemy.
For we who write
    the verse you do not read
        already plead your cause
before
    that cold tribunal
        while you're unaware
they hold their session.
    Our language is our land
        that we'll
not waste or sell
    against a promised mess
        of pottage that we may not taste.
For who has known
    the seasons' sweet succession
        and would still
exchange them for a whim, a wish
    or swim into
        a mill-race for an unglimpsed fish?

Winter-Piece

You wake, all windows blind – embattled sprays
grained on the medieval glass.
Gates snap like gunshot
as you handle them. Five-barred fragility
sets flying fifteen rooks who go together
silently ravenous above this winter-piece
that will not feed them. They alight
beyond, scavenging, missing everything
but the bladed atmosphere, the white resistance.
Ruts with iron flanges track
through a hard decay
where you discern once more
oak-leaf by hawthorn, for the frost
rewhets their edges. In a perfect web

blanched along each spoke
and circle of its woven wheel,
the spider hangs, grasp unbroken
and death-masked in cold. Returning
you see the house glint-out behind
its holed and ragged glaze,
frost-fronds all streaming.

History

It is the unregarded congruence:
The boy who cries 'Bull'
Because he is leading one
Past the antique cart
Which the winter's advent
Will convert to firewood.
He does not mark it
Nor will he mark its absence –
Himself, the guardian
Of a continuity he cannot see
And – grant him means –
Would injure readily:
Admire, but not revere
This inarticulate philosopher.

Lines

You have seen a plough
the way it goes breeds
furrows line on line
until they fill a field?

What I admire in this
is less the page complete
and all the insatiable
activity towards it

than when, one furrow
more lies done with
and the tractor hesitates:
another line to be begun

and then it turns and drags
the blade in tow and that
turns too along the new
and growing groove

and each reversal thus
in mitigating mere aggression
prepares for the concerted
on-rush of the operation

and then the dark the cool
the dew corroding the intent
abandoned mechanism
that contemplates accomplishment.

Canal

Swans. I watch them
come unsteadying
the dusty, green
and curving arm
of water. Sinuously
both the live
bird and the bird
the water bends
into a white and wandering
reflection of itself,
go by in grace
a world of objects.
Symmetrically punched
now empty rivet-
holes betray
a sleeper fence:
below its raggedness
the waters darken

and above it rear
the saw-toothed houses
which the swinging
of the waters makes
scarcely less regular
in repetition. Swans
are backed by these, as
these are by
a sky of silhouettes,
all black and almost
all, indefinite.
A whitish smoke
in drifting diagonals
accents, divides
the predominance of street
and chimney lines,
where all is either
mathematically supine
or vertical, except
the pyramids of slag.
And, there, unseen
among such angularities –
a church, a black
freestanding witness
that a space of graves
invisibly is also
there. Only
its clock identifies
the tower between
the accompaniment of stacks
where everything
repeats itself –
the slag, the streets
and water that repeats
them all again
and spreads them rippling
out beneath
the eye of the discriminating
swans that seek
for something else
and the blank brink
concludes them without conclusion.

John Maydew or The Allotment

Ranges
    of clinker heaps
        go orange now:
through cooler air
    an acrid drift
        seeps upwards
from the valley mills;
    the spoiled and staled
        distances invade
these closer comities
    of vegetable shade,
        glasshouses, rows
and trellises of red-
    ly flowering beans.
        This
is a paradise
    where you may smell
        the cinders
of quotidian hell beneath you;
    here grow
        their green reprieves
for those
    who labour, linger in
        their watch-chained waistcoats
rolled-back sleeves –
    the ineradicable
        peasant in the dispossessed
and half-tamed Englishman.
    By day, he makes
        a burrow of necessity
from which
    at evening, he emerges
        here.
A thoughtful yet unthinking man,
    John Maydew,
        memory stagnates
in you and breeds
    a bitterness; it grew
        and rooted in your silence

from the day
        you came
                unwitting out of war
in all the pride
        of ribbons and a scar
                to forty years
of mean amends...
        He squats
                within his shadow
and a toad
        that takes
                into a slack and twitching jaw
the worms he proffers it,
        looks up at him
                through eyes that are
as dimly faithless
        as the going years.
                For, once returned
he found that he
        must choose between
                an England, profitlessly green
and this —
        a seamed and lunar grey
                where slag in lavafolds
unrolls beneath him.
        The valley gazes up
                through kindling eyes
as, unregarded at his back
        its hollows deepen
                with the black, extending shadows
and the sounds of day
        explore its coming cavities,
                the night's
refreshed recesses.
        Tomorrow
                he must feed its will,
his interrupted pastoral
        take heart into
                those close
and gritty certainties that lie
        a glowing ruse
                all washed in hesitations now.

He eyes the toad
        beating
                in the assuagement
of his truce.

Steel

the night shift

Slung from the gantries cranes
patrol in air and parry
lights the furnaces fling up at them.
Clamour is deepest in the den beneath,
fire fiercest at the frontier where
an arm of water doubles
and disjoints it. There is a principle, a pulse
in all these molten and metallic contraries,
this sweat unseen. For men
facelessly habituated to the glare
outstare it, guide the girders
from their high and iron balconies
and keep the simmering slag-trucks
feeding heap on heap
in regular, successive, sea-on-shore
concussive bursts of dry
and falling sound. And time
is all this measured voice would seem
to ask, until it uncreate
the height and fabric of the light-
lunged, restive, flame-eroded night.

Crow

The inspecting eye
shows cold
amid the head's
disquieted iridescence.
The whole bird sits
rocking at a vantage
clumsily. The glance
alone is steady
and a will behind it
rights the stance,
corrects all disposition
to ungainly action.
Acting, it will be
as faultless as its eye
in a concerted drop
on carrion; or watch
it fly – the insolence
transfers to wing-tip
and the action wears
an ease that's merciless,
all black assumption,
mounting litheness.
The blown bird,
inaccessible its intimations
of the wind, 'Stay
where you are' is
what it says and we
poor swimmers
in that element
stay, to bear
with clumsy eye
affronted witness at its ways in air.

Walking to Bells

The spray of sound
(Its echo rides
As bodied as metal
Whose echoes'
Echo it is)
Stunned, released
Where the house-walls
Stand or cease
Blows, or does not
Into the unfilled space
Accordingly; which
Space whose Adam wits
Slept on till now,
Kindles from cold
To hold the entire
Undoubling wave
Distinct in its jewelled collapse,
And the undertone
Sterner and broader than such facile beads
Gainsays
Not one from the toppling hoard its tensed back heaves.

The Farmer's Wife: At Fostons Ash

Scent
        from the apple-loft!
                I smelt it and I saw
in thought
        behind the oak
                that cupboards all your wine
the store in maturation
        webbed
                and waiting.
There
        we paused in talk,
                the labyrinth of lofts

above us and the stair
        beneath, bound
                for a labyrinth of cellars.
Everywhere
        as darkness
                leaned and loomed
the light was crossing it
        or travelled through
                the doors you opened
into rooms that view
        your hens and herds,
                your cider-orchard.
Proud
        you were
                displaying these
inheritances
        to an eye
                as pleased as yours
and as familiar almost
        with them. Mine
                had known,
had grown into the ways
        that regulate such riches
                and had seen
your husband's mother's day
        and you had done
                no violence to that recollection,
proving it
        by present fact.
                Distrust
that poet who must symbolize
        your stair into
                an analogue
of what was never there. Fact
                has its proper plenitude
that only time and tact
        will show, renew.
                It is enough
those steps should be
        no more than what they were, that your
                hospitable table

overlook the cowshed.
                    A just geography
                                completes itself
with such relations, where
                    beauty and stability can be
                                each other's equal.
But building is
                    a biding also
                                and I saw
one lack
                    among your store of blessings.
                                You had come
late into marriage
                    and your childlessness
                                was palpable
as we surveyed
                    the kitchen, where four unheraldic
                                sheep-dogs kept the floor
and seemed to want
                    their complement of children.
                                Not desolateness
changed the scene I left,
                    the house
                                manning its hill,
the gabled bulk
                    still riding there
                                as though it could
command the crops
                    upwards
                                out of willing land;
and yet
                    it was as if
                                a doubt
within my mood
                    troubled the rock of its ancestral certitude.

The Hand at Callow Hill Farm

Silence. The man defined
The quality, ate at his separate table
Silent, not because silence was enjoined
But was his nature. It shut him round
Even at outdoor tasks, his speech
Following upon a pause, as though
A hesitance to comply had checked it –
Yet comply he did, and willingly:
Pause and silence: both
Were essential graces, a reticence
Of the blood, whose calm concealed
The tutelary of that upland field.

Harvest Festival: At Ozleworth

Here, Romans owned the need – to give
    The giver gifts. I saw again
The shadow of the old propitiation
    In this ritual of preparing: women
Deft amid that fruit, those blooms
    Were priestesses at hecatombs of pear and apple,
Building their banks of leaves beneath
    Leaved capitals. The chancel arch
Seemed like the chosen counter-bass
    To show the theme weaving about it. There
Thorns were the crown to all the fruits: the hand
    That faultlessly had spanned the space, had cut
For a crossing in the stone, the spines
    Which Christ had worn, long lobes
In interlacing, shadowed grey. Cruel, these
    Cool fingers, tip to tip, and yet
Whoever wove them had not lost delight
    In the conception. Though they stood for more
Than we could ever be or bear, they fed
    The eye with regularity, humanized the hurt.
This, growing kind, could thus

Remind us of the necessary pain that none
Is proof against, and even stone
   Must neighbour. The garlands took the theme
Back to delight again, to gratitude,
   Scent, earth and (since the season
Brings in death) delight and death
   Ran in this canon graced to sanctify
Ceres with the chastened music of our festivity.

The Picture of J.T. in a Prospect of Stone

What should one
    wish a child
        and that, one's own
emerging
    from between
        the stone lips
of a sheep-stile
    that divides
        village graves
and village green?
    – Wish her
        the constancy of stone.
– But stone
    is hard.
        – Say, rather
it resists
    the slow corrosives
        and the flight
of time
    and yet it takes
        the play, the fluency
from light.
    – How would you know
        the gift you'd give
was the gift
    she'd wish to have?
        – Gift is giving,

gift is meaning:
     first
          I'd give
then let her
     live with it
          to prove
its quality the better and
     thus learn
          to love
what (to begin with)
     she might spurn.
          – You'd
moralize a gift?
     – I'd have her
          understand
the gift I gave her.
     – And so she shall
          but let her play
her innocence away
     emerging
          as she does
between
     her doom (unknown),
          her unmown green.

Four Kantian Lyrics

for Paul Roubiczek

1   On a Theme of Pasternak

I stared, but not to seize
the point of things: it was an incidental
sharpness held me there,
watching a sea of leaves
put out the sun. Spark
by spark, they drew it slowly down
sifting the hoard in glints

and pinheads. Rents of space
threatened to let it through
but, no – at once, the same
necessity that tamed the sky
to a single burning tone
would drag it deeper. Light
was suddenly beneath the mass
and silhouette of skirts and fringes,
shrinking to a glow on grass.
With dark, a breeze comes in
sends staggering the branches'
blackened ledges till they rear
recoiling. And now the trees are there
no longer, one can hear it climb
repeatedly their sullen hill
of leaves, rake and rouse them,
then their gathered tide
set floating all the house on air.

2   *What It Was Like*

It was like the approach of flame
treading the tinder, a fleet
cascade of it taking tree-toll,
halting below the hill and then
covering the corn-field's dryness
in an effortless crescendo. One heard
in the pause of the receding silence
the whole house grow
tense through its ties, the beams
brace beneath pantiles
for the coming burst. It came
and went. The blinded pane
emerged from the rainsheet
to an after-water world,
its green confusion brought
closer greener. The baptism
of the shining house was done
and it was like the calm
a church aisle harbours
tasting of incense, space and stone.

3   *An Insufficiency of Earth*

The wind goes over it. You see
the broken leaf-cope breathe
subsidingly, and lift itself
like water levelling. Stemmed,
this cloud of green, this mammoth
full of detail shifts
its shimmering, archaic head
no more. You think it for a second
hugely dead, until the ripple
soundless on the further corn,
is roaring in it. We cannot pitch
our paradise in such a changeful
nameless place and our encounters
with it. An insufficiency of earth
denies our constancy. For,
content with the iridescence of the moment,
we must flow with the wood-fleece
in a war of forms, the wind
gone over us, and we
drinking its imprints, faceless as the sea.

4   *How It Happened*

It happened like this: I heard
from the farm beyond, a grounded
churn go down. The sound
chimed for the wedding of the mind
with what one could not see,
the further fields, the seamless
spread of space, and then,
all bestial ease, the cows
foregathered by the milking place
in a placid stupor. There are two
ways to marry with a land –
first, this bland and blind
submergence of the self, an act
of kind and questionless. The other
is the thing I mean, a whole
event, a happening, the sound

that brings all space in
for its bound, when self is clear
as what we keenest see and hear:
no absolute of eye can tell
the utmost, but the glance
goes shafted from us like a well.

Up at La Serra

The shadow
    ran before it lengthening
        and a wave went over.
Distance
    did not obscure
        the machine of nature:
you could watch it
    squander and recompose itself
        all day, the shadow-run
the sway of the necessity down there
    at the cliff-base
        crushing white from blue.
Come in
    by the arch
        under the campanile parrocchiale
and the exasperation of the water
    followed you,
        its *Soldi, soldi*
unpicking the hill-top peace
    insistently.
        He knew, at twenty
all the deprivations such a place
    stored for the man
        who had no more to offer
than a sheaf of verse
    in the style of Quasimodo.
        Came the moment,
he would tell it
    in a poem

                    without rancour, a lucid
testament above his name
                    Paolo
                            Bertolani
— *Ciao, Paolo!*
            — *Ciao*
                    Giorgino!
He would put them
        all in it —
                    Giorgino going
over the hill
        to look for labour;
                    the grinder
of knives and scissors
        waiting to come up, until
                    someone would hoist his wheel
on to a back, already
        hooped to take it,
                    so you thought
the weight must crack
        the curvature. And then:
                    Beppino and Beppino
friends
        who had in common
                    nothing except their names and friendship;
and the sister of the one
        who played the accordion
                    and under all
the *Soldi, soldi,*
        sacra conversazione
                    del mare —
della madre.
        Sometimes
                    the men had an air of stupefaction:
La Madre:
        it was the women there
                    won in a truceless enmity.
At home
        a sepia-green
                    Madonna di Foligno
shared the wall
        with the October calendar —

                    Lenin looked out of it,
Mao
          blessing the tractors
                    and you told
the visitors:
          We are not communists
                    although we call ourselves communists
we are what you English
          would call... socialists.
                    He believed
that God was a hypothesis,
          that the party would bring in
                    a synthesis, that he
would edit the local paper for them,
          or perhaps
                    go northward to Milan;
or would he grow
          as the others had – son
                    to the puttana-madonna
in the curse,
          chafed by the maternal knot and by
                    the dream of faithlessness,
uncalloused hands,
          lace, white
                    at the windows of the sailors' brothels
in the port five miles away?
          Soldi –
                    soldi –
some
          worked at the naval yards
                    and some, like him
were left between
          the time the olives turned
                    from green to black
and the harvest of the grapes,
          idle
                    except for hacking wood.
Those
          with an acre of good land
                    had vines, had wine
and self-respect. Some
          carried down crickets

                to the garden of the mad Englishwoman
who could
    not
        tolerate
crickets, and they received
        soldi, soldi
            for recapturing them...
The construction
        continued as heretofore
                on the villa of the Milanese dentist
as the evening
        came in with news:
                – *We have won*
the election.
        – *At the café*
            the red flag is up.
He turned back
        quickly beneath the tower.
                Giorgino
who wanted to be a waiter
        wanted to be commissar
                piling *sassi*
into the dentist's wall.
        Even the harlot's mother
                who had not dared
come forth because her daughter
        had erred in giving birth,
                appeared by the *Trattoria della Pace.*
She did not enter
        the masculine precinct,
                listening there, her shadow
lengthened-out behind her
        black as the uniform of age
                she wore
on back and head.
        This was the Day
                which began all reckonings
she heard them say
        with a woman's ears;
                she liked
the music from the wireless.
        The padre

                    pulled
        at his unheeded angelus
            and the Day went down behind
                the town in the bay below
    where – come the season –
        they would be preparing
            with striped umbrellas,
    for the *stranieri* and *milanesi* –
        treason so readily compounded
            by the promiscuous stir
    on the iridescent sliding water.
            He had sought
                the clear air of the cliff.
    – Salve, Giorgino
        – Salve
            Paolo, have you
    heard
            that we have won the election?
                – I am writing
    a poem about it:
        it will begin
            here, with the cliff and with the sea
    following its morning shadow in.

Rhenish Winter

a montage after Apollinaire

    In the house
        of the vine-grower
            women were sewing
    Lenchen
        pile up the stove
            put on
    water for the coffee
        – Now that the cat
            has thawed itself
    it stretches-out flat

        – Bans are in
            at last for Gertrude
and Martin her neighbour
        The blind nightingale
           essayed a song
but quailed in its cage
        as the screech-owl wailed
           The cypress out there
has the air of the pope
        setting out in snow
           – That's the post
has stopped for a chat
        with the new schoolmaster
           – This winter is bitter
the wine
        will taste all the better
           – The sexton
the deaf and lame one
        is dying
           – The daughter
of the old burgomaster
        is working
           a stole in embroidery
for the priest's birthday
        Out there
           thanks to the wind
the forest gave forth
        with its grave organ voice
           Dreamy Herr Traum
turned up with his sister
        Frau Sorge
           unexpectedly
Mended
        you call these
           stockings mended Käthe
Bring
        the coffee the butter the spread
           bread in Set
the jam and the lard and
        don't forget milk
        – Lenchen
a little more

of that coffee please
            — You could imagine
that what the wind says
            was in Latin
                    — A little more
Lenchen
        — Are you sad
                Lotte my dear
I think
        she's sweet on somebody
                — God
keep her clear
        of that — As for me
                I love nobody
but myself — Gently
        gently
                grandmother's telling her rosary
— I need
        sugar candy
                I've a cough Leni
— There's Paul
        off with his ferret
                hunting for rabbits
The wind
        blew on the firs
                till they danced in a ring
Love makes
        a poor thing of Lotte
                Ilse
isn't life bright
        In the snarled stems
                the night
was turning the vineyards
        to charnels of snow
                shrouds
lay there unfolded
        curs
                bayed at cold travellers
He's dead
        listen
                from the church
the low bell-tone

The sexton had gone
Lise
the stove's dwindled to nothing
rekindle it
The women
made the sign of the cross
and the night
abolished their outline.

The Archer

for James Dickey

A lyre at rest:
you fingered it awake
your bow, and showed me
how the tensely-
tempered wood
responded, grew
nimble, lithe
against the bowstring
as you drew. I felt
at once the power
pent in such an instrument
and what your apollonian stance
must now constrain;
then saw the arrows
launch into the lane
of force, and hit
a bale of straw,
impale and pass it
for the earth beyond.
Each time, the string
sang behind their cruel
feathered going
as the sound and scene
combined to one effect –
all rending speed

eyed only
in the aiming, ending.
Mind could not divorce
the wedded terror,
graceful force, and
now must hold their music
single in the silence when
unarrowed, stilled
once more the bow
lay innocent
of what had filled
and bent it to its certainty,
a lyre unstrung,
a kill unsung.

At Wells: Polyphony

The unmoving vault
    receives their movement
        voices
falling flights
    niched
        on the sudden, providential hand
of air
    daring to reassume
        the height that
spanned and hemmed un-
    til (like light
        entering amber)
they take and hold it
    and their time
        its space
sustain
    in a single element the chord of grace.

Sea Poem

A whiter bone:
    the sea-voice
        in a multiple monody
crowding towards that end.
    It is as if
        the transparencies of sound
composing such whiteness
    disposed many layers
        with a sole movement
of the various surface,
    the depths, bottle-glass green
        the bed, swaying
like a fault in the atmosphere, each
    shift
        with its separate whisper, each whisper
a breath of that singleness
    that 'moves together
        if it moves at all',
and its movement is ceaseless,
    and to one end –
        the grinding
a whiter bone.

Maillol

    These
        admonitory images
            begotten where
    despair alone
        seemed powerful to create
            images commensurate
    and durable:
        these
            refusals
    of embittered counsels
        of engrossed affections

                    celebrate
the earthbound body and
        the full repose,
                or (where
massive Rousillon
        cedes to the glancing grace
                of the Île-de-France)
the delicate
        and perennial recurrences
                of the vineyard and the almond tree.
Paris is sick
        Pomona
                opposes her
carries
        in either extended hand
                the unbitten fruit;
the River
        that still yet flowing
                statue at play
large with its own delight
        and to the shore's
                unfelt restraint
leaning an earthward ear,
        chides the uncivil city
                pours reproof
through its pride of limb.
        These
                caught between sea and mountain
Mediterranean appearances
        were fed
                by adversity:
no innocence
        unearned
                could glean
what blindness gave
        Aristide Maillol, who
                turned by its threat
from tapestry toward
        an art
                where hand and eye
must marry,
        became

                    Maillol the sculptor.
Rather than to express
            his trials or
                    his times
in an intricate bravura
            adequate
                    to their twists,
he resisted them,
            admired it
                    and mistrusted
that flickering frenzy
            of Rodin.
                    For poverty had taught
the essential bareness
            bar between
                    a plenitude and a luxury.
What tempered
            this disregard for all
                    save fecund fact
first principle? –
            Only integrity
                    can wear
the bather's bronze
            antique nudity
                    and bear
no mirror
            measure
                    of the eye's complicity:
here
            hand and eye
                    did what conception
bade them do
            enriching it
                    with the unforeseen
beauty of the act.
            What fisher
                    his customary boat
in measured waters
            can predict
                    the catch he fishes?
He knows his net
            but knowledge

                    must reassess its ground
        to comprehend
                the mystery of fact
                    supple in sunlight
        teeming from the sound.

Flame

Threshing from left to right, whose
    Anger is this? Or whose delight?
For it is volatile like thought, stained-through like mind
    With odour and reminiscence of those seams
Darker and deeper than its shifting scope.
    The mind, that rooted flame
Reaches for knowledge as the flame for hold –
    For shapes and discoveries beyond itself. A slow
Crescendo of crepitations through burning music,
    It mines in its element, shines-out its ores.

Head Hewn with an Axe

        The whittled crystal: fissured
        For the invasion of shadows.

        The stone book, its
        Hacked leaves
        Frozen in granite.

        The meteorite, anatomized
        By the geometer. And to what end?
        To the enrichment of the alignment:
        Sun against shade against sun:
        That daily food, which
        Were it not for such importunities
        Would go untasted:

The suave block, desecrated
In six strokes. The light
Is staunching its wounds.

Last Judgement

Flame in the pit, flame
In the open height. The same
Unseizable element runs
Bounded and burning
Through that circle of singers
As the damned feel, overflowed
In liquid disorder. Hell
Is the fulfillment which stifles their desire
By granting it.

The Beech

Nakedly muscular, the beech no longer regrets
Its lost canopy, nor is shamed
By its disorder. The tatters lie
At the great foot. It moves
And what it moves is itself.

The Tree

I had seen a tree before,
the amputated trunk
merely a table-top
set on a single claw
of roots. But that
was not like this:

this lay awry
even before they cut it;
this – propped up
on the elbows of its boughs
– spanned half a hill
and bridged the green
dank slot
a narrow stream
had worn into the flank
beyond. On end
it leaned against
the rising slope.
Leafless? It was never
leafless. Leaves
climbed with it, roots
socketed and spread into
the layered marl.
And leaves were on it now
that pierced the air
with crumpled wedges –
you could sense the injury
in that half-completed gesture
and before you knew
the cause of it.
This might have seemed
an occasion for regret,
had not the effect
been incontestable.
The saw had entered
sideways the knot of roots,
and the plane it left,
resistant, vertical,
exposed a map
of grains and stains,
a mud-splashed
scored relief
held by a frame,
an inlay lip,
where the rind enclosed it.
The sections of the trunk
greeted each other
from opposing banks

nakedly. A third
irregularly fluted,
now erect,
completed the triangulation,
tugged the group
afresh into a unity
from where it stood
and finally a rain
had cleansed it, freshened,
flushed the colour through.
The reservoir of content,
dammed behind
the mask of form,
the tree's geometry
still put the same
unanswerable question
as the living tree,
though framed it
with a difference, and I
between its Janus faces,
was compelled to echo it,
as though the repetition could
reconsecrate this altar of discarded wood.

The Gossamers

Autumn. A haze is gold
By definition. This one lit
The thread of gossamers
That webbed across it
Out of shadow and again
Through rocking spaces which the sun
Claimed in the leafage. Now
I saw for what they were
These glitterings in grass, on air,
Of certainties that ride and plot
The currents in their tenuous stride
And, as they flow, must touch

Each blade and, touching, know
Its green resistance. Undefined
The haze of autumn in the mind
Is gold, is glaze.

The Barometer

It runs ahead. And now
Like all who anticipate
Must wait. Rain was what
Peremptorily it said and
Rain there is none. The air
As still as it, has dimmed
But not with drops, nor with
That sudden progress – when
All that is not black is green –
From intensity to purity. Rain
The repetitive, unmoving finger
Still insists, the name
With numerical corroboration under
Its arrow index. The storm
Hides in the stormhead still
That, heaping-over, spreads
And smokes through the zenith, then
Yields to a sordid-white
Identical image of itself
That climbs, collapsing as before.
The glass door reveals
The figured face, the one
Certainty in all these shifts
Of misty imponderables, pale
Seeping pervasions of each tone,
And the baleful finger
Balances, does not record them.

Cloud Change

First light – call it
First doubt among shadows
As the seam splits
At sky-level. The dark
Scarcely disperses.
The partial light
Drifts into it from beneath,
Flushes the atmosphere
Transparent. Call it
Dismissal, elemental
Reprimand to reluctance:
The dark is losing
In the day-long sway
That neither can win. Call it –
Defeat into dialogue.

Letter from Costa Brava

Its crisp sheets, unfolded,
Give on to a grove, where
Citrons conduct the eye
Past the gloom of foliage
Towards the glow of stone. They write
Of a mesmeric clarity
In the fissures of those walls
And of the unseizable lizards, jewelled
Upon them. But let them envy
What they cannot see:
This sodden, variable green
Igniting against the grey.

Chaconne for Unaccompanied Violin

Here
    walls are cool
        and coolness is
the firm exclusion of a day
    that burns and beats
        dances at thresholds
and defies
    this moving well
        content
with the ripple-run
    reflected
        in a core of shade.
This
    is the measure
        of a solitude
to feel
    resisting
        all that eludes its scope –
to recognize
    that music which awaits
        the permissive gesture to invade
carrying the single voice against its wave.

Ship's Waiters

for Marianne Moore

Waiters
    'gliding'
        with the accuracy
and the inscrutable
    intuition of the bat,
        that avoids collision
even by dark. Nothing
    can diminish
        that peculiar concert

of either the gliding
        man, or the infallible
                freaked quadruped, but one
can equal it –
        I mean
                the leaning fathoms
their pulse
        its arterial unpredictable beat
                teasing precision from those harried feet.

The Flight

Foam lips
        waters
                in following folds
the slow
        irrefutable insistence
                of the unheard argument
is now behind us
        and the immense palm
                unrolling its map of wrinkles
bares
        Dakota's rock –
                the Chinese
predicted
        and depicted this
                where cream-white
rises into a wall
        which pinestems (red)
                horizontality of branch
and leaf-mass (rhythmically repeated)
        'decorate' is the word.
                Europe
could not foretell
        that prime vernacular
                made keen
by silence. Lower
        and may the hovering eye
                particularize.

Over Brooklyn Bridge

Mayakovsky
has it! –
   'in the place
of style, an austere
  disposition of bolts'.
    The poet cedes
his elocutionary function
   to the telephone book:
     Helmann
Salinas
  Yarmolinsky,
    words
reciprocally
   kindling one another
     like the train of fire
over a jewel box.
   Miss Moore
    had a negress
for a maid whose father
   was a Cherokee.
     'No,' she said
'I do not live in town
   I live in Brooklyn.
   I was afraid
you wouldn't like it here –
   it's gotten so ugly.'
    I liked Brooklyn
with its survival
   of wooden houses
    and behind trees
the balconies colonnaded.
    And what I liked
    about the bridge
was the uncertainty
   the way

'The poet cedes his elocutionary function…' is a slightly travestied version of a famous passage from Mallarmé's 'Crise de vers': 'l'oeuvre pure implique la disparation élocutoire du poète, qui cède l'initiative aux mots…'

                    the naked steel
would not go naked
          but must wear
                    its piers of stone –
as the book says
          'stylistically
                    its weakest feature'.
I like
          such weaknesses, the pull
                    the stone base
gives to the armature.
          I live
                    in a place of stone
if it's still there
          by the time I've sailed to it.
                    Goodbye
Miss Moore
          I hope
                    the peacock's feather you once saw
at the house of Ruskin
          has kept its variegations.
                    Jewels
have histories:
          'I never did
                    care for Mallarmé,'
she said
          and the words
                    in the book of names
are flames not bolts.

Ode to Arnold Schoenberg

on a performance of his concerto for violin

          At its margin
                    the river's double willow
                              that the wind
          variously
                    disrupts, effaces

and then restores
in shivering planes:
        it is
            calm morning.
The twelve notes
        (from the single root
            the double tree)
and their reflection:
        let there be
            unity – this,
however the winds rout
        or the wave disperses
            remains, as
in the liberation of the dissonance
        beauty would seem discredited
            and yet is not:
redefined
        it may be reachieved,
            thus to proceed
through discontinuities
        to the whole in which
            discontinuities are held
like the foam in chalcedony
        the stone, enriched
            by the tones' impurity.
The swayed mirror
        half-dissolves
            and the reflection
yields to reflected light.
            Day. The bell-clang
                goes down the air
and, like a glance
        grasping upon its single thread
            a disparate scene,
crosses and re-creates
        the audible morning.
            All meet at cockcrow
when our common sounds
        confirm our common bonds.
            Meshed in meaning
by what is natural
        we are discontented

NEW COLLECTED POEMS

for what is more,
until the thread
of an instrument pursue
a more than common meaning.
But to redeem
both the idiom and the instrument
was reserved
to this exiled Jew – to bring
by fiat
certainty from possibility.
For what is sound
made reintelligible
but the unfolded word
branched and budded,
the wintered tree
creating, cradling space
and then
filling it with verdure?

AMERICAN SCENES

AND OTHER POEMS

1966

Face and Image

Between
the image of it
and your face: Between
is the unchartable country,
variable, virgin
terror and territory.

The image –
that most desperate act
of portraiture –
I carry and my mind
marries it willingly,
though the forfeiture's
foreknown already: admit
the reality and you see
the distance from it.

The face –
mouth, eyes and forehead,
substantial things,
advance their frontier
clear against all imaginings:

And yet –
seeing a face, what
do we see?
It is not
the one
incontrovertible you or me.

For, still, we must
in all the trust of seeing
trace
the face in the image, image in the face.

To love
is to see,
to let be
this disparateness
and to live within
the unrestricted boundary between.

Even an uncherished face
forces us
to acknowledge
its distinctness, its continuance thus;
then how should these
lips not compound the theme
and being of all appearances?

The Snow Fences

They are fencing the upland against
the drifts this wind, those clouds
would bury it under: brow and bone
know already that levelling zero
as you go, an aching skeleton,
in the breathtaking rareness of winter air.

Walking here, what do you see?
Little more, through wind-teased eyes,
than a black, iron tree
and, there, another, a straggle
of low and broken wall between, grass
sapped of its greenness, day going.

The farms are few: spread
as wide, perhaps, as when
the Saxons who found them, chose
these airy and woodless spaces
and froze here before they fed
the unsuperseded burial ground.

Ahead, the church's dead-white
limewash will dazzle the mind
as, dazed, you enter to escape:
despite the stillness here, the chill
of wash-light scarcely seems
less penetrant than the hill-top wind.

Between the graves, you find
a beheaded pigeon, the blood and grain
trailed from its bitten crop, as alien to all
the day's pallor as the raw
wounds of the earth, turned above
a fresh solitary burial.

A plaque of staining metal
distinguishes this grave among
an anonymity whose stones
the frosts have scaled, thrusting under
as if they grudged the ground
its ill-kept memorials.

The bitter darkness drives you
back valleywards, and again you bend
joint and tendon to encounter
the wind's force and leave behind
the nameless stones, the snow-shrouds
of a waste season: they are fencing
the upland against those years, those clouds.

The Fox

When I saw the fox, it was kneeling
in snow: there was nothing to confess
that, tipped on its broken forepaws
the thing was dead – save for its stillness.

A drift, confronting me, leaned down
across the hill-top field. The wind
had scarped it into a pennine wholly of snow, and
where did the hill go now?

There was no way round:
I drew booted legs
back out of it, took to my tracks again,
but already a million blown snow-motes were
flowing and filling them in.

Domed at the summit, then tapering,
the drift still mocked
my mind as if the whole
fox-infested hill were the skull of a fox.

Scallops and dips
of pure pile rippled and shone, but what
should I do with such beauty
eyed by that?

It was like clambering between its white temples
as the crosswind tore
at one's knees, and each
missed step was a plunge at the hill's blinding interior.

Bone

I unearthed
what seemed like the jawbone of an ass –
and what a weapon it was
that Samson wielded! For the first time
as I drew the soil-stained
haft of it out, I knew.

It balanced
like a hand-scythe, bladed
weighted and curved for an easy blow
that would transmit
the whole of the arm's force as it rose
dropped and dealt it.

How many
was it he slaughtered thus
in a single bout
with just such a boomerang of teeth
grained, greened and barbarous?

But no. Not until I'd cleaned
the weapon did I see
how candidly fleshless
that jawbone must have shone
out of the desert brightness.

A sill now restores it
into perspective, emblem
for a quarrel of deadmen where it lies,
brilliant obstacle beside its shadow
across the pathway of appearances.

The Door

Too little
has been said
of the door, its one
face turned to the night's
downpour and its other
to the shift and glisten of firelight.

Air, clasped
by this cover
into the room's book,
is filled by the turning
pages of dark and fire
as the wind shoulders the panels, or unsteadies that burning.

Not only
the storm's
breakwater, but the sudden
frontier to our concurrences, appearances,
and as full of the offer of space
as the view through a cromlech is.

For doors
are both frame and monument
to our spent time,
and too little
has been said
of our coming through and leaving by them.

The Weathercocks

Bitten and burned into mirrors of thin gold,
the weathercocks, blind from the weather,
have their days of seeing as they
grind round on their swivels.

A consciousness of pure metal
begins to melt when (say)
that light 'which never was'
begins to be

And catches the snow's accents
in each dip and lap, and the wide
stains on the thawed ploughland are like continents
across a rumpled map.

Their gold eyes hurt
at the corduroy lines come clear whose grain
feels its way over the shapes of the rises
joining one brown accord of stain and stain.

And the patterning stretches, flown
out on a wing of afternoon cloud that the sun
is changing to sea-wet sandflats,
hummocked in tiny dunes like the snow half-gone –

As if the sole wish of the light
were to harrow with mind matter, to shock
wide the glance of the tree-knots and the stone-eyes
the sun is bathing, to waken the weathercocks.

A Given Grace

Two cups,
a given grace,
afloat and white
on the mahogany pool
of table. They unclench
the mind, filling it
with themselves.
Though common ware,
these rare reflections,
coolness of brown
so strengthens and refines
the burning of their white,
you would not wish
them other than they are –
you, who are challenged
and replenished by
those empty vessels.

Saving the Appearances

The horse is white. Or it
appears to be under this
November light that could
well be October. It goes
as nimbly as a spider does
but it is gainly: the great
field makes it small
so that it seems
to crawl out of the distance
and to grow not larger
but less slow. Stains
on its sides show where
the mud is and the power
now overmasters the fragility
of its earlier bearing. Tall
it shudders over one and bends

a full neck, cropping
the foreground, blotting
the whole space back
behind those pounding feet.
Mounted, one feels the sky
as much the measure of the event
as the field had been, and all
the divisions of the indivisible
unite again, or seem
to do as when the approaching
horse was white, on this
November unsombre day
where what appears, is.

In Winter Woods

1   Snow Sequence

A just-on-the-brink-of-snow feel,
a not-quite-real
access of late daylight. I tread
the puddles' hardness: rents
spread into yard-long splinters –
galactic explosions, outwards
from the stark, amoebic
shapes that air has pocketed
under ice. Even the sky
marbles to accord with grass
and frosted tree: the angles
of the world would be all knives, had not
the mist come up
to turn their edges,
just as the sun began
to slide from this precipice, this pause:
first flakes simultaneously
undid the stillness, scattering
across the disk
that hung, then dropped,

a collapsing bale-fire-red
behind the rimed, now snow-spanned
depth of a disappearing woodland.

2   *The Meeting*

Two stand
admiring morning.
A third, unseen as yet
approaches across upland
that a hill and a hill's wood
hide. The two
halving a mutual good,
both watch a sun
entering sideways
the slope of birches
a valley divides them from.
A gauzy steam
smokes from the slope: this
and the light's obliquity
puzzle their glance; they see
thin tree stems:
the knuckled twiggery above
(relieved on sky)
rises more solid
than the thread-fine boles
supporting it – boles that the eye
through its shuttered pane
construes as parallel
scratchings, gold runnels
of paint-drip on the sombre
plane of deeper dark
where the wood evades
the morning. 'But who is this?'
As the third climbs in
down the slope, and the sunlight
clambers with him, on face
and form, 'Who is this?'
they say, who should have asked
'What does he see?' and turned
to answer: a high, bare

unlit hill behind
two faceless visitants
sharing a giant shadow
the night has left: two
at an unseen door
stilled by their question,
whom movement suddenly
humanizes as they
begin descending
through a common day
on to the valley floor.

3 *Nocturnal*

Shade confounds shadow now. Blue
is the last tone left
in a wide view
dimming in shrinking vista.
Birds, crossing it,
lose themselves rapidly
behind coverts where all the lines
are tangled, the tangles
hung with a halo of cold dew.
The sun smearily edges
out of the west, and a moon
risen already, will soon
take up to tell in its own style
this tale of confusions:
that light which seemed
to have drawn out after it
all space, melting in horizontals,
must yield now
to a new, tall beam,
a single, judicious eye: it will have
roof behind roof once more, and these
shadows of buildings
must be blocked-in
and ruled with black, and shadows
of black iron must flow
beneath the wrought-iron trees.

4 *Focus*

Morning has gone
before the day begins,
leaving an aftermath
of mist, a battleground
burnt-out, still smoking: mist
on the woodslopes like a blue
dank bloom that hazes
a long-browned photograph:
under that monotone
sleep ochres, reds,
and (to the eye
that sees) a burning
of verdure at the vapour's edge
seems to ignite
those half-reluctant tones –
then, having kindled
fails them. Green
in that grey contagion
leads the eye
homewards, to where a black
cut block of fallen beech
turns, in the weathers,
to a muddy anvil:
there, the whole, gigantic
aperture of the day
shuts down to a single
brilliant orifice: a green
glares up through this
out of a dark of whiteness
from the log – a moss
that runs with the grain-mark, whirled
like a river
over a scape of rapids
into a pool of mingling
vortices. And the mind
that swimmer, unabashed
by season, encounters
on entering, places
as intimate as a fire's
interior palaces: an Eden

on whose emerald tinder,
unblinded and unbounded
from the dominance of white,
the heart's eye enkindles.

The Cavern

Obliterate
mythology as you unwind
this mountain-interior
into the negative-dark mind,
as there
the gypsum's snow
the limestone stair
and boneyard landscape grow
into the identity of flesh.

Pulse of the water-drop,
veils and scales, fins
and flakes of the forming
leprous rock,
how should these
inhuman, turn
human with such chill affinities?

Hard to the hand,
these mosses not of moss,
but nostrils, pits
of eyes, faces
in flight and prints
of feet where no feet ever were,
elude the mind's
hollow that would contain
this canyon within a mountain.

Not far
enough from the familiar,
press

in under a deeper dark until
the curtained sex
the arch, the streaming buttress
have become
the self's unnameable and shaping home.

Arizona Desert

Eye
drinks the dry orange ground,
the cowskull
bound to it by shade:
sun-warped, the layers
of flaked and broken bone
unclench into petals,
into eyelids of limestone:

Blind glitter
that sees
spaces and steppes expand
of the purgatories possible
to us and
impossible.

Upended trees
in the Hopi's desert orchard
betoken
unceasing unspoken war,
return
the levelling light,
imageless arbiter.

A dead snake
pulsates again
as, hidden, the beetles' hunger
mines through the tunnel of its drying skin.

Here, to be,
is to sound
patience deviously
and follow
like the irregular corn
the water underground.

Villages
from mud and stone
parch back
to the dust they humanize
and mean
marriage, a loving lease
on sand, sun, rock and
Hopi
means peace.

A Death in the Desert

in memory of Homer Vance

There are no crosses
on the Hopi graves. They lie
shallowly
under a scattering
of small boulders. The sky
over the desert
with its sand-grain stars
and the immense equality
between
desert and desert sky,
seem
a scope and ritual
enough to stem
death and to be its equal.

'Homer
is the name,' said

the old Hopi doll-maker.
I met him in summer. He was dead
when I came back that autumn.

He had sat
like an Olympian
in his cool room
on the rock-roof of the world,
beyond the snatch
of circumstance
and was to die
beating a burro out of his corn-patch.

'That',
said his neighbour
'was a week ago.' And the week
that lay
uncrossably between us
stretched into sand,
into the spread
of the endless
waterless sea-bed beneath
whose space outpacing sight
receded as speechless and as wide as death.

On the Mountain

Nobody there:
no body,
thin aromatic air
pricking the wide nostrils
that inhale the dark.

Blank brow freezing
where the blaze of snow
carries beyond the summit
up over a satin cloud meadow
to confront the moon.

Nobody sees
the snow-free tree-line,
the aspens weightlessly shivering
and the surrounding pine
that, hardly
lifting their heavy
pagodas of leaves,
yet make a continuous
sound as of sea-wash
around the mountain lake.

And nobody climbs
the dry collapsing ledges
down to the place
to stand
in solitary, sharpened reflection
save for that swaying moon-face.

Somebody
finding nobody there
found gold also:
gold gone, he
(stark in his own redundancy)
must needs go too
and here, sun-warped
and riddled by moon, decays
his house which nobody occupies.

Las Trampas USA

for Robert and Priscilla Bunker

I go through hollyhocks
in a dry garden, up
to the house,
knock, then ask
in English for the key
to Las Trampas church.

The old woman
says in Spanish: I
do not speak English
so I say: Where
is the church key
in Spanish.
– You see those
three men working: you
ask them. She
goes in, I
go on
preparing to ask
them in Spanish:
Hi, they say
in American. Hello
I say and ask
them in English
where is the key
to the church and they
say: He has it
gesturing to a fourth
man working
hoeing a corn-field
nearby, and to him
(in Spanish): Where is
the church key? And he:
I have it. – OK
they say in
Spanish–American:
You bring it (and
to me in English)
He'll bring it. You
wait for him
by the church door.
Thank you, I say and they
reply in American
You're welcome. I go
once more and
await in shadow
the key: he
who brings it is not
he of the hoe, but

one of the three
men working, who
with a Castilian grace
ushers me in
to this place
of coolness out
of the August sun.

Arroyo Seco

A piano, so long untuned
it sounded like a guitar
was playing *Für Elise*:
the church was locked: graves
on which the only flowers
were the wild ones
except for the everlasting
plastic wreaths and roses,
the bleached dust making
them gaudier than they were
and they were gaudy:

SILVIANO
we loved him

LUCERO

and equal eloquence in
the quotation, twisted and
cut across two pages
in the statuary book:

THY | LIFE
WILL | BE
DO | NE

Old Man at Valdez

No books, no songs
belong in the eighty-
year-old memory:
he knows where
the Indian graves are
in the woods, recalls
the day the Apaches
crept into Valdez
carrying away
a boy who
forty years later
came back
lacking one arm and said:
'I could hear you all
searching, but I
dursn't cry out
for fear they'd…'
The Indians
had trained their prize
to be a one-armed thief.
'And we never did', the old man says,
'see a thief like him
in Valdez.'

New Mexico

Mr Brodsky

I had heard
before, of an
American who would have preferred
to be an Indian;
but not
until Mr Brodsky, of one
whose professed and long
pondered-on passion

was to become a Scot,
who even sent for haggis and oatcakes
across continent.
Having read him
in Cambridge English
a verse or two
from MacDiarmid,
I was invited
to repeat the reading
before a Burns Night Gathering
where the Balmoral Pipers
of Albuquerque would
play in the haggis
out of its New York tin.
Of course, I said
No. No. I could *not* go
and then
half-regretted I had not been.
But to console
and cure the wish, came
Mr Brodsky, bringing
his pipes and played
until the immense, distended
bladder of leather seemed
it could barely contain its water –
tears (idle
tears) for the bridal of Annie Laurie
and Morton J. Brodsky.
A bagpipe in a dwelling is
a resonant instrument
and there he stood
lost in the gorse
the heather or whatever
six thousand
miles and more
from the infection's source,
in our neo-New Mexican parlour
where I had heard
before of an
American who would have preferred
to be merely an Indian.

Chief Standing Water

or my night on the reservation

Chief Standing Water
explained it

all to me –
the way he

left the reservation
(he was the only

Indian I ever
knew who

favoured explanation
explanation)

then his
conversion

(*Jesus Saves
Courtesy pays* –

the house
was full of texts)

and his
reversion to

'the ways of my people'
though he had

never (as he said)
forfeited

what civilization
taught him –

the house
was full of books

books like *The Book
of Mormon*

a brochure
on the Coronation

a copy of Blavatsky
(left by a former guest)

– her *Secret Doctrine*:
had he

read it? Oh he
had read

it. I like
my reading

heavy
he said:

he played
his drum

to a song
one hundred thousand

years old –
it told

the way his people
had come

from Yucatan
it predicted

the white-man:
you heard

words
like

*Don't know
OK*

embedded in
the archaic line

quite dis-
tinctly

and listen
he said

there's *Haircut*
and he sang it

again and look
my hair

is cut:
how's that now

for one hundred thousand
years ago

the archaeologists
don't-know-

nothin: and
in farewell:

this is not
he said

a motel but
Mrs Water and me

we
have our

plans for one
and the next

time that
you come

maybe...
I paid

the bill
and considering

the texts
they lived by

he and
Mrs Water

it was a
trifle high

(*Jesus pays*
Courtesy saves)

and that was my
night

on the
reservation.

At Barstow

Nervy with neons, the main drag
was all there was. A placeless place.
A faint flavour of Mexico in the tacos
tasting of gasoline. Trucks refuelled
before taking off through space. Someone lived
in the houses with their houseyards wired
like tiny Belsens. The Götterdämmerung
would be like this. No funeral pyres, no choirs
of lost trombones. An Untergang
without a clang, without
a glimmer of gone glory
however dimmed. At the motel desk
was a photograph of Roy Rogers
signed. It was here
he made a stay. He did not
ride away on Trigger
through the high night, the tilted
Pleiades overhead, the Pole Star low, no

going off until
the eyes of beer-cans
had ceased to glint at him
and the desert darknesses
had quenched the neons. He was spent.
He was content. Down he lay.
The passing trucks patrolled his sleep,
the shifted gears contrived
a muffled fugue against the fading of his day
and his dustless, undishonoured stetson rode
beside the bed,
glowed in the pulsating, never-final twilight
there, at that execrable conjunction
of gasoline and desert air.

Arizona Highway

To become the face of space,
snatching a flowing mask
of emptiness
from where the parallels meet.

One is no more
than invaded transparency, until
on falling asleep, one can feel
them travelling through one still.

The windshield drinks
the telegraphed desert miles,
the tarmac river: tyranny,
glass identity,
devouring and dusty eye,
pure duration, all
transition, transformation.

We have driven into day,
get down to eat:
in a disappearing shadow
under our feet, the dry

pale Sienese reds and oranges
are distinct crystals
that sleep cannot snatch away.

But sleep
expands through senses
that distance has rifled.

When I wake,
hands and head
are in sand, ants are shifting,
inspecting the remains of breakfast,
and on the lips and tongue
burns the fine-ground glass of the sand grains.

Two Views of Two Ghost Towns

I

Why speak of memory and death
on ghost ground? Absences
relieve, release. Speak
of the life that uselessness
has unconstrained. Rusting
to its rails, the vast obese
company engine that will draw
no more, will draw no more:
Keep Off
the warning says, and all
the mob of objects, freed
under the brightly hard
displacement of the desert light
repeat it: the unaxled wheels,
doorless doors and windowless
regard of space. Clear
of the weight of human
meanings, human need,
gradually
houses splinter to the ground
in white and red, two

rotting parallels beneath
the sombre slag-mound.

II

How dry the ghosts
of dryness are. The air
here, tastes of sparseness
and the graveyard stones
are undecorated. To the left
the sea and, right, the shadows
hump and slide, climbing
the mountainside as clouds go over.
The town has moved away,
leaving a bitten hill
where the minehead's visible. Brambles
detain the foot. Ketchum,
Clay, Shoemake, Jebez O'Haskill
and Judge H. Vennigerholz
all (save for the judge's
modest obelisk) marked
by a metal cross; and there are four
crosses of wood, three
wooden stakes (unnamed)
that the sun, the frost, the sea-
wind shred alternately
in sapless scars. How dry
the ghosts of dryness are.

Ute Mountain

'When I am gone,'
the old chief said
'if you need me, call me,'
and down he lay, became stone.

They were giants then
(as you may see),
and we
are not the shadows of such men.

The long splayed Indian hair
spread ravelling out
behind the rocky head
in groins, ravines;

petered across the desert plain
through Colorado,
transmitting force
in a single undulant unbroken line

from toe to hair-tip: there
profiled, inclined away from one
are features, foreshortened, and the high
blade of the cheekbone.

Reading it so, the eye
can take the entire great
straddle of mountain-mass,
passing down elbows, knees and feet.

'If you need me, call me.'
His singularity dominates the plain
as we call to our aid his image:
thus men make a mountain.

In Connecticut

White, these villages. White
their churches without altars. The first snow
falls through a grey-white sky
and birch-twig whiteness turns
whiter against the grey. White
the row of pillars (each
of them is a single tree), the walls
sculptureless. 'This church was gathered
in 1741. In 1742
by act of the General Assembly of Connecticut
this territory was incorporated

and was named Judea.'
The sun passes, the elms
enter as lace shadows, then
go out again. White...
'Our minister is fine. He's a minister
in church, and a man outside.' – delivered
with the same shadowless conviction
as her invitation, when
lowering, leaning
out of the window she was cleaning
she had said: 'Our doors
are always open.'

Maine Winter

Ravenous the flock
who with an artist's
tact, dispose
their crow-blue-black
over the spread of snow –
Trackless, save where
by stalled degrees
a fox flaringly goes
with more of the hunter's caution than
of the hunter's ease.

The flock
have sighted him, are his match
and more, with their artist's eye
and a score of beaks against
a fox, paws clogged, and a single pair of jaws.

And they mass to the red-on-white
conclusion, sweep
down between
a foreground all snow-scene and a distance
all cliff-tearing seascape.

Letters from Amherst

for Edith Perry Stamm

Letters from Amherst came. They were written
In so peculiar a hand, it seemed
The writer might have learned the script by studying
The famous fossil bird-tracks
In the museum of that college town. Of punctuation
There was little, except for dashes: 'My companion
Is a dog,' they said. 'They are better
Than beings, because they know but do not tell.'
And in the same, bird-like script: 'You think
My gait "spasmodic". I am in danger, sir.
You think me uncontrolled. I have no tribunal.'
Of people: 'They talk of hallowed things aloud
And embarrass my dog. I let them hear
A noiseless noise in the orchard. I work
In my prison where I make
Guests for myself.' The first of these
Letters was unsigned, but sheltered
Within the larger package was a second,
A smaller, containing what the letter lacked –
A signature, written upon a card in pencil,
As if the writer wished
To recede from view as far as possible
In the upstairs room
In the square cool mansion where she wrote
Letters from Amherst...

In Longfellow's Library

Sappho
and the Venus de Milo
gaze out past
the scintillations from
the central
candelabrum

to where
(on an upper shelf)
plaster Goethe
in a laurel
crown, looks
down divided
from a group
dancing a
tarantella, by
the turquoise butterfly
that Agassiz
brought back
dead: below
these, the busts of
Homer, Aeschylus
and Sophocles still
pedestalled where
they ambushed Hiawatha.

On Eleventh Street

A mosaicist of minute
attentions composed it,
arranged the gravel
walks, where there is not
room for any, and the neat
hedges of privet: the complete
Second Cemetery
of the Spanish and Portuguese
Synagogue, Shearith
Israel, in the City of
New York
eighteen-five to
twenty-nine, could be
cut out, and carried
away by three
men, one at each
corner: a tight

triangle between two
building ends, the third
side a wall, white-washed
topped by a railing, and a gate
in it on to the street.

A Garland for Thomas Eakins

for Seymour Adelman

I

He lived
from his second year
at seventeen twentynine
Mount Vernon Street
Philadelphia
Pennsylvania where
he painted his
father and his sisters
and he died
in Pennsylvania in
Philadelphia at
seventeen twentynine
Mount Vernon Street.

II

Anatomy, perspective
and reflection: a boat
in three inclinations:
to the wind, to the waves
and to the picture-frame.
Those are the problems. What
does a body propose
that a boat does not?

III

Posing the model
for 'The Concert Singer' he

stood her
relative to a grid
placed vertically
behind her. There was a spot
before her
on the wall that
she must look at.
To her dress
by the intersections
of the grid he tied
coloured ribbons, thus
projecting her
like an architect's elevation
on a plane
that was vertical, the canvas
at a right angle
to the eye and perpendicular
to the floor.
What does the man
who sees
trust to
if not the eye? He trusts
to knowledge
to right appearances.

IV

– And what do you think of
that, Mr Eakins? (A Whistler)
– I think that that
is a very cowardly way to paint.

V

A fat woman
by Rubens
is not a fat
woman but a fiction.

VI

The Eakins portrait
(said Whitman)
sets me down
in correct style

without feathers.
And when they
said to him:
Has Mr. Eakins no
social gifts? he said
to them: What are
'social gifts'? –
The parlour puts
quite its own
measure upon social gifts.

VII

The figures of perception
as against
the figures of elocution.
What they wanted
was to be Medici
in Philadelphia
and they survive
as Philadelphians.

VIII

The accord with that
which asked
only to be recorded:
'How beautiful,' he said,
'an old lady's skin is:
all those wrinkles!'

IX

Only
to be recorded!
and his stare
in the self-portrait
calculates the abyss
in the proposition. He dies
unsatisfied, born
to the stubborn
anguish of
those eyes.

The Well

in a Mexican convent

Leaning on
the parapet stone
Listening down
the long, dark
sheath through which the standing
shaft of water
sends its echoings up
Catching, as it stirs
the steady seethings
that mount and mingle
with surrounding sounds
from the neighbouring
barrack-yard: soldiery
– heirs, no doubt
of the gunnery that gashed
these walls of tattered
frescoes, the bullet-
holes now socketed
deeper by sunlight
and the bright gaps
giving on to the square
and there revealing
strollers in khaki
with their girls Aware
of a well-like
cool throughout
the entire, clear
sunlit ruin,
of the brilliant cupids
above the cistern
that hold up
a baldachin of stone
which is not there
Hearing the tide
of insurrection
subside through time
under the still-

painted slogans
Hemos servido
lealmente
la revolución

On a Mexican Straw Christ

This is not the event. This
Is a man of straw,
The legs straw-thin
The straw-arms shent
And nailed. And yet this dry
Essence of agony must be
Close-grained to the one
They lifted down, when
Consummatum est the event was done.
Below the baroque straw-
Haloed basket-head
And the crown, far more
Like a cap, woven
For a matador than a crown of thorn,
A gap recedes: it makes
A mouth-in-pain, the teeth
Within its sideways-slashed
And gritted grin, are
Verticals of straw, and they
Emerge where the mask's
Chin ceases and become
Parallels plunging down, their sum
The body of God. Beneath,
Two feet join in one
Cramped culmination, as if
To say: 'I am the un-
Resurrection and the Death.'

On the Tlacolula Bus

On the Tlacolula bus
'I flew for the Fuehrer'
it says: *Yo vole*
para el Fuehrer signed
Lukenbac in Gothic.
The Fuehrer is dead and Lukenbac
does not drive today:
instead, a Mexican with the brown
face of a Mayan
is in his place and under
a sign *No distraer*
al Operador is
chatting across his shoulder.
Would Lukenbac? And does he
care for this country, or long
for a land of hygiene and Christmas trees
where he would not dare
write up his boast in Gothic?
As we swing
out of the market square
a goat on a string
being led by someone
stops, stands and while
the bus passes by
into history, turns
on the succession of windows
its narrow stare, looking
like Lukenbac in exile.

The Oaxaca Bus

Fiat Voluntas Tua:
over the head of the driver
an altar. No end to it,
the beginning seems to be
Our Lady of Solitude
blessing the crowd

out of a double frame –
gilt and green. Dark
mother by light,
her neighbour, the Guadalupe Virgin
is tucked away under the right-
hand edge as if
to make sure
twice over and (left)
are the legs of a protruding
postcard crucifixion
mothered by both. A cosmos
proliferates outwards
from the mystery, starts
with the minute, twin
sombreros dangling there, each
with embroidered brims
and a blood-red cord
circling the crown of each.
The driving mirror
catches their reflection, carries on
the miraculous composition
with two names – serifs
and flourishes –: *Maria,*
Eugenia: both
inscribed on the glass and
flanked at either end
by rampant rockets
torpedoing moonwards. Again
on either side,
an artificial vine
twines down: it is tied
to rails in the aisle
and, along it, flower –
are they nasturtiums? They are
pink like the bathing dresses
of the cut-out belles
it passes in descending,
their petals are pleated
like the green
of the fringed curtain that borders the windshield:
they are lilies
of the field of Mexico,

plastic godsend,
last flourish
of that first *Fiat* from sister goddesses
and (yes)
the end...

Constitution Day

Subject for Eisenstein
but in reversion:
proletariat
flowing in cinematic streams
all going the wrong way
to pray
to the Dark Virgin of Tepeyac hill.

Ablaze
in his laundered white
an adolescent recites
a poem on the Constitution
and, *Juarez*, *Madero*, *Cárdenas*
the names go by
like faces in a fresco
just as Diego
would have painted them. It's all
very bad, but it's a poem.

While the brass band
finger their instruments for another fanfare
– *Juarez*, *Lopez Mateos* –
penitents come pouring in
to the gold interior and effigy,
deaf to the Day and seeking
the promise of a more than human mercy.

The committee
platformed behind the spouting child
are quite the best-
dressed Mexicans I have seen,

perched there beyond the doom
of the ragged rest,
of God's desolate mother, Eisenstein
dead of a weakened heart
and Stalin rifled from his tomb.

The Bootblack

What does he think about
down there? His hair is immaculate
and all that I can glimpse
save for a pair of hands
in a mess of turpentine, the back
thin, its twin shoulder-blades
rucking the shirt. What does he see?
Does he see me? Or the penitents
behind him, crossing the plaza
by the Basilica de Guadalupe
and climbing
up into the shrine
taking the steps on shuffled knees?
It's Constitution Day.
Does he care? Does he hear
the processions of bobbing straw sombreros
on sandalled feet
liquid-footed as sheep
feeding the city from the villages?
Ask your questions, and they
reply with smiles you cannot interpret.
He has done
spreading the stain
from naked fingers, has put on
the shine. I say: 'The shoes
are fit for a king.' And he smiles.
Will he be
angry or mirthful when he
inherits the earth?

Mexico City

Theory of Regress

Seven bulls of a Sunday:
corrida for the crowd, carcasses
for the penitentiary. *And you descend
said Artaud, to this
when you began
with human
sacrifice?*

In Michoacán

A poor church
but an obstinate devotion
had filled it
with flowers.

What power drew
those flower-fraught Indians down
by narrow trails
no one knew

Until the earthquake:
after it, the altar
split wide open
like a hell-mouth,

And inside the wreck
there sat
its guardian idol:
squat, smiling, Aztec.

Weeper in Jalisco

A circle of saints, all
hacked, mauled, bound,
bleed in a wooden frieze
under the gloom of the central
dome of gold. They
are in paradise now
and we are not –
baroque feet gone
funnelling up, a blood-
bought, early resurrection
leaving us this
tableau of wounds, the crack
in the universe sealed
behind their flying backs.
We are here, and a woman
sprawls and wails to them
there, the gold screen
glistening, hemming her
under, till her keening
fills the stone ear
of the whole, hollow sanctum
and she is the voice
those wounds cry through
unappeasably bleeding where
her prone back shoulders
the price and weight
of forfeited paradise.

Landscape

after Octavio Paz

Rock and precipice,
More time than stone, this
Timeless matter.

Through its cicatrices
Falls without moving
Perpetual virgin water.

Immensity reposes here
Rock over rock,
Rocks over air.

The world's manifest
As it is: a sun
Immobile, in the abyss.

Scale of vertigo:
The crags weigh
No more than our shadows.

Idyll

Washington Square, San Francisco

A door:
   PER L'UNIVERSO
     is what it says
above it.
    You must approach
      more nearly
(the statue
    of Benjamin Franklin watching you)
      before you see
La Gloria di Colui
   che tutto muove
     PER L'UNIVERSO
– leaning
   along the lintel –
    penetra e risplende
across this church
   for Italian Catholics:
    Dante

unscrolling in rhapsody.
      Cool
            the January sun.
that with an intensity
      the presence of the sea
           makes more exact,
chisels the verse with shade
      and lays
           on the grass
a deep and even
      Californian green,
           while a brilliance
throughout the square
      flatters the meanness of its architecture.
           Beyond
there is the flood
      which skirts this pond
           and tugs the ear
towards it: cars
      thick on the gradients of the city
           shift sun and sound –
a constant ground-bass
      to these provincialisms of the piazza
           tasting still
of Lerici and Genova.
      Here
           as there
the old men sit
      in a mingled odour
           of cheroot and garlic
spitting;
      they share serenity
           with the cross-legged
Chinese adolescent
      seated between them
           reading, and whose look
wears the tranquility of consciousness
      forgotten in its object –
           his book
bears for a title
      SUCCESS
           in spelling.

How
         does one spell out this
                  che penetra e risplende
from square
         into the hill-side alley-ways
                  around it, where
between tall houses
         children of the Mediterranean
                  and Chinese element
mingle
         their American voices?...
                  The dictionary
defines idyllium
         as meaning
                  'a piece, descriptive
chiefly of rustic life';
         we
                  are in town: here
let it signify
         this poised quiescence, pause
                  and possibility in which
the music of the generations
         binds into its skein
                  the flowing instant,
while the winter sun
         pursues the shadow
                  before a church
whose decoration
         is a quotation from *Paradiso*.

Small Action Poem

for Robert and Bobbie Creeley

To arrive
　　　unexpectedly
　　　　　from nowhere:
then:
　　　having done
　　　　　what it was
one came for,
　　　to depart.
　　　　　The door
is open now
　　　that before
　　　　　was neither
open
　　　nor was it there.
　　　　　It is like
Chopin
　　　shaking
　　　　　music from the fingers,
making that
　　　in which
　　　　　all is either
technique
　　　heightened to sorcery
　　　　　or nothing but notes.
To arrive
　　　unexpectedly
　　　　　at somewhere
and the final
　　　chord, the final
　　　　　word.

THE WAY OF A WORLD

1969

Y tanto se da el presente
Que el pie caminante siente
La integridad del planeta.
Jorge Guillén, Perfección

Swimming Chenango Lake

Winter will bar the swimmer soon.
   He reads the water's autumnal hesitations
A wealth of ways: it is jarred,
   It is astir already despite its steadiness,
Where the first leaves at the first
   Tremor of the morning air have dropped
Anticipating him, launching their imprints
   Outwards in eccentric, overlapping circles.
There is a geometry of water, for this
   Squares off the clouds' redundances
And sets them floating in a nether atmosphere
   All angles and elongations: every tree
Appears a cypress as it stretches there
   And every bush that shows the season,
A shaft of fire. It is a geometry and not
   A fantasia of distorting forms, but each
Liquid variation answerable to the theme
   It makes away from, plays before:
It is a consistency, the grain of the pulsating flow.
   But he has looked long enough, and now
Body must recall the eye to its dependence
   As he scissors the waterscape apart
And sways it to tatters. Its coldness
   Holding him to itself, he grants the grasp,
For to swim is also to take hold
   On water's meaning, to move in its embrace
And to be, between grasp and grasping, free.
   He reaches in-and-through to that space
The body is heir to, making a where
   In water, a possession to be relinquished
Willingly at each stroke. The image he has torn
   Flows-to behind him, healing itself,
Lifting and lengthening, splayed like the feathers
   Down an immense wing whose darkening spread
Shadows his solitariness: alone, he is unnamed
   By this baptism, where only Chenango bears a name
In a lost language he begins to construe –
   A speech of densities and derisions, of half-
Replies to the questions his body must frame

Frogwise across the all but penetrable element.
Human, he fronts it and, human, he draws back
   From the interior cold, the mercilessness
That yet shows a kind of mercy sustaining him.
   The last sun of the year is drying his skin
Above a surface a mere mosaic of tiny shatterings,
   Where a wind is unscaping all images in the flowing obsidian
The going-elsewhere of ripples incessantly shaping.

Prometheus

Summer thunder darkens, and its climbing
   Cumuli, disowning our scale in the zenith,
Electrify this music: the evening is falling apart.
   Castles-in-air; on earth: green, livid fire.
The radio simmers with static to the strains
   Of this mock last-day of nature and of art.

We have lived through apocalypse too long:
   Scriabin's dinosaurs! Trombones for the transformation
That arrived by train at the Finland Station,
   To bury its hatchet after thirty years in the brain
Of Trotsky. Alexander Nikolayevitch, the events
   Were less merciful than your mob of instruments.

Too many drowning voices cram this waveband.
   I set Lenin's face by yours –
Yours, the fanatic ego of eccentricity against
   The systematic son of a schools inspector
Tyutchev on desk – for the strong man reads
   Poets as the antisemite pleads: 'A Jew was my friend.'

Cymballed firesweeps. Prometheus came down
   In more than orchestral flame and Kerensky fled
Before it. The babel of continents gnaws now
   And tears at the silk of those harmonies that seemed
So dangerous once. You dreamed an end
   Where the rose of the world would go out like a close in music.

Population drags the partitions down
    And we are a single town of warring suburbs:
I cannot hear such music for its consequence:
    Each sense was to have been reborn
Out of a storm of perfumes and light
    To a white world, an in-the-beginning.

In the beginning, the strong man reigns:
    Trotsky, was it not then you brought yourself
To judgement and to execution, when you forgot
    Where terror rules, justice turns arbitrary?
Chromatic Prometheus, myth of fire,
    It is history topples you in the zenith.

Blok, too, wrote The Scythians
    Who should have known: he who howls
With the whirlwind, with the whirlwind goes down.
    In this, was Lenin guiltier than you
When, out of a merciless patience grew
    The daily prose such poetry prepares for?

Scriabin, Blok, men of extremes,
    History treads out the music of your dreams
Through blood, and cannot close like this
    In the perfection of anabasis. It stops. The trees
Continue raining though the rain has ceased
    In a cooled world of incessant codas:

Hard edges of the houses press
    On the after-music senses, and refuse to burn,
Where an ice cream van circulates the estate
    Playing Greensleeves, and at the city's
Stale new frontier even ugliness
    Rules with the cruel mercy of solidities.

'Prometheus' refers to the tone-poem by Scriabin and to his hope of transforming the world by music and rite.

A Dream

or the worst of both worlds

Yevtushenko, Voznesensky and I
are playing to a full house: I lack their verve
(I know) their red reserve
of Scythian corpuscles, to ride in triumph through
Indianapolis. They read. Libido roars
across the dionysian sluice of the applause
and the very caryatids lean down
to greet them: youth towers (feet
on shoulders) into instant acrobatic pyramids –
human triforia to shore up the roof
cheering. I come on
sorting my pages, searching for the one
I've failed to write. It's October
nineteen seventeen once more. But is it me
or Danton from the tumbril, stentoriously
starts delivering one by one my bits of ivory?
No matter. I still ride their tide of cheers
and I could read the whole sheaf
backwards, breasting effortlessly
the surge of sweat and plaudits to emerge
laurelled in vatic lather, brother, bard:
they hear me out who have not heard one word,
bringing us back for bows, bringing down the house
once more. The reds return to their homeground stadia,
their unforeseen disgraces; I
to the sobriety of a dawn-cold bed, to own
my pariah's privilege, my three-inch spaces,
the reader's rest and editor's colophon.

A Word in Edgeways

Tell me about yourself they
say and you begin to
tell them about yourself and

that is just the way I
am is their reply: they play
it all back to you in another
key, their key, and then in mid-
narrative they pay you a
compliment as if to say what a good
listener you are I am
a good listener my stay
here has developed my faculty I will
say that for me I will not
say that every literate male in
America is a soliloquist, a
ventriloquist, a strategic
egotist, an inveterate
campaigner-explainer over and
back again on the terrain of him-
self – what I will
say is they are not un-
interesting: they are simply
unreciprocal and yes it was a
pleasure if not an unmitigated
pleasure and I yes I did enjoy our
conversation goodnightthankyou

Eden

I have seen Eden. It is a light of place
   As much as the place itself; not a face
Only, but the expression on that face: the gift
   Of forms constellates cliff and stones:
The wind is hurrying the clouds past,
   And the clouds as they flee, ravelling-out
Shadow a salute where the thorn's barb
   Catches the tossed, unroving sack
That echoes their flight. And the same
   Wind stirs in the thicket of the lines
In Eden's wood, the radial avenues
   Of light there, copious enough

To draft a city from. Eden
   Is given one, and the clairvoyant gift
Withdrawn, 'Tell us', we say
   'The way to Eden,' but lost in the meagre
Streets of our dispossession, where
   Shall we turn, when shall we put down
This insurrection of sorry roofs? Despair
   Of Eden is given, too: we earn
Neither its loss nor having. There is no
   Bridge but the thread of patience, no way
But the will to wish back Eden, this leaning
   To stand against the persuasions of a wind
That rings with its meaninglessness where it sang its meaning.

Adam

Adam, on such a morning, named the beasts:
   It was before the sin. It is again.
An openwork world of lights and ledges
   Stretches to the eyes' lip its cup:
Flower-maned beasts, beasts of the cloud,
   Beasts of the unseen, green beasts
Crowd forward to be named. Beasts of the qualities
   Claim them: sinuous, pungent, swift:
We tell them over, surround them
   In a world of sounds, and they are heard
Not drowned in them; we lay a hand
   Along the snakeshead, take up
The nameless muzzle, to assign its vocable
   And meaning. Are we the lords or limits
Of this teeming horde? We bring
   To a kind of birth all we can name
And, named, it echoes in us our being.
   Adam, on such a morning, knew
The perpetuity of Eden, drew from the words
   Of that long naming, his sense of its continuance
And of its source – beyond the curse of the bitten apple –
   Murmuring in wordless words: 'When you deny

The virtue of this place, then you
    Will blame the wind or the wide air,
  Whatever cannot be mastered with a name,
    Mouther and unmaker, madman, Adam.'

Night Transfigured

Do you recall the night we flung
    Our torch-beam down in among
The nettle towers? Stark-white
    Robbed of their true dimension
Or of the one we knew, their dense
    World seemed to be all there was:
An immense, shifting crystal
    Latticed by shadow, it swayed from the dark,
Each leaf, lodged blade above blade
    In serrated, dazzling divisions.
What large thing was it stood
    In such small occurence, that it could
Transfigure the night, as we
    Drew back to find ourselves once more
In the surrounding citadel of height and air?
    To see then speak, is to see with the words
We did not make. That silence
    Loud with the syllables of the generations, and that sphere
Centred by a millennial eye, all that was not
    There, told us what was, and clothed
The sense, bare as it seemed, in the weave
    Of years: we knew that we were sharers,
Heirs to the commonalty of sight, that the night
    In its reaches and its nearnesses, possessed
A single face, sheer and familiar
    Dear if dread. The dead had distanced,
Patterned its lineaments, and to them
    The living night was cenotaph and ceaseless requiem.

Assassin

The rattle in Trotsky's throat and his wild boar's moans
Piedra de Sol, Octavio Paz

Blood I foresaw. I had put by
    The distractions of the retina, the eye
That like a child must be fed and comforted
    With patterns, recognitions. The room
Had shrunk to a paperweight of glass and he
    To the centre and prisoner of its transparency.

He rasped pages. I knew too well
    The details of that head. I wiped
Clean the glance and saw
    Only his vulnerableness. Under my quivering
There was an ease, save for that starched insistence
    While paper snapped and crackled as in October air.

Sound drove out sight. We inhabited together
    One placeless cell. I must put down
This rage of the ear for discrimination, its absurd
    Dwelling on ripples, liquidities, fact
Fastening on the nerve gigantic paper burs.
    The gate of history is straiter than eye's or ear's.

In imagination, I had driven the spike
    Down and through. The skull had sagged in its blood.
The grip, the glance – stained but firm –
    Held all at its proper distance and now hold
This autumnal hallucination of white leaves
    From burying purpose in a storm of sibilance.

I strike. I am the future and my blow
    Will have it now. If lightning froze
It would hover as here, the room
    Riding in the crest of the moment's wave,
In the deed's time, the deed's transfiguration
    And as if that wave would never again recede.

The blood wells. Prepared for this
  This I can bear. But papers
Snow to the ground with a whispered roar:
  The voice, cleaving their crescendo, is his
Voice, and his the animal cry
  That has me then by the roots of the hair.

Fleshed in that sound, objects betray me,
  Objects are my judge: the table and its shadow,
Desk and chair, the ground a pressure
  Telling me where it is that I stand
Before wall and window-light:
  Mesh of the curtain, wood, metal, flesh:

A dying body that refuses death,
  He lurches against me in his warmth and weight,
As if my arm's length blow
  Had transmitted and spent its strength
Through blood and bone; and I, spectred,
  The body that rose against me were my own.

Woven from the hair of that bent head,
  The thread that I had grasped unlabyrinthed all –
Tightrope of history and necessity –
  But the weight of a world unsteadies my feet
And I fall into the lime and contaminations
  Of contingency; into hands, looks, time.

Against Extremity

Let there be treaties, bridges,
  Chords under the hands, to be spanned
Sustained: extremity hates a given good
  Or a good gained. That girl who took
Her life almost, then wrote a book
  To exorcize and to exhibit the sin,
Praises a friend there for the end she made
  And each of them becomes a heroine.

The time is in love with endings. The time's
    Spoiled children threaten what they will do,
And those they cannot shake by petulance
    They'll bribe out of their wits by show.
Against extremity, let there be
    Such treaties as only time itself
Can ratify, a bond and test
    Of sequential days, and like the full
Moon slowly given to the night,
    A possession that is not to be possessed.

In the Fullness of Time

a letter to Octavio Paz

The time you tell us is the century and the day
    Of Shiva and Parvati: immanent innocence,
Moment without movement. Tell us, too, the way
    Time, in its fullness, fills us
As it flows: tell us the beauty of succession
    That Breton denied: the day goes
Down, but there is time before it goes
    To negotiate a truce in time. We met
Sweating in Rome and in a place
    Of confusions, cases and telephones: and then
It was evening over Umbria, the train
    Arriving, the light leaving the dry fields
And next the approaching roofs. As we slowed
    Curving towards the station, the windows ahead swung
Back into our line of vision and flung at us
    A flash of pausing lights: the future
That had invited, waited for us there
    Where the first carriages were. That hesitant arc
We must complete by our consent to time –
    Segment to circle, chance into event:
And how should we not consent? For time
    Putting its terrors by, it was as if
The unhurried sunset were itself a courtesy.

Music's Trinity

Lugar de las nupcias impalpables

(for Octavio and Marie José)

Motion: not things
moving, where the harp's
high swan
sailing out across
clear water
has all our ear.

Time: not the crabbed
clock's, but the force
and aggregation as the horns'
cumuli mass
rising to rob the sky
of silence.

Space: not between
but where: as,
out of a liquid
turbulence, a tremulousness gives place
to Atlantis.

Logic

A trailed and lagging grass, a pin-point island
Drags the clear current's face it leans across
In ripple-wrinkles. At a touch
It has ravelled the imaged sky till it could be
A perplexity of metal, spun
Round a vortex, the sun flung off it
Veining the eye like a migraine – it could
Scarcely be sky. The stones do more, until we say
We see there meshes of water, liquid
Nets handed down over them, a clear

Cross-hatching in the dance of wrinkles that
Re-patterns wherever it strikes.
So much for stones. They seem to have their way.
But the sway is the water's: it cannot be held
Though moulded and humped by the surfaces
It races over, though a depth can still
And a blade's touch render it illegible.
Its strength is here: it must
Account for its opposite and yet remain
Itself, of its own power get there.
Water is like logic, for it flows
Meeting resistance arguing as it goes:
And it arrives, having found not the quickest
Way, but the way round, the channel which
Entering, it may come to a level in,
Which must admit, in certain and crowding fusion,
The irrefutable strength which follows it.

The Way of a World

Having mislaid it, and then
    Found again in a changed mind
The image of a gull the autumn gust
    Had pulled upwards and past
The window I watched from, I recovered too
    The ash-key, borne-by whirling
On the same surge of air, like an animate thing:
    The scene was there again: the bird,
The seed, the windlines drawn in the sidelong
    Sweep of leaves and branches that only
The black and supple boughs restrained –
    All would have joined in the weightless anarchy
Of air, but for that counterpoise. All rose
    Clear in the memory now, though memory did not choose
Or value it first: it came
    With its worth and, like those tree-tips,
Fine as dishevelling hair, but steadied
    And masted as they are, that worth
Outlasted its lost time, when

The cross-currents had carried it under.
In all these evanescences of daily air,
    It is the shapes of change, and not the bare
Glancing vibrations, that vein and branch
    Through the moving textures: we grasp
The way of a world in the seed, the gull
    Swayed toiling against the two
Gravities that root and uproot the trees.

Descartes and the Stove

Thrusting its armoury of hot delight,
    Its negroid belly at him, how the whole
Contraption threatened to melt him
    Into recognition. Outside, the snow
Starkened all that snow was not –
    The boughs' nerve-net, angles and gables
Denting the brilliant hoods of it. The foot-print
    He had left on entering, had turned
To a firm dull gloss, and the chill
    Lined it with a fur of frost. Now
The last blaze of day was changing
    All white to yellow, filling
With bluish shade the slots and spoors
    Where, once again, badger and fox would wind
Through the phosphorescence. All leaned
    Into that frigid burning, corded tight
By the lightlines as the slow sun drew
    Away and down. The shadow, now,
Defined no longer: it filled, then overflowed
    Each fault in snow, dragged everything
Into its own anonymity of blue
    Becoming black. The great mind
Sat with his back to the unreasoning wind
    And doubted, doubted at his ear
The patter of ash and, beyond, the snow-bound farms,
    Flora of flame and iron contingency
And the moist reciprocation of his palms.

The Question

Having misread the house, 'What
　　Room is it', she said, 'lies beyond
That?' And towards the door
　　Which did not exist, leaned
The room of air, the thousand directions
　　Ungoverned by any eye save one –
The blind house-wall, that for its two
　　Centuries had faced away
From that long possession of the moon and sun,
　　Room of the damasked changes where
Tonight, a pentecostal storm-light
　　Flashed and died through its patternings
And each invisible scene replied
　　In echo, tree-lash and water-voice
With the gift of tongues. In the room of storm
　　Rain raked the confine with its dense
Volley, the old house staining
　　Through wall and floor, as the sodden
Clamorous earth exuded, locked
　　Round on its soundlessness, but turned
Towards her question: 'What
　　Room is it lies beyond that?'

The View

The woods are preparing to wait out winter.
　　Gusts blow with an earnest of all there is to be done
Once frost will have entered the apple and the sun.
　　Of the view, there is no tale to tell you.
Its history is incidental. One would not date
　　The window that stands open like a gate
In the opposing house-face. It is dark inside.
　　The façade is a dirty white, and yet it seems
The right colour to stand there between
　　The dull green of the foreground trees
Still bearing leaves, and the autumnal glare

From the others framing it, foregoing theirs.
The dark of the window square might be
      A mineshaft of pure shadow, a way
Through to the heart of the hill – the black
      Centre, if centre there were where
Sight must travel such drops and intervals,
      And an undulation of aspens along the slope
Is turning the wind to water and to light,
      Unpivoting place amid its shaken coins,
While under a shuddering causeway, a currency,
      The season is dragging at all the roots of the view.

Weatherman

Weather releases him from the tyranny of rooms,
      From the white finality of clapboard towns.
The migrations have begun: geese going
      Wake him towards dawn, as they stream south
Drawing the north behind them, the long threat
      That disquiets his blood. He rises and roams
In the grey house. In the dark
      Height, geese yelp like a pack
Hunting through space. Unseen, they drive the eye
      Of the mind the way they go, through the opal
Changes of dawn light on the light of snow.
      The sun looks full at the town, at each
House with its double fringe of icicles
      And their shadows. He can hear no more
The cries that had woken him, but through eyes
      That wincing away from it, blink back
The radiance that followed the flock, he drinks in
      Human his inheritance and retrieved his kin
With that clamour, this cold, those changes-to-come from skies
      Now a stained-glass blue in the whiteness of the weather.

On the Principle of Blowclocks

three-way poem

The static forces
not a ball of silver
of a solid body
but a ball of air
and its material strength
whose globed sheernesses
derive from
shine with a twofold glitter:
not the quantity of mass:
once with the dew and once
an engineer would instance
with the constituent bright threads
rails or T beams, say
of all its spokes
four planes constructed to
in a tense surface
contain the same volume as
in a solid cloud of stars
four tons of mass

Clouds

How should the dreamer, on those slow
    Solidities, fix his wandering adagio,
Seizing, bone-frail, blown
    Through the diaphanous air of their patrols,
Shadows of fanfares, grails of melting snow?

A reading of 'On the Principle of Blowclocks' should include (a) the italicized lines, (b) the unitalicized, (c) the whole as printed.

How can he hope to hold that white
Opacity as it endures, advances,
    At a dream's length? Its strength
 Confounds him with detail, his glance falls
    From ridge to ridge down the soft canyon walls,
And, fleece as it may seem, its tones
    And touch are not the fleece of dream,
But light and body, spaced accumulation
    The mind can take its purchase on:
Cloudshapes are destinies, and they
    Charging the atmosphere of a common day,
Make it the place of confrontation where
    The dreamer wakes to the categorical call
And clear cerulean trumpet of the air.

Words for the Madrigalist

Look with the ears, said Orazio Vecchi,
    Trusting to music, willing to be led
Voluntarily blind through its complete
    Landscape of the emotion, feeling beneath the feet
Of the mind's heart, the land fall, the height
    Re-form: Look with the ears – they are all
Looking with the eyes, missing the way:
    So, waiting for sleep, I look
With the ears at the confused clear sounds
    As each replenished tributary unwinds
Its audible direction, and dividing
    The branchwork of chime and counterchime
Runs the river's thick and drumming stem:
    Loud with their madrigal of limestone beds
Where nothing sleeps, they all
    Give back – not the tune the listener calls
But the measure of what he is
    In the hard, sweet music of his lack,
The unpremeditated consonances: and the words
    Return it to you over the ground-
Bass of their syllables, Orazio Vecchi:
    Hear with the eyes as you catch the current of their sounds.

Anecdote

Carlos Trujillo
killed this mountain wolf
that killed his calf,

and strung it
high on a pinebranch
below Mt Lobo:

when I asked him, 'Why? –
for all the other
coyotes to see?'

his reply was:
'I did it
so the birds should have meat.'

Kiowa Ranch

Arroyo Hondo

Twice I'd tried
to pass the
bastard outside
of Arroyo Hondo:
each time, the same
thing: out he
came in a
wobbling glide
in that beat-up
pick-up, his
head bent
in affable accompaniment,
jawing at
the guy who sat
beside him: the third
time (ready

for him) I
cut out wide,
flung him
a passing look as I
made it: we almost
made it together
he and I: the same
thing, out he
came, all crippled speed
unheeding: I could not
retreat and what
did I see? I
saw them
playing at cards
on the driving seat.

The Matachines

Where, but here
would you
find – not
ten miles
from the city limit,
on an afternoon
graced by the feast-
day of Saint
Antony of Padua;
where, but here
all ranged
in a double line
masked as Moors
and dancing the morris
– the Moorish dance,
to the repetitions
of a high
fiddle and a low
guitar – where
but in this

play
of the way the Moors
were beaten in Spain,
that became
the story
in which Cortés
conquered
Moctezuma of Mexico
helped by his
Indian mistress
the Malinche: she
and the daughter
of the Moroccan emperor
(dual betrayal)
meet
in the white
minute girl
dancing in her
communion dress
between
the lines of men;
and where the bull
came from
nobody says
or why she
must betray
him too,
waving her
scarf of red
confusing his
tied-on horns,
his head
of a wrinkled
Spanish parishioner:
it is a
dance of
multiform confusions –
she
the Malinche
the Moorish bride
and the holy
Virgin all

in one:
conquistadores
all these
dressed-up Moors
before the saint,
and now, backwards
they dance to church,
the saint's
canopy carried
after them, until
by the door the double
line pause
and there the saint
passes in between them:
following, they
enter dancing
as if to say,
we are here
whatever we
do or
mean in this
dance
of the bull
and the betrayal:
whatever we
do we mean
as praise, praise
to the saint
and the occasion,
to the high
altar and its
ponderous crucifix
above: it is
done:
it is clear
the music
in the cool aisle
that the open
air dispersed:
we are here.

San Antonio, New Mexico

Before the Dance

at Zuni

The dance
is not yet
and when it will begin
no one says:
the waiting
for the Indian
is half the dance,
and so they wait
giving a quality
to the moment
by their refusal
to measure it:
the moment
is expansible
it burns
unconsumed
under the raw bulbs
of the dancing chamber:
the Navajo faces
wear
the aridity of the landscape
and 'the movement
with the wind
of the Orient and
the movement against
the wind
of the Occident'
meet
in their wrinkles:
they wait, sitting
(the moment)
on the earth floor
(is expansible)
saying very little
or sleep
like the woman
slipping along the wall

sideways
to wake
in the clangour of the pulse of time
at the beginning
drum...

A Sense of Distance

The door is shut.
The red rider
no longer crosses the canyon floor
under a thousand feet of air.

The glance that fell
on him, is shafting
a deeper well:
the boughs of the oak are roaring
inside the acorn shell.

The hoofbeats – silent, then –
are sounding now
that ride
dividing a later distance.

For I am in England,
and the mind's embrace
catches-up this English
and that horizonless desert space
into its own, and the three there
concentrically fill a single sphere.

And it seems as if a wind
had flung wide a door
above an abyss, where all
the kingdoms of possibilities shone
like sandgrains crystalline in the mind's own sun.

The Instance

They do say said
the barber running
his cold shears
downwards and over
the neck's sudden
surprised flesh:
They do say frost
will flow in
through the gap of a hedge
like water, and go
anywhere and I
believe it. I believe
him – a gardener,
he knows. The tepid
day erases
his wisdom and he
is out of mind
until at night
I grope for a way
between darkness and door
and passing a hand
down over
a parked car's
roof feel
the finger tips
burn at the crystal
proof of a frost
that finding a hole
in the hedge
has flowed through like water.

A Little Night Music

A shimmer at the ear: a sheen
the all-but-done day
would still detain it with:
a dying hoard of

wholly-unseen-now,
just-heard visitations:
small sounds poise
superimpose, then shift
as lightly as summer-flies
go glinting down
the drift of late air cooling:
a spate of sibilances: a maze
in motion where the foursquare
frontier of tree girths, the million
leaves beating there, are
spread weed in sleep's underwater: a
wincing and wandering of evanescences:
a not-listening ear.

The Awakening

The storm wind
was tearing at sleep: as it struck
a tremor through rafter and dream,
you might have been a rook
clinging in the swung tree.

Clear-cut, the canon beat on
beneath dark: the predictable
seashore simmer-then-crash as the flood
of air flung itself
into an uproar of woodland.

In here, out there – where
were you? You were
all at once awake. And it was not the storm
had lopped the branches of your dream
but the quiet: the wind had dropped.

What the pane now showed
was unquivering rainbuds loading
a rose-bare tangle of bush and, magnified
in the still, grey air of the lapse,
ponderous beech-boles, like silence solidified.

The Windshield

You took it in
at a glance: the March
snow-clouds seemed to be dancing
as the gale impelled
their glittering reflections over the windshield.

No snow fell. A gusty sun
was switching the shadows off and on,
making the steepness a deeper blue
that the reflections were broken across
and sailing through. Your glance

gave back a sense of the force
contained by the framing glass;
so seen, crag and shelf
of the cloud grew exact in power,
for sky is sky and no measure of itself.

Under the roar of the black
veinwork of branches, the whole city lay
open to the illumination
that pierced between door and car-door
out of the random fierceness of season and day.

Last Days of the Miser

An immaculate
December garden
of ranked cabbages
glows green
before his smoky door which stands
half-open: the room
behind it is a flue
the fume prefers
to the unswept chimney
and on the wall, a black

glass, or picture
it could be, is all
that hangs there.
Bread, cup and spoon
have drunk the same
impenetrable tone
at the lonely table,
along-side which he
sits, coloured like them.
He is crying
silently with the smoke,
as unaware of it
as of the tears
or what it is that works
his jaws unceasingly,
drawing his lost
look downwards.
His palate hoards
nothing, the irreducible
bolus, and the something
he still is, expends
all of its poor
power against it
swelling within him,
stopping his mouth
with the taste of time
wasted and of time
yet to be
gnawed small
to the same grist.

His mind's tooth
can find
less sustenance
than the mice
among his tattered notes
(has he forgone the recollection
even of them?).
An hour and more
I have been
sitting with him, before he
rouses to a stare and I

feed the silence
with That's a smoky
chimney you've got
in here. His reply
absently judicious,
slow to come –
I got, he says,
a smokier one at home,
which is where he is.

Rumour

we called him – with his three
chins, earnest
of as many tongues,
and Rumour had it and Rumour
spread it that we
were moving away
because we'd sold the table:
Rumour could elevate
the bare stone of a truth into
the instant architecture of a fable.
Your duck is
serving was the word
he used, your goose:
I've been watching them
for an hour behind the house
said voyeur Rumour.
An hour? An hour.
Is it possible, I said
wondering at the result –
Possible, he replied
but difficult.
Deciding
to woo Circumstance
Rumour will come on
wearing the look of Indigence.
Sorry for him, I

offer strawberries from a basket:
You haven't a fag, he asks.
No. I haven't a fag,
so with a great
reluctance, he manages to eat
one of them. But with his
You can believe me,
I'm telling you no lie
it's not long before
he's laying claim
to his proper glory,
his own construction
put upon plain
fact, and launched
on a likely story
to exercise his chins
Rumour is Rumour once again.

Terminal Tramps

The first is female.
In the station restaurant,
taking tea
that some thirsty traveller
had found too hot
for drinking, she sips
at the unmeasured time of her
terrible leisure.
The eyes of the mad
have a restless candour:
even their furtiveness
betrays itself openly:
there seems, in the way
she declares to the entire
room: *I expect
a civil answer* —
the appearance of an honesty.
It is distinct from the absurd

sobriety in the drunk
tramp's gesture
carrying on
in the corner, an imitation
conversation, with one
as craftily glanced as he
but sober. All
three inhabit
this shifting place
on whose fluidities the clocks
impose a certainty.
The room is aware of them.
The room is tolerant
in its curiosity and waits
to see, but to see
what? The Indian
personnel pretend
that the three are not
there – even the mad
woman has had
sense to avoid
in this two-roomed
restaurant, the white
management next door.
What does occur
is this – this
and no more: she picks
out of the air and starts
to repeat the word
Eisenhower. She takes
apart into its four
syllables the arbitrary
sound, then feels
her way out
over them, as though
they might have led
her somewhere, stretched
from here to there, –
might have proved
there there, but the mind's
needle merely
chokes on its repetitions

until, with an accumulating
force, the vortex
spins her on
into inconsequence.
The drunk walks
suddenly half
the room's length,
balanced tensely
by the strength of one
determination – to make it;
and to complete the demonstration
he flings with a total
accuracy into the slot
of a litter bin
his emptied bottle.
Her babble stops him.
He attends, and for the first
time sees her:
she takes him in,
her din rises
raging against the mere
shape he makes there:
it is her voice not she
gets up to accost him
and to demand her civil
answer. Answer
she has, but whether
she hears, or whether
she can interpret
the sharp transition
as with half a threat
he gestures at her, then
lets the gesture
drift, die out across
the air… with an
Ach! – the dawning
sense of her daftness –
he goes back
aiming himself at his former
corner, and gets
there on both
feet, as neat

as bottle into bin-slot –
to resume (he has clearly
forgotten her) his parody
of someone perfectly
self-possessed. The room
holding its breath
for his fall
is relieved. The room
has seen it all and now
inches out daughters
and sons into the loud
sane ambience
of train-sounds.
Under the dome
of stale air,
two Indians are
going their rounds,
swabbing the tables.
They circle the one
she sits at
with her all-but-spent
babble, her syllable-
chopping search
for the right sound,
the word to express
her groundless humanity,
hunched, alien
and intent amid
the new invasion
of travellers with a destination.

The Fox Gallery

A long house –
the fox gallery you called
its upper storey, because
you could look down to see
(and did) the way a fox would

cross the field beyond
and you could follow out, window
to window, the fox's way
the whole length of the meadow
parallel with the restraining line
of wall and pane, or as far
as that could follow the sense of all
those windings. Do you remember
the morning I woke you with the cry
Fox fox and the animal
came on – not from side
to side, but straight
at the house and we craned
to see more and more, the most
we could of it and then
watched it sheer off deterred
by habitation, and saw
how utterly the two worlds were
disparate, as that perfect
ideogram for agility
and liquefaction flowed
away from us rhythmical
and flickering and
that flare was final.

Frost

clings to the shadows, a wan silhouette
mapping out the house
in flat projection. Fields freeze still
under the hill's cold shoulder,
but winter cannot keep white
for long this shadowy frontier. Crowns
of rime (no reason to climb for them)
ring the under-oak grass, where one
by one the sunlight is melting them down.

Composition

for John Berger

Courbet might have painted this
gigantic head: heavy, yellow
petal-packed bloom of the chrysanthemum.

He would have caught the way
the weight of it looms from the cheap-green
vase this side the window it lolls in.

But he would have missed the space
triangled between stalk and curtain
along a window-frame base.

The opulence of the flower
would have compelled him to ignore
the ship-shape slotted verticals

of the door in the house beyond
dwarfed by the wand of the stem;
and the gate before it would not

have echoed those parallels to his eye
with its slatted wood, its two
neat side-posts of concrete.

The triangle compacts the lot: there
is even room in it for the black
tyre and blazing wheel-hub of a car

parked by the entrance. But the eye
of Courbet is glutted with petals
as solid as meat that press back the sky.

The Beautiful Aeroplane

Under its hangar the afternoon
waits for a less brilliant time,
a time of less dry sunlight
on shapes grown uncertain.

The nailheads of the first flowers
will be rustier then, the coming
grass ground-out under the treads
of the speculator's assistant

as he moves on down the first
hill and the next, his yellow
bulldozer arbitrarily cheerful
where now there can be

no confusion in sequence
as you pass between
the spaced-out parts – they
that a touch might slide together

and the wing united to the fuselage
the balancing tail tower, a high
axis between and above
the articulate shining assembly.

To be Engraved on the Skull of a Cormorant

across the thin
façade, the galleried-
with-membrane head:
narrowing, to take
the eye-dividing
declivity where
the beginning beak
prepares for flight
in a still-

perfect salience:
here, your glass
needs must stay
steady and your gross
needle re-tip
itself with reticence
but be
as searching as the sea
that picked and pared
this head yet spared
its frail acuity.

Gull

for Louis and Celia

Flung
far down,
as the
gull rises,
the black
smile of
its shadow
masking its
underside
takes
the heart
into the height
to hover
above the ocean's
plain-of-mountains'
moving quartz.

Oppositions

debate with Mallarmé

for Octavio Paz

The poet must rescue etymology from among the footnotes, thus moving up into the body of the text, '*cipher:* the Sanskrit word *sunya* derived from the root *svi*, to swell.'

To cipher is to turn the thought word into flesh. And hence 'the body of the text' derives its substance.

The master who disappeared, taking with him into the echo-chamber the ptyx which the Styx must replenish, has left the room so empty you would take it for fullness.

Solitude charges the house. If all is mist beyond it, the island of daily objects within becomes clarified.

Mistlines flow slowly in, filling the land's declivity that lay unseen until that indistinctness had acknowledged them.

If the skull is a memento mori, it is also a room, whose contained space is wordlessly resonant with the steps that might cross it, to command the vista out of its empty eyes.

Nakedness can appear as the vestment of space that separates four walls, the flesh as certain then and as transitory as the world it shares.

The mind is a hunter of forms, binding itself, in a world that must decay, to present substance.

Skull and shell, both are helmeted, both reconcile vacancy with its opposite. *Abolis bibelots d'inanité sonore.* Intimate presences of silent plenitude.

'*Oppositions*' *replies to one of Mallarmé's most famous sonnets,* '*Ses purs ongles très haut dédiant leur onyx*', *whose* '*ptyx*' *is explained as being a sea shell.*

Autumn

The civility of nature overthrown, the badger must fight in the roofless colosseum of the burning woods.

The birds are in flight, and the sky is in flight, raced by as many clouds as there are waves breaking the lakes beneath it.

Does Tristan lie dying, starred by the oak leaves? Tristan is on horseback, in search, squat, with narrow eyes, saddleless, burner of cities.

The field mouse that fled from the blade, flattened by wheels, has dried into the shape of a leaf, a minute paper escutcheon whose tail is the leaf stalk.

Yet the worm still gathers its rings together and releases them into motion… You too must freeze.

The horses of Attila scatter the shed foliage under the splashed flags of a camp in transit.

A truce: the first rime has not etched the last oak-shocks; the rivermist floats back from the alders and the sun pauses there.

Peace? There will be no peace until the fragility of the mosquito is overcome and the spirals of the infusoria turn to glass in the crystal pond.

These greens are the solace of lakes under a sun which corrodes. They are memorials not to be hoarded.

There will be a truce, but not the truce of the rime with the oak leaf, the mist with the alders, the rust with the sorrel stalk or of the flute with cold.

It will endure? It will endure as long as the frost.

Tout Entouré de Mon Regard

Surrounded by your glance – shapes at the circumference of its half-circle staring back into foreground shapes –, you measure the climbing abyss up to the birds that intersect in contrary directions the arc of winter air.

To the question you did not ask, comes the reply of arriving and departing cloud, the intensifying violet skyline that throws forward its patterns of boughs, the spaces between them flushed with a glowing obscurity.

It is like a phalanx of moth-wings with their separations of line and darkly incandescent tints, pressed against a window which is no window and behind which, burning towards them, a late sun hangs.

Surrounded by your glance, you are the pivot of that scale half of which balances in darkness behind you. And you feel its insistence held over against the light, the yellowing sky, the colliding of imitation mountains that presage more snow.

To see, is to feel at your back this domain of a circle whose power consists in evading and refusing to be completed by you.

It is infinity sustains you on its immeasurable palm.

Skullshapes

Skulls. Finalities. They emerge towards new beginnings from undergrowth. Along with stones, fossils, flint keel-scrapers and spoke-shaves, along with bowls of clay pipes heel-stamped with their makers' marks, comes the rural detritus of cattle skulls brought home by children. They are moss-stained, filthy with soil. Washing them of their mottlings, the hand grows conscious of weight, weight sharp with jaggednesses. Suspend them from a nail and one feels the bone-clumsiness go out of them: there is weight still in their vertical pull downwards from the nail, but there is also a hanging fragility. The two qualities fuse and the brush translates this fusion as wit, where leg-like appendages conclude the skulls' dangling mass.

Shadow explores them. It sockets the eye-holes with black. It reaches like fingers into the places one cannot see. Skulls are a keen instance of this duality of the visible: it borders what the eye cannot make out, it transcends itself with the suggestion of all that is there beside what lies within the eyes' possession: it cannot be possessed. Flooded with light, the skull is at once manifest surface and labyrinth of recesses. Shadow reaches down out of this world of helmeted cavities and declares it.

One sees. But not merely the passive mirrorings of the retinal mosaic – nor, like Ruskin's blind man struck suddenly by vision, without memory or conception. The senses, reminded by other seeings, bring to bear on the act of vision their pattern of images; they give point and place to an otherwise naked and homeless impression. It is the mind sees. But what it sees consists not solely of that by which it is confronted grasped in the light of that which it remembers. It sees possibility.

The skulls of birds, hard to the touch, are delicate to the eye. Egg-like in the round of the skull itself and as if the spherical shape were the result of an act like glass-blowing, they resist the eyes' imaginings with the blade of the beak which no lyrical admiration can attenuate to frailty.

The skull of nature is recess and volume. The skull of art – of possibility – is recess, volume and also lines – lines of containment, lines of extension. In seeing, one already extends the retinal impression, searchingly and instantaneously. Brush and pen extend the search beyond the instant, touch discloses a future. Volume, knived across by the challenge of a line, the raggedness of flaking bone countered by ruled, triangular facets, a cowskull opens a visionary field, a play of universals.

The Daisies

All evening, daisies outside the window, have gone on flying, stalk-anchored, towards the dark. Still, vibrant, swaying, they have stood up through dryness into beating rain: stellar cutouts, arrested explosions; too papery thin to be 'flower-heads' – flower-faces perhaps; upturned hands with innumerable fingers. Unlike the field daisies, they do not shut with dark: they stretch as eagerly towards it as they did to the sun, images of flight. And your own image, held by the pane, diffuses your features among those of the daisies, so that you flow with them until your hand, lifted to close the window, becomes conscious of its own heaviness. It is their stalks thrust them into flight as much as their launching-out of winged fingers, all paper accents, *grave* thrusting on acute, acute on *grave*. Cut the stalks and they fall, they do not fly; let them lose their bond and they, too, would grow, not lighter, but suddenly heavy with the double pull of their flower flesh and of the rain clinging to them.

Poem

The muscles which move the eyeballs, we are told, derive from a musculature which once occupied the body end to end... Sunblaze as day goes, and the light blots back the scene to iris the half-shut lashes. A look can no longer extricate the centre of the skyline copse. But the last greys, the departing glows caught by the creepers bearding its mass, prevail on the half-blinded retina. Branches deal with the air, vibrating the beams that thread into one's eye. So that 'over there' and 'in here' compound a truce neither signed – a truce that, insensibly and categorically, grows to a decree, and what one hoped for and what one is, must measure themselves against those demands which the eye receives, delivering its writ on us through a musculature which occupies the body end to end.

Ceci n'est pas une pipe

(Magritte)

This is not a pipe, but an explosion of the lips, the mouth unseaming rapidly and the lips exploding once more.

This is not only a statement. It has roots. And they are unpleasant, as though the possibility distinctly existed that lips should explode without benefit of quotation marks.

Our words surround us with contingencies. The mouth unseaming rapidly may do so like an unstitched wound. This is not a pipe.

We summon our terrors before us, to cohabit with clocks, plants, window-panes and apples, as if we would always know the worst.

But we are scarcely to be trusted. Our 'sinnes of fear' remain as incorrigible as our groundless optimisms.

So we terrorize ourselves fictitiously, with the body that has become a face, or the face that has become a body. But 'this is not a pipe'.

Such a face disproves itself. It could terrorize only by existing.

There is this comfort in the hypotheses of fancy: they restore the world to us by denying its premises.

This is not a stone because it is flying. This is not a bird because it is made of stone.

Yet the flying stone impends over the landscape by abstracting all the qualities of the real one. And the density of the stone bird is negated by the contours of flight.

This is not a pipe, but it entails the rider that the stone will interpose an irremovable 'and yet –', and the bird spread wings of bone and feather towards its point of high vantage.

'Ceci n'est pas une pipe' is the caption to a painting of a pipe – one that you smoke, not play – by Magritte.

A Process

A process; procession; trial.

A process of weather, a continuous changing. Thus, the gloom before darkness engenders its opposite and snow begins. Or rain possesses the night unbrokenly from the dazzle on the lit streets to the roar, dense, ubiquitous and incessant, that overcomes the hills drinking-in their black harvest. Its perfect accompaniment would be that speech of islanders, in which, we are told, the sentence is never certainly brought to an end, its aim less to record with completeness the impression an event makes, than to mark its successive aspects as they catch the eye, the ear of the speaker.

To process: to walk the bounds to lay claim to them, knowing all they exclude.

A procession, a body of things proceeding, as in the unending commerce of cloud with the seamless topology of the ground. Or a procession of waters: the whole moving belt of it swallows itself in sudden falls to be regurgitated as combed-over foam. Flung in reverse against the onrush that immediately pushes it forward, it is replaced by its own metamorphosis into this combed-back whiteness.

A trial: the whole of the proceedings, including the complication and the unravelling. One accords the process its reality, one does not deify it; inserted among it, one distinguishes and even transfigures, so that the quality of vision is never a prisoner of the thing seen. The beginnings have to be invented: thus the pictograph is an outline, which nature, as the poet said, does not have. And the ends? The ends are windows opening above that which lay unperceived until the wall of the house was completed at that point, over that sea.

The Chances of Rhyme

The chances of rhyme are like the chances of meeting –
   In the finding fortuitous, but once found, binding:
They say, they signify and they succeed, where to succeed
   Means not success, but a way forward
If unmapped, a literal, not a royal succession;
   Though royal (it may be) is the adjective or region
That we, nature's royalty, are led into.
   Yes. We are led, though we seem to lead
Through a fair forest, an Arden (a rhyme
   For Eden) – breeding ground for beasts
Not bestial, but loyal and legendary, which is more
   Than nature's are. Yet why should we speak
Of art, of life, as if the one were all form
   And the other all Sturm-und-Drang? And I think
Too, we should confine to Crewe or to Mow
   Cop, all those who confuse the fortuitousness
Of art with something to be met with only
   At extremity's brink, reducing thus
Rhyme to a kind of rope's end, a glimpsed grass
   To be snatched at as we plunge past it –
Nostalgic, after all, for a hope deferred.
   To take chances, as to make rhymes
Is human, but between chance and impenitence
   (A half-rhyme) come dance, vigilance
And circumstance (meaning all that is there
   Besides you, when you are there). And between
Rest-in-peace and precipice,
   Inertia and perversion, come the varieties
Increase, lease, re-lease (in both
   Senses); and immersion, conversion – of inert
Mass, that is, into energies to combat confusion.
   Let rhyme be my conclusion.

The End

All those who have not died have married.
    A Pompeian pause arrests
Merton beside his window, and the view
    Below is parkland, final as none
Could be, but the moment after she
    Whose name is on the card he holds
Has gone. The sliver of pasteboard framed
    By the great window, now, forever,
He is perfected in regret. Dalton
    Hailing the cab that will carry him
Out of the book, the motif on his lips
    (*So much for London, then*) for the last time,
The last chord chimes, tolling the solitudes
    Of the vast mind they moved in.
Such ends are just. But let him know
    Who reads his time by the way books go,
Each instant will bewry his symmetries
    And Time, climbing down from its pedestal
Uncrown the settled vista of his loss.
    Is it autumn or spring? It is autumn or spring.
Before door and window, the terrible guest
    Towers towards a famine and a feast.

WRITTEN ON WATER

1972

On Water

'Furrow' is inexact:
no ship could be
converted to a plough
travelling this vitreous ebony:

seal it in sea-caves and
you cannot still it:
image on image bends
where half-lights fill it

with illegible depths
and lucid passages,
bestiary of stones,
book without pages:

and yet it confers
as much as it denies:
we are orphaned and fathered
by such solid vacancies:

Mackinnon's Boat

Faced to the island, Mackinnon's boat
  Arcs out: the floats of his creels
Cling to the shelter half a mile away
  Of Tarner's cliff. Black, today
The waters will have nothing to do with the shaping
  Or unshaping of human things. No image
Twists beside the riding launch, there to repeat
  Its white and blue, its unrigged mast
Slanting from the prow in which a dog
  Now lies stretched out – asleep
It seems, but holds in steady view
  Through all-but-closed eyes the grey-black
Water travelling towards it. The surface,
  Opaque as cliffstone, moves scarred
By a breeze that strikes against its grain

In ruffled hatchings. Distance has disappeared,
Washed out by mist, but a cold light
    Keeps here and there re-touching it,
Promising transparencies of green and blue
    Only to deny them. The visible sea
Remains a sullen frontier to
    Its unimaginable fathoms. The dog eyes
Its gliding shapes, but the signs he can recognize
    Are land signs: he is here
Because men are here, unmindful
    Of this underworld of Mackinnon's daily dealings.
As the creels come in, he'll lie
    Still watching the waters, nostrils
Working on seasmells, but indifferent
    To the emerging haul, clawed and crawling.
The cliff lifts near, and a guttural cry
    Of cormorants raises his glance: he stays
Curled round on himself: his world
    Ignores this waste of the in-between,
Air and rock, stained, crag-sheer
    Where cormorants fret and flock
Strutting the ledges. The two men
    Have sited their destination. Mackinnon
Steering, cuts back the engine and Macaskill
    Has the light floats firm and then
The weight of the freighted creels is on his rope –
    A dozen of them – the coil spitting
Water as it slaps and turns on the windlass
    Burning Macaskill's palms paying it in.
As the cold, wet line is hauled, the creels
    Begin to arrive. And, inside, the flailing
Seashapes pincered to the baits, drop
    Slithering and shaken off like thieves
Surprised, their breath all at once grown rare
    In an atmosphere they had not known existed.
Hands that have much to do yet, dealing
    With creel on creel, drag out the catch
And feeling the cage-nets, re-thread each fault.
    Crabs, urchins, dogfish, and star,
All are unwanted and all are
    Snatched, slaughtered, or flung to their freedom –
Some, shattering on the cordage
    They too eagerly clung to. Hands must be cruel

To keep the pace spry to undo and then
    To re-tie, return the new-baited traps
To water, but an ease makes one
    The disparate links of the concerted action
Between the first drawing in
    And the let down crash of stone-weighted baskets.
There is more to be done still. The trough of the gunwhale
    Is filled with the scrabbling armour of defeat;
Claw against claw, not knowing
    What it is they fight, they swivel
And bite on air until they feel
    The palpable hard fingers of their real
Adversary close on them; and held
    In a knee-grip, must yield to him.
The beaked claws are shut and bound
    By Mackinnon. Leaning against the tiller,
He impounds each one alive
    In the crawling hatch. And so the boat
Thrusts on, to go through a hundred and more creels
    Before the return. Macaskill throws
To Mackinnon a cigarette down the length
    Of half the craft. Cupping,
They light up. Their anonymity, for a spell,
    Is at an end, and each one
Free to be himself once more
    Sharing the rest that comes of labour.
But labour must come of rest: and already
    They are set towards it, and soon the floats
Of the next creel-drift will rise
    Low in the water. An evasive light
Brightens like mist rolling along the sea,
    And the blue it beckoned – blue
Such as catches and dies in an eye-glance –
    Glints out its seconds. Making a time
Where no day has a name, the smells
    Of diesel, salt, and tobacco mingle:
They linger down a wake whose further lines
    Are beginning to slacken and fall back to where
Salt at last must outsavour name and time
    In the alternation of the forgetful waters.

Ullinish

The Thief's Journal

Only this book of love will be real. What of the facts which served as its pretext?
I must be their repository.

Genet

How much there was had escaped him:
The suns were outpacing his vagrancy:
He had crossed Andalusia. Andalusia
Was what it was still to be
Without him. It tantalized imagination
The taste of the fish he had eaten there without salt or bread
At his sea-wrack fire whose ashes
The careful sea had long-since appropriated.

Rower

A plotless tale: the passing hours
    Bring in a day that's nebulous. Glazes of moist pearl
Mute back the full blaze of a sea,
    Drifting continually where a slack tide
Has released the waters. Shallows
    Spread their transparency, letting through
A pale-brown map of sandbanks
    Barely submerged, where a gull might wade
Thin legs still visible above its blurred reflection.
    It seems nothing will occur here until
The tide returns, ferrying to the shore its freshness,
    Beating and breaking only to remake itself
The instant the advancing line goes under.
    And nothing does. Except for the inching transformations
Of a forenoon all melting redundancies
    Just beyond eyeshot: the grey veils
Drink-in a little more hidden sunlight,
    Shadows harden, pale. But then
Out into the bay, towards deeper water,
    Sidles the rower, gaining speed

As he reaches it. Already his world
    Is sliding by him. Backwards
He enters it, eyes searching the past
    Before them: that shape that crowns the cliff,
A sole, white plane, draws tight his gaze –
    A house, bereft so it seems of time
By its place of vantage, high
    Over cleft and crack. When, as momentarily,
He steals a glance from it to fling
    Across his travelling shoulder, his eyes
Soon settle once more along that line
    Tilted towards the shoremark. And though the ripple
Is beneath him now – the pull and beat
    Unfelt when further in – he cuts athwart it
Making his way, to the liquid counterpulse
    Of blades that draw him outwards to complete
The bay's half-circle with his own. Muscle
    And bone work to that consummation of the will
Where satisfaction gathers to surfeit, strain
    To ease. Pleased by his exertions, he abandons them
Riding against rested oars, subdued
    For the moment to that want of purpose
In sky and water, before he shoots
    Feathering once more baywards, his face
To the direction the tide will take when
    Out of the coherent chaos of a morning that refuses
To declare itself, it comes plunging in
    Expunging the track of his geometries.

The Lighthouse

The lighthouse is like the church of some island sect
    Who have known the mainland beliefs and have defected
Only to retain them in native purity
    And in the daily jubilation of storm and sea,
But adding every day new images
    To their liturgy of changes – each one
Some myth over and done with now

Because sea has rebegotten land and land
The sea, and all is waiting to declare
   That things have never been praised for what they were,
                                 emerging
Along promontory on enfiladed promontory.

Two Poems on Titles Proposed by Octavio and Marie José Paz

I *Le Rendez-Vous des Paysages*

The promenade, the plage, the paysage
all met somewhere
in the reflection of a reflection
in midair: cars, unheard,
were running on water: jetplanes
lay on their backs
like sunbathers
in a submarine graveyard
about to resurrect into the fronds
of ghost-palms boasting
'We exist'
to the sea's uncertain mirrors
to the reversed clocktowers that had lost
all feeling for time
suspended
among the overlapping vistas
of promenade, plage, paysage.

II *La Promenade de Protée*

Changing, he walks the changing avenue:
this blue and purple are the blue
and purple of autumn underwater:
they are changing to green and he
is changing to an undulated statue
in this sea-floor park

and does not know
if the iced green will undo him
or which are real
among the recollections that cling
to him and seem to know him:
and hears overhead the shudder of departing keels.

Stone Speech

Crowding this beach
are milkstones, white
teardrops; flints
edged out of flinthood
into smoothness chafe
against grainy ovals,
pitted pieces, nosestones,
stoppers and saddles;
veins of orange
inlay black beads:
chalk-swaddled babyshapes,
tiny fists, facestones
and facestone's brother
skullstone, roundheads
pierced by a single eye,
purple finds, all
rubbing shoulders:
a mob of grindings,
groundlings, scatterings
from a million necklaces
mined under sea-hills, the pebbles
are as various as the people.

The Sea is Open to the Light

The sea is open to the light:
the image idling
beneath the skerry
is the unmoving
skerry's own
rockbound foundation
travelling down and down
to meet in the underdeeps
the spread floor
shadowed where the fish
flash in their multitude
transmitting and eluding
the illumination.

Variation on Paz

Hay que… soñar hacia dentro y tambien hacia afuera

We must dream inwards, and we must dream
  Outwards too, until – the dream's ground
Bound no longer by the dream – we feel
  Behind us the sea's force, and the blind
Keel strikes gravel, grinding
  Towards a beach where, eye by eye,
The incorruptible stones are our witnessess
  And we wake to what is dream and what is real
Judged by the sun and the impartial sky.

The Compact: At Volterra

The crack in the stone, the black filament
  Reaching into the rockface unmasks
More history than Etruria or Rome

Bequeathed this place. The ramparted town
Has long outlived all that; for what
    Are Caesar or Scipio beside
The incursion of the slow abyss, the daily
    Tribute the dry fields provide

Trickling down? There is a compact
    To undo the spot, between the unhurried sun
Edging beyond this scene, and the moon,
    Risen already, that has stained
Through with its pallor the remaining light:
    Unreal, that clarity of lips and wrinkles
Where shadow investigates each fold,
    Scaling the cliff to the silhouetted stronghold.

Civic and close-packed, the streets
    Cannot ignore this tale of unshorable earth
At the town brink; furrow, gully,
    And sandslide guide down
Each seeping rivulet only to deepen
    The cavities of thirst, dry out
The cenozoic skeleton, appearing, powdering away,
    Uncovering the chapped clay beneath it.

There is a compact between the cooling earth
    And every labyrinthine fault that mines it –
The thousand mouths whose language
    Is siftings, whisperings, rumours of downfall
That might, in a momentary unison,
    Silence all, tearing the roots of sound out
With a single roar: but the cicadas
    Chafe on, grapevine entwines the pergola

Gripping beyond itself. A sole farm
    Eyes space emptily. Those
Who abandoned it still wire
    Their vines between lopped willows:
Their terraces, fondling the soil together,
    Till up to the drop that which they stand to lose:
Refusing to give ground before they must,
    They pit their patience against the dust's vacuity.

The crack in the stone, the black filament
    Rooting itself in dreams, all live
At a truce, refuted, terracing; as if
    Unreasoned care were its own and our
Sufficient reason, to repair the night's derisions,
    Repay the day's delight, here where the pebbles
Of half-ripe grapes abide their season,
    Their fostering leaves outlined by unminding sky.

Two Poems of Lucio Piccolo

I   *Unstill Universe*

Unstill universe of gusts
of rays, of hours without colour, of perennial
transits, vain displays
of cloud: an instant and –
look, the changed forms
blaze out, milennia grow unstable.
    And the arch of the low door and the step
worn by too many winters, are a fable
in the unforeseen burst from the March sun.

II   *Veneris Venefica Agrestis*

She springs from the ground-clinging thicket, her face
– gay now, now surly – bound in a black
kerchief, a shrivelled chestnut it seems: no fine fleece
the hair that falls loose, but a lock
of curling goat-hair; when she goes by
(is she standing or bending?) her gnarled and dark
foot is a root that suddenly juts from the earth and walks.
    Be watchful she does not offer you her cup of bark,
its water root-flavoured that tastes of the viscid leaf,
either mulberry or sorb-apple, woodland fruit that flatters with lies
the lips but the tongue ties.
    She governs it seems
the force of rounding moons

that swells out the rinds of trees
and alternates the invincible ferments,
flow of the sap and of the seas...
  Pronubial, she, like the birds that bring
seeds from afar: arcane
the breeds that come of her grafting.
  And the mud walls of the unstable
cottage where the nettle grows
with gigantic stalk, are her realms of shadows:
she ignites the kindlings in the furnaces of fable.
  And round the door, from neighbouring orchard ground
the fumes that rise
are the fine, unwinding muslins of her sibylline vespers.
  She appears in the guise
of the centipede among the darknesses
by water-wheels that turn
no more in the maidenhair fern.
  She is the mask that beckons
and disappears, when the light
of the halfspent wicks
makes voracious the shadows in the room where
they are milling by night, working at the presses,
and odours of crushed olives are in the air,
kindled vapours of grapejuice; and lanterns come
swayed to the steps of hobnailed boots.
  The gestures of those who labour
in the fields, are accomplices
in the plots she weaves:
the stoop of those who gather up dry leaves
and acorns... and the shoeless tread and measured bearing
under burdened head, when you cannot see
the brow or the olives of the eyes
but only the lively mouth... the dress
swathes tight the flanks, the breasts, and has comeliness –
passing the bough she leaves behind
an odour of parching...
or the gesture that raises the crock
renewed at the basin of the spring.
  She bends, drawing a circle:
her sign sends forth
the primordial torrent out of the fearful earth
(and the foot that presses the irrigated furrow

and the hand that lifts
the spade-power of a different desire summons them now);
she draws strength
from the breaths of the enclosures,
the diffused cries, the damp and burning
straw of the litters, the blackened
branches of the vine, and the shadow that gives back
the smell of harnesses of rope and sack,
damp baskets, where who stands
on the threshold can descry
the stilled millstone, hoes long used to the grip of rural hands:
the rustic shade ferments with ancestral longings.

    Rockroses, thistles, pulicaria, calaminths – scents
that seem fresh and aromatic, are
(should your wariness pall) the lures
of a spiral that winds-in all,
(night bites into silver
free of all alloy of sidereal ray) she will
blur in a fume of dust the gentle hill-curve.

    Now, she's in daylight, one hand against an oak,
the other hangs loose – filthy and coaxing,
her dress black as a flue-brush...
and the sudden rush of wind
over the headland, sets at large
and floods with blue
a tangle of leaves and flourishing bough.
She promises, too, discloses the ardour,
freshness, vigour of the breath that frees
peach and the bitter-sweet
odour of the flowering almond tree; under coarse leaf
are fleshy and violent mouths, wild offshoots,
between the ferns' long fans
obscure hints of mushroom growths,
uncertain glances of water glint through the clovers,
and a sense of bare
original clay is there
near where the poplar wakes unslakeable thirst
with its rustling mirages of streams
and makes itself a mirror of each breeze,
where, in the hill's shade,
steep sloping,
the valley grows

narrow and closes
in the mouth of a spring
among delicate mosses.
    If, for a moment,
cloud comes to rest
over the hill-crest or the valley threshold,
in the living shade
the shaft of that plough now shows
which shakes which unflowers unleafs
the bush and the forest rose.

At Sant' Antimo

Flanking the place,
a cypress
stretches itself, its surface
working as the wind
travels it in a continual
breathing, an underwater
floating of foliage
upwards, till
compact and wavering
it flexes a sinuous
tip that chases
its own shadow
to and fro
across the still
stone tower.

Tarquinia

Vince Viet Cong! The testimony of walls.
What do they mean – 'is winning'
Or 'let win'? In the beginning Tarquinia
Lorded ten provinces and has come to this,
A museum of tombstones, a necropolis.

Walls built of walls, the run-down
Etruscan capital is a town
Of bars and butchers' shops
Inside the wreck of palaces.
The Tomb of the Warriors. They are painted there
Carousing, drinking to victory. Said Forster,
'Let yourself be crushed.' They fought and were.
A woman goes past, bent by the weight
Of the trussed fowl she is trailing. The cross
Swings from her neck in accompaniment.
The eyes of the winged horses
That rode on the citadel are still keen
With the intelligence of a lost art.
Vince Viet Cong! What is it they mean?

Santa Maria delle Nevi

Santa Maria
stands open
to the heat, a cave
of votive flames
that lure the eye
into the gloom
surrounding them. Lost
at first, one looks
for the ground and closure
to that fresh recess,
shallowly tunnelled-out
between its walls
and, in the end,
grasps it is the white
of painted snow
irradiates the altar-piece:
from bowl and salver
it overflows,
in snowballs like fruit,
an offering to
the Madonna of the Snows
and to the child
whom her restraining hands

hold steady,
its fingers curious
at the inexplicable
intimation of the cold:
an August dream,
and so exactly
does it fit the day
it seems to tally
with its opposite
in strength of fact,
where Santa Maria
hoards up the glow
of winter recollected
and summer inlays the street
as bright as snow.

The Square

A consolidation
of voices in the street
below, a wave
that never reaches
its destination: the higher
voices of children
ride it and the raucous
monomaniac bikes
hunting their shadows
into the sunlight of the square
to a drum-roll
of metal shutters
sliding: and above it all
the reflection
hung on the open
pane (it opens
inwards) of the bell
over Santa Maria delle Nevi,
not even slightly
swung in the hot
evening air.

Ariadne and the Minotaur

When Theseus went down
she stood alone surrounded
by the sense of what finality it was
she entered now: the hot rocks offered her
neither resistance nor escape, but ran
viscous with the image of betrayal:
the pitted and unimaginable face
the minotaur haunted her with
kept forming there
along the seams and discolorations
and in the diamond sweat
of mica: the sword and thread
had been hers to give, and she
had given them, to this easer of destinies:
if she had gone
alone out of the sun and down where he
had threaded the way for her,
if she had gone
winding the ammonite of space
to where at the cold heart
from the dark stone the bestial warmth
would rise to meet her
unarmed in acquiescence, unprepared
her spindle of packthread... her fingers felt now
for the image in the sunlit rock, and her ears
at the shock of touch took up a cry
out of the labyrinth
into their own, a groaning
that filled the stone mouth
hollowly: between the lips of stone
appeared he whom she had sent
to go where her unspeakable
intent unspoken had been to go
herself, and heaved unlabyrinthed at her feet
their mutual completed crime –

'Ariadne and the Minotaur' was suggested initially by Picasso's series of drawings. It ignores as they do the question of the actual kinship between Ariadne and the Minotaur. Perhaps she, too, was unaware of it.

a put-by destiny, a dying
look that sought her
out of eyes the light extinguished,
eyes she should have led
herself to light: and the rays
that turned to emptiness in them
filling the whole of space with loss,
a waste of irrefutable sunlight spread
from Crete to Naxos.

Machiavelli in Exile

A man is watching down the sun. All day,
Exploring the stone sinew of the hills,
For his every predilection it has asked
A Roman reason of him. And he has tried
To give one, tied to a dwindling patrimony
And the pain of exile. His guileless guile,
Trusted by nobody, he is self-betrayed.

And yet, for all that, Borgia shall be praised
Who moved and, moving, saved by sudden action:
The Florentines, despite their words, will have
Faction and the blood that comes of faction:
The work of France and Spain others begin –
Let him who says so exercise his powers
With dice and backgammon at a country inn;

Where, for his day's companions, he must choose
Such men as endure history and not those
Who make it: with their shadows, magnified
And spread behind them, butcher, publican,
Miller, and baker quarrel at their cards,
And heights and hill-roads all around are filled
With voices of gods who do not know they're gods.

Nor are they, save for a trick of light and sound:
Their fate is bound by their own sleeping wills.

Though lateness shadows all that's left to do,
Tarde non furon mai grazie divine:
The sun that lit his mind now lights the page
At which he reads and words, hard-won, assuage
What chance and character have brought him to.

He enters that courtly ancient company
Of men whose reasons may be asked, and he,
Released from tedium, poverty, and threat,
Lives in the light of possibility:
Their words are warm with it, yet tempered by
The memory of its opposite, else too soon
Hopes are a mob that wrangle for the moon.

Adversity puts his own pen in hand,
First torture, then neglect bringing to bear
The style and vigilance which may perfect
A prince, that he whom history forsook
Should for no random principle forsake
Its truth's contingency, his last defeat
And victory, no battle, but a book.

Hawks

Hawks hovering, calling to each other
    Across the air, seem swung
Too high on the risen wind
    For the earth-clung contact of our world:
And yet we share with them that sense
    The season is bringing in, of all
The lengthening light is promising to exact
    From the obduracy of March. The pair,
After their kind are lovers and their cries
    Such as lovers alone exchange, and we

'Tarde non furon mai grazie divine' (Divine graces were never late) is Machiavelli's misquotation of Petrarch's 'Ma tarde non fur mai grazie divine'. It begins the letter to Francesco Vettori on which 'Machiavelli in Exile' is, in part, based.

Though we cannot tell what it is they say,
 Caught up into their calling, are in their sway,
And ride where we cannot climb the steep
 And altering air, breathing the sweetness
Of our own excess, till we are kinned
 By space we never thought to enter
On capable wings to such reaches of desire.

Of Beginning Light

The light of the mind is poorer
than beginning light: the shades
we find pigment for
poor beside the tacit
variety we can all see
yet cannot say: of beginning light
I will say this, that it dispenses
imperial equality to everything
it touches, so that purple
becomes common wear, but purple
resolving in its chord
a thousand tones
tinged by a thousand
shadows, all
yielding themselves
slowly up: and the mind,
feeling its way among
such hesitant distinctions,
is left behind as they
flare into certainties that
begin by ending them
in the light of day.

Carscape

Mirrored
the rear window
holds a glowing
almost–gone–day
scene, although the day
across this upland
has far to go: one drives
against its glare
that by degrees a moving
Everest of cloud
will shadow–over
while amid these
many vanishings
replenished, the wintry
autumnal afternoon
could still be dawn.

Drive

First light strikes
across a landmass
daylight hides: horizon
rides above horizon
momentarily
like a region of cloud:
I return driving
to the same view undone:
the windscreen takes it in
as a high and brilliant
emptiness that lies to one
of no depth, stretched above
palpabilities morning could touch:
and one feels for the features of the lost
continent (it seems)
of day's beginnings, recollection
seizing on the mind

with what infinity of unmarked
mornings, of spaces unsounded
habit abjures, in the cross-
tides of chaos, till we
believe our eyes (our lies)
that there is nothing there
but what we see –
and drive

Legend

Midas eyes the seasonable glints:
    Pennywise, he hears the cash-crop
Clashing its foliage under the wind,
    As the buzz-saw in his mind
Bores through the pastoral irrelevance:
    Seen from this vantage, every view
Becomes a collector's item, and the atmosphere
    Squares off each parcel of bright worth
In bounding it: limbs to matchwood,
    Skyline saw-toothed to raw angles
Roof on roof, as Midas
    Stares the future into being, melts down
Season into season, past distinction,
    While the leaves too slowly
Deal their lightness to the air that lifts
    Then releases them on suppled boughs,
Time present beyond all bargain, liquid gifts.

Autumn Piece

Baffled
by the choreography of the season
the eye could not
with certainty see
whether it was wind
stripping the leaves or
the leaves were struggling to be free:

They came at you
in decaying spirals
plucked flung and regathered by the same
force that was twisting
the scarves of the vapour trails
dragging all certainties out of course:

As the car resisted it
you felt it in either hand
commanding car, tree, sky,
master of chances,
and at a curve was a red
board said 'Danger':
I thought it said dancer.

The White Van

new coated
a winter white
rides on ahead
through the brightness of
late autumn weather,
as the low and rising
side sun
flings from hedgerow
and from sky on to
its moving screen
a shadow show:

trees, half-unleafed,
fretted and pierced now
by sudden skylights,
come dancing down,
angle and mass and bough,
birds drawing them together
in their reflected flight:
this is all shape
and surface, you might say,
this black and white
abstraction of a coloured
day, but here
is no form so far
from what we see
it does not take the glow
and urgency of all
those goings-on
surrounding us: chance
unblinds certitude
with a fourth eye (the third
one is the mind's),
the paint of autumn
showing the more intense
for these pied
anatomies and
as the white van turns
right, distance
ahead of us
re-opens its density
of gold, green, amethyst.

In October

A weather of flashes, fragments
of Pentecost restored
and lost before the tongue
has time for them. The word
is brought to nothing

that caught at burning bushes
gone already and at vistas
where there are none. For now
it must speak of the wreck
two rainbows make that
half-expunged, hang
one broken above the other
footlessly balancing.

Urlicht

At the end of an unending war:
Horizons abide the deception
Of the sky's bright truce

But the dispersals have begun
There are no more roads
Only an immense dew

Of light
Over the dropped leafage
And in the room where

On the music-stand
The silent sonata lies
Open

Poem

space
window
that looks into itself

a facing
both and
every way

colon
between green apple:
and vase of green

invisible
bed and breath
ebb and air-flow

below an unflawed
iridescence
of spiderweb

Appearance

Snow brings into view the far hills:
   The winter sun feels for their surfaces:
Of the little we know of them, full half
   Is in the rushing out to greet them, the restraint
(Unfelt till then) melted at the look
   That gathers them in, to a meeting of expectations
With appearances. And what appears
   Where the slant-sided lit arena opens
Plane above plane, comes as neither
   Question nor reply, but a glance
Of fire, sizing our ignorance up,
   As the image seizes on us, and we grasp
For the ground that it delineates in a flight
   Of distances, suddenly stilled: the cold
Hills drawing us to a reciprocation,
   Ask words of us, answering images
To their range, their heights, held
   By the sun and the snow, between pause and change.

Ars Poetica

in memoriam A.A.

What is it for
this form of saying, truce
with history in a language
no one may wish to use?

Who was it said
'a form of suicide'? – meaning
you drive yourself up to the edge
or as near as you can ride

without dropping over.
Some drop, wit-
less – and we
are to praise them for it?

Well, if mourning
were all we had,
we could settle for a great simplicity,
mourn ourselves mad.

But that is only half
the question: blight
has its cures and hopes
come uninvited.

What is it for? Answers
should be prepaid. And no Declines
of the West Full Stop
No selling lines.

Mélisande

For Mélisande
flower-child of the forest
there were certain lacunae
in the short history of
her life: stoned
so many times
she could not recall
and she kept losing things
rings and things:
there was so little of her
she was mostly hair
and an impregnable innocence
gave an unthinking
rightness to whatever
she did or did not
do: the men she knew
slipped away
almost unnoticed
(she was not tenacious)
like rings and things:
– I had, she said
when she ended up
'beginning all over again'
and went home – I had
what you might call
a vision: and she needed one:
her mother
had forgotten to tell her
things and there was
nothing at all
half-way in her life such as
sorry or thankyou…
but they were together now
and in the evenings
mother sat
and read to her
The Greening of America
and other books like that
and so they lived
vapidly ever after

Dialectic

for Edoardo Sanguineti

Life is the story of a body, you say:
the cough in the concert-hall is the story
of a body that cannot contain itself,
and the Waldstein the story of a life
refusing to be contained
by its body, the damaged ear
rebegetting its wholeness in posterities
of notes. I uncramp
bent knees. Side by side
all these itching legs! straining
to give back to the body
the rhythm out of the air and
heel-tap it into the ground.
A dropped programme tells
of a body lost to itself
and become all ear – ear
such as only the deaf
could dream of, with its gigantic
channels and circuits, its
snailshell of cartilage
brimming and quivering with the auricle's
passed-on story where
life is the breaking of silences
now heard, the daily remaking a body
refleshed of air.

The Night-Train

composed
solely of carbon and soot-roses
freighted tight
with a million
minuscule statuettes
of La Notte (Night)

stumbles on
between unlit halts
till daylight begins
to bleed its jet
windows white, and the night–
train softly
discomposes, rose
on soot-rose,
to become – white
white white –
the snow-plough
that refuses to go.

Event

Nothing is happening
Nothing

A waterdrop
Soundlessly shatters
A gossamer gives

Against this unused space
A bird
Might thoughtlessly try its voice
But no bird does

On the trodden ground
Footsteps
Are themselves more pulse than sound

At the return
A little drunk
On air

Aware that
Nothing
Is happening

Comedy

It was when he began to see fields
As arguments, the ribbed ploughland
Contending with the direction of its fence:
If you went with the furrows, the view
From the fence disputed with you
Because you couldn't see it. If you sat still
The horizontals plainly said
You ought to be walking, and when you did
All you were leaving behind you proved
That you were missing the point. And the innumerable views
Kept troubling him, until
He granted them. Amen.

Three Wagnerian Lyrics

I   *Liebestod*

Tannhäuser wandered in the Venusberg:
　　Spring's goddess had him for a season,
And no love living ever gave
　　All that he knew there, and still craved
At his return. What could his lady
　　Do but die? – She drew him after her
Deeper than ever spring could stir him.

II   *The Potion*

King Mark who
Unwilling prognosticator
Of the *grand guignol viennois*
Despaired of ruling
His libidinal relatives,
Apologized
To them for them: 'The potion!
It was not your fault.'

Children of the times,
Absolved, they did not hear
The excuses he came to bring,
For one was dead and the other kept on singing.

III *Good Friday*

Easter and the resurrection
  Of the grass. Humbled Kundry
Dries the anointed feet of Parsifal
  With her hair. It is the imprisoned blood
Of Venus glows in the grail cup.

Over Elizabeth Bridge: A Circumvention

to a friend in Budapest

… my heart which owes this past a calm future.
Attila József, *By the Danube*

Three years, now, the curve of Elizabeth Bridge
Has caught at some half-answering turn of mind –
Not recollection, but uncertainty
Why memory should need so long to find
A place and peace for it: that uncertainty
And restless counterpointing of a verse
'So wary of its I', Iván, is me:

Why should I hesitate to fix a meaning?
The facts were plain. A church, a riverside,
And, launched at the further bank, a parapet
Which, at its setting-out, must swerve or ride
Sheer down the bulk of the defenceless nave,
But with a curious sort of courteousness,
Bends by and on again. That movement gave

A pause to thoughts, which overeagerly
Had fed on fresh experience and the sense
That too much happened in too short a time
In this one city: self-enravelled, dense
With its own past, even its silence was
Rife with explanations, drummed insistent
As traffic at this church's window-glass.

How does the volley sound in that man's ears
Whom history did not swerve from, but elected
To face the squad? Was it indifference,
Fear, or sudden, helpless peace reflected
In the flash, for Imre Nagy? – another kind
Of silence, merely, that let in the dark
Which closed on Rajk's already silenced mind?

Here, past is half a ruin, half a dream –
Islanded patience, work of quiet hands,
Repainting spandrels that out-arched the Turk
In this interior. These are the lands
Europe and Asia, challenging to yield
A crop, or having raised one, harvest it,
Used for a highroad and a battlefield.

The bridge has paid the past its compliment:
The far bank's statuary stand beckoning
Where it flows, in one undeviating span,
Across the frozen river. That reckoning
Which József owed was cancelled in his blood,
And yet his promise veered beyond the act,
His verse grown calm with all it had withstood.

László Rajk: Hungarian Foreign Minister, executed during the Stalinist period; Imre Nagy: Prime Minister and leader of the 1956 revolution, also executed. The poet Attila József killed himself in the thirties.

NEW COLLECTED POEMS

In Memoriam Thomas Hardy

How to speak with the dead
so that not only
our but their
words are valid?

Unlike their stones,
they scarcely resist us,
memory adjusting
its shades, its mist:

they are too like their photographs
where we can fill
with echoes of our regrets
brown worlds of stillness.

His besetting word
was 'afterwards' and it released
their qualities, their restlessness
as though they heard it.

Remembering Williams

'Wish we could talk today'
you wrote – no more
than that: the time before
it was: 'I stumbled
on a poem you had written', but the theme
lost itself, you forgot to say
what it was
'that called to mind
something over which
we had both been working, but had not
worked out by half.' Your wife
said she had done her mourning
while you still lived. Life
is a hard bed to lie on dying.

The Apparition

I dreamed, Justine, we chanced on one another
   As though it were twenty years ago. Your dark
Too vulnerable beauty shone
   As then, translucent with its youth,
Unreal, as dreams so often are,
   With too much life. 'Tomorrow',
You said, 'we plough up the pastureland.'
   The clear and threatening sky
New England has in autumn – its heightened blue,
   The promise of early snow – were proofs enough
Of the necessity, though of what pastureland
   You spoke, I'd no idea. Then
Reading the meaning in your face, I found
   Your pastureland had been your hallowed ground which now
Must yield to use. And all of my refusals,
   All I feared, stood countered
By the resolve I saw in you and heard:
   While death itself, its certain thread
Twisted through the skein of consequence
   Seemed threatened by the strength
Of those dead years. It was a dream –
   No more; and you whom death
And solitude have tried, must know
   The treachery of dreams. And yet I do not think it lied,
Because it came, without insistence,
   Stood for a moment, spoke and then
Was gone, that apparition,
   Beyond the irresolute confines of the night,
Leaving me to weigh its words alone.

Juliet's Garden

J'ai connu une petite fille qui quittait son jardin bruyamment, puis s'en revenait à pas de loup pour 'voir comment il était quand elle n'était pas là'.

Sartre

Silently…
she was quieter than breathing now,
hearing the garden seethe
behind her departed echo:

flowers merely grew,
showing no knowledge of her:
stones hunching their hardnesses
against her not being there:

scents came penetratingly,
rose, apple, and leaf-rot,
earthsmell under them all,
to where she was not:

such presences could only
rouse her fears,
ignoring and perfuming
this voluntary death of hers:

and so she came rushing back
into her garden then,
her new-found lack
the measure of all Eden.

Against Portraits

How, beyond all foresight
or intention, light
plays with a face
whose features play with light:

frame on gilded frame,
ancestor on ancestor,
the gallery is filled
with more certainty than we can bear:

if there must be
an art of portraiture,
let it show us ourselves as we
break from the image of what we are:

the animation of speech, and then
the eyes eluding
that which, once spoken,
seems too specific, too concluding:

or, entering a sudden slant
of brightness, between dark and gold,
a face half-hesitant,
face at a threshold:

Green Quinces

Ripening there
among the entanglement of leaves
that share their colour –
green quinces:
fragrantly free
from the contaminations
of daily envy,
the sight and suddenness
of green unknot
all that which thought
has ravelled where it cannot span
between the private and the public man –
between the motive
and the word:
the repeated and absurd
impulse to justify

oneself, knows
now its own
true colours:
it was the hardest-to-be-
put-down
vanity – desire
for the regard
of others. And how wrong
they were who taught us
green was the colour
should belong
to envy: they envied green.

During Rain

Between
slats of the garden
bench, and strung
to their undersides
ride clinging
rain-drops, white
with transmitted
light as the bench
with paint: ranged
irregularly
seven staves of them
shine out
against the space
behind: untroubled
by the least breeze they
seem not to move
but one
by one as if
suddenly ripening
tug themselves free
and splash
down to be
replaced by an identical
and instant twin:

the longer you
look at it
the stillness proves
one flow unbroken
of new, false pearls,
dropped seeds of now
becoming then.

Elegy for Henry Street

for George and Mary Oppen

After the flight, the tired body
    Clung to the fading day of Henry Street:
There, it was hardly at an end, but midnight
    Weighed on the pulse of thought, its deep
Inconsistency working behind the eye
    That watched the lights come on – lights
Of the further shore, Manhattan's million
    Windows, floor on floor repeated
By the bay. I liked the street for its sordid
    Fiction of a small town order,
For its less and dingier glass
    As it let one down and back
Slowly out of transatlantic into human time,
    And its sooted bricks declared they were there
As they no longer are. 'Duck!' you cried, George,
    The day the militia filed out with rifles
At a Shriner celebration, but that was the pastoral era
    Of sixty-six, and how should we or they
Have known, as taps were blowing, and the echoes,
    Trapped in each scarred hallway
Meanly rhymed memory with civility,
    They were bugling the burial of a place and time?

Mistlines

Watching the mistlines flow slowly in
   And fill the land's declivities that lay
Unseen until that indistinctness
   Had acknowledged them, the eye
Grasps, at a glance, the mind's own
   Food and substance, shape after shape
Emerging where all shapes drown;
   For the mind is a hunter of forms:
Finding them wherever it may – in firm
   Things or in frail, in vanishings –
It binds itself, in a world that must decay,
   To present substance, and the words
Once said, present and substance
   Both belie the saying. Mist
Drives on the house till forms become
   The shapes of nearness, densities of home
Charged by their solitude – an island of
   Daily objects mist has clarified
To the transparent calm in which you wear
   The vestment of space that separates four walls,
Your flesh as certain and transitory as the world you share.

Movements

I

I want that height and prospect such as music
   Brings one to – music or memory,
When memory gains ground drowned-out
   By years. I want the voyage of recovery,
The wind-torn eyrie and the mast-top
   Sight of the horizon island,
Look-out tower compounded from pure sound:
   Trough on trough, valley after valley
Opens across the waves, between the dancing
   Leaves of the tree of time, and the broken chords

Space a footing for melody, borne-out above
    The haven of its still begetting, the hill
Of its sudden capture, not disembodied
    But an incarnation heard, a bird-flight
Shared, thrust and tendon and the answering air.

II

The sky goes white. There is no bright alternation now
    Of lit cloud on blue: the scene's finality
Is robbed of a resonance. The day will end
    In its misting-over, its blending of muffled tones,
In a looking to nearnesses. A time
    Of colourlessness prepares for a recomposing,
As the prelude of quiet grows towards the true
    Prelude in the body of the hall. Anew we see
Nature as body and as building
    To be filled, if not with sound, then with
The thousand straying filamented ways
    We travel it by, from the inch before us to the height
Above, and back again. For travelling, we come
    To where we were; as if, in the rhymes
And repetitions and the flights of seeing,
    What we sought for was the unspoken
Familiar dialect of habitation – speech
    Behind speech, language that teaches itself
Under the touch and sight: a text
    That we must write, restore, complete
Grasping for more than the bare facts warranted
    By giving tongue to them. The sound
Of the thick rain chains us in liberty to where we are.

III

Man, in an interior, sits down
    Before an audience of none, to improvise:
He is biding his time, for the rhymes
    That will arise at the threshold of his mind –
Pass-words into the castle-keep,
    The city of sleepers. Wakened by him,

Stanza by stanza (room by room)
    They will take him deeper in. Door
Opens on door, rhyme on rhyme,
    And the circling stair is always nearer
The further it goes. At last,
    He will hear by heart the music that he feared
Was lost, the crossing and the interlacing,
    The involutions of its tracery and the answering of part
By part, as the melody recedes, proceeds
    Above the beat, to twine, untwine
In search of a consonance between
    The pulse of the exploration and the pulse of line.

IV

How soon, in the going down, will he
    Outdistance himself, lose touch to gain
The confidence of what would use him? Where
    Does he stand – beyond the customary ritual,
The habitual prayer? We live
    In an invisible church, a derisible hurt,
A look-out tower, point of powerlessness:
    The kingdom he has entered is a place
Of sources not of silences; memory does not rule it,
    But memory knows her own there
In finding names for them, reading
    By the flames the found words kindle
Their unburnable identities: the going down
    Is to a city of shapes, not a pit of shades
(For all ways begin, either from the eyes out
    Or the eyes in): to a Piazza del Campo
For spirits blessed by a consequence of days;
    For all that would speak itself aloud, a season
Of just regard, a light of sweetened reason.

V

Man, in an exterior, sits down to say
    What it is he sees before him: to say
Is to see again by the light of speech

Speechless, the red fox going
With intent, blind-eyed to all
    But prey. Human, our eyes
Stay with the green of an environment
    He only moves through, and man
In an exterior, tutelary spirit
    Of his own inheritance, speaks
To celebrate, entering on this action
    That is a sort of acting, this assumption
Of a part where speech must follow
    As natural to the occasion, a doing which
Acts out the doer's being,
    Going beyond itself to clarify
The thing it is. But an actor
    May rehearse, sewing the speech behind his thoughts,
Readying them to come into his mind
    Before the words. Yet here, to think
Is say is see: and the red fox
    Caught where it patrols its cruel Eden,
Sets at a counter-pause
    The track of thought, as mounting the unsteady
Wall of crumbled ragstone, it halts its progress,
    A clear momentary silhouette, before it
Dips and disappears into wordlessness.

VI *Written on Water*

One returns to it, as though it were a thread
    Through the labyrinth of appearances, following-out
By eye, the stream in its unravelling,
    Deep in the mud-flanked gash the years
Have cut into scarpland: hard to read
    The life lines of erratic water
Where, at a confluence of two ways
    Refusing to be one without resistance,
Shoulderings of foam collide, unskein
    The moving calligraphy before
It joins again, climbing forward
    Across obstructions: but do you recall
That still pool – it also fed its stream –
    That we were led, night by night,

To return to, as though to clarify ourselves
    Against its depth, its silence? We lived
In a visible church, where everything
    Seemed to be at pause, yet nothing was:
The surface puckered and drew away
    Over the central depth; the foliage
Kept up its liquid friction
    Of small sounds, their multiplicity
A speech behind speech, continuing revelation
    Of itself, never to be revealed:
It rendered new (time within time)
    An unending present, travelling through
All that we were to see and know:
    'Written on water', one might say
Of each day's flux and lapse,
    But to speak of water is to entertain the image
Of its seamless momentum once again,
    To hear in its wash and grip on stone
A music of constancy behind
    The wide promiscuity of acquaintanceship,
Links of water chiming on one another,
    Water-ways permeating the rock of time.

Curtain Call

The dead in their dressing rooms
sweat out the sequel
through greasepaint and brocade.
O to have died
on the last note of a motif, flangeing home
the dovetails of sweet necessity… But the applause
draws them on to resurrection.
No one has won.
Time has undone the incurables
by curing them. The searoar of hands
throbbing, ebbing, each castaway
starts to explore his island. Vans
are standing outside now,

ready for palaces and caverns where
past hoardings and houses
boarded against demolition
a late-night traffic
turning its headlamps towards the peripheries gives
caller and called
back to their own unplotted lives.

THE WAY IN
AND OTHER POEMS

1974

The Way In

The needle-point's swaying reminder
    Teeters at thirty, and the flexed foot
Keeps it there. Kerb-side signs
    For demolitions and new detours,
A propped pub, a corner lopped, all
    Bridle the pressures that guide the needle.

I thought I knew this place, this face
    A little worn, a little homely.
But the look that shadows softened
    And the light could grace, keeps flowing away from me
In daily change; its features, rendered down,
    Collapse expressionless, and the entire town

Sways in the fume of the pyre. Even the new
    And mannerless high risers tilt and wobble
Behind the deformations of acrid heat –
    A century's lath and rafters. Bulldozers
Gobble a street up, but already a future seethes
    As if it had waited in the crevices:

A race in transit, a nomad hierarchy:
    Cargoes of debris out of these ruins fill
Their buckled prams: their trucks and hand-carts wait
    To claim the dismantlings of a neighbourhood –
All that a grimy care from wastage gleans,
    From scrap-iron down to heaps of magazines.

Slowing, I see the faces of a pair
    Behind their load: he shoves and she
Trails after him, a sexagenarian Eve,
    Their punishment to number every hair
Of what remains. Their clothes come of their trade –
    They wear the cast-offs of a lost decade.

The place had failed them anyhow, and their pale
    Absorption staring past this time
And dusty space we occupy together,
    Gazes the new blocks down – not built for them;
But what they are looking at they do not see.
    No Eve, but mindless Mnemosyne,

She is our lady of the nameless metals, of things
    No hand has made, and no machine
Has cut to a nicety that takes the mark
    Of clean intention – at best, the guardian
Of all that our daily contact stales and fades,
    Rusty cages and lampless lampshades.

Perhaps those who have climbed into their towers
    Will eye it all differently, the city spread
In unforeseen configurations, and living with this,
    Will find that civility I can only miss – and yet
It will need more than talk and trees
    To coax a style from these disparities.

The needle-point's swaying reminder
    Teeters: I go with uncongealing traffic now
Out onto the cantilevered road, window on window
    Sucked backwards at the level of my wheels.
Is it patience or anger most renders the will keen?
    This is a daily discontent. This is the way in.

Night Ride

The lamps are on: terrestrial galaxies,
    Fixed stars and moving. How many lights,
How many lives there are, cramped in beside
    This swathe of roadway. And its sodium circuits
Have ousted the glimmer of a thousand hearths
    To the margins of estates whose windows
Blaze over pastoral parentheses. Scatterings
    Trace out the contours of heights unseen,
Drip pendants across their slopes.
    Too many of us are edging behind each other
With dipped beams down the shining wet.
    Our lights seem more beautiful than our lives
In the pulse and grip of this city with neither
    Time nor space in which to define
Itself, its style, as each one feels
    His way among the catseyes and glittering asterisks
And home on home reverberates our wheels.

At Stoke

I have lived in a single landscape. Every tone
  And turn have had for their ground
These beginnings in grey-black: a land
  Too handled to be primary – all the same,
The first in feeling. I thought it once
  Too desolate, diminished and too tame
To be the foundation for anything. It straggles
  A haggard valley and lets through
Discouraged greennesses, lights from a pond or two.
  By ash-tips, or where the streets give out
In cindery in-betweens, the hills
  Swell up and free of it to where, behind
The whole vapoury, patched battlefield,
  The cows stand steaming in an acrid wind.
This place, the first to seize on my heart and eye,
  Has been their hornbook and their history.

Hokusai on the Trent

This milky sky of a dragging afternoon
  Seems a painter's sky – the vision of a lack,
A thwarted possibility that broods
  On the meanness and exclusion. This could well be
An afternoon sunk in eternity
  But for the traffic tolling the rush hour
Among blackened houses, back to back
  And the tang of the air (its milk is sour):
And what painting could taste of such dragging afternoons
  Whose tints are tainted, whose Fujiyamas slag?

Etruria Vale

Nineteen-thirty, our window had for view
The biggest gasometer in England.
Time, no doubt, has robbed that record, too.
The waste ground disappeared beneath the houses.
Faced with the scale of all this, I'm as lost
As if I were Josiah Wedgwood's ghost
Compelled to follow out the tow-path through
The place he named Etruria. In the darkness
He might still bark his shins against the rungs
His barges moored beside. His sooted house
Flares nightly in the gusty lightnings as
The foundries pour their steel. The plan had been
A factory and model cottages,
A seat and prospect for a gentleman,
But history blackened round him, time drank up
The clear wine of his intention, left the lees
Staining the bottom of the valley's cup.
The gas tank has the air of an antique.
And nineteen-thirty was another century.

Gladstone Street

It was the place to go in nineteen-thirty,
And so we went. A housemaid or two
Still lingered on at the bigger houses.
A miner and his family were the next
To follow us there, had scarcely settled in
When the wife began dying, whitely visible
Through the bay window in their double bed.
At the back, the garden vanished
Under grass and a ramshackle shed.
People were sure the street was going downhill.
It literally was: cracks in our hall
Opened as the house started to subside
Towards the mines beneath. Miners were everywhere
Under that cancerous hill. My mother swore

That you could hear them tapping away below
Of a quiet night. Miners unnerved her so
Ever since one sat beside her on the train
And soiled her with his pit dirt. But it wasn't miners
Undid the street. The housemaids lasted
Until the war, then fed the factories.
Flat-dwellers came and went, in the divided houses,
Mothers unwedded who couldn't pay their rent.
A race of gardeners died, and a generation
Hacked down the walls to park their cars
Where the flowers once were. It was there it showed,
The feeble-minded style of the neighbourhood
Gone gaudily mad in painted corrugations,
Botches of sad carpentry. The street front has scarcely changed.
No one has recorded the place.
Perhaps we shall become sociology. We have outpaced
Gladstone's century. We might have been novels.

Dates: Penkhull New Road

It was new about eighteen-sixty.
Eighteen-sixty had come to stay, and did
Until the war – the second war, I mean.
Wasn't forty-five our nineteen-seventeen –
The revolution we had all of us earned?
Streamers and trestles in the roadway:
Even the climate rhymed with the occasion
And no drop fell. Eighteen-sixty
The architecture still insisted, gravely neat:
Alleyways between the houses, doors
That opened onto a still car-less street.
Doorsteps were once a civil place. There must have been a date
It came to be thought common and too late
In time, to be standing shouting out there
Across to the other side – the side
I envied, because its back-yards ran sheer
To the factory wall, warm, black, pulsating,
A long, comforting brick beast. I returned

In seventy-three. Like England,
The place had half-moved with the times – the 'other side'
Was gone. Something had bitten a gap
Out of the stretch we lived in. Penkhull still crowned
The hill, rebuilt to a plan – may as well scrap
The architectural calendar: that dream
Was dreamed up by the insurance-man
And we've a long time to live it yet.
The factory wore a half-bereaved, half-naked look...
It took time to convince me that I cared
For more than beauty: I write to rescue
What is no longer there – absurd
A place should be more fragile than a book.

Portrait of the Artist I

One day, his mother took him on the tram.
An octogenarian in a mackintosh
Who still possessed the faculty for veneration,
Leaned across the aisle to her and said:
'That boy of yours has a remarkable forehead –
He'll live to be lord mayor.' He didn't rise
To that, but forehead letting instinct choose,
Betrayed him into verse. So Whittington
Never turned again, his mother strayed
Bemused between the prophecy and its failure.
The tram-lines were dragged up the very next year.

Portrait of the Artist II

Season of mists and migraines, rich catarrhs,
Pipes in the public library throbbed and hissed
Against your advent. Parks were emptying.
Soaked benches and a wind that brought the grime
Smoking across the beds, now flowerless,

Drove old men indoors to the reading room.
They took their time, pored over magazines
They scarcely saw, and breathed in dust and newsprint,
Clearing their throats to splatter on the floor.
Across the street, the high school lunch-hour raged.
He brought his sandwiches inside. Of course,
It was forbidden. The old illiterates, too,
Dragged orts and fragments from their paper bags.
A schoolboy and a dozen ancients, they
Watched for the librarian's bureaucracy
Who tried to spy them out, but seldom could –
They'd grown so adept at their secret feeding,
Bent at those tables others used for reading...
Did the old guilt stick? For now, he wrote
His verses furtively, on blotters, minutes,
As though back there, that surreptitious snack
Still hidden by *The Illustrated London News*.

The Tree

This child, shovelling away
what remains of snow –
a batter of ash and crystals –
knows nothing of the pattern
his bent back lifts
above his own reflection:
it climbs the street-lamp's stem
and cross-bar, branching
to take in all the lines
from gutter, gable, slates
and chimney-crowns to the high
pillar of a mill chimney
on a colourless damp sky:
there in its topmost air
and eyrie rears that tree
his bending sends up
from a treeless street, its roots
in the eye and in the net the shining
flagstones spread at his feet.

Midlands

Rain baptizes the ravaged counties
    In the name of some god who can remember
The way the land lay, the groundswell
    Under it all. The football club,
Treading back to mud their threadbare pitch,
    Move garish on the grey, hemmed-
In by a throng of sodden houses
    Whose Sunday kitchens grow savoury for them.

In the Ward

Old women come here to die. Nurses
    Tend them with a sort of callous zest
That keeps their youthful patience, guarantees it
    In face of all they do not wish to be:
Shrunk limbs, shrunk lives, the incontinence.
    A woodland scene is hanging on the wall,
To rectify some lost connection
    With a universe that goes on shepherding its flock
Of fogs out there, its unkillable seasons.
    Dying, these old have for an ally still
That world of repetitions for, once gone,
    They are replaced incessantly. In the ward
The picture-glass gives back the outlines
    Of both old and young, in a painted
Sunlight and among the twines of trees.

The Marl Pits

It was a language of water, light and air
    I sought – to speak myself free of a world
Whose stoic lethargy seemed the one reply

To horizons and to streets that blocked them back
In a monotone fume, a bloom of grey.
   I found my speech. The years return me
To tell of all that seasoned and imprisoned:
   I breathe familiar, sedimented air
From a landscape of disembowellings, underworlds
   Unearthed among the clay. Digging
The marl, they dug a second nature
   And water, seeping up to fill their pits,
Sheeted them to lakes that wink and shine
   Between tips and steeples, streets and waste
In slow reclaimings, shimmers, balancings,
   As if kindling Eden rescinded its own loss
And words and water came of the same source.

Class

Those midland *a*'s
once cost me a job:
diction defeated my best efforts –
I was secretary at the time
to the author of *The Craft of Fiction*.
That title was full of class.
You had only to open your mouth on it
to show where you were born
and where you belonged. I tried
time and again I tried
but I couldn't make it
that top *A* – *ah*
I should say –
it sounded like gargling.
I too visibly shredded his fineness:
it was clear the job couldn't last
and it didn't. Still, I'd always thought him an ass
which he pronounced arse. There's no accounting for taste.

The Rich

I like the rich – the way
they say: 'I'm not made of money':
their favourite pastoral
is to think they're not rich at all –
poorer, perhaps, than you or me,
for they have the imagination of that fall
into the pinched decency
we take for granted. Of course,
they do want to be wanted
by all the skivvies and scrapers
who neither inherited nor rose.
But are they daft or deft,
when they proclaim themselves
men of the left, as if prepared
at the first premonitory flush
of the red dawn
to go rushing onto the street
and, share by share,
add to the common conflagration
their scorned advantage?
They know that it can't happen
in Worthing or Wantage:
with so many safety valves
between themselves and scalding,
all they have to fear
is wives, children, breath and balding.
And at worst
there is always some sunny
Aegean prospect. I like the rich –
they so resemble the rest
of us, except for their money.

Bridges

The arteries, red lane on lane,
  Cover the engineers' new maps:
England lies lost to silence now:
  On bridges, where old roads cross
The chasm of the new, the idlers
  Stand staring down. Philosophers
Of the common run, some masticate pipe-stems,
  And seem not to hear the roar in Albion's veins,
As though the quiet, rebegotten as they lean, survived
  Through them alone, its stewards and sustainers,
For all these advancing and disappearing lives.

At Saint Mary's Church

The high nave, in a place of ships,
  Seems like the invitation to some voyage
Long deferred. It will not be undertaken now.
  Saint Mary's shares a horizon
With blocks in a mock stone-brown
  Meant to resemble hers. This cheek by jowl affair
Labours to prove we can equal or outdo
  Those eras of cholera, fear of the mob.
If that is true, it is not true here.
  Elizabeth thought this church the comeliest
She had seen, and haunts it still, solid
  In painted wood, and carved by the same
Hands as those, that in a place of ships,
  Shaped gaudy figure-heads. And though
That voyage is not to be undertaken, she,
  All bright will, female insouciance,
Might well have been the thrust and prow
  To such a venture now forsaken
In the dust of abolished streets, the land –
  Locked angles of a stale geometry.

Bristol

In a Brooklyn Park

'To people these lands with civil men',
   George Jackson said. There is civility enough
Inside this place, if one could spread it:
   A woman is trying to reconcile
Two fighting boys who still refuse
   To smile with the bright persuasion of her smile;
An old man sits learning from a book
   Inglés sin Maestro, while among the trees
Wander three generations of the Jews.

Under the Moon's Reign

Twilight was a going of the gods: the air
   Hung weightlessly now – its own
Inviolable sign. From habit, we
   Were looking still for what we could not see –
The inside of the outside, for some spirit flung
   From the burning of that Götterdämmerung
And suffused in the obscurity. Scraps
   Of the bare-twigged scene were floating
Scattered across scraps of water – mirrors
   Shivered and stuck into a landscape
That drifted visibly to darkness. The pools
   Restrained the disappearing shapes, as all around
The dusk was gaining: too many images
   Beckoned from that thronging shade
None of which belonged there. And then the moon
   Drawing all into more than daylight height
Had taken the zenith, the summit branches
   Caught as by steady lightning, and each sign
Transformed, but by no more miracle than the place
   It occupied and the eye that saw it
Gathered into the momentary perfection of the scene
   Under transfigured heavens, under the moon's reign.

Foxes' Moon

Night over England's interrupted pastoral,
  And moonlight on the frigid lattices
Of pylons. The shapes of dusk
  Take on an edge, refined
By a drying wind and foxes bring
  Flint hearts and sharpened senses to
This desolation of grisaille in which the dew
  Grows clearer, colder. Foxes go
In their ravenous quiet to where
  The last farm meets the first
Row from the approaching town: they nose
  The garbage of the yards, move through
The white displacement of a daily view
  Uninterrupted. Warm sleepers turn,
Catch the thin vulpine bark between
  Dream on dream, then lose it
To the babbling undertow they swim. These
  Are the fox hours, cleansed
Of all the meanings we can use
  And so refuse them. Foxes glow,
Ghosts unacknowledged in the moonlight
  Of the suburb, and like ghosts they flow
Back, racing the coming red, the beams
  Of early cars, a world not theirs
Gleaming from kindled windows, asphalt, wires.

After a Death

A little ash, a painted rose, a name.
  A moonshell that the blinding sky
Puts out with winter blue, hangs
  Fragile at the edge of visibility. That space
Drawing the eye up to its sudden frontier
  Asks for a sense to read the whole
Reverted side of things. I wanted
  That height and prospect such as music brings –

Music or memory. Neither brought me here.
　　This burial place straddles a green hill,
Chimneys and steeples plot the distances
　　Spread vague below: only the sky
In its upper reaches keeps
　　An untarnished January colour. Verse
Fronting that blaze, that blade,
　　Turns to retrace the path of its dissatisfactions,
Thought coiled on thought, and only certain that
　　Whatever can make bearable or bridge
The waste of air, a poem cannot.
　　The husk of moon, risking the whole of space,
Seemingly sails it, fraily launched
　　To its own death and fullness. We buried
A little ash. Time so broke you down,
　　Your lost eyes, dry beneath
Their matted lashes, a painted rose
　　Seems both to memorialize and mock
What you became. It picks your name out
　　Written on the roll beside a verse –
Obstinate words: measured against the blue,
　　They cannot conjure with the dead. Words,
Bringing that space to bear, that air
　　Into each syllable we speak, bringing
An earnest to us of the portion
　　We must inherit, what thought of that would give
The greater share of comfort, greater fear –
　　To live forever, or to cease to live?
The imageless unnaming upper blue
　　Defines a world, all images
Of endeavours uncompleted. Torn levels
　　Of the land drop, street by street,
Pitted and pooled, its wounds
　　Cleansed by a light, dealt out
With such impartiality you'd call it kindness,
　　Blindly assuaging where assuagement goes unfelt.

Elemental

A last flame,
sole leaf
flagging at the tree tip,
is dragged through the current
down into the water
of the air, and in this final
metamorphosis, spiralling
swims to earth.

In December

Cattle are crowding the salt-lick.
The gruel of mud icily thickens.
On the farm-boy's Honda a sweat of fog drops.
They are logging the woodland, the sole standing crop.

Hyphens

'The country's love-
liness', it said:
what I read was
'the country's love-
lines' – the unnec-
essary 's'
passed over by
the mind's blind-
ly discriminating eye:
but what I saw
was a whole scene
restored: the love-
lines drawing
together the list

'loveliness' capped
and yet left
vague, unloved:
lawns, gardens, houses,
the encircling trees.

In March

These dry, bright winter days,
   When the crow's colour takes to itself
Such gloss, the shadows from the hedge
   Ink-stain half way across
The road to where a jagged blade
   Of light eats into them: light's guarded frontier
Is glittering everywhere, everywhere held
   Back by naked branchwork, dark
Fissurings along the creviced walls,
   Shade side of barn and house, of half-cut stack
Strawing the ground, in its own despite
   With flecks of pallid gold, allies to light:
And over it all, a chord of glowing black
   A shining, flying shadow, the crow is climbing.

Discrepancies

That year, March began in April.
Wasn't it floes from Greenland
Going south, they said, and the earthquake
In Nicaragua – a collision between
The seismic and the atmospheric that released
An effervescence into the air? Its tang and sting
Excited the nostrils of the yearling,
The dead leaves circling rose again –
But the clouds said, 'Snow, snow',
The sun melting the threat before it fell.

Nicaragua blazed into the chaos,
A polar glittering of gulls
Swung round and round on the mid-air currents
Over the windswept bed of their inland sea.
Nature has evolved beyond us –
You couldn't have painted it, I mean,
Unless on the whirlpool's fish-eye mirror
Where the blinding navel winds all discrepancies in.

The Last of Night

Mist after frost. The woodlands
stretch vague in it, but catch
the rising light on reefs
of foliage above the greyish
'sea' I was about to say,
but sun so rapidly advances
between glance and word,
under that leafy headland
mist lies a sea no more:
a gauze visibly fading
burns out to nothing, lets grow
beneath each mid-field bush
a perfect shadow, and among
frost-whitened tussocks
the last of night recedes along
tracks the animals have taken
back into earth and wood.

The Witnesses

Now that the hillside woods are dense with summer,
One enters with a new, an untaught sense
Of heights and distances. Before,
Lacking the profusion, the protrusion of the leaves,

Spaces seemed far shallower that, now,
   Thronged with ledges of overhanging green,
Bear down on the air beneath. One can no longer see
   The high recession stretching beyond each tree,
But the view, shut round, lets through
   The mind into a palpitation of jostled surfaces.
Nudging, they overlap, reach out
   Beckoning, bridging the underdeeps that stir
Unsounded among the foliage of a hundred trees
   That fill an aerial city's every thoroughfare
With the steady vociferation of unhuman witnesses.

Hill Walk

for Philippe and Anne-Marie Jaccottet

Innumerable and unnameable, foreign flowers
   Of a reluctant April climbed the slopes
Beside us. Among them, rosemary and thyme
   Assuaged the coldness of the air, their fragrance
So intense, it seemed as if the thought
   Of that day's rarity had sharpened sense, as now
It sharpens memory. And yet such pungencies
   Are there an affair of every day – Provençal
Commonplaces, like the walls, recalling
   In their broken sinuousness, our own
Limestone barriers, half undone
   By time, and patched against its sure effacement
To retain the lineaments of a place.
   In our walk, time used us well that rhymed
With its own herbs. We crested idly
   That hill of ilexes and savours to emerge
Along the plateau at last whose granite
   Gave on to air: it showed us then
The place we had started from and the day
   Half gone, measured against the distances
That lay beneath, a territory travelled.
   All stretched to the first fold

Of that unending landscape where we trace
    Through circuits, drops and terraces
The outworks, ruinous and overgrown,
    Where space on space has labyrinthed past time:
The unseizable citadel glimmering back at us,
    We contemplated no assault, no easy victory:
Fragility seemed sufficiency that day
    Where we sat by the abyss, and saw each hill
Crowned with its habitations and its crumbled stronghold
    In the scents of inconstant April, in its cold.

Lacoste

De Sade's rent walls let in
    Through faceless windows, a sky
As colourless as the stones that framed them:
    All tenacity, a dry ivy grew
Bristling against the grey. But wild thyme
    Sweetened anew the memory of the spot,
Its scent as fresh as a single fig-tree's
    Piercing greenness. The only words
I heard in that place were kind ones –
    'If you would care to visit my house...'
– And came from the old woman who
    Paused in climbing the broken street
At meeting us: but we were *en voyage*
    So she, wishing us a good one, bent on
Once more against the devious, sloped track,
    We winding down a descent that led
Back to the valley vineyards' spread geometry.

How Far

How far from us
even the nearest are
among these close leaves
crowding the window:

what we know
of that slow then sudden
bursting into green is merely
what we have seen of it and not

(fermenting at its heart)
darkness such as the blind might hear:
for us, there is no way in where
across these surfaces

the light is a white lie
told only to hide the dark
extent from us
of a seafloor continent.

Tiger Skull

Frozen in a grimace, all cavernous threat,
onslaught remains its sole end still:
handle it, and you are taught the weight
such a thrust to kill would carry.

The mind too eagerly marries a half truth. This carapace
lies emptied of the memory of its own sated peace,
its bestial repose and untensed pride
under the equanimity of sun and leaf,

where to be tiger is
to move through the uncertain terrain supple-paced:
how little this stark and armoured mouth can say
of the living beast.

The Greeting

One instant of morning
he cast a glance
idly, half blindly
into the depths of distance:

space and its Eden
of green and blue
warranted more watching
than such gazing through:

but the far roofs gave
a 'Good day' back,
defeating that negligence
with an unlooked-for greeting:

it was the day's one time
that the light on them
would carry their image
as far as to him

then abandon the row,
its lit-up walls
and unequal pitches,
its sharpness to shadow:

one instant of morning
rendered him time
and opened him space,
one whole without seam.

The Insistence of Things

paragraphs from a journal

At the edge of conversations, uncompleting all acts of thought, looms the insistence of things which, waiting on our recognition, face us with our own death, for they are so completely what we are not. And thus we go on trying to read them, as if they were signs, or the embodied message of oracles. We remember how Orpheus drew voices from the stones.

It takes so long to become aware of the places we inhabit. Not so much of the historic or geographic facts attaching to them, as of the moment to moment quality of a given room, or of the simple recognitions that could be lured to inhabit a paragraph, a phrase, a snatch of words – and thus speak to us.

A stump of stone juts up out of the grass, glittering drily like weathered cedar. A cloud of gnats dances over it on a now mild December day. It is the remains of a mounting block, disused beside this fenced-off bridge. The gnats haunt the stone as if it held warmth, grey against grey. One can scarcely make out what they are, and their winter dance seems such a weightless celebration of improbables (how did they escape last night's frost? – the birds of the day before?) that what one actually sees is more than the sight – an instance radiating unlooked-for instances, a swarm of unreasoning hopes suddenly and vulnerably brought into the open.

Snow keeps trying the currents of the air – a haze, a smoke of crystals – but each time it is about to take solid shape, the wind whirls it apart into specks of white dust, just visible on the blackness of the surrounding woodland. The thin cry of an early lamb is brought in on the blustering wind that crashes endlessly against the trees. There is an almost metallic edge to that frail voice with which a new energy has entered among the leafless branches, the sudden sun-gashes in dark cloud and lancings of green over shallow grass where the rays emerge.

Beech leaves on a small beech, crowded and protected by the closeness of an ill-kept wood. For all the storms, they are still firmly anchored and look like brittle, even fragments of brown paper, their veining very clear and regular. The wind in them hisses faintly, a distinct and crisper hiss than that of the water which fills the distances. The coming and going breaths of the wind: hiss, silence, hiss. The pale brown of the leaves seems among the dark branches to attract light into these scalloped and cupped handshapes.

Towards the end of a warm spring day, the evening air, echoing with bird-calls, prepares for frost. A distant half moon in its halo. No cloud near it, only down low on the western horizon where it lies shapeless, thick and pink-purple, more like a mist. In the east, a few feathery drifters also catching the pink, last flare. The map on the moon is visible. A sound as clearly isolated as the moon (a shut door) breaks off from the farm building. The thin cry of lambs, a discussion of rooks above the wood, the insistence of bird-calls. The sound of a farm van winds away through the mingled callings. The rooks are flying round and round in the twilight over the wood, like dirty sediment rising and falling in the water of the air. They argue (or agree? – which?) on one concerted note. A sudden intervention from two wild ducks. An owl takes up the broken note of the ducks, rounds it, mellows it, hollows it to a scream, hoarsely answering a second owl in a new dialogue. As the daylight disappears, the moon casts pallid shadows.

Idrigill

Roofless, the wreck of a house and byre
    Lies like a stone boat, the tide
Behind, inching, ebbing. A high
    Sea could almost float it out
Across that plain of water, to where
    Those who abandoned it still try
To account for their lives here
    Levelled too long, too soon:
Working the waves, they gather up salt sheaves
    That, collapsing, break their hold and spread
In abysses of candour, scatterings of fools' gold.
    That boat would take them in,
Beach them by sea-caves where they might lie
    And face out the storms in sea-cleansed effigy,
If grass had not matted its decks and clasped them down
    To a tranquil earth its owners could never own.

Of Lady Grange

Of Lady Grange
    that ill-starred daughter
    of Chiesly of Dalry: he
    who when the Lord President
    sat in adverse judgement
    murdered him:

She inherited
    the violence of her father, was married
    some say against her will, others
    so that she might spy on him
    to Erskine, my Lord Grange,
    Jacobite, profligate and bigot:

He
    and the family she bore him
    detested her: but when a separation
    was arranged, my Lady Grange went on
    molesting him, opposed as she was
    to his politics and his person:

One night –
    it was a decade and more
    after the rebellion and its failure –
    her husband and his friends
    gathered, each to rehearse his part
    in the restoration of the house of Stuart:

The lives
    of men of great family
    were at stake when she, concealed
    it is said beneath a sofa
    or a day-bed where they sat,
    burst forth and threatened to betray them:

James Erskine
    judging her capable of that,
    two gentlemen (attended)
    called at her lodging: her resistance
    cost her two teeth as they forced her
    first into a sedan, then on to horse:

Her husband
    had it given out that she
    was sick of a fever: the next day
    she 'died' of it and he
    saw to it that her funeral should
    have all of the ceremony due to blood:

Her journey
    was as cold as the earth
    her coffin lay in:
    air, spray and the spread of water
    awaited the living woman
    her stone mocked greyly:

They rode
    from Edinburgh to Stirling and despite
    storms, robbers, Highland
    tracks and the lack of them,
    reached the deserted Castle Tirrim
    at Moidart loch:

Thence
    on by boat, and out
    into the Atlantic: Heiskir
    was to house her two years,
    until the single family there
    could no longer tolerate her

And said so:
    from a ship, two men
    appeared and carried her
    on board to Kilda, where
    no one could speak her language,
    nor would she learn theirs:

She learned
    to spin and in a clew
    of yarn sent with her neighbours' wool
    to Inverness, she hid a message,
    though she had neither pen nor pencil:
    this was the sixth year of her exile:

To Hope,
 her misnamed lawyer,
 the letter seemed
 to be written in blood: a ship
 chartered, fitted and sent
 found without its tenant

The house
 on Kilda, chimneyless, earth-floored:
 for her, once more
 the inevitable sea, Skye
 at last and the sand of a sea-cave
 where fish-nets hung to dry

At Idrigill:
 nor could this place
 keep the secret long:
 though the cliffs hung sheer,
 the fishers came
 to cure their catch and to sleep here:

Again
 she must be moved on
 and over to Uist: a large
 boulder, knotted in a noose,
 lay in the boat: a guard stood
 ready to sink his charge

If
 rounding a headland of the cliff
 the ship, sighting them,
 should pursue: out into the surge
 oars drew them where
 the three wrecked women

Emerge
 from the sea in stone:
 they were set for the further isles:
 Bracadale sank down
 behind them into its mist:
 now they could only trust

Time
  to weary what vigilance
  might try, and time
  so ruffled and so smoothed
  the sea-lanes they went by,
  was it from Uist, Harris or Assynt

That she
  came back to Skye?
  Of the life she had
  in Vaternish, all we hear
  is of the madness of her last
  and fifteenth year

In exile,
  of 'the poor, strange lady
  who came ashore
  and died', and of the great
  funeral which the Macleod
  of Ramsay's portrait, paid for:

Yet still
  no ordinary end
  attended that lonely woman:
  'for reasons unknown'
  the coffin at Duirinish
  held stones only:

But there
  where Kilconan church
  still points at variable skies
  a roofless gable, the square
  stone of a later year
  confesses her corpse:

She
  is well buried above that sea,
  the older dead beside her
  murdered in the burning church
  and, below, their slayers on the same
  day slain, the dyke-wall toppled to cover them.

The Promise

The tide goes down, uncovering its gifts:
    Rocks glint with the silver of slivered wood,
Like the piecemeal skeleton of some great boat,
    That this light of resurrection, if it could
Would draw together again, and the next tide find
    As solid as the cliff that looms behind
Its absence now. But part of a scene
    That is flawed and flowing, the pieces lie
Under a fragmented rainbow's promise
    Of the changes in their unbroken sufficiency.

Marine

The water, wind-impelled, advancing
    Along the promontory side, continually
Shaves off into spray, where its flank
    Grazes against rock, each white
In-coming rush like a vast
    Wheel spun to nothing, a wing
Caught down from flight to feathers.

Rubh An' Dunain

(The Point of the Forts)

Mouthings of water at the end of a world.
Pictish masons have outreached their enemy
In stone. But who won, or what gods
Saved the bare appearances of it all
Is written in no history.
Their pantheon was less powerful than this wall.

Couplet

Light catches the sudden metal of the streams:
Their granite captive is stirring in its chains.

Beethoven Attends the C Minor Seminar

That was the day they invited
Ludmilla Quatsch, the queen of the sleevenote.
Her works cannot be quoted
Without permission. I shall not quote.

Think and drink were to be paid for
Out of the Gabbocca Fund.
Her theme was 'Arguing About Music'. Her arguments
Had driven T. Melvin Quatsch into the ground.

She challenged Beethoven on the Heiliger Dankgesang:
Too long. Too long. She argued
For a C Minor without final chords
And a Hymn to joy without the words.

Ah, if only he were here in spirit to agree!
(She knew that she had him confuted)
And suddenly, inexplicably there he was –
Some confusion of levels in the celestial computer

Had earthed him. It was the briefest of appearances,
But up out of vagueness wavering
He seemed to savour her points, and she
Clutched for his attention, all cadenzas and fortissimi.

She had sensed at once the urgency of the event,
Packed-in and pressure-cooked her argument:
By now, the laity were quite lost
As she pitched her apophthegms at that height, that ghost.

He seemed to grow very deaf, and then
(After a slight cybernetic adjustment overhead)
Very dead and disappeared.
Had all she was saying gone unheard?

She thought she still could descry him –
He of the impregnable ear, still quick
To catch only the most hidden sound:
His silence was as unanswerable as his music.

Doubt diminished her. They helped her out.
After which those sleevenotes were never the same
(Too complicated, as I have said, to quote)
– Rumour insisted it was another hand from which they came.

When they invited Ludmilla, all had hoped
That she might return to fill the chair,
But that untimely vision balked
Them and her of twenty years of talk.

Consolations for Double Bass

You lament your lot at the bottom of an abyss
    Of moonlight. And yet you would not
Change it for all that bland redundance
    Overhead, the great theme leaping
Chromatic steeps in savage ease.
    The trumpets on their fugal stair
Climb each other's summits pair by pair:
    A memorial of remissive drums. The hero falls.
A race of disappointed generals, we mourn him
    Nobilmente. Confluence of a hundred streams
In one lambency of sound, our grief
    Beckons the full orchestra, 'Come on –
Crash in like a house collapsing
    On top of its hardware.' And you?
All that you can do is state, repeat,
    For repetition is the condition for remembering
What must come – the moment
    For the return to earth, to blood-beat.
Good gut, resonant belly,
    You are the foot a hundred others
Tread by, the bound of their flying islands
    And their utopias of sound. Tristan is being sung to

Like a drowsy suckling: you
    Are sanchoing still: that, I know,
Is the story of another hero – but you have ridden
    With them all to their distress, and lived
To punctuate it, unastounded in your endless
    Unthanked *Hundesleben*, nose to ground.

Melody

Song is being...
    Rilke

That phrase in the head – that snatch repeated
    Could have led nowhere, but for the will
To hear the consequence of it – the reply
    To 'I am dying, I am denying, I, I...'
A shred of the self, an unease: its pleasure
    Would not please the hearer long who heard it
Only within: a violin carries it
    To surrounding air, letting it meet
That first and silent pressure, come
    To test its setting out, its hovering
Over a spun doubt, its own questioning.
    Through a second instrument it flows,
But a third goes counter to it, and a fourth
    Derides both the pride and pains
It has taken to stay proud; and forces,
    Frees it to a singing strength
Until that thread of song, defied,
    Gathering a tributary power, must find
The river course, winding in which
    It can outgo itself – can lose
Not the reality of pain, but that sense
    Of sequestration: the myth of no future
And no ancestry save ache. *Gesang*
    Ist Dasein? Song is the measure, rather,
Of being's spread and height, the moonrise
    That tips and touches, recovering from the night
The lost hill-lines, the sleeping prospects:

It is the will to exchange the graph of pain
Acknowledged, charted and repeated, for the range
    Of an unpredicted terrain. Each phrase
Now follows the undulations of slope, rise
    And drop, released along generous contours
And curving towards a sea where
    The play of light across the dark immensity,
Moves in a shimmering completeness. The tide
    Ridden in unexulting quiet, rides
Up against the craft that sails it
    Tossed and tried, through the groundswell
To the dense calm of unfathomable silence.

Da Capo

And so
they go back: violin
against piano
to know once more
what it was
they had felt before:

But reapproaching
all they knew
though they touch (almost)
they cannot encroach there:
to know what they knew
and, knowing, seize it,
how should time grow and how
should they reappraise it?

Time beyond all repeal,
they know that they must feel
now what they know,
and going back
to unenterable Eden, they
enter a time new-made
da capo

THE SHAFT

1978

Charlotte Corday

O Vertu! le poignard, seul espoir de la terre,
Est ton arme sacrée...

Chénier

Courteously self-assured, although alone,
With voice and features that could do no hurt,
Why should she not enter? They let in
A girl whose reading made a heroine –
Her book was Plutarch, her republic Rome:
Home was where she sought her tyrant out.

The towelled head next, the huge batrachian mouth:
There was a mildness in him, even. He
Had never been a woman's enemy,
And time and sickness turned his stomach now
From random execution. All the same,
He moved aside to write her victims down,
And when she approached, it was to kill she came.

She struck him from above. One thrust. Her whole
Intent and innocence directing it
To breach through flesh and enter where it must,
It seemed a blow that rose up from within:
Tinville reduced it all to expertise:
– What, would you make of me a hired assassin?

– What did you find to hate in him? – His crimes.
Every reply was temperate save one
And that was human when all's said and done:
The deposition, read to those who sit
In judgement on her, 'What has she to say?'
'Nothing, except that I succeeded in it.'

– You think that you have killed all Marats off?
– I think perhaps such men are now afraid.
The blade hung in its grooves. How should she know
The Terror still to come, as she was led
Red-smocked from gaol out into evening's red?
It was to have brought peace, that faultless blow.

Fouquier Tinville: the public prosecutor.

Uncowed by the unimaginable result,
She loomed by in the cart beneath the eye
Of Danton, Desmoulins and Robespierre,
Heads in a rabble fecund in insult:
She had remade her calendar, called this
The Fourth Day of the Preparation of Peace.

Greater than Brutus was what Adam Lux
Demanded for her statue's sole inscription:
His pamphlet was heroic and absurd
And asked the privilege of dying too:
Though the republic raised to her no statue,
The brisk tribunal took him at his word.

What haunted that composure none could fault?
For she, when shown the knife, had dropped her glance –
She 'who believed her death would raise up France'
As Chénier wrote who joined the later dead:
Her judge had asked: 'If you had gone uncaught,
Would you have then escaped?' 'I would,' she said.

A daggered Virtue, Clio's roll of stone,
Action unsinewed into statuary!
Beneath that gaze what tremor was willed down?
And, where the scaffold's shadow stretched its length,
What unlived life would struggle up against
Death died in the possession of such strength?

Perhaps it was the memory of that cry
That cost her most as Catherine Marat
Broke off her testimony… But the blade
Inherited the future now and she
Entered a darkness where no irony
Seeps through to move the pity of her shade.

Marat Dead

the version of Jacques Louis David

*Citoyen, il suffit que je sois bien malheureuse
pour avoir droit à votre bienveillance.*

Charlotte Corday to Marat

They look like fact, the bath, the wall, the knife,
The splintered packing-case that served as table;
The linen could be priced by any housewife,
As could the weapon too, but not the sable
Suggestion here that colours all we feel
And animates this death-scene from the life
With red, brown, green reflections on the real.

Scaled back to such austerity, each tone
Now sensuous with sadness, would persuade
That in the calm the ugliness has gone
From the vast mouth and from the swaddled head;
And death that worked this metamorphosis
Has left behind no effigy of stone
But wrought an amorous languor with its kiss.

'Citizen, it is enough that I should be
A most unhappy woman to have right
To your benevolence': the heeded plea
Lies on his desk, a patch of bloodied white,
Taking the eye beside the reddening bath,
And single-minded in duplicity,
Loud in the silence of this aftermath.

Words in this painting victimize us all:
Tyro or tyrant, neither shall evade
Such weapons: reader, you grow rational
And miss those sharp intentions that have preyed
On trusting literacy here: unmanned
By generosity and words you fall,
Sprawl forwards bleeding with your pen in hand.

She worked in blood, and paint absolves the man,
And in a bathtub laves all previous stains:

She is the dark and absence in the plan
And he a love of justice that remains.
Who was more deft, the painter or the girl?
Marat's best monument with this began,
That all her presence here's a truthless scrawl.

A Self-Portrait: David

This is the face behind my face. You see
At every trembling touch of paint laid-in
To haunt the ground with shade, enough of me
To tell you what I am. This flesh puts by
The mind's imperious geometry,
The signature of will among the things
That will must change. From this day forth, distrust
Whatever I may do unless it show
A startled truth as in these eyes' misgivings,
These lips that, closed, confess 'I do not know.'

For Danton

Bound to the fierce Metropolis…
The Prelude, Book X

*In the autumn of 1793 – the year in which he had instituted the Revolutionary
Tribunal – Danton went back to his birthplace, Arcis-sur-Aube. After his
return in November, he was to be arrested, tried and condemned.*

Who is the man that stands against this bridge
And thinks that he and not the river advances?
Can he not hear the links of consequence
Chiming his life away? Water is time.
Not yet, not yet. He fronts the parapet
Drinking the present with unguarded sense:

The stream comes on. Its music deafens him
To other sounds, to past and future wrong.
The beat is regular beneath that song.
He hears in it a pulse that is his own;
He hears the year autumnal and complete.
November waits for him who has not done

With seeings, savourings. Grape-harvest brings
The south into the north. This parapet
Carries him forward still, a ship from Rheims,
From where, in boyhood and on foot, he'd gone
'To see', he said, 'the way a king is made',
The king that he himself was to uncrown –

Destroyed and superseded, then secure
In the possession of a perfect power
Returned to this: to river, town and plain,
Walked in the fields and knew what power he'd lost,
The cost to him of that metropolis where
He must come back to rule and Robespierre.

Not yet. This contrary perfection he
Must taste into a life he has no time
To live, a lingered, snatched maturity
Before he catches in the waterchime
The measure and the chain a death began,
And fate that loves the symmetry of rhyme
Will spring the trap whose teeth must have a man.

Lines Written in the Euganean Hills

1

The tiles of the swimming pool are azure,
    Dyeing on breast and wings the swifts
That, transfigured, hunt its surface:
    This is man's landscape, all transfigurings
Across the thrust of origin – of rock
    Under schists and clays, their erratic
Contours cross-ruled by vine on vine:

Over the table, flies are following-out the stains
Tasting the man-made, the mature stale wine.

2

An aridity haunts the edges of the fields:
   The irrigation jet, irising, arching
Across the cloud of its own wet smoke,
   Puts a gloss on the crop. But the cricket
Is raucous, the hoarse voice of that dust
   That whitening the grassroots of the burnt-out ditches,
Has webbed-over the spider's net with chalk.

3

Unshuttering vistas
mournfully the wizened
female custodian recites
snatches of Petrarch
whose statue cramped
in the cellarage gesticulates
beside his mummified cat, Laura.

4

D'Annunzio saw it all behind golden mist,
A wavering of decay, vegetable, vast,
That had taken hold on each statue, each relief,
And was eating and unmaking them, as if leaf by leaf.
Two wars, and the mathematic of the humanist
Re-declares itself in white persistence,
Slogans scaling the plinths and walls where Mao
And Lenin dispute the Palladian ratio.

Death in Venice

Glass gauds from Murano.
The band at Florian's are drowsing
drowned in the syrup of their rhapsody.
A high stack

flaring-off waste from Mestre
hangs beaconed across water
where each outboard's wake
is flexing, unmaking those marble
images, bridals of stone
and sea, restless to have
that piled longevity
down and done.

Near Corinium

The recalcitrance
                    of whorl-wheel fossils
of belemnite teeth
                    shatterings
from the meteors
                    gods had hurled
according
            to those who also
lie in the subsoil these inlay:
                    'I, Caius Martius restored
                        this Jupiter column
                            the Christians had defaced'
                                            of which
only the limestone base…
                            those who,
these which –
                history's particles refusing
both completion
                    and extinction:
traceries
            finer than the lines
of spider floss:
                    it is as though
this torn tapestry
                    faded calligraphy
were whole
            if only one could adjust

one's eyes to them:
                    excavations
for the by-pass:
                    the dust–motes turning like stars
which the air–currents lift

Casarola

for Attilio Bertolucci

Cliffs come sheering down into woodland here:
    The trees – they are chestnuts – spread to a further drop
Where an arm of water rushes through unseen
    Still lost in leaves: you can hear it
Squandering its way towards the mill
    A path crossing a hillslope and a bridge
Leads to at last: the stones lie there
    Idle beside it: they were cut from the cliff
And the same stone rises in wall and roof
    Not of the mill alone, but of shed on shed
Whose mossed tiles like a city of the dead
    Grow green in the wood. There are no dead here
And the living no longer come
    In October to crop the trees: the chestnuts
Dropping, feed the roots they rose from:
    A rough shrine sanctifies the purposes
These doors once opened to, a desolation
    Of still-perfect masonry. There is a beauty
In this abandonment: there would be more
    In the slow activity of smoke
Seeping at roof and lintel; out of each low
    Unwindowed room rising to fill
Full with essences the winter wood
    As the racked crop dried. Waste
Is our way. An old man
    Has been gathering mushrooms. He pauses
To show his spoil, plumped by a soil
    Whose sweet flour goes unmilled:

Rapid and unintelligible, he thinks we follow
  As we feel for his invitations to yes and no:
Perhaps it's the mushrooms he's telling over
  Or this place that shaped his dialect, and where nature
Daily takes the distinctness from that signature
  Men had left there in stone and wood,
Among waning villages, above the cities of the plain.

Portobello Carnival 1973

A malleability
              a precision
with which they keep the beat
                            their bodies
overflowing to the house-doors
                            dancing
so that the street
              is a jostled conduit
that contains them (just):
                        the steel-band ride,
their pace decided
              by the crowd's pace
before their open truck
              to a music
of detritus
        wheelhubs, cans:
the tempered oil-drums
                    yield a Caribbean sweetness
belied by the trumpet
                    that gliding on
ahead of the ostinato
              divides
what the beat unites:
              the trumpeter knows
and through his breath
                    and fingers the knowledge
flows into acid sound:
              you will not go back

to the fronds, the sands
                    Windward, Leeward
and all those islands
               the banner bears forward
under the promise
          FOREVER:
below
        human peacocks and imaginary birds,
a devil
       hoisting as a flag
his black bat-wings
              that have come unpinned (unpinioned):
in all the sweat
           and garish conglomeration of dress
there is a rightness
           to every acrylic splash
spattering the London grey,
                the unrelenting trumpet deriding
the drum-beat fable
          of a tribal content
on this day of carnival,
          the dissonance
half-assuaged in the sway of flesh
              holding back time
dancing off history.

Prose Poem

for John and Lisbeth

If objects are of two kinds – those
    That we contemplate and, the remainder, use,
I am unsure whether its poetry or prose
    First drew us to this jar. A century
Ago, an apothecary must have been its owner,
    Thankful that it was airtight. And in spite of time
It remains so still. Its cylinder of glass,
    Perfectly seamless, has the finality and satisfaction
Of the achieved act of an artisan. Indeed,

The stopper of ground glass, that refused
To be freed from the containing neck,
    Was almost too well-made. What had to be done
If we were to undo it, was to pass
    A silk cord round the collar of glass
And rub it warm – but this friction
    Must be swift enough not to conduct its heat
Inside – the best protection against which
    (Only a third hand can ensure this feat)
Is a cube of ice on top of the stopper.
    Whether it was the rubbing only, or the warm
Grasp that must secure the bottle's body,
    The stopper, once more refusing at first,
Suddenly parted – breathed-out
    (So to speak) by the warmed expanding glass.
Remaining ice-cool itself, when
    Lightly oiled, it was now ready again
For use – but not before we had tried
    Jar against ear to find the sound inside it.
It gave off – no seashell murmur –
    A low, crystalline roar that wholly
Possessed one's cavities, a note (as it were)
    Of unfathomable distance – not emptiness,
For this dialogue between air and ear
    Was so full of electric imponderables, it could compare
Only with that molecular stealth when the jar
    Had breathed. There is one sole lack
Now that jar and stopper are in right relation –
    An identifiable aroma: what we must do
Is to fill it with coffee, for use, scent and contemplation.

Departure

You were to leave and being all but gone,
    Turned on yourselves, to see that stream
Which bestows a flowing benediction and a name
    On our house of stone. Late, you had time
For a glance, no more, to renew your sense
    Of how the brook – in spate now –

Entered the garden, pooling, then pushing
    Over a fall, to sidle a lock or two
Before it was through the confine. Today,
    The trail of your jet is scoring the zenith
Somewhere, and I, by the brink once more,
    Can tell you now what I had to say
But didn't then: it is here
    That I like best, where the waters disappear
Under the bridge-arch, shelving through coolness,
    Thought, halted at an image of perfection
Between gloom and gold, in momentary
    Stay, place of perpetual threshold,
Before all flashes out again and on
    Tasseling and torn, reflecting nothing but sun.

Images of Perfection

        ...What do we see
In the perfect thing? Is our seeing
Merely a measuring, a satisfaction
    To be compared? How do we know at sight
And for what they are, these rarenesses
    That are right? In yesterday's sky
Every variety of cloud accompanied earth,
    Mares' tails riding past mountainous anvils,
While their shadows expunged our own:
    It was pure display – all a sky could put on
In a single day, and yet remain sky.
    I mean, you felt in the air the sway
Of sudden apocalypse, complete revelation:
    But what it came to was a lingering
At the edge of time, a perfect neighbouring,
    Until the twilight brought it consummation,
Seeping in violet through the entire scene.
    Where was the meaning, then? Did Eden
Greet us ungated? Or was that marrying
    Purely imaginary and, if it were,
What do we see in the perfect thing?

Rhymes

Perfect is the word I can never hear
   Without a sensation as of seeing –
As though a place should grow perfectly clear,
   The light on the look of it agreeing
To show – not all there is to be seen,
   But all you would wish to know
At a given time. Word and world rhyme
   As the penstrokes might if you drew
The spaciousness reaching down through a valley view,
   Gathering the lines into its distances
As if they were streams, as if they were eye-beams:
   Perfect, then, the eye's command in its riding,
Perfect the coping hand, the hillslopes
   Drawing it into such sight the sight would miss,
Guiding the glance the way perfection is.

The Perfection

There is that moment when,
the sun almost gone,
red gains and deepens on
neighbouring cloud:

and the shadows that seam
and grain it take
to themselves
indelible black:

yet we never know it
until it has been
for the moment it is
and the next has brought in

a lost pitch,
a lack-lustre pause
in the going glow
where the perfection was.

The Hesitation

Spring lingers-out its arrival in these woods:
   A generation of flowers has been and gone
Before one tree has put on half its leaves:
   A butterfly wavers into flight yet scarcely wakes:
Chill currents of the air it tries to ride
   Cannot fulfill the promises of the sun
To favoured coverts sheltered beneath a hillside:
   Is it may blossom smokes on the thicket crest,
Or the pallor of hoar-frost whitening its last?

The Faring

That day, the house was so much a ship
   Clasped by the wind, the whole sky
Piling its cloud-wrack past,
   To be sure you were on dry land
You must go out and stand in that stream
   Of air: the entire world out there
Was travelling too: in each gap the tides
   Of space felt for the earth's ship sides:
Over fields, new-turned, the cry
   And scattered constellations of the gulls
Were messengers from that unending sea, the sky:
   White on brown, a double lambency
Pulsed, played where the birds, intent
   On nothing more than the ploughland's nourishment,
Brought the immeasurable in: wing on wing
   Taking new lustres from the turning year
Above seasonable fields, they tacked and climbed
   With a planet's travelling, rhymed here with elsewhere
In the sea-salt freshnesses of tint and air.

The Metamorphosis

Bluebells come crowding a fellside
  A stream once veined. It rises
Like water again where, bell on bell,
  They flow through its bed, each rope
And rivulet, each tributary thread
  Found-out by flowers. And not the slope
Alone, runs with this imaginary water:
  Marshes and pools of it stay
On the valley-floor, fed (so the eye would say)
  From the same store and streamhead.
Like water, too, this blueness not all blue
  Goes ravelled with groundshades, grass and stem,
As the wind dishevels and strokes it open;
  So that the mind, in salutary confusion,
Surrendering up its powers to the illusion,
  Could, swimming in metamorphoses, believe
Water itself might move like a flowing of flowers.

Below Tintern

The river's mirrorings remake a world
  Green to the cliff-tops, hanging
Wood by wood, towards its counterpart:
  Green gathers there as no green could
That water did not densen. Yet why should mind
  So eagerly swim down and through
Such towering dimness? Because that world seems true?
  And yet it could not, if it were,
Suspend more solid castles in the air.
  Machicolations, look-outs for mind's eye
Feed and free it with mere virtuality
  Where the images elude us. For they are true enough
Set wide with invitation where they lie
  Those liquid thresholds, that inverted sky
Gripped beneath rockseams by the valley verdure,
  Lost to reflection as the car bends by.

Providence

It is May: 'A bad winter,'
    They prophesy, the old women – they
Who remember still – for I cannot –
    Years when the hawthorns were as thick as now:
Spray on spray hangs over
    In heavy flounces, white swags
Weigh down the pliancy of branches,
    Drag at a whole tree until it bends:
I thought it must be these snow-brides, snow-ghosts
    Brought-on their unseasonable dream of frosts:
But old women know the blossoms must give way
    To berry after berry, as profuse as they,
On which, come winter, the birds will feed:
    For what in the world could justify and bring
Inexplicable plenty if not the birds' need? –
    And winter must be harsh for appetite
Such as they have the means now to requite:
    Old women reason providentially
From other seasons, remembering how
    Winter set out to hunt the sparrows down
In years when the hawthorns were as thick as now.

Mushrooms

for Jon and Jill

Eyeing the grass for mushrooms, you will find
A stone or stain, a dandelion puff
Deceive your eyes – their colour is enough
To plump the image out to mushroom size
And lead you through illusion to a rind
That's true – flint, fleck or feather. With no haste
Scent-out the earthy musk, the firm moist white,
And, played-with rather than deluded, waste
None of the sleights of seeing: taste the sight
You gaze unsure of – a resemblance, too,
Is real and all its likes and links stay true

To the weft of seeing. You, to begin with,
May be taken in, taken beyond, that is,
This place of chiaroscuro that seemed clear,
For realer than a myth of clarities
Are the meanings that you read and are not there:
Soon, in the twilight coolness, you will come
To the circle that you seek and, one by one,
Stooping into their fragrance, break and gather,
Your way a winding where the rest lead on
Like stepping stones across a grass of water.

In the Intensity of Final Light

In the intensity of final light
    Deepening, dyeing, moss on the tree-trunks
Glares more green than the foliage they bear:
    Hills, then, have a way of taking fire
To themselves as though they meant to hold
    In a perpetuity of umber, amber, gold
Those forms that, by the unstable light of day,
    Refuse all final outline, drift
From a dew-cold blue into green-shot grey:
    In the intensity of final light
A time of loomings, then a chime of lapses
    Failing from woodslopes, summits, sky,
Leaving, for the moonrise to untarnish,
    Hazed airy fastnesses where the last rays vanish.

The Spring Symphony

This is the Spring Symphony. Schumann
    Wrote it in autumn. Now it is June.
Nothing to deny, nothing to identify
    The season of this music. Autumn in the cellos
Is proverbial, yet these consent
    To be the perfect accompaniment to such a day

As now declares itself: on the flexed grass
New sheen: the breeze races in it
Blent with light as on the face of waters:
The returning theme – new earth, new sky –
Filled the orchestral universe until,
On fire to be fleshed-out, leaf and seed
Became their dream and dazzle in freshness still:
Yet, self-consuming, these
Emanations, energies that press
In light and wind to their completeness,
Seem half irate: invaded by this music
The summer's single theme might be
The mind's own rage against mortality
In wasting, hastening flight towards
The sum of all, the having done.
This summer sound is the Spring Symphony
Written in autumn. Death is its ground,
Life hurrying to death, its urgency,
Its timelessness, its melody and wound.

Nature Poem

This August heat, this momentary breeze,
First filtering through, and then prolonged in it,
Until you feel the two as one, this sound
Of water that is sound of leaves, they all
In stirrings and comminglings so recall
The ways a poem flows, they ask to be
Written into a permanence – not stilled
But given pulse and voice. So many shades,
So many filled recesses, stones unseen
And daylight darknesses beneath the trees,
No single reading renders up complete
Their shifting text – a poem, too, in this,
They bring the mind half way to its defeat,
Eluding and exceeding the place it guesses,
Among these overlappings, half–lights, depths,
The currents of this air, these hiddennesses.

The Whip

We are too much on the outside
in the inside of the ear
to sort clear at first
the unrolling of the thunder: then
deserting the distances, all
that sunken mumbling turns
to a spine of sound, a celestial
whipline, the crack at the end
of each lash implied under the first
spreading salvo the ears
had been merely fumbling with:
one sky-track now
flashes through them as keen
as the lightning dancing to the eye
the shape of the whip that woke
in them its uncoiling soundscape.

To See the Heron

To see the heron rise
detaching blue from the blue
that, smoking, lies along
field-hollows, shadowings
of humidity: to see it
set off that blaze
where ranks of autumn trees
are waiting just for this
raised torch, this touch,
this leisurely sideways
wandering ascension to unite
their various brightnesses, their fire-
music as a voice might
riding sound: risen
it is darkening now
against the sullen sky blue,
so let it go

unaccompanied save by the thought
that this is autumn and the stream
whose course its eye is travelling
the source of fish: to see the heron
hang wondering where
to stoop, to alight and strike.

One Day of Autumn

One day of autumn
sun had uncongealed
the frost that clung
wherever shadows spread
their arctic greys among
October grass: mid–
field an oak still
held its foliage intact
but then began
releasing leaf by leaf
full half,
till like a startled
flock they scattered
on the wind: and one
more venturesome than all
the others shone far out
a moment in mid-air,
before it glittered off
and sheered into the dip
a stream ran through
to disappear with it

October

Autumn seems ending: there is lassitude
Wherever ripeness has not filled its brood
Of rinds and rounds: all promises are fleshed
Or now they fail. Far gone, these blackberries –
For each one that you pull, two others fall
Full of themselves, the leaves slick with their ooze:
Awaiting cold, we welcome in the frost
To cleanse these purples, this discandying,
As eagerly as we shall look to spring.

Old Man's Beard

What we failed to see
was twines of the wild clematis
climbing all summer
through each burdened tree:

not till the leaves were gone
did we begin to take
the measure of what strength
had fed from the limestone

that roof of feathered seed
bearding the woods now
in its snowy foliage
yet before fall of snow

and what silent cordage bound
the galaxy together where
December light reflected
from star on hairy star

innumerably united
in a cascade, a cloud, a wing
to hang their canopy above
the roots they were strangling.

...Or Traveller's Joy

I return late
on a wintry road: the beam
has suddenly lit
flowers of frost, or so they seem:

Traveller's Joy! the recognition
flares as soon, almost,
as the headlights quit
those ghosts of petals:

a time returns, when men
fronting the winter starkness
were travellers travailing
against hail, mud, dark:

then, whoever it was,
much road behind him,
coming, perhaps, at dawn
with little to remind him

he was cared for, kinned,
saw from the road
the hedgerow loaded
and thought it rimed:

and so it was: the name
he drew from that sudden brightness
came as if his joy
were nature's, too:

and the sweet illusion
persists with the name
into present night,
under the travelling beam.

In the Balance

The cold came. It has photographed the scene
With so exact a care, that you can look
From field-white and from wood-black to the air
Now that the snow has ceased, and catch no shade
Except these three – the third is the sky's grey:
Will it thicken or thaw, this rawness menacing?
The sky stirs: the sky refuses to say:
But it lets new colour in: its thinning smoke
Opens towards a region beyond snow,
Rifts to a blueness rather than a blue:
Brought to a sway, the whole day hesitates
Through the sky of afternoon, and you beneath,
As if questions of weather were of life and death.

The Death of Will

The end was more of a melting:
as if frost turned heavily to dew
and the flags, dragged down by it,
clung to their poles: marble becoming glue.

Alive, no one had much cared
for Will: Will no sooner gone,
there was a *je ne sais quoi*, a *ton*
'fell from the air':

And how strange that, Will once dead,
Passion must die, too,
although they'd had nothing to do
with each other, so it was said:

It was then everyone stopped looking
for the roots of decay,
for curative spears and chapels perilous
and the etymology of 'heyday':

Parents supine, directionless,
looked to their wilful children now:
was this metempsychosis?
was Will reborn in them somehow?

Someone should record Will's story.
Someone should write a book on *Will and Zen*.
Someone should trace all those who
knew Will, to interview them. Someone

A Night at the Opera

When the old servant reveals she is the mother
   Of the young count whose elder brother
Has betrayed him, the heroine, disguised
   As the Duke's own equerry, sings *Or'*
Che sono, pale from the wound she has received
   In the first act. The entire court
Realize what has in fact occurred and wordlessly
   The waltz song is to be heard now
In the full orchestra. And we, too,
   Recall that meeting of Marietta with the count
Outside the cloister in Toledo. She faints:
   Her doublet being undone, they find
She still has on the hair-shirt
   Worn ever since she was a nun
In Spain. So her secret is plainly out
   And Boccaleone (blind valet
To the Duke) confesses it is he (*Or' son'io*)
   Who overheard the plot to kidnap the dead
Count Bellafonte, to burn by night
   The high camp of the gipsy king
Alfiero, and by this stratagem quite prevent
   The union of both pairs of lovers.
Now the whole cast packs the stage
   Raging in chorus round the quartet – led
By Alfiero (having shed his late disguise)
   And Boccaleone (shock has restored his eyes):

Marietta, at the first note from the count
    (Long thought dead, but finally revealed
As Alfiero), rouses herself, her life
    Hanging by a thread of song, and the Duke,
Descending from his carriage to join in,
    Dispenses pardon, punishment and marriage.
Exeunt to the Grand March, Marietta
    (Though feebly) marching, too, for this
Is the 'Paris' version where we miss
    The ultimate dénouement when at the command
Of the heroine (*Pura non son'*) Bellafonte marries
    The daughter of the gipsy king and

In the Studio

'Recorded ambience' – this
is what they call
silences put back
between the sounds:
leaves might fall
on to the roof-glass to compound
an instant ambience
from the drift of sibilants:
but winter boughs
cannot enter – they
distort like weed
under the glass water:
this (sifted) silence
now recording (one
minute only of it)
comprises what
you did not hear before
you began to listen –
the sighs that
in a giant building
rise up trapped between
its sound-proofed surfaces
murmuring, replying

to themselves, gathering
power like static
from the atmosphere: you do
hear this ambience?
it rings true: for silence
is an imagined thing.

Misprint

for L.S. Dembo

'Meeting' was what
I had intended:
'melting' ended
an argument that
should have led
out (as it were)
into a clearing, an
amphitheatre
civic or sylvan
where what could not be
encompassed stood
firmly encompassing
column on column, tree on tree
in their clear ring:
there I had hoped to come
into my true
if transitory kingdom:
instead, one
single letter has un-
made, punned
meaning away into
a statuary circle
becoming snow
and down I dissolve with it
statue on statue
gobbet on slithering gobbet

Maintenant

for Samuel Menashe

Hand
holding on to this
instant metamorphosis,
the syllables maintain
against the lapse
of time that they remain
here, where all else escapes

Sky Writing

A plane goes by,
and the sky takes hold
on the frail, high chalk-line
of its vapour-trail, picks
it apart, combs out
and spreads the filaments
down either side
the spine of a giant plume
which rides written on air now:
that flocculent, unwieldy sceptre
begins its sway with
an essential uncertainty, a
veiled threat tottering it
slowly to ruin, and the sky
grasping its tatters
teases them thin,
letting in blue until,
all flaxen cobblings, lit
transparencies, they
give up their ghosts
to air, lost in their opposite.

Into Distance

Swift cloud
across still cloud
drifting east
so that the still
seems also on the move
the other way: a vast
opposition throughout the sky
and, as one stands
watching the separating
gauzes, greys, the eyes
wince dizzily away from them:
feeling for roots anew
one senses the strength
in planted legs, the pull
at neck, tilted
upwards to a blue that
ridding itself of all
its drift keeps now
only those few, still
island clouds to occupy
its oceanic spread
where a single, glinting plane
bound on and over
is spinning into distance and ahead
of its own sound

Embassy

A breeze keeps fleshing the flag:
    I watch it droop, then reassemble
On air an emblem I do not know:
    Nor does that woman know the part
She plays in this rhymescheme that no art
    Has prompted: for the breeze begins
Feeling along the dyed silk of her hair,
    Unfurling its viking platinum to the same

Rhythm with which the flag bursts into flame:
  Steam seeps from a manhole in the asphalt:
And that, too, leans to the common current,
  Goes upward taking shape from the unseen
In this unpremeditable action where
  A wind is having its way with all swayable things,
Combing through flag and steam, streaming-out hair.

The Race

These waters run secretively until
  Rushing the race where a mill stood once
The weight comes drumming down,
  Crushing-out whiteness as they fall
And fill with a rocking yeast this pool
  They clamour across: clamour and clamber
Blindly till again they find their leat
  And level, narrow-out into
A now-smooth riverlane and pouring on
  Go gathering up the silence where they run.

In Arden

This is the forest of Arden...

Arden is not Eden, but Eden's rhyme:
  Time spent in Arden is time at risk
And place, also: for Arden lies under threat:
  Ownership will get what it can for Arden's trees:
No acreage of green-belt complacencies
  Can keep Macadam out: Eden lies guarded:
Pardonable Adam, denied its gate,
  Walks the grass in a less-than-Eden light
And whiteness that shines from a stone burns with his fate:
  Sun is tautening the field's edge shadowline

Along the wood beyond: but the contraries
  Of this place are contrarily unclear:
A haze beats back the summer sheen
  Into a chiaroscuro of the heat:
The down on the seeded grass that beards
  Each rise where it meets with sky,
Ripples a gentle fume: a fine
  Incense, smelling of hay smokes by:
Adam in Arden tastes its replenishings:
  Through its dense heats the depths of Arden's springs
Convey echoic waters – voices
  Of the place that rises through this place
Overflowing, as it brims its surfaces
  In runes and hidden rhymes, in chords and keys
Where Adam, Eden, Arden run together
  And time itself must beat to the cadence of this river.

The Roe Deer

We must anticipate the dawn one day,
Crossing the long field silently to see
The roe deer feed. Should there be snow this year
Taking their tracks, searching their colours out,
The dusk may help us to forestall their doubt
And drink the quiet of their secrecy
Before, the first light lengthening, they are gone.
One day we must anticipate the dawn.

The Shaft

for Guy Davenport

The shaft seemed like a place of sacrifice:
  You climbed where spoil heaps from the hill
Spilled out into a wood, the slate
  Tinkling underfoot like shards, and then

316   NEW COLLECTED POEMS

You bent to enter: a passageway:
  Cervix of stone: the tick of waterdrops,
A clear clepsydra: and squeezing through
  Emerged into cathedral space, held-up
By a single rocksheaf, a gerbe
  Buttressing-back the roof. The shaft
Opened beneath it, all its levels
  Lost in a hundred feet of water.
Those miners – dust, beards, mattocks –
  They photographed seventy years ago,
Might well have gone to ground here, pharaohs
  Awaiting excavation, their drowned equipment
Laid-out beside them. All you could see
  Was rock reflections tunneling the floor
That water covered, a vertical unfathomed,
  A vertigo that dropped through centuries
To the first who broke into these fells:
  The shaft was not a place to stare into
Or not for long: the adit you entered by
  Filtered a leaf-light, a phosphorescence,
Doubled by water to a tremulous fire
  And signalling you back to the moist door
Into whose darkness you had turned aside
  Out of the sun of an unfinished summer.

De Sole

after Ficino

for Homero Aridjis

If once a year
the house of the dead
stood open
and those dwelling
under its roof
were shown the world's
great wonders, all
would marvel beyond every other thing at
the sun

Macduff

This wet sack, wavering slackness
    They drew out silent through the long
Blood-edged incision, this black
    Unbreathing thing they must first
Hoist from a beam by its heels and swing
    To see whether it could yet expel
Death through each slimy nostril,
    This despaired-of, half-born mishap
Shuddered into a live calf, knew
    At a glance mother, udder and what it must do
Next and did it, mouthing for milk.
    The cow, too, her womb stitched back inside,
Her hide laced up, leans down untaught
    To lick clean her untimely firstborn:
'Pity it's a male.' She looms there innocent
    That words have meanings, but long ago
This blunt lapsarian instinct, poetry,
    Found life's sharpest, readiest
Rhyme, unhesitating – it was knife –
    By some farm-yard gate, perhaps,
That led back from nature into history.

Tree

I took a tree for a guide – I mean
    Gazing sideways, I had chosen idly
Over walls, fields and other trees,
    This single elm, or it had chosen me:
At all events, it so held my mind,
    I did not stop to admire as otherwise I should
The charlock all in yellow fire against
    A sky of thunder-grey: I walked on,
Taking my bearings from that trunk
    And, as I moved, the tree moved too
Alongside, or it seemed to do. Seemed?
    Incontrovertibly the intervening hedgerows occupied

Their proper place, a mid-ground
    In a bounded scene, myopically vague
At each extremity. But the elm
    Paced as if parallel for half a mile
Before I could outstrip it and consign
    The sight into the distances. A trick
Of the eye no doubt, but one not easily
    Put out of mind: that branch-crowned tower,
That stalking memorial of Dunsinane
    Reared alien there, but it was I
Was the stranger on that silent field,
    Gazing unguarded, guideless at a frontier
I could never cross nor whose image raze.

The Gap

It could be that you are driving by.
    You do not need the whole of an eye
To command the thing: the edge
    Of a merely desultory look
Will take it in – it is a gap
    (No more) where you'd expect to see
A field-gate, and there well may be
    But it is flung wide, and the land so lies
All you see is space – that, and the wall
    That climbs up to the spot two ways
To embrace absence, frame skies:
    Why does one welcome the gateless gap?
As an image to be filled with the meaning
    It doesn't yet have? As a confine gone?
A saving grace in so much certainty of stone?
    Reason can follow reason, one by one.
But the moment itself, abrupt
    With the pure surprise of seeing,
Will outlast all after-knowledge and its map –
    Even, and perhaps most then, should the unseen
Gate swing-to across that gap.

The Scream

Night. A dream so drowned my mind,
  Slowly it rose towards that sound,
Hearing no scream in it, but a high
  Thin note, such as wasp or fly
Whines-out when spider comes dancing down
  To inspect its net. Curtains –
I dragged them back – muffled the cry:
  It rang in the room, but I could find
No web, wasp, fly. Blackly
  Beyond the pane, the same sound
Met the ear and, whichever way
  You pried for its source, seemed to be everywhere.
Torch, stair, door: the black
  Was wavering in the first suffusion
Of the small hours' light. But nothing
  Came clearly out of that obscure
Past-midnight, unshaped world, except
  The shrill of this savaging. I struck uphill
And, caught in the torchbeam, saw
  A lustre of eye, a dazzle on tooth
And stripe: badger above its prey
  Glared worrying at that strident thing
It could neither kill nor silence. It swung
  Round to confront the light and me,
Sinewed, it seemed, for the attack, until
  I flung at it, stoned it back
And away from whatever it was that still
  Screamed on, hidden in greyness. A dream
Had delivered me to this, and a dream
  Once more seemed to possess one's mind,
For light could not find an embodiment for that scream,
  Though it found the very spot and tussock
That relentlessly breathed and heaved it forth.
  Was it a sound half-underground? Would badger
Bury its prey? Thoughts like these
  No thoughts at all, crowded together
To appall the mind with dream uncertainties.
  I flashed at the spot. It took reason
To unknot the ravel that hindered thought,

And reason could distinguish what was there,
But could no more bear the cry
　　Than the untaught ear. It was the tussock lived
And turned, now, at the touch of sight
　　– You could eye the lice among its spines –
To a hedgehog. Terrible in the denial
　　Of all comfort, it howled on here
For the lease that was granted it, the life
　　That was safe, and which it could not feel
Was its own yet. It howled down death
　　So that death might meet with its equal
Ten times the size of the despised life
　　It had hunted for. In this comedy
Under the high night, this refusal
　　To die with a taciturn, final dignity
A wolf's death, the scream
　　In its nest of fleas took on the sky.

Translating the Birds

The buzzard's two-note cry falls plaintively,
　　And, like a seabird's, hesitates between
A mewing, a regret, a plangent plea,
　　Or so we must translate it who have never
Hung with the buzzard or above the sea.

It veers a haughty circle with sun-caught breast:
　　The small birds are all consternation now,
And do not linger to admire the sight,
　　The flash of empery that solar fire
Lends to the predatory ease of flight.

The small birds have all taken to the trees,
　　Their eyes alert, their garrulousness gone:
Beauty does not stir them, realists to a man,
　　They know what awe's exacted by a king,
They know that now is not the time to sing.

They'll find their way back into song once more
    Who've only sung in metaphor and we
Will credit them with arias, minstrelsy,
    And, eager always for the intelligible,
Instruct those throats what meaning they must tell.

But supply pulsing, wings against the air,
    With yelp that bids the silence of small birds,
Now it is the buzzard owns the sky
    Thrusting itself beyond the clasp of words,
Word to dance with, dally and outfly.

The Scar

That night, the great tree split
    Where it forked, and a full half lay
At morning, prone by the other
    To await decay. The scar
Of cleavage gleams along the trunk
    With such a tall and final whiteness,
It is the living tree seems dead
    That rears from its own done life
Preparing to put on leaf. Buds
    Bead and soon the leaves will cover
That sapless-seeming wintershape all over.
    A debris clings there and claws
At the tree-foot, spills out
    Up half a hill in bone-white antlerings:
Over it all, the scar glints down,
    And a spring light pulsating ashen,
You would swear that through the shuddered trunk
    Still tremors the memory of its separation.

At Dawn

in memoriam F.M.D.

The blue took you, a wing of ash:
   Returning from the summit where
We had released you into the sky
   And air of earliest day, we saw
Deer at gaze, deer drinking
   Before the blaze of desert sun
Dispersed them: that liquid look
   So held us, it was less a thing
Consolatory than a fact of morning,
   Its freshness returning us to time,
Its farness acknowledging the claim
   Of such distance as we shall only know
On a wing of ash, absorbed against the blue.

THE FLOOD

1981

Snow Signs

They say it is waiting for more, the snow
   Shrunk up to the shadow-line of walls
In an arctic smouldering, an unclean salt,
   And will not go until the frost returns
Sharpening the stars, and the fresh snow falls
   Piling its drifts in scallops, furls. I say
Snow has left its own white geometry
   To measure out for the eye the way
The land may lie where a too cursory reading
   Discovers only dip and incline leading
To incline, dip, and misses the fortuitous
   Full variety a hillside spreads for us:
It is written here in sign and exclamation,
   Touched-in contour and chalk-followed fold,
Lines and circles finding their completion
   In figures less certain, figures that yet take hold
On features that would stay hidden but for them:
   Walking, we waken these at every turn,
Waken ourselves, so that our walking seems
   To rouse some massive sleeper out of winter dreams
Whose stretching startles the whole land into life,
   As if it were us the cold, keen signs were seeking
To pleasure and remeasure, repossess
   With a sense in the gathered coldness of heat and height.
Well, if it's for more the snow is waiting
   To claim back into disguisal overnight,
As though it were promising a protection
   From all it has transfigured, scored and bared,
Now we shall know the force of what resurrection
   Outwaits the simplification of the snow.

Their Voices Rang

Their voices rang
through the winter trees:
they were speaking and yet it seemed they sang,
the trunks a hall of victory.

And what is that and where?
Though we come to it rarely,
the sense of all that we might be
conjures the place from air.

Is it the mind, then?
It is the mind received,
assumed into a season
forestial in the absence of all leaves.

Their voices rang
through the winter trees and time
catching the cadence of that song
forgot itself in them.

The Double Rainbow

to Ulalume Gonzalez de Leon

When I opened your book
a rainbow shaft
looked into it
through the winter window:

a January light
searching the pane
paused there refracted
from white onto white:

so words become
brides of the weather
of the day in the room
and the day outside:

in the light of the mind
the meanings loom
to dance in their own
glimmering spectrum

For Miriam

I

I climbed to your high village through the snow,
   Stepping and slipping over lost terrain:
Wind having stripped a dead field of its white
   Had piled the height beyond: I saw no way
But hung there wrapped in breath, my body beating:
   Edging the drift, trying it for depth,
Touch taught the body how to go
   Through straitest places. Nothing too steep
Or narrow now, once mind and muscle
   Learned to dance their balancings, combined
Against the misdirections of the snow.
   And soon the ground I gained delivered me
Before your smokeless house, and still
   I failed to read that sign. Through cutting air
Two hawks patrolled the reaches of the day,
   Black silhouettes against the sheen
That blinded me. How should I know
   The cold which tempered that blue steel
Claimed you already, for you were old.

II

Mindful of your death, I hear the leap
   At life in the *resurrexit* of Bruckner's mass:
For, there, your hope towers whole:
   Within a body one cannot see, it climbs
That spaceless space, the ear's
   Chief mystery and mind's, that probes to know
What sense might feel, could it outgo
   Its own destruction, spiralling tireless
Like these sounds. To walk would be enough
   And top that rise behind your house
Where the land lies sheer to Wales,
   And Severn's crescent empties and refills
Flashing its sign inland, its pulse
   Of light that shimmers off the Atlantic:
For too long, age had kept you from that sight
   And now it beats within my eye, its pressure

A reply to the vein's own music
   Here, where with flight-lines interlinking
That sink only to twine and hover the higher,
   A circling of hawks recalls to us our chains
And snow remaining hardens above your grave.

III

You wanted a witness that the body
   Time now taught you to distrust
Had once been good. 'My face,' you said –
   And the Shulamite stirred in decembering flesh
As embers fitfully relit – 'My face
   Was never beautiful, but my hair
(It reached then to my knees) was beautiful.'
   We met for conversation, not conversion,
For you were that creature Johnson bridled at –
   A woman preacher. With age, your heresies
Had so multiplied that even I
   A pagan, pleaded for poetry forgone:
You thought the telling-over of God's names
   Three-fold banality, for what you sought
Was single, not (and the flame was in your cheek)
   'A nursery rhyme, a jingle for theologians.'
And the incarnation? That, too, required
   All of the rhetoric that I could bring
To its defence. The frozen ground
   Opened to receive you a slot in snow,
Re-froze, and months unborn now wait
   To take you into the earthdark disincarnate.

IV

A false spring. By noon the frost
   Whitens the shadows only and the stones
Where they lie away from light. The fields
   Give back an odour out of earth
Smoking up through the haysmells where the hay
   – I thought it was sunlight in its scattered brightness –
Brings last year's sun to cattle wintering:
   The dark will powder them with white, and day
Discover the steaming herd, as beam

On beam, and bird by bird, it thaws
Towards another noon. *Et resurrexit:*
   All will resurrect once more,
But whether you will rise again – unless
   To enter the earthflesh and its fullness
Is to rise in the unending metamorphosis
   Through soil and stem… This valediction is a requiem.
What was the promise to Abraham and his seed?
   That they should feed an everlasting life
in earthdark and in sunlight on the leaf
   Beyond the need of hope or help. But we
Would hunger in hope at the shimmer of a straw,
   Although it burned, a mere memory of fire,
Although the beauty of earth were all there were.

V

In summer's heat, under a great tree
   I hear the hawks cry down.
The beauty of earth, the memory of your fire
   Tell of a year gone by and more
Bringing the leaves to light: they spread
   Between these words and the birds that hang
Unseen in predatory flight. Again,
   Your high house is in living hands
And what we were saying there is what was said.
   My body measures the ground beneath me
Warm in this beech-foot shade, my verse
   Pacing out the path I shall not follow
To where you spoke once with a wounded
   And wondering contempt against your flock,
Your mind crowded with eagerness and anger.
   The hawks come circling unappeasably. Their clangour
Seems like the energy of loss. It is hunger.
   It pierces and pieces together, a single note,
The territories they come floating over now:
   The escarpment, the foreshore and the sea;
The year that has been, the year to be;
   Leaf on leaf, a century's increment
That has quickened and weathered, withered on the tree
   Down into this brown circle where the shadows thicken.

The Recompense

The night of the comet,
Sunset gone, and shadow drawing down
Into itself landscape, horizon, sky,
We climbed the darkness. Touch
Was all we had to see by, as we felt
For a path among the crowding trees:
Somehow, we threaded them, came through
At last to the vantage we had aimed for:
It was viewless: a sole star,
The cold space round which seemed
The arena a comet might be found
Sparkling and speeding through, if only
One waited long enough. We waited.
No comet came, and no flame thawed
The freezing reaches of our glance: loneliness
Quelled all we saw – the wide
Empire of that nightworld held
To the sway of centuries, sidereal law,
And the silent darkness hiding every star
Save one: had we misheard the date?
A comet, predicted, might be late
By days perhaps? Chilled, but unwillingly
We took the tree-way down; and ran
Once feet, freed from obstruction,
Could feel out the smoothest path for us
From wood to warmth. Now that we faced away
From the spaces we had scanned for light,
A growing glow rose up to us,
Brought the horizon back once more
Night had expunged: it travelled contrary
To any comet, this climbing brightness:
We wound the sight towards us as we went,
The immense circle of the risen moon
Travelling to meet us: trees
Wrote themselves out on sea and continent,
A cursive script where every loop and knot
Glimmered in hieroglyph, clear black:
We – recompense for a comet lost –
Could read ourselves into those lines

Pulsating on the eye and to the veins,
Thrust and countercharge to our own racing down,
Lunar flights of the rooted horizon.

Poem

It falls onto my page like rain
the morning here
and the ink-marks run
to a smoke and stain, a vine-cord, hair:

this script that untangles itself
out of wind, briars, stars unseen,
keeps telling me what I mean
is theirs, not mine:

I try to become all ear
to contain their story:
it goes on arriving from everywhere:
it overflows me

and then:
a bird's veering
into sudden sun
finds me for a pen

a feather on grass,
a blade tempered newly
and oiled to a gloss
dewless among dew:

save for a single
quicksilver drop –
one from a constellation
pearling its tip

In April

I thought that the north
wind was treating the wood
as a thunder-sheet it was
thunder itself had
merged with the roar
of the air in a vast
voice a judgement chord
and the winter that would not go
was blocking spring
through the upper sky piling
ledges of cold onto
ridges of ripening warmth
quaking across the entire
expanse and pushing sun
back into a livid
pre-world light as it
rolled end and beginning
up in a single emphatic
space-travelling verb breath word

The Order of Saying

'As soon as the blackthorn comes in flower
    The wind blows cold,' she says:
I see those bushes tossed and whitening,
    Drawing the light and currents of the air
Into their mass and depth; can only see
    The order of her saying in that flare
That rises like a beacon for the wind
    To flow into, to twist and wear
Garment and incandescence, flag of spring.

The Lesson

The larks, this year,
fly so early and so high,
it means, you tell me, summer
will be dry and hot,
and who am I
to gainsay that prophecy?
For twenty years here have not
taught me to read with accuracy
the signs either of earth or sky:
I still keep the eye of a newcomer,
a townsman's eye:
but there is time yet
to better my instruction
in season and in song:
summer on summer

Hay

The air at evening thickens with a scent
That walls exude and dreams turn lavish on –
Dark incense of a solar sacrament
Where, laid in swathes, the field-silk dulls and dries
To contour out the land's declivities
With parallels of grass, sweet avenues:
Scent hangs perpetual above the changes,
As when the hay is turned and we must lose
This clarity of sweeps and terraces
Until the bales space out the slopes again
Like scattered megaliths. Each year the men
Pile them up close before they build the stack,
Leaving against the sky, as night comes on,
A henge of hay-bales to confuse the track
Of time, and out of which the smoking dews
Draw odours solid as the huge deception.

The Conspiracy

My writing hand moves washed in the same light now
   As the beasts in the field beneath this window:
The hot day hangs in the glitter and the shade:
   Those toys of Arden, seeing and half-seeing,
The rocking of the leaves, the slow berceuse,
   The airs advancing to invade the heat
But warming to a world of ease, all
   Breathe together this conspiracy:
Butterflies tongue the nectaries and summer
   Is hiving time against the centuries.

The Gate

Someone has set up a gate here
   In this unfenced field. Waiting for its fence
It teases the sight. Is it that one feels half-blind,
   The mind demanding an enclosure that the eye
Cannot supply it with? Or is it an X-ray eye
   One has, melting wall to a nothing,
And the grass greening up at one, that returns
   A look with intimations of a place unspaced
And thus not quite there? The mocked mind,
   Busy with surroundings it can neither bound nor unbind,
Cedes to the eye the pleasure of passing
   Where, between the gate's five bars,
Perpetual seawaves play of innumerable grasses.

At the Edge

The offscape, the in-folds, secreted
   Water-holes in the boles of trees,
Abandoned bits, this door of water
   On the wood's floor (knock with the breath

And enter a world reverted, a catacomb
    Of branching ways where the roots splay):
Edges are centres: once you have found
    Their lines of force, the least of gossamers
Leads and frees you, nets you a universe
    Whose iridescent weave shines true
Because you see it, but whose centre is not you:
    Through the wheel of a web today I saw
The wren, that mere mouse of a bird
    Hurry from its hole and back again
With such an energy of glancing lightness
    It made me measure all the force unspied
That stirred inside that bank, still
    As it seemed, beside the flashing watercourse
That came straight on contrary to my direction and
    Out of the dereliction of an edge of woodland.

The Near and the Far

It is autumn and there are no flowers in this desert garden. Open to the breeze and to the light, it gauges near against far and resolves them. For the breeze, that pushes to and fro the shadows of the hanging pods of the catalpa tree, is stirring the dust over hundreds of desert miles, lifting it in a veil before the long mass of the Sandía Mountains and picking to pieces the vapour trails of the jets that scar the high and intense blue. As for the light: it reveals sandy distances, ripening the tints, as shadows lengthen, to dusty reds and deep yellows. Here, in the eyes' immediate reaches, it brings out each facet of bark still armouring the stakes that fence the dry yard. Yet they do not fence it in: the endless streaming of light through the cottonwoods, whose leaves are sapless but dazzling, reaches us from an unseen source, a blinding immensity. The sky is full of cross-roads of jet-trails, downy tracks gigantically decaying. At foot level, ants are busy in their moonworld of dust and craters.

This desert garden lies at the town's edge, open to the breath of a thousand miles. The engine of a passing truck grinds by with the silence of desert spaces first surrounding then absorbing it. A train passes. Its siren seems to sound out the distances it is entering and, as it were, creating. Waves of wind are rolling across the sky. And from the cottonwoods come the rattle of their leaves, crepitations, lulls, whispers, splashings, like a sea breaking against shore and jetty, where no shore or jetty ever was, on this dried-up bed of a vanished ocean.

Rooted in dust, what do they feed on, these great trees, whose abundance of falling leaves attests the fullness of their summer? In this desert garden there is no succulence. The spiny plants catch at one's ankles, one's shoes are perpetually powdered over. Cottonwood leaves leap across the ground in the wind, side by side with the cicadas that land with a metallic crashing sound among the already shed foliage.

Red ants, dwarfed by their own gangling shadows, carry high their polished abdomens, rushing out on some frantic mission through the warm dust and its maze of cat- and dogpaw prints, shoe-shapes, trails where the hose has been dragged across it. The ant nests are composed of a circular wall of dust like a tiny Celtic fortification raised on the desert. Cruzita will not kill the ants because they are part of a divine and unsoundable dispensation. However, she has stood empty jam jars up to their necks in sand, so that the ants can fall into them if that dispensation permits them to. She, the tutelary spirit of this house and garden, has brought into their enclosure the memory of that wisdom which has made life possible across desert and mesa.

She has lit her morning fire. The piñon of which it is built sends out an upland fragrance of pinewoods over the ragged edges of the suburb. The smoke tells the nostrils of the rarer, cooler autumnal air in those fastnesses, recalls to the mind's eye the mesa villages and the sight of trees growing along the mesa top that, seen from afar, look like the stubble of a beard. The light-blue, rising smoke winding above the house, spreading, perfuming the atmosphere, brings to a lingering resolution in its chord of colour, the blue shadows exploring the heights, the dust-haze that the breeze has lifted and a sense of possibility that, investing space, pours into this garden with the light and air.

Albuquerque

Driving once more
on Central – though what
it is central to
now the town has spread

up to the foothills –
I caught one thing
out of the past that
still was there –

the Kimo Kinema
built in my birth year –
tile, fresco and cement-adobe –
style, tribal art-deco:

Corbusier
could scarcely have applauded
architecture so little tectonic
or so tawdry

and yet a
pupil of his
aware that this
is neither Ronchamps nor Sabbioneta

is actually here
restoring that memory
of a gone year:
I am antique already

Jemez

When we were children said
Eva they told us
the trees on the skyline there
– we turned to see

the trees on the skyline there
stand staring down –
were the kachinas and we
believed them but today
if you say to children
the trees on the skyline there
– the skyline trees stand
calling up sap out of rock and sand –
are the kachinas they
reply kachinas?
they're nothing but trees

Cochiti

The cries
of the eagle
dancers at Cochiti
rise to such a
complete complicity
with the way it is
when eagles
speak what they have to say
that the sky
brings down
over thinning snow
unfurling the black
line of wings
slackening then
tautening them back
to take the thrust
of the wind and mount it
to wander away
above the pocked snow-whitenesses
of plain hills mesas
an eagle

Kachinas: tribal spirits

Abiquiu

Rattlesnakes I've had them
in every room of this house
she said: one
lay there suspended
– it might have been in mid-air –
on the down of a piled rug
as if it were swimming:
then one night
I opened the patio
door and the cat
sat there faced
by a snake: neither
moved but the snake kept up
its warning rattle:
day or night
I wouldn't step
right out there
onto the patio
without looking first:
do you know
it's not from that
tight coil
that a rattler strikes:
it's – she twisted her fingers together –
from a tangle
that has no shape
but I tell you
whatever its reputation
a rattlesnake is a gentleman:
before he strikes he
always lets you know

Quarai

Two dogs
wait for the crumbs
from our desert meal:
they are not importunate
but thoughtful in their anticipation:
I recognize their pondering courtesy
in the custodian – they belong to him –
opening his show for us
– artefacts and a plan
of the vanished pueblo –
under a leaking roof
which come spring days
he must he says mend:
La Purisima Concepcion
where the inquisition spied
for witches and blasphemers
cannot account for him:
it died and dwindled
into sky-roofed sandstone here
through pestilence, famine
drought and massacre
unprepared for this
accommodating gentleness
that says: You
hurry on back
whenever you want to

Under the Bridge

Where the ranch-house disappeared its garden
seeded and the narcissi
began through a slow mutation
to breed smaller and smaller stars
unimpaired in scent: beside these
the horns of the cala lilies
each scroll protruding an insistent

yellow pistil seem from their scale
and succulent whiteness to belong
to an earlier world:
if there were men in it the trellises
that brace these stanchions
would fit the scale
of their husbandry and
if they made music it would
shudder and rebound
like that which travels down
the metal to the base
of this giant instrument
bedded among teazle, fennel, grass
in a returning wilderness
under the bridge

San Francisco

Cronkhite Beach

They look surreal
you said: you meant
the figures along the cliff
above us that the evening light
was thrusting forward in silhouette as if
the sheer stance of curiosity
– they were all stillness facing out to sea –
had magnified them: wave
after wave was entering
from the horizon: moving mountains
which as they sailed-in threw
the surf backwards from their peaks
each like a separate volcano:
and the diminishing force unspent
you could measure by the pitch
of the offshore buoy
belling the shallows as the sea
tugged past it to become

white on the darkening beach
a frayed rope of foam: and there
were the peaceful Brobdignagians still
stationed out massively along that hill:
tall as the objects of their contemplation
they looked surreal: so real

Poolville, NY

Brekekekex?
The frogs of upstate speak
with a mellifluousness as ungreek
as their names – 'spring peepers':
neither hoarse nor flatulent
like the ones elsewhere, this
breed were never peasantry
like those in Ovid's metamorphosis,
but nature's aristocracy –
'We are all princes here':
and thus will never ask
for a log for king
and end up with a stork:
they must sing four nights and then
they've safely brought the springtime in
past tardy drifts and up the trees
to a music that outdates
Ovid and Aristophanes.

Parsnips

for Ted Chamberlin

A mixed crop. I dig a clump:
Crotches seamed with soil,
Soil clinging to every hair,
To excrescences and mandrake mandibles.

Poor bare forked earth-stained animals,
One comes up whole and white,
A vegetable Adam. I take the lot
And wash them at the stream.
Rubbing, rinsing, I let fall
Inevitably this image of perfection,
Then rush for a garden rake
To fish it back again and run
Trying to out-race the current's
Rain-fed effervescence:
Fit image of the poet, he
In the waterproof, with the iron comb who goes
Hunting a prey that's halfway to the sea.

Programme Note

Reading this, you are waiting for the curtain
    To go up on a glade, vistaed valley
Or colonnade of lath. Yet you are not here
    To view a painting – the painted thing
Like the written word, is there for the hearing –
    To which end the tympanist stretches his ear
To interrogate a drumskin, hangs over
    Undistracted by bell note or forest murmur
In horn and harp. Cellist pursues
    An intent colloquy with his instrument,
Urging nerve and string up to that perfection
    He may falter at. For, the aria done,
It is he alone who must comment on
    The meaning of it, and bars he is testing now
Climb then on a faultless bow
    Out of the darkened pit as the hero pauses
To resume in song. He, too, unseen
    Sweating into his paint, runs through
(In mind, that is) the perils of a part
    That from start to finish (and this is true
Of every bubble and iota of these tuning notes)
    Raises its fragment to build a single arc

Of sound. Yet suppose that you are here
    Tonight to share in the good conscience
Of all masquerade, that this wood or square
    Waits to be filled with cadences in which
Taking leave of the humid north,
    The steam of Niebelheim, you find yourself
With time and light enough to feel
    The filigree of things, and dare to be
Superficial out of profundity: suppose
    This composer of yours had for a beginning
The merest ravelled thread of a plot –
    The sort of thing a poet would wince at
Or a bad poet write –, it flows
    Out from his musician's mind, not
As the Gesammtkunstwerk (let that dragon sleep),
    The streambed's deep self-inspection,
But the purest water where reflection
    Pooling for a moment, is drawn along
Over drops and through recesses, to emerge
    Strong though contained, a river of song:
You feel that you could leap it from side to side:
    Its dazzle and deftness so take hold,
They convince the mind that it might be
    Equally agile, equally free:
Are you the swift that dips here, or the course
    Of sheer, unimpeded water, the counterforce
Of rock and stone? But images lie –
    Not the Ding-an-sich, but the light to see it by:
And no river could convey the artifice
    And no landscape either, the pulse of this:
A closer thing, it is as if thought might sing
    To the bloodbeat, set it racing;
As if… and yet a man shaped this
    Who read the fragile story from the start
As that which his art would make of it –
    So that, in the mind, the body dances
To this flowing fiction – soprano, tenor
    And basso buffo – believing all,
Limpid, unpsychological: and finding true
    A wholly imaginary passion – passion spaced until
Meted and metred-out, its urgency
    Does not merely billow up to fill

The gallery with sound. But I have said
    Enough and the musicians mouthed and bowed
Their accordant A; the light glows out
    On the gildings, and here is the man in black
And white who holds this world of yellow and green and red
    Together, and his first chord cuts the last whisper back.

On a Pig's Head

Once it had gorged itself
to a pitch of succulence, they slew it:
it was the stare in the eyes
the butcher hated, and so removed
with a quick knife,
transforming the thing
to a still life, hacked
and halved, cross-cutting it
into angles with ears.
It bled no more,
though the black pearls
still lurked on its rawness.
The ears were streaked with wax,
the teeth stained near the roots
like an inveterate smoker's.
It was the nose looked freshest –
a rubbery, soft pink.
With a spill of paper, I cleaned
the orifice of each ear,
and played water into the nostrils.
The brain was a mere thimble of brain,
and the tongue, smaller than a sheep's
sliced neatly. The severed ears
seemed delicate on their plate
with their maze of veins.
When we submerged it in brine
to change it to brawn and galantine,
it wouldn't fit the bowls:
evidently, it had been conceived

for a more capacious age.
Divided, it remained massive
leaving no room for reflection
save that peppercorns, cloves
of garlic, bay-leaves and wine
would be necessary for its transformation.
When set to boil, it required
a rock, a great
red one
from Macuilxochitl
to keep it down.

Ritornello

Wrong has a twisty look like wrung misprinted
Consider! and you con the stars for meaning
Sublime comes climbing from beneath the threshold
Experience? you win it out of peril
The pirate's cognate. Where did the words arise?
Human they sublimed out of the humus
Surprised by stars into consideration
You are wrung right and put into the peril
Of feelings not yet charted lost for words
Abstraction means something pulled away from
Humus means earth place purchase and return

San Fruttuoso

the divers

Seasalt has rusted the ironwork trellis
at the one café. Today
the bathers are all sunbathers
and their bodies, side by side,
hide the minute beach:

the sea is rough and the sun's
rays pierce merely fitfully
an ill-lit sky. Unvisited,
the sellers of lace and postcards
have nothing to do, and the Dorias
in their cool tombs under the cloisters
sleep out history unfleshed.
Oggi pesce spada
says the café sign, but we
shall eat no swordfish today:
we leave by the ferry
from which the divers are arriving.
We wait under an orange tree
that produces flowers but no oranges.
They litter the rocks with their gear
and begin to assume
alternative bodies, slipping
into black rubbery skins with *Caution*
written across them.
They are of both sexes. They strap on
waist weights, frog feet,
cylinders of oxygen,
they lean their heaviness which water will lighten
back against rock, resting there
like burdened seals.
They test their cylinders
and the oxygen hisses at them.
They carry knives
and are well equipped to encounter
whatever it is draws them downwards
in their sleek black flesh.
The postcards show Christ –
Cristo del mare –
sunk and standing on his pedestal
with two divers circling
as airy as under-water birds
in baroque, ecstatic devotion
round the bad statue.
Will they find calm down there
we wonder, stepping heavily
over the ship-side gap,
feeling already the unbalancing

pull of the water under us.
We pass the granular rocks
faulted with long scars.
The sea is bristling up to them.
The straightness of the horizon
as we heave towards it
only disguises the intervening
sea-roll and sea-chop, the clutching glitter.
I rather like
the buck of the boat. What I dislike
with the sea tilting at us
is the thought of losing one's brains
as one slides sideways
to be flung at the bulwarks
as if weightless, the 'as if'
dissolving on impact
into bone and blood.
The maternal hand tightens
on the push-chair
that motion is dragging at:
her strapped-in child is asleep.
Perhaps those invisible divers –
luckier than we are –
all weight gone
levitate now
around the statue,
their corps de ballet
like Correggio's sky-
swimming angels, a swarm
of batrachian legs:
they are buoyed up by adoration,
the water merely an accidental aid
to such staggeringly
slow-motion pirouettes
forgetful of body, of gravity.
The sea-lurch snatches
and spins the wheels of his chair
and the child travels the sudden gradient
caught at by other hands,
reversed in mid-flight
and returned across the up-
hill deck to his mother:

a visitor,
she has the placid
and faintly bovine look
of a Northern madonna
and is scarcely surprised; he, too,
stays perfectly collected
aware now of what it was he had forgotten
while sleeping – the stuff
he was chewing from a packet,
which he continues to do.
He has come back to his body once more.
How well he inhabits his flesh:
lordly in unconcern,
he is as well accoutred as those divers.
He rides out the storm chewing and watching,
trustfully unaware
we could well go down
– though we do not, for already
the town is hanging above
us and the calm quay water.
From the roofs up there
perhaps one could see the divers
emerging, immersing,
whatever it is they are at
as we glide forward
up to the solid, deck to dock,
with salted lips.
That same sea
which wrecked Shelley
goes on rocking behind
and within us, hiding
its Christ, its swordfish,
as the coast reveals
a man-made welcome to us
of wall, street, room,
body's own measure and harbour,
shadow of lintel, portal
asking it in.

Above Carrara

for Paolo and Francesco

Climbing to Colonnata past ravines
    Squared by the quarryman, geometric gulfs
Stepping the steep, the wire and gear
    Men use to pare a mountain: climbing
With the eye the absences where green should be,
    The annihilating scree, the dirty snow
Of marble, at last we gained a level
    In the barren flat of a piazza, leaned
And drank from the fountain there a jet
    As cold as tunnelled rock. The place –
Plane above plane and block on block –
    Invited us to climb once more
And, cooled now, so we did
    Deep between church- and house-wall,
Up by a shadowed stairway to emerge
    Where the village ended. As we looked back then
The whole place seemed a quarry for living in,
    And between the acts of quarrying and building
To set a frontier, a nominal petty thing,
    While, far below, water that cooled our thirst
Dyed to a meal now, a sawdust flow,
    Poured down to slake those blades
Slicing inching the luminous mass away
    Above Carrara...

Fireflies

The signal light of the firefly in the rose:
Silent explosions, low suffusions, fire
Of the flesh-tones where the phosphorus touches
On petal and on fold: that close world lies
Pulsing within its halo, glows or goes:
But the air above teems with the circulation
Of tiny stars on darkness, cosmos grows

Out of their circlings that never quite declare
The shapes they seem to pin-point, swarming there
Like stitches of light that fleck and thread a sea,
Yet unlike, too, in that the dark is spaces,
Its surfaces all surfaces seen through,
Discovered depths, filled by a flowering,
And though the rose lie lost now to the eye,
You could suppose the whole of darkness a forming rose.

Thunder in Tuscany

Down the façade lean statues listening:
Ship of the lightning-gust, ship of the night,
The long nave draws them into dark, they glisten
White in the rainflash, to shudder-out blackbright:
The threads of lightning net and resinew form
In sudden fragments – line of a mouth, a hem –
Taut with the intent a body shapes through them
Standing on sheerness outlistening the storm.

Giovanni Diodati

from the Italian of Attilio Bertolucci

My astonishment almost felicity
when I discovered Giovanni Diodati –
whose Protestant Bible which I was reading
somehow entered my household – Catholic

if only tepidly with tenacious roots –
was the friend of that John Milton
whom today – late – I count among those poets
I care for most. The shimmer

of his lines – when he depicts Eve naked
garnishing a cloth
with reddening fruits in the autumn
of Paradise its noonday corruscating

at the guest's approach – Raphael
the Archangel – for a meal for three –
isn't it just the same as in the prose
of the exile from Lucca beside Lake Leman

where the Bride of the Canticle appears
suggesting to the intent adolescent –
fiery twilight coming slantwise in
to the resonant granary of wheat
hiding-place in air vertigo

of a plain black with swallows – the saliva of kisses?

On a May Night

after the prose of Leopardi's journal

Gloom in my mind: I leaned
at a window that showed the square:
two youths on the grass-grown
steps before the abandoned church
fooling and falling around
sat there beneath the lamp: appears
the first firefly of that year:
and one of them's up already
to set on it: I ask
within myself mercy for the poor thing
urging it *Go go* but he
battered and beat it low then turned
back to his friend: meantime
the coachman's daughter
comes up to a window
to wash a platter

and turning tells those within
Tonight it will rain
no matter what:
it's as black as a hat out there
and then the light at that
window vanishes: the firefly
in the interval has come round:
I wanted to – but the youth
found it was moving turned
swore and another
blow laid out the creature
and with his foot he made
a shining streak of it
across the dust until
he'd rubbed it out: arrived
a third youth from an alley-way
fronting the church
who was kicking the stones and
muttering: the killer laughingly
leaps at him bringing him down
then lifts him bodily:
as the game goes on
the din dies but the loud
laughs come volleying through:
I heard the soft voice
of a woman I neither knew nor saw:
Let's go Natalino: it's late:
For godsake he replies
it isn't daybreak yet: I heard
a child that must surely be
hers and carried by her
babblingly rehearse
in a milky voice
inarticulate laughing sounds
just now and then out of its own
quite separate universe: the fun
flares up again: *Is there any*
wine to spare at Girolamo's?
they ask of someone passing:
wine there was none:
the woman began laughing softly –
trying out

proverbs that might fit
the situation: and yet that wine
was not for her and that
money would be
coin purloined from the family
by her husband:
and every so often she
repeated with a laughing patience
her hint *Let's go*
in vain: at last a cry
Oh look comes from them
it's raining: it was a light spring rain:
and all withdrew bound homewards:
you could hear the sound
of doors of bolts
and this scene
which pleased drawing me from myself
appeased me.

Instead of an Essay

for Donald Davie

Teacher and friend, what you restored to me
Was love of learning; and without that gift
A cynic's bargain could have shaped my life
To end where it began, in detestation
Of the place and man that had mistaught me.
You were the first to hear my poetry,
Written above a bay in Italy:
Lawrence and Shelley found a refuge once
On that same coast – exiles who had in common
Love for an island slow to learn of it
Or to return that love. And so had we
And do – you from the far shore of the sea
And I beside a stream in Gloucestershire
That feeds it. Meeting maybe once a year
We take the talk up where we left it last,

Forgetful of which fashions, tide on tide –
The Buddha, shamanism, suicide –
Have come and passed.
Brother in a mystery you trace
To God, I to an awareness of delight
I cannot name, I send these lines to you
In token of the prose I did not write.

Barque Nornen

Barque Nornen broken by the storms
vanishes in shifting sand:
tides reshape the terrain and
unsilt the ship's clear hollow form:

Berrow church-tower looks out on
the ruin of that other nave
its sides like an inverted wave
and rib on rib as hard as stone.

The Littleton Whale

in memory of Charles Olson

What you wrote to know
was whether
the old ship canal
still paralleled the river
south
of Gloucester (England)…

What I never told
in my reply
was of the morning
on that same stretch

(it was a cold
January day in '85)
when Isobel Durnell
saw the whale...

She was up at dawn
to get her man off on time
to the brickyard and
humping up over the banks
beyond Bunny Row
a slate-grey hill showed
that the night before
had not been there...

They both ran outside
and down to the shore:
the wind was blowing
as it always blows
so hard that the tide
comes creeping up under it
often unheard...

The great grey-blue thing
had an eye
that watched wearily
their miniature motions as they
debated its fate
for the tide
was already feeling beneath it
floating it away...

It was Moses White
master mariner
owner of the sloop *Matilda*
who said the thing to do
was to get chains and a traction engine
– they got two from Olveston –
and drag it ashore:
the thing was a gift:
before long it would be
drifting off to another part of the coast
and lost to them
if they didn't move now...

And so the whale –
flukes, flesh, tail
trembling no longer
with a failing life –
was chained and hauled
installed above the tideline...

And the crowds came
to where it lay
upside down
displaying a
belly evenly-wrinkled
its eye lost to view
mouth skewed and opening into
an interior of tongue and giant sieves
that had once
filtered that diet of shrimp
its deep-sea sonar
had hunted out for it
by listening to submarine echoes
too slight
for electronic selection...

And Hector Knapp
wrote in his diary:
Thear was a Whal
cum ashore at Littleton Pill
and bid thear a fortnight
He was sixty eaight feet long
His mouth was twelve feet
The Queen claim it at last
and sould it for forty pound
Thear supposed to be
forty thousen pepeal to se it
from all parts of the cuntry...

The Methodist preacher
said that George Sindry
who was a very religious man
told himself when that whale came in
he'd heard so many arguments
about the tale of Jonah not being true

that he went to Littleton to
'satisfy people'. He was a tall man
a six footer
'but I got into that whale's mouth' he said
'and I stood in it
upright…'

The carcass
had overstayed its welcome
so they sent up a sizeable boat
to tow it to Bristol
and put it on show there
before they cut the thing down stinking
to be sold
and spread for manure…

You can still see the sign
to Whale Wharf as they renamed it
and Wintle's Brickworks became
the Whale Brick
Tile and Pottery Works…

Walking daily onto
the now-gone premises
through the 'pasture land
with valuable deposits of clay thereunder'
when the machine- and drying sheds
the five kilns, the stores and stables
stood permanent in that place
of their disappearance
Enoch Durnell still
relished his part in all that history begun
when Bella shook
and woke him with a tale that the tide
had washed up a whole house
with blue slates on it into Littleton Pill
and that house was a whale…

The Flood

It was the night of the flood first took away
   My trust in stone. Perfectly reconciled it lay
Together with water – and does so still –
   In the hill-top conduits that feed into
Cisterns of stone, cisterns echoing
   With a married murmur, as either finds
Its own true note in such a unison.
   It rained for thirty days. Down chimneys
And through doors, the house filled up
   With the roar of waters. The trees were bare,
With nothing to keep in the threat
   And music of that climbing, chiming din
Now rivers ran where the streams once were.
   Daily, we heard the distance lessening
Between house and water-course. But floods
   Occur only along the further plains and we
Had weathered the like of this before
   – The like, but not the equal, as we saw,
Watching it lap the enclosure wall,
   Then topping it, begin to pile across
And drop with a splash like clapping hands
   And spread. It took in the garden
Bed by bed, finding a level to its liking.
   The house-wall, fronting it, was blind
And therefore safe: it was the doors
   On the other side unnerved my mind
– They and the deepening night. I dragged
   Sacks, full of a mush of soil
Dug in the rain, and bagged each threshold.
   Spade in hand, why should I not make
Channels to guide the water back
   Into the river, before my barricade
Proved how weak it was? So I began
   Feeling my way into the moonless rain,
Hacking a direction. It was then as though
   A series of sluices had been freed to overflow
All the land beneath them: it was the dark I dug
   Not soil. The sludge melted away from one
And would not take the form of a trench.

This work led nowhere, with no bed
To the flood, no end to its sources and resources
    To grow and to go wherever it would
Taking one with it. It was the sound
    Struck more terror than the groundlessness I trod,
The filth fleeing my spade – though that, too,
    Carried its image inward of the dissolution
Such sound orchestrates – a day
    Without reprieve, a swealing away
Past shape and self. I went inside.
    Our ark of stone seemed warm within
And welcoming, yet echoed like a cave
    To the risen river whose tide already
Pressed close against the further side
    Of the unwindowed wall. There was work to do
Here better than digging mud – snatching
    And carrying such objects as the flood
Might seep into, putting a stair
    Between the world of books and water.
The mind, once it has learned to fear
    Each midnight eventuality,
Can scarcely seize on what is already there:
    It was the feet first knew
The element weariness had wandered through
    Eyeless and unreasoning. Awakened eyes
Told that the soil-sacked door
    Still held, but saw then, without looking,
Water had tried stone and found it wanting:
    Wall fountained a hundred jets:
Floor lay awash, an invitation
    To water to follow it deriding door
On door until it occupied the entire house.
    We bailed through an open window, brushing
And bucketing with a mindless fervour
    As though four hands could somehow find
Strength to keep pace, then oversway
    The easy redundance of a mill-race. I say
That night diminished my trust in stone –
    As porous as a sponge, where once I'd seen
The image of a constancy, a ground for the play
    And fluency of light. That night diminished
Yet did not quite betray my trust.

For the walls held. As we tried to sleep,
And sometimes did, we knew that the flood
   Rivered ten feet beneath us. And so we hung
Between a dream of fear and the very thing.
   Water-lights coursed the brain and sound
Turned it to the tympanum of an ear. When I rose
   The rain had ceased. Full morning
Floated and raced with water through the house,
   Dancing in whorls on every ceiling
As I advanced. Sheer foolishness
   It seemed to pause and praise the shimmer
And yet I did and called you down
   To share this vertigo of sunbeams everywhere,
As if no surface were safe from swaying
   And the very stone were as malleable as clay.
Primeval light undated the day
   Back into origin, washed past stain
And staleness, to a beginning glimmer
   That stilled one's beating ear to sound
Until the flood-water seemed to stream
   With no more burden than the gleam itself.
Light stilled the mind, then showed it what to do
   Where the work of an hour or two could
Hack a bank-side down, let through
   The stream and thus stem half the force
That carried its weight and water out of course.
   Strength spent, we returned. By night
The house was safe once more, but cold within.
   The voice of waters burrowed one's dream
Of ending in a wreck of walls:
   We were still here, with too much to begin
That work might make half-good.
   We waited upon the weather's mercies
And the December stars frosted above the flood.

Severnside

We looked for the tide, for the full river
    Riding up the expanse to the further cliff:
But its bed lay bare – sand
    That a brisk wind planed towards us.
Perpetual shore it seemed, stretch
    And invitation to all we could see and more:
Hard to think of it as the thoroughfare for shoals:
    At the edge, a cracked mosaic of mud,
Even shards of it dried in the sunny wind –
    A wind whose tidal sound mocked tidelessness,
Mocked, too, the grounded barges grass now occupied
    Dense on the silt-filled holds. Sad,
But a glance told you that land had won,
    That we would see no swell today
Impelled off the Atlantic, shelving
    And channelling riverwards in the hour we had.
And so we turned, and the wind possessed our ears,
    Mocked on, and our talk turned, too,
Mind running on future things,
    Null to all save the blind pull of muscle
In a relegated present. When we paused
    The sands were covered and the channels full:
We had attended the wind too long, robbed
    Of distinction between the thing it was
And what it imitated. But the rise we stood on,
    Reawakening our eyes, gave back suddenly
More than the good that we had forfeited:
    Ahead – below – we could sight now
The present, as it were, spread to futurity
    And up the river's bend and bed
The waters travelling, a prow of light
    Pushing the foam before them in its onrush
Over the waiting sand. And we who seemed
    To be surfing forward on that white
Knew that we only dreamed of standing still
    Here where a tide whose coming we had missed
Rode massed before us in the filled divide.

In the Estuary

This is the way it goes, the tide:
  A stain through the water, a first sign
That the light is getting down to layers
  Under the flowing surface: then
Colour brought up out of the depths
  To reveal suddenly a ledge of sand
Turning into a glassy island that reflects
  The further shore. The swimming birds
Are left standing, and walk to and fro
  Across their mirrored landscape, each
Accompanying its own white reflection.
  The channel shallowing, two rocks
(To begin with) and then a chain
  Of rock on rock, space out an archipelago
Of islets before the continental mass
  Which was the sand. You could not map
This making and unmaking. Every gap
  Is losing water. Every rise
Tussocked with grass that greens and fattens
  In the tidal flow, shows now
As an inland island above mudflats
  Through which the veins of channels hurry-off
What's left of the river from its bed.
  Reading the weather from such skies –
Cloud promise and cloud countermand –
  As cover this searun neither sea nor land,
You end in contraries like the bight itself,
  Where an unseen moon is pulling the place from focus
And the lunar ripple runs woven with the sunlight.

The Epilogue

It was a dream delivered the epilogue:
　　I saw the world end: I saw
Myself and you, tenacious and exposed,
　　Smallest insects on the largest leaf:
A high trail coasted a ravine
　　Eyes could not penetrate because a wood
Hung down its slope: a fugue of water
　　Startled the ear and air with distances
Around and under us, as if a flood
　　Came pouring in from every quarter:
Our trail and height failed suddenly,
　　Fell sheer away into a visibility
More terrible than what the trees might hide:
　　Fed by a fall, wide, rising
Was it a sea? claimed all the plain
　　And climbed towards us, smooth
And ungainsayable. We turned and knew now
　　That no law steadied a sliding world,
For what we saw was an advancing wave
　　Cresting along the height. An elate
Despair held us together silent there
　　Waiting for that wall to fall and bury
Us and the love that taught us to forget
　　To fear it. I woke then to this room
Where first I heard the sounds that dogged that dream,
　　Caught back from epilogue to epilogue.

NOTES FROM NEW YORK
AND OTHER POEMS
1984

The Landing

Banking to land, as readily as birds
   We tilt down in. Manhattan
Beyond us is holding on to the rays
   Of a tawny strip of sun of late afternoon,
That catches on spire and pinnacle and then
   Shafts out the island entire:
A blaze across the Verrazano Narrows
   Conflagrates suburbs, the Jersey woods, and we
In our circling the only ones to see
   The total and spreading scope of it,
The Passaic flowing with fire towards the sun
   Just when one thinks the sundown over and done:
Scaling the silhouettes above the water
   In the eyries of the town the lights come on.

Above Manhattan

Up in the air
among the Iroquois: no:
they are not born
with a head for heights:
their girder-going
is a learned, at last
a learnèd thing
as sure as instinct:
beneath them
they can see in print
the newssheet of the city
with a single rent where three
columns, clipped out of it,
show the Park was planted:
webbed and cradled
by the catenary

The Iroquois are employed in high construction work.

distances of bridge on bridge
the place is as real
as something imaginary:
but from where they are
one must read with care:
for to put
one foot wrong
is to drop
more than a glance
and though
this closeness and that distance
make dancing difficult a dance
it is that the mind is led
above Manhattan

At the Trade Center

Paused at the more than Brocken summit,
    Hand outstretched to touch and cover
The falling height beneath, I watch
    Between the nakedness of fingers – light
On each knuckled promontory of flesh
    And shadows tremulous between the gaps –
The map of land, the map of air:
    Rivers both sides of this island
Tug the gaze askance from the grid of streets
    To the sea- and bird-ways, the expanse
That drinks the reverberation of these energies.
    What can a hand bring back into a view
No rule of thumb made possible? It spans
    The given rigours and the generous remissions
Of ocean, of the ferryings to-and-fro
    Between the harbour and the islands. As you climb
The more you see of waters and of marsh
    Where, angle-poised, the heron
Stands within earshot of this city
    Back to the horizon, studying its pool.
The horizon is where we are:

The Bridge is small from this new vantage,
The view in space become a view in time:
    Climbing we see an older city's fall –
The waterfront is down: the clerks are hived
    Window on window where the town began
And spread. I spread my fingers
    And the traffic runs between. The elevator grounds
Us back to streets where in the cracks
    Between immeasurable buildings beggars
From their domains of dust and paper-bags
    Hold out one hand deep in the traffic sounds.

On Madison

We walk up Madison. It is the end
    Of a winter afternoon: the mist
Has cancelled out the reaches of the vista
    As the rivers (we cannot see them)
Assert their right to the island they enclose.
    So much of the surrounding, the unseen –
The homelessness beyond the mist-lopped towers –
    Presses upon us at this hour:
We savour the wine of the solitude of spaces
    In the same instant as we choose the street
That seems like a home returned to, grown
    Suddenly festive as we enter it
With the odour of chestnuts on the corner braziers.

What Virginia Said

I like the crush here
we were standing by the stair
trying to insert our bodies
into the upward flow
out of the Liberty Express

I mean after that college town
I like that too
we were getting through now
But in a crowd you
always feel safe
especially at night
which is not true there
and were climbing
and were half-way
to the upper floors –
the drunks, the sleepy
addicts, the derelicts
outside the doors
of Penn Station
and she swimming on
ahead with a retrospective
laugh and one
hand waving *See you see you*
feeling safe

Crossing Brooklyn Ferry

To cross a ferry that is no longer there,
The eye must pilot you to the farther shore:
It travels the distance instantaneously
And time also: the stakes that you can see
Raggedly jettying into nothingness
Are the ghosts of Whitman's ferry: their images
Crowding the enfilade of steel and stone
Have the whole East River to reflect upon
And the tall solidities it liquefies.

In Verdi Square

A minute garden
you must not enter
and whose birds (there are notices)
you are forbidden to feed:

Verdi surveys it all
stone cloak on arm
as if about to quit
his pigeoned pedestal:

without coming down
he knows perfectly well
what operas are in town:
at the Ansonia Hotel

across the square
they have been practising
ever since Destinn and Caruso
and do so now:

ranged at his feet, stands
Falstaff beside
Aida and Leonora
watching a cast of thousands

pour into 72nd Street
as various as if the entire
complement of the complete
thirty operas were on stage at once

and crowding towards the green
silhouette of the Park
Olmsted had foreseen
against their advent, in '56 –

the year *La Traviata*
arrived amid the brownstones and
vista on unfinished vista mapped
a half-empty island.

Lament for Doormen

In vestibules the doormen
shift red-headed pins
on the chart of rooms: these
figures in their landscape
are the ins and outs
abstracted to essences:
Mrs Schwamm has left for Tuba City
Mr Guglielmi has gone to his office
the Du Plessis are still sleeping
but the poetry of names
strikes little fire in the vestibule.
Spring: and the yellow cabs
go by each
with its Sun King
inside and leave
doormen to their dark.
The lull of afternoon
brings them out under awnings
to rake the roadway for event
yawning into the quiet.
And you forget them
street on street of them
until a furtive movement
in the penumbra and
crossing the floor
of the confine ahead of you
one of them has the elevator
door open for your ascent.

All Afternoon

All afternoon the shadows have been building
A city of their own within the streets,
Carefully correcting the perspectives
With dark diagonals, and paring back
Sidewalks into catwalks, strips of bright

Companionways, as if it were a ship
This counter-city. But the leaning, black
Enjambements like ladders for assault
Scale the façades and tie them to the earth,
Confounding fire-escapes already meshed
In slatted ambiguities. You touch
The sliding shapes to find which place is which
And grime a finger with the ash of time
That blows through both, the shadow in the shade
And in the light, that scours each thoroughfare
To pit the walls, rise out of yard and stairwell
And tarnish the Chrysler's Aztec pinnacle.

The Arrival

Sailing at dawn into the Narrows,
The cliffs once passed and, level with the spokes
Of light that radiate the streets, we veer
At the edge of this great solar wheel
Whose axis buildings hide: here beam on beam
Haloes the place once more with all the hopes
Time has renewed in it, lost and recovered
Where expectation shrinks to a single yard,
A concourse of four gables round one tree
Straggling towards its sun, as ships unseen
Sway into their anchorage raying back
The incandescence of beginning day.

Byzantium

In that 'corridor of garments'
Orchard Street the cry
of a gigantic nightingale or thrush
drops out of the sky.

Out of the sky?
Out of the water-whistle
of a vendor of plastic birds –
and with so much of pastoral artifice

that the Sundaying Jews
in their cars on
Delancey Street might be
tourists along the Vale of Hebron.

I choose a bird all green
for the colour that is not here
to testify to the birds of Gloucestershire
where it is I have been.

For, once I have gone
back, such a roulade
and cataract will never come
to the ear as on the sidewalks of Byzantium.

The Mirror in the Roadway

Nature here
is the multiplicity of luck
such as furniture in the street
when a mirror
hoisting the image
of a stopped truck
on to a dresser top
encloses its mass
inside the glass square
bevelled at the lip:
the mirror
has sheered away
all save the rear view –
a cargo of chairs, a piece
to be inserted elsewhere
in the jigsaw as the truck

moves off and leaves this high
fragment of deserted space
for the street to stare into
and where the chairs had hung
people it with the reflections of passers-by

Hero Sandwiches

for John

Tuesday and Friday
are Hero Sandwich Day:
all other days
heroes must feed
on sandwiches
for the common breed of men
not these
vast open
energy-providers
Siegfried in search
of dragons or a bride
might breakfast on:
why do you never make
Hero Sandwiches
other days of the week
I ask the man
at the Delicatessen:
all he replies is
Tuesdays and Fridays
are our Blue Collar Special:
one cannot confute
logic so ready and so resolute:
clearly one must wait until
Blue Collar Special Day
arrives decreeing that
heroes in overalls
heroes in canticles
Whitman might have written

shall be provendered and provided
for their journey down-
stream with the Rhine
of the lunch-hour traffic
flowing through mid-town

Of the Winter Ball Game

for Bill Humphrey

Of the winter ball game –
not that I could follow the play
and given my inability to
recognize until half-way through
which team was 'ours' – I must
say there was enough incidental
counterpoint to set
those Mars-men with padded shoulders
and the haphazard choreography of majorette
on majorette into one
seamless music as when
a black dog
suddenly crossed the pitch
as confused as I was
and out of a desolate sky
the sun appeared (just once)
and lit up the whole stadium
and everyone cheered to see
nature participate: the band
was playing I got plenty of nothin' and
nothin's plenty for me: something
kept dragging the day from focus –
the cold mostly that reddened
the bare legs of the cheer-leaders
and made them dance the harder:
it drove us home before
we knew what the score was: the event
our desertion excepted was a draw
between persistence and winter

Ice Cream at Blauenberg

The restaurant serving Char-Broiled Meats
Flavored in Flame, Welsh Farms Ice Cream,
Stands at a four-way stop between
A Dutch cemetery and an antique shop.

Eating our purchase in the scent of char-broil,
We read the tombs – all one great clan
It seems, named Voorhees or Van Zandt,
Inherit beneath these cenotaphs Jersey soil.

A dog without dignity or character
Of any sort comes cringing up to beg us
For whatever surplus overflows our cones,
All eyes, all blandishments, all shamelessness.

The sun is autumnal, but it melts our ices,
The stone is durable and free from moss,
Father, Mother, Our Parents, the lettering says:
They are buried without the drama of a cross

Which would seem, perhaps, presumptuous on this hill –
Even the crowning urns suggest they'd be
Useful if only you could reach them down
Out of the blue of this American day.

The urns are immovable whites and greys,
The ices keep running down our fingers,
Our cones are sticky – they were overfilled –
The dog with the sweet tooth sidles still and lingers.

Our aim had been the house named Rockingham
Washington lived in – in my mind's eye
I caught him at supper there, his campaigns done
Pictured him (painted by Leutze) Crossing the Delaware.

However, a wrong road was to bring us out
To the hush of these Dutchmen and this dog:
We give it the butts of our cones and the slush that's left,
Get back inside the car and turn about

Into the current of history going on,
Past the antique shop, then cutting back
Counter to the route the armies followed,
In the Sunday traffic and the shortening sun.

From the Motorway

Gulls flock in to feed from the waste
    They are dumping, truck by truck,
Onto a hump of land three roads
    Have severed from all other:
Once the seeds drift down and net together
    This shifting compost where the gulls
Are scavenging a winter living,
    It will grow into a hill – for hawks
A hunting ground, but never to be named:
    No one will ever go there. How
Shall we have it back, a belonging shape?
    For it will breed no ghosts
But only – under the dip and survey
    Of hawk-wings – the bones of tiny prey,
Its sodium glow on winter evenings
    As inaccessible as Eden…

To Ivor Gurney

Driving north, I catch the hillshapes, Gurney,
    Whose drops and rises – Cotswold and Malvern
In their cantilena above the plains –
    Sustained your melody: your melody sustains
Them, now – Edens that lay
    Either side of this interminable roadway.
You would recognize them still, but the lanes
    Of lights that fill the lowlands, brim
To the Severn and glow into the heights.

You can regain the gate: the angel with the sword
Illuminates the paths to let you see
    That night is never to be restored
To Eden and England spangled in bright chains.

The Question

The curve of lamps that climbs into the dark
    And distances of moorland, leads-on the road
Past where the excavation first laid bare
    Secretive farms: our beams explore them there –
Gaunt hill-top shapes, slab-roofed
    And dour, although their panes give back
The festive scintillation of our lights. Within,
    The televisions fade and waver, their images
Unseamed by the unending cavalcade
    To north and south. When no one came,
Was silence as oppressive as our sounds?
    We could scarcely be welcome here: and yet
May not time have so habituated them
    To all the accumulated shifts and strangenesses
That none can any longer feel what change
    Those resonant rooms have brought into their lives
Eased into sleep now by incessant wheels?

Black Brook

Black Brook is brown. It travels
    With the hillside in it – an upside-down
Horizon above a brackened slope – until
    It drops and then: rags and a rush of foam
Whiten the peat-stained stream
    That keeps changing note and singing
The song of its shingle, its shallowness or its falls.
    I pace a parallel track to that of the water:

It must be the light of a moorland winter
    Let them say that black was fair name
For such a stream, making it mirror
    Solely the granite and the grey
As no doubt it can. But look! Black Brook
    Has its horizon back, and a blue
Inverted sky dyeing it through to a bed
    Of dazzling sand, an ore of gravel
It has washed out beneath rock and rowan
    As it came here homing down
To the valley it brightens belying its name.

Poem for my Father

I bring to countryside my father's sense
Of an exile ended when he fished his way
Along the stained canal and out between
The first farms, the uninterrupted green,
To find once more the Suffolk he had known
Before the Somme. Yet there was not one tree
Unconscious of that name and aftermath
Nor is there now. For everything we see
Teaches the time that we are living in,
Whose piecemeal speech the vocables of Eden
Pace in reminder of the full perfection,
As oaks above these waters keep their gold
Against the autumn long past other trees
Poised between paradise and history.

The Journey

The sun had not gone down. The new moon
    Rose alongside us, set out as we did:
Grateful for this bright companionship
    We watched the blade grow sharp against the night

And disappear each time we dipped:
   A sliver of illumination at the crest
Awaited us, a swift interrogation
   Showed us the shapes we drove towards
And lost them to the intervening folds
   As our way descended. It was now
The travelling crescent suddenly began
   To leap from side to side, surprising us
At every fresh appearance, unpredictably
   Caught among the sticks of some right-hand tree
Or sailing left over roof and ridge
   To mock us. I know the explanation
But explanations are less compelling than
   These various returns and the expectancy that can
Never quite foresee the way
   The looked-for will look back at us
Across the deviousness of distances that keep on
   Lapsing and renewing themselves under a leaping moon.

The Arch

Good at maps and vistas, poor
At the varieties of grass and flower,
A car has at all events this to be said in its favour:
It has an eye for metamorphosis –
As when the windscreen frames the image
Of one of those tree-roofs arching the road
All apparent mass and solidity
Until you swing in under and fragments
(Or so the glance would say) start
Falling away and let the sky show
As you are passing beneath, staring up into
A shattered canopy, a leaf-floor
Swaying apart. The past
Receding into the tunnel mouth
That has instantly re-formed behind you,
Ledge on ledge of green masonry where you have gone
Flows back into place to close
Finally round an immovable keystone.

Hedgerows

for Peter Porter

In Suffolk they are no longer there:
    The post-modern landscape has gone medieval:
The stuff for the staff of life you townsmen
    Still lean on, Peter, flows up to the tarmac
An inland sea. Once they begin to disappear
    You see what an urbanity hedgerows are:
Feeling their way across the featureless land,
    Shutting out swamp and gripping the soil together,
They contain, compel as civilly as stanzas
    In the cultivator's poem of earth and sun
Where harvests fatten to be freighted up for London.

The Shout

Somebody's shout displaces the horizon:
    Distance rushes at foreground things
Like a flare of lengthening light
    And tears at one's steps with the sound of the shout.
It was in play no doubt, but whoever raised it
    Has gone on unaware of the way the air
Roused and rippled outwards to give it space.
    Besides me, the rooks have taken it in,
Rising and wheeling in a blank sky
    On which the early dark is stiffening
Its silhouettes at the reverberations of that cry.

High Summer

Buzzards bring out their young one
    Circling, show it the map of woods,
The fields of prey, drive at it
    Diving it downwards and away, then
Let it rise to take up space
    Under its wings, their incessantly insisting
Note teaching it what kingdom
    It is the prince of, crying it awake to things:
They lead it aloft now feeling
    The currents pull through emptiness – emptiness
That is full of the invitation to height and flight –,
    Through blue where only a combed-out floss
Presaging fair weather faintly clouds
    The zenith they are climbing. Down that height
The currents tremor earthwards, tug
    And turn up the undersides of leaves
Into the light until they give it back
    As if from a turning of those wings
One can no longer see: the two
    High Aztec messengers of the sun
Telling over and over the sources of blood
    Hang dark and far against the upper blue
Pulsating beside their studious progeny.

The Quarry

The gap where the quarry is keeps moving away,
    As each year they cut and fill
The hillside, draw out its veins
    Of stone until the cranes are ready
To lift them in severed lengths
    Leaving the rifts behind – and soon
They, too, disappear. The house
    That clung to the brink is sailing back
On a tide of green. One day it will be
    Out of sight of all this activity and dust,
And the gap itself finally close,

When a field, whose hedge no longer greys
To the tone of the stone-meal, has covered it,
    And other eyes in travelling this way
Will feel the difference and appraise it then.

The Beech

Blizzards have brought down the beech tree
    That, through twenty years, had served
As landmark or as limit to our walk:
    We sat among its roots when buds
Fruitlike in their profusion tipped the twigs –
    A galaxy of black against a sky that soon
Leaf-layers would shut back. The naked tree
    Commanded, manned the space before it
And beyond, dark lightnings of its branches
    Played above the winter desolation:
It seemed their charge had set the grass alight
    As a low sun shot its fire into the valley
Splitting the shadows open. Today that sun
    Shows you the place uncitadelled,
A wrecked town centred by no spire,
    Scattered and splintered wide. At night
As the wind comes feeling for those boughs
    There is nothing now in the dark of an answering strength,
No form to confront and to attest
    The amplitude of dawning spaces as when
The tower rebuilt itself out of the mist each morning.

After the Storm

Waters come welling into this valley
    From a hundred sources. Some
Sealed by the August heat, dry back
    From a dusty bed and only when the leaves
Are down again, rustle and rush

In their teeming gulley after the storm.
Today – just once – the sun looks forth
    To catch the misty emanations of our north
Rising in spirals underneath the hill:
    Here, like a steaming beast, a house
Emerges into its beams, the mist
    Smoking along them into a vapour veil
That trails up into soaked branches
    Sending down shower on shower.
The sky is clear for an hour. Where the sun
    Is going under it seems to impose
That silence against which the streams keep telling
    Over and over in the ebbing light
In their voices of liquid suasion, of travelling thunder
    From what depths they have drunk and from what heights.

Confluence

Where the hillside stream unearths itself
    You can catch nothing but its urgent voice
Laying claim to the air and bearing down
    On all that lies below. Then, finding
A bed to flow into, submitting
    To go the way a valley goes, it silences.
The mind goes with the water feeling free,
    Yields itself to the sea's gravity.
Following downhill I no longer hear
    The querulousness of the emerging spring:
New the sound that fills the mind's ear now,
    Each vein and voice of the watershed
Calling to the estuary as they near,
    Tuning themselves to the slopes and stones
They flow across: the weirs and the thresholds
    Of the bridges cleared, a singleness
Out of all the confluences pours on
    To a music of what shapes, what stays and passes
Between this island and its seas,
    Off sandstone, moorslope, shales and scarp
Creation overleaping its seven days.

In December

The fog, as it enters the lowland, is smoothing away
    All demarcations, transforming into a bay
Of white and level waters the valley mouth:
    The tide keeps running and rising
Until it fills from side to side
    The whole of the space before us and its cold
Is on our faces now. This grey lava,
    Gliding apocalypse undoes the promise
Of the bay it has hardly formed,
    Climbs like water coming to a level
It cannot find until it closes
    The narrowing parallel between the skyline
And itself: a house goes down
    Into an underwater world, a core
Of warmth in the sea that minutes since
    Was merely a shore. But in this play
Of the last or is it the first day
    By midnight the sky is clear: no sign
Of what has passed save in the transformation
    Of mist to the drops that star the grass:
The horizon is keeping its distance and its nearness
    Between the glittering of earth and galaxies,
Worlds within worlds encircling our walls
    From the recesses and recessions of winter skies.

At a Glance

The mountains, from this downward turn in the road,
    Are sometimes there of a morning, sometimes gone:
Today, you could almost rest your hand upon
    Their bulky ripple and feel it
Flow out like paint at a brush-tip,
    Feel also the exact resistance of that flow:
It is an abyss one looks across –
    Whole tracts and counties melted in a glance
That, meeting the sky-line limit,

Turns it into a nearness as if such
Ease of the sight were in possession of the touch.
    And so it is. Light touches the sense awake,
First fiat crossing the aeons to an eye
    That sees it is still good, its touch a healing
Where yesterday revealed at this turn of the hill
    Only a void and formlessness of sky.

The Glacier

            We climbed that day
        Up into a region where the mist
Stagnated over beds of slate – a waste
        Of mountain ground we had approached
Through grass and moss, themselves as grey
        As the accumulating dust (for it was summer)
That soiled the trickling glacier where it lay.
        Over the blackened razors of the slate
Crumbling as they cut, we slithered by
        One eye upon the blades beneath our feet,
One searching the source that fed a slow
        Continuous water out of ice and snow
Into this carious mass. That source
        Contouring round the mountain's form
Coiled along the ledges with a hold
        Slackened by thaw, then frozen firm by cold –
The glacier's edge, eating at the track
        That faltered past it. We trusted that faint line
To take us back and down, and so it did:
        The glacier, overshadowing our minds,
In a sordid glistening outwaited our descent
        To where the final macerations, siftings
Of moraines staining the torrents brown,
        Had turned, at last, to the soil which fructifies
In the plains a wide and level shore.

Night Fishers

After the autumn storms, we chose a night
    To fish the bay. The catch
I scarcely recollect. It was the climb,
    The grasp at slipping rock unnerved
All thought, thrust out of time
    And into now the sharp original fear
That mastered me then. I do not think
    I ever looked so far down into space
As through the clefts we over-leapt:
    Beams of our torches given back
Off walls and water in each rift
    Crossed and recrossed one another, so the mind
Recalling them, still seems to move
    Inside a hollow diamond that the dark
As shadows shift, threatens to unfacet:
    It was no jewel, it was the flesh would shatter.
And yet it did not. Somehow we arrived
    And crouched there in the cool. The night
Save for the whispered water under-cliff,
    The hiss of falling casts, lay round
Thick with silence. It seemed
    A sky spread out beneath us, constellations
Swimming into view wherever fish
    Lit up its dark with phosphor. A thousand
Points of light mapped the expanse
    And depth, and yet the cliff-top height
Hinted no pull of vertigo along
    Its sudden edge: through diaphanous waters
The radium in the flowing pitchblende glowed
    Holding both mind and eye
Encompassed by a stir of scattered lambency:
    And unalarmed, I could forget
As night-bound we fished on unharmed,
    The terrors of the way we'd come, put by
The terrors of return past fault and fall,
    Watching this calm firmament of the sea.

Near Hartland

We came by night,
  Drove the great avenue of beech
– A mile of them – in a dark
  That lopped their summits. Dead they seemed
To the glare that raked the boughless trunks
  Lichened, spare. Daylight restored
Their foliage: each westerly tree
  Taking its inclination from the sea-wind
East, had knit with its neighbour opposite
  A straining arch above the roadway.
We left through the colonnade we came by
  And watched above us the Atlantic breathe and pile
Its airy tonnage down that aisle of branches
  Trying the roof-ties between side and side:
Like travellers in the maelstrom's eye
  We rode closed in a ring of force
That flowed from roots to tree-tip,
  Coiled back to carry and withstand
The long swell out of Labrador
  Pouring across this heaving mile of England.

Morwenna's Cliff

The glance drops here like a hawk falling,
  Grasps, from above, the tide-edge
Gliding in and shaping itself to a profile,
  To a certainty of nose, full lips and chin:
The face comes imaging up from chaos
  Just where the bedrock forces water
To an instant of definition, lost
  Till the next wave meets with white
The same resistance. Hawks hang
  And the fine bones bleach where conies
Lurk in their warrened cliff, where only
  A man could trace out a human face
Printing and reprinting itself as the waters mass.

Near Ceibwr

The castle has gone into the cliff:
    These rocks that recall the origins of earth
Cannot remember it. Only the roots
    Of the bracken suspect the whereabouts
Of unguarded threshold stones. But they
    Are deaf to the searching whisper of the sea
That startles our ears with the very tone
    That flowed up to the sentry looking down.

At the Hill Fort

Walls, from its looted stones, defend
    Hayfields against the Irish Sea: today
More boisterous than belligerent a westerly
    Lifts and then lets fall as if in play
A flock of jackdaws that nest along the outcrop:
    They rise like chaff, hover like thistledown
Between a scooping-up and a droop, a drop.
    Hard to say which is at play with which
As they ride up the air yet again,
    A pattern, at first, of filings uncertainly
Magnetized together; toil and toy
    With the wind and let it tame them,
Flung back at their rock in alternations
    Of secure possession and a daring joy
In their world above walls within earshot of the sea.

The Moment

Watching two surfers walk toward the tide,
Floating their boards beside them as the shore
Drops slowly off, and first the knee, then waist
Goes down into the elemental grasp,

I look to them to choose it, as the one
Wave gathers itself from thousands and comes on:
And they are ready for it facing round
Like birds that turn to levitate in wind:
All is assured now as they slide abreast:
Much as I envy them their bodies' skill
To steady and prolong the wild descent,
I choose that moment when their choice agrees
And, poised, they hesitate as though in air
To a culmination half theirs and half the sea's.

Writing on Sand

Birds' feet and baby feet,
Man Friday prints,
dog-pads
cramponned with claws,
ribbed shoe-soles –
hints there
of a refusal
to bare oneself
to the elemental,
a pacing parallel
to the incoming onrush, a
careful circuiting
of the rock pools:
the desire to stay
dry to be read
in the wet dust.
By what way
did that one
return? – he
of the stark striders,
the two perfect five-toed
concaves aimed
direct at the waves
whose own aim is
to remove

all clues
under the primeval slidings,
to erase them
to a swimming Braille,
an illegible Ogham,
to wash the slate clean.

Van Gogh

I thought, once, that your hillshapes swam and swayed
Only in rhythm with that rising tide
Which mastered and unmade you at the last.
Yet if they did, there's this I judged awry:
It was such health you felt for in those hills
As madness robbed you of: your haste to fill
The no man's land of space between the eye
And what it reached at, was a sanity,
For you abhorred both vacuum and dream:
It was not seeming, but solidities
That took your glance: it was a love of substance
Bound you to Arles. The apocalyptic night
Strained at the mysteries you could not see,
But sight asked to be fed, and chose for food
The daily bread of street, of room and bed.
The nebular revelations of the sky
Hovered and coiled, yet earth held till that day
When hills no longer pressed their bulwarks round
But shattered to echoes as if it were they had ceased.

Legend

The hill-top schloss
with its roots of stone
cellar on cellar
feels through and down

into the soil
the saecular dark
where space turns blind
and time is murk

from root to tower
an ascension seeks
for the lighted room
where someone sleeps

then waking goes
to the source of sun
the slit of a window
that gives out on

Bluebeard's domain
that will never
surrender space
to the torture chamber

to the clink of the treasury
the walled-in garden
the lake of tears
or the armourer's burden

in this kingdom's light
an undertone
shares the phosphorescence
of a pool in limestone

that cupped by the rock
of the underground
spreads opaque and thick
to its glinting bound

and this is well
for the deep and the high
riding horizons
replenish the eye

with all that terrain
it cannot see
on which it must raise
the hive and immensity

of a hill-top schloss
with roots of stone
cellar on cellar
feeling through and down

The Sound of Time

When the clock-tick fades
out of the ear
you can listen to time
in the flow of fire:

and there a cascade
streams up the coals:
loud as Niagara
these climbing falls:

it pours within
forked and fleering
over the thresholds
of a deafened hearing

till the superfluity
of the room's recess
has filled the auricle
with time's abyss

History of a Malady

Plangebant aliae proceris tympana palmis
Catullus

I

'Others beat timbrels with uplifted hands':
  Across the words a ripple drifted
As if the onomatopoeia had excited
  The eyes themselves, fluttering a pulse in them:
But what, as it guttered and renewed,
  The ripple did was wake one to that pitch
The body had reached already: the same
  Thing would have chanced without the words:
For had I been outside, a ripple
  Would have travelled across the distances
Drawing a comet-train behind it,
  The patterned flashes sparking to a pulse
Till the whole field of sight
  Blossomed corollas of disintegrating rays:
We live at the surface of our bodies
  With only the pain to tell the presence there
Of a history whose pressure we ignored:
  To follow out that history from its source
One would have needed to retreat
  Turning away from life and listening
Only to the roar of blood. Today
  As the migraine fluttered and then burst
In a swarm of lights, I knew the body
  Had been travelling in darkness and for days
Towards this consummation in confusion
  When the body's quiet and its spongy dark
Wince with neon gleams, a corridor
  In the invaded citadel where messengers
Arrive with excited and uncertain news,
  With memory, beset by malady, of when
The unquestioning mind inhabited its flesh
  And, moving in time and rhyme with the body's ease,
We beat the timbrels with uplifted hands.

II

Not Dostoevsky's fit and fall: gentler
    Than that: yet with a violence of its own:
A velocity of the cells seizes the mind,
    The speed of this flare on flare
Taking pace from the recurring nightmare
    Of a week of dreams, the hurtling journey
Nowhere that, waking, one forgot. This dislocation
    Between sleep and seeing, what did it mean
Save that the body had made off alone
    Blind to direction – that one lacked by day
A measure of its urgency? Times are
    When a superabundance of the senses
Preludes this familiar disarray. Why
    Does one take no warning then
From their elation? It has occurred before
    And one should know it: unknowing
Breeds another dislocation: this time
    Body has not gone off alone –
One has gone with it exulting in its tone
    And capabilities: the eye exults also
Finding all colours prime – the humid
    Blues, the greys of dust. Forms
Now are all that they should be: a tree
    With its shock of foliage sways
Precise as the flower-head of a rose,
    As undeclared, too – move the glance
An inch and there is so much that is new
    To be read in that unpossessable shape
That could be said now with a perfect adequacy
    Or so it seems. But one took warning
Neither from dreams nor this. One should have entered
    Suspiciously this Eden of the sight
As one attends to the brittle brightness
    That on a day of spring spells rain:
Instead, sharpness turns its edge
    As the first distorting ripple
Starts to spread and first lights
    Flare the eye, powering it to the pulse
Of rapped and clinking tambourines Catullus
    Heard and trapped beating into the words.

III

Beating into the words?
Verse does not know
where malady becomes melody
nor can rehearse:

this is the gift
I did not bargain for:
I would not choose it
nor can I refuse:

circling and dancing
so it seems –
despite the double
violence of dreams and light:

this is the angel with the sword
the shining double-bladed word
a lingering at the gate
of Eden late or early.

Desert Autumn

Dead grasshoppers'
bone-white
hollow shells
swirl with the dry
leaves in the ditch:
a month since
they – flat eye,
thin legs –
shone with a lustre
dust could not
utterly tarnish,
striped black
striped brown
like the beadwork
Indian hands

had patterned:
weeds and sand
are the world
they sprang through
and the leathery stalks,
sunflowers,
poor corn, all
faded yellow
like grasshoppers' wings
still kept then the bright
green of spring as they
first leapt into sunlight.

Mictlantecuhtli

I saw past the door, today,
into the death god's palace:
it was a look, no more,
a place of snow and ice:

as the plane rose up
it was then I saw it
high over the valley and
at the volcano's summit:

a crater of blown snows,
snow caught in each fold
where the lava paths led
from the drifted threshold:

the accurate Aztecs
carved the skull god's device
out of rock crystal
as transparent as ice:

when the conquerors climbed
from the heat to his doorway
his icicle fence they brought
dripping back to the valley:

yet out of the whole vast
melted hierarchy
one sole god has lasted
and that is he

At Trotsky's House

A barrel-organ
assails the suburb
with *Tales from the Vienna Woods*:
in Calle Viena
the garden is guarded
by wall and turret
and an aleatory score
of bullet holes
pocks the interior.
Lev Davidovich slept here
and this is the table
at which he wrote,
the goatee shedding its stray hairs
over the books, the pamphlets.
Words, words… there are cylinders
for the silent dictaphone
and a bottle of Waterman's Ink long dry.
And this is the way he
left things
the day of the assassination?
Más o menos, sí.
He is courteous in three languages
the great man's grandson –
Does he never return to Europe?
De temps en temps.
Under the palm outside
whose rind is peeling,
Europe, or one's own part of it,
seems a distant planet:
and the Moscow
to which the urn of ashes
is awaiting its return
lies kremlined forever in historic snow.

Los Pobrecitos

Caridad para los pobrecitos
she is saying, her hand
outstretched as she
sways towards me:
diminutives sweeten
between beggar and giver
the injustices of living:
hers is a courteous race
accustomed to endure:
gentle and cunning is what they are
these sitters in shadows,
dogging the porches where
they are both prologue and epilogue
to each gold interior.

Teotihuacán

Compra? compra? – the street cry
of the pyramids:
will you buy? will you buy?
It is the gods they are selling.
The girl with her *idolitos*
offers us *La Diosa de la Muerte*
– *Genuine*, she adds.
                          Genuine
comes echoing back
the whole way up this pyramid:
it seems to be inhabited
by a priesthood of vendors,
each one
vouching for the authenticity
of his own particular god.
Now the gods are dead
their houses greet a sky
freed of their weight

and from a summit that is a plain
the flat-topped pyramids repeat
the volcanic horizons of this high terrain
that cone on cone
opens its fastnesses to a mythless sun.

Valle de Oaxaca

for Roberto Donis

Trumpeters
from the Comandancia militar
in the last glare of day
are practising a fanfare:

their notes float off
buffeted by walls
into a shower of chromatics
that falls round the ears of the women at the washing trough:

a celebration? You might call it that
as it harmonizes with the tones
that toll from Santo Domingo –
a celebration, but of what?

Oh it's a desultory enough affair
I know: perhaps little more
than that the sun is shining
and they are standing where they are

under a tree's wide shade
where they've begun
to lay their instruments down
as they cross to the other side

of the barrack yard
to join the talkers there,
easy as unhurried men should be
conversing in the cooling air:

the abandoned instruments
gleam on, a heap
the low sun grazes
tracing the glinting contours of a sleep

tomorrow's dawn will scatter as
trumpeters set lips to brass
to waken also us as they
shake down reveilleing echoes over town and valley

Sight and Flight

Flying south-west – say Washington to Albuquerque – unlulled by
printed matter, stoical at the colour and taste of airline food, one
can see things that were once only imagined.

I like that moment when, as the plane rises, its shadow shrinks
smaller and smaller, until it looks like an accompanying black bird
down there. Then it gets lost in the mathematic of the suburbs, as
the first clouds drift past and one climbs through them to emerge
high above their flocculent plain. They become one's horizon now.
In doing so, they intensify for one that sense of things always
moving, disintegrating, re-forming – the sense of a world which is
never quite *there* because light and time have changed it. The clouds
are no longer exactly a plain: they are cloud herds, cloud flocks,
cloud islands, floes packing a seascape, and below that extend the
map-lines of an undersea land whose houses are dotting a sea-floor.

Over Dakota a cloudy vagueness mists the squared-off fields, as
though a colourless sandstorm were streaming across them. There
is an odd pathos about the patchwork quiet of the mapped-out land,
as if someone had undertaken to measure accurately this immeas-
urable continent, only to be frustrated by the encroaching of
mountain-masses, lakeshapes, rivercourses, saltflats, the humping
and wrinkling of the terrain countering the human insistence on
angles and straight lines.

Sight becomes a double mystery up here, because so frequently
one cannot make out what precisely it is that one is looking at.
Again, this merely intensifies a daily experience. Indeed, before
embarking, and while driving into the airport this morning, I caught

sight of what seemed to be an injured gull struggling on the tarmac: a second later, beaked, bent and rocking in the wind, it resolved itself into a scrap of twisted paper. In flight, we climb above hill-folds, then mountains: a white smoke over their highest point solidifies into snow hooding a peak. It is an exact replica of snow until the eye distinguishes a faint movement in it: cloud! It is the perfect cloak to this mountain inaccessibility, closing off one of the Bible's 'high places', a sierra Sinai, under the purest fleece.

Sight and flight: we are flying and so is the day. Sunset lies along the edge of our cloud horizon, flushing it a deeper royal purple, holding to the west in an orange stripe just ahead of the darkening cloud-edge. Behind us all is black. We fly towards that sunset where it is transfusing cloud-stuff with its orange fire while beneath us the clouds spread opaquely ocean-like, sliding back in even waves into the darkness. A sunset, enduring beyond the normal event, draws us westward, a nocturne in four bands of ascending colours, blue, yellow, orange, black, striped like a Mexican blanket. It glows on out of the dusk, retreating while we manage to keep it just in sight. Like the angles and lines of fields and roads across the landscape, the plane, in its westward trajectory, seems to partake of that same desire to bring the universe under the rule of measure. It will abolish space, or at least shrink it, and it will defy time as it chases the sunset – that sunset which remains so tantalizingly how many hundred miles ahead, securely eluding us.

In this world which is never quite there, because the light has passed on, and 'everything flows', the plane lifts us across a conti-nent and will soon deposit us among the ordinary demands of our lives. The Sinai peak lies behind us now, along with the sky-seas and the cloud-continents. But they persist to haunt the mind, rising sheer beyond us, not mocking us, but reassessing us, not so much scaling us down as redefining for us that universe of which we too are a part.

THE RETURN

1987

In the Borghese Gardens

for Attilio Bertolucci

Edging each other towards consummation
On the public grass and in the public eye,
Under the Borghese pines the lovers
Cannot tell what thunderheads mount the sky,
To mingle with the roar of afternoon
Rumours of the storm that must drench them soon.

Cars intersect the cardinal's great dream,
His parterres redesigned, gardens half-gone,
Yet Pluto's grasp still bruises Proserpine,
Apollo still hunts Daphne's flesh in stone,
Where the Borghese statuary and trees command
The ever-renewing city from their parkland.

The unbridled adolescences of gods
Had all of earth and air to cool their flights
And to rekindle. But where should lovers go
These torrid afternoons, these humid nights
While Daphne twists in leaves, Apollo burns
And Proserpine returns, returns, returns?

Rome is still Rome. Its ruins and its squares
Stand sluiced in wet and all its asphalt gleaming,
The street fronts caged behind the slant of rain-bars
Sun is already melting where they teem:
Spray-haloed traffic taints your laurel leaves,
City of restitutions, city of thieves.

Lovers, this giant hand, half-seen, sustains
By lifting up into its palm and plane
Our littleness: the shining causeway leads
Through arches, bridges, avenues and lanes
Of stone, that brought us first to this green place –
Expelled, we are the heirs of healing artifice.

Deserted now, and all that callow fire
Quenched in the downpour, here the parkland ways
Reach out into the density of dusk,
Between an Eden lost and promised paradise,
That overbrimming scent, rain-sharpened, fills,
Girdled within a rivercourse and seven hills.

Revolution

Piazza di Spagna

REVOLUTION it says
painted in purple along
the baluster of the Spanish
Steps and yes
you can return
by the other side
of this double stair
to where the word
is guiding you
(a little breathless)
down, up and back:
returning
you must run a ring
round the sun-browned
drop-outs
who litter the ascent:
their flights are inward
unlike these,
unfolding by degrees
what was once a hill,
each step a lip
of stone and what they say
to the sauntering eye
as clear as the day
they were made
to measure out and treasure
each rising inch

that nature had mislaid:
for only art
can return us to an Eden where
each plane and part
is bonded, fluid, fitting and
fits like this stair.

Fountain

Art grows from hurt, you say. And I must own
Adam in Eden would have need of none.
Yet why should it not flow as a Roman fountain,
A fortunate fall between the sun and stone?
All a fountain can simulate and spread –
Scattering a music of public places
Through murmurs, mirrors, secrecy and shade –
Makes reparation for what hurt gave rise
To a wish to speak beyond the wound's one mouth,
And draw to singleness the several voices
That double a strength, diversify a truth,
Letting a shawl of water drape, escape
The basin's brim reshaping itself to fill
A whole clear cistern with its circling calm,
And the intricacies of moss and marble
With echoes of distance, aqueduct and hill.

In San Clemente

What deer are these stand drinking at the spring?
Ask of the child the saint is carrying
Across a stream in spate. The steps that flow
Downwards through the sonorous dark beneath,
Should be a water-stair, for where they go,
A child that angels bring forth on the wall
Has lived a whole year on the ocean bed;

Then, down once more, and past the humid cave
Of Mithras' bull and shrine, until they lead
To a wall of tufa and – beyond – the roar
Of subterranean waters pouring by
All of the centuries it takes to climb
From Mithras to the myth-resisting play
Of one clear jet chiming against this bowl
In the fountained courtyard and the open day.

In the Gesù

All frescoed paradise in adoration,
Saints choir the unanimity each atom feels,
And hearts that cannot rise to the occasion
Are spurned to earth beneath angelic heels.
This is the church triumphant, not so loving
As winged with a resistless certainty:
This is the despotism of the dove,
The empire of love without love's comity.

The Wind from Africa

Wind ransacks every colonnade and corner,
Rattles the empty Coke cans, drags shutters back
To show St Peter's palled in dusty fog.
A cat creeps down the Campidoglio steps –
A stage-set fit to play the Roman on –,
Then blows to the stairfoot like a weightless rag
And slides and sidles out across the square.
Sahara's particles have greyed to London
The whole of Rome, complete with a paper snow-storm:
'And if it comes from Africa,' an old man says, 'why is the wind
                                          not warm?'

The Return

to Paolo Bertolani

I *The Road*

I could not draw a map of it, this road,
Nor say with certainty how many times
It doubles on itself before it climbs
Clear of the ascent. And yet I know
Each bend and vista and could not mistake
The recognitions, the recurrences
As they occur, nor where. So my forgetting
Brings back the track of what was always there
As new as a discovery. And now
The summit gives us all that lies below,
Shows us the islands slide into their places
Beyond the shore and, when the lights come on,
How all the other roads declare themselves
Garlanding their gradients to the sea,
How the road that brought us here has dropped away
A half-lost contour on a chart of lights
The waters ripple and spread across the bay.

II *Between Serra and Rocchetta*

Walking to La Rocchetta, thirty years
Would not be long enough to teach the mind
Flower by flower their names and their succession.
Walking to La Rocchetta, leave behind
The road, the fortress and the radar tower
And turn across the hill. From thirty years
I have brought back the image to the place.
The place has changed, the image still remains –
A spot that, niched above a half-seen bay,
Climbs up to catch the glitter from beyond
Of snow and marble off the Apennines.
But where are the walls, the wells, the living lines
That led the water down from plot to plot?
Hedges have reached the summits of the trees

Over the reeds and brambles no one cut.
When first I came, it was a time of storms:
Grey seas, uneasily marbling, scourged the cliff:
The waters had their way with skiff on skiff
And, beached, their sides were riven against stone,
Or, anchored, rode the onrush keels in air
Where hope and livelihood went down as one.
Two things we had in common, you and I
Besides our bitterness at want of use,
And these were poetry and poverty:
This was a place of poverty and splendour:
All unprepared, when clarity returned
I felt the sunlight prise me from myself
And from the youthful sickness I had learned
As shield from disappointments: cure came slow
And came, in part, from what I grew to know
Here on this coast among its reefs and islands.
I looked to them for courage across time,
Their substance shaped itself to mind and hand –
Severe the grace a place and people share
Along this slope where Serra took its stand:
For years I held those shapes in thought alone,
Certain you must have left long since, and then
Returning found that you had never gone.
What is a place? For you a single spot.
Walking to La Rocchetta we can trace
In all that meets the eye and all that does not
Half of its history, the other lies
In the rise, the run, the fall of voices:
Innumerable conversations chafe the air
At thresholds and in alleys, street and square
Of those who climbed this slope to work its soil,
And phrases marrying a tongue and time
Coil through the mind's ear, climbing now with us
Through orchids and the wild asparagus:
For place is always an embodiment
And incarnation beyond argument,
Centre and source where altars, once, would rise
To celebrate those lesser deities
We still believe in – angels beyond fable
Who still might visit the patriarch's tent and table
Both here and now, or rather let us say

They rustle through the pages you and I
Rooted in earth, have dedicated to them.
Under the vines the fireflies are returning:
Pasolini spoke of their extinction.
Our lookout lies above a poisoned sea:
Wrong, he was right, you tell us – I agree,
Of one thing the enigma is quite sure,
We have lived into a time we shall not cure.
But climbing to La Rocchetta, let there be
One sole regret to cross our path today,
That she, who tempered your beginning pen
Will never take this road with us again
Or hear, now, the full gamut of your mastery.

III *Graziella*

We cannot climb these slopes without our dead;
We need no fiction of a hillside ghosted,
A fade-out on the tremor of the sea.
The dead do not return, and nor shall we
To pry and prompt the living or rehearse
The luxuries of self-debating verse.
Their silence we inhabit now they've gone
And like a garment drawn the darkness on
Beyond all hurt. This quiet we must bear:
Put words into their mouths, you fail to hear
What once they said. I can recall the day
She imitated my clipped, foreign way
Of saying *Shakespeare*: English, long unheard,
Came flying back, some unfamiliar bird
Cutting a wing-gust through the weight of air
As she repeated it – *Shakespeare Shakespeare* –
Voice-prints of a season that belongs
To the cicadas and the heat, their song
Shrill, simmering and continuous.
Why does a mere word seem autonomous
We catch back from the grave? The wave it rides
Was spent long-since, dissolved within the tides
Of space and time. And yet the living tone
Shaped to that sound, and mocking at its own,
A voice at play, amused, embodied, clear,

Spryer than any ghost still haunts the ear.
The dog days, the cicada had returned
And through that body more than summer burned
A way and waste into its dark terrain,
Burned back and back till nothing should remain,
Yet could not dry the mind up at its source:
Clear as her voice-print, its unyielded force
Would not be shadowed out of clarity
Until the moment it had ceased to be.
Downhill, between the olives, more than eye
Must tell the foot what path it travels by;
The sea-lights' constellations sway beneath
And we are on the Easter side of death.

IV *The Fireflies*

I have climbed blind the way down through the trees
(How faint the phosphorescence of the stones)
On nights when not a light showed on the bay
And nothing marked the line of sky and sea –
Only the beating of the heart defined
A space of being in the faceless dark,
The foot that found and won the path from blindness,
The hand, outstretched, that touched on branch and bark.
The soundless revolution of the stars
Brings back the fireflies and each constellation,
And we are here half-shielded from that height
Whose star-points feed the white lactation, far
Incandescence where the single star
Is lost to sight. This is a waiting time.
Those thirty, lived-out years were slow to rhyme
With consonances unforeseen, and, gone,
Were brief beneath the seasons and the sun.
We wait now on the absence of our dead,
Sharing the middle world of moving lights
Where fireflies taking torches to the rose
Hover at those clustered, half-lit porches,
Eyelid on closed eyelid in their glow
Flushed into flesh, then darkening as they go.
The adagio of lights is gathering
Across the sway and counter-lines as bay

And sky, contrary in motion, swerve
Against each other's patternings, while these
Tiny, travelling fires gainsay them both,
Trusting to neither empty space nor seas
The burden of their weightless circlings. We,
Knowing no more of death than other men
Who make the last submission and return,
Savour the good wine of a summer's night
Fronting the islands and the harbour bar,
Uncounted in the sum of our unknowings
How sweet the fireflies' span to those who live it,
Equal, in their arrivals and their goings,
With the order and the beauty of star on star.

Tyrrhenian

from the train

Not recognizing the thing it was, I caught
For a moment an elsewhere in the view:
It seemed a luminous steppe, a plain of blue
Had risen up suddenly beneath the sky –
A grass ocean, yet neither grass nor wave
Stirred on this calm that would persuade the eye
It was as deep and changeless as the grave.
This Blue Grass was a country of the mind,
And yet its sheer impossibility
Brought home unmediated sea, a crop
That had sprung up overnight but always been
There rustling and ready to be seen,
Though the eye rode past it at a glance
Filled with the certainty that sea was sea.

Travelling

poem ending with a line of Emerson

The storm, as it closed in, blackening round the train,
    Flushed back the yellows of the passing field
To twilit vanishings, as if the sense
    Faltering, had gone out. Rain
Rushed the sleeping ear into wakefulness;
    At every window it crashed and rang
Like gravel against the glass, like clashed keys flung
    As, all forms gone, we swung through the daylight dark
And on, in a tumultuous privacy of storm.

Palermo

The road to Palermo flows through a tunnel of trees –
    An asphalt waterway, a discovery
The car-lights keep extending
    Ahead of themselves. Fencing back
Mountains, plains and sea, this dense
    Illusion of a forest seems more real
Than the vista replacing it, a perspective
    Down decaying streets that stops
At the water's margin beneath the impartial
    Cranes conferring together above roof-tops.

Catacomb

A Capuchin – long acquaintance with the dead
    Has left him taciturn – stands guard
At gate and stairhead. Silent, he awaits
    The coin we drop into his dish, and then
Withdraws to contemplation – though his eye

Glides with a marvellous economy sideways
Towards the stair, in silent intimation
    You may now descend. We do – and end up
In a corridor with no end in view: dead
    Line the perspective left and right
Costumed for resurrection. The guidebook had not lied
    Or tidied the sight away – and yet
Eight thousand said, unseen, could scarcely mean
    The silence throughout this city of the dead,
Street on street of it calling into question
    That solidity the embalmer would counterfeit.
Mob-cap, cape, lace, stole and cowl,
    Frocked children still at play
In the Elysian fields of yesterday
    Greet each morning with a morning face
Put on a century ago. Why are we here? –
    Following this procession, bier on bier
(The windowed dead, within), and those
    Upright and about to go, but caught
Forever in their parting pose, as though
    They might have died out walking. Some
Face us from the wall, like damaged portraits;
    Some, whose clothing has kept its gloss,
Glow down across the years at us
    Why are you here? And why, indeed,
For the sunlight through a lunette overhead
    Brightens along a sinuous bole of palm:
Leaves catch and flare it into staring green
    Where a twine of tendril sways inside
Between the bars. Light from that sky
    Comes burning off the bay
Vibrant with Africa; in public gardens
    Tenses against the butterflies' descent
The stamens of red hibiscus. Dead
    Dressed for the promenade they did not take,
Are leaning to that light: it is the sun
    Must judge them, for the sin
Of vanity sits lightly on them: it is the desire
    To feel its warmth against the skin
Has set them afoot once more in this parade
    Of epaulette, cockade and crinoline. We are here
Where no northern measure can undo

So single-minded a lure – if once a year
The house of the dead stood open
    And these, dwelling beneath its roof,
Were shown the world's great wonders,
    They would marvel beyond every other thing
At the sun. Today, the dead
    Look out from their dark at us
And keep their counsel. The Capuchin
    Has gone off guard, to be replaced
By a brother sentry whose mind is elsewhere –
    Averted from this populace whose conversion
Was nominal after all. His book
    Holds fast his eyes from us. His disregard
Abolishes us as we pass beyond the door.

Palermo

The Unpainted Mountain

There was a storm of wind and light. The rock
Darkened to shadow and then flared to chalk.
All of the mountain seemed disparity
That I could neither think to one, nor see
Save as a tomb of stones, a livid chine
That blocked back distance. The horizon line
Straddled a mass of salt, of quarried snow.
Where were the folds, the facets that we knew –
The confirmation of the view we wanted,
Where was the mountain that the painter painted?
It was the light, you said, had changed it all,
Sapped out the warmth and left this interval
Of limestone where a pulse no longer beat
Between the scintillations of a heat
That wove the slope, the summit and the glance
Together in one dancing radiance.
Two tones – between-tones, both – pink-grey, green-black,
Flushed through the scene whenever sun came back:
The whole place hovered, image upon image:

A flank of marble or a crumpled page,
The bushes dotted a rucked leopard skin:
What we were seeing was unpainted mountain.
A blue recession, then, of mass gone-by,
Took a new colour out of space and sky:
The height was shepherding its shadows in
Out of the wind-torn vistas of the plain.
Distance and hills had hidden it from view
Till, unforeseen, a twist of road let through
An image that we knew from foot to crown,
As suddenly a seam of light ran down
The western slope and left it separate
Before that place where, soon, the sun would set
Though out of eye-shot, and already sent
A glow and earnest up the whole extent
Of Mont Ste-Victoire, altar more than hill.
Before us, now, new shapes began to fill
The poised horizon where the Luberon
Massed to our approach as night came on.

The Miracle of the Bottle and the Fishes

I

What is it Braque
would have us see in this
piled-up table-top of his?

One might even take it for
a cliff-side, sky-high
accumulation opening door on door

of space. We do not know
with precision or at a glance
which is space and which is substance,

nor should we yet: the eye must stitch
each half-seen, separate
identity together

in a mind delighted and disordered by
a freshness of the world's own weather.

II

To enter space anew:
to enter a new space
inch by inch and not
the perspective avenue
cutting a swathe through mastered distance
from a viewpoint that is single:
'If you painted nothing but profiles
you would grow to believe
men have only one eye.'
Touch must supply
space with its substance and become
a material of the exploration
as palpable as paint,
in a reciprocation where
things no longer stand
bounded by emptiness: 'I begin,'
he says, 'with the background
that supports the picture
like the foundation of a house.'

III

These layered darknesses
project no image of a mind
in collusion with its spectres:
in this debate
of shadow and illumination fate
does not hang heavily
over an uncertain year
(it is nineteen-twelve) for the eye
leaves fate undone
refusing to travel straitened
by either mood or taken measure:
it must stumble, it must touch
to guess how much of space
for all its wilderness
is both honeycomb and home.

Soutine at Céret

The mistral is tearing at trunks: they flow in it.
   Cypresses lean in file, nodding and bowing
With the ceremonious automatism of trees.
   The heaped-up land hoists dwellings
Above rock-packs stacked
   And collapsing sideways and yet
Holding on. Here, olives angle themselves
   To cling to slopes, bending their backs
Like the old man climbing village steps:
   His legs strengthlessly weigh down
Drawn to the inertia of the stone in walls
   That circle and scale these hills. You feel
The mistral could billow out the houses
   With their windows and their doors
Into funfair mirror grimaces.
   The painter chose his landscape all too well
To fix the flux and turmoil of his hell,
   Deaf to the steady counsel of the rocks
And their refusal, anchorages firm,
   To liquefy to the impasto of his brushstrokes.

Self-Portrait

Grey on white, the pencil congregates
   Its immutable wisps, its flecks of form:
He is drafting a portrait of himself
   As someone else – sheer image
Without biography. Inhabiting the skin
   No longer from inside, he declares it there
As pure stranger, a bush of lines
   Growing before his eyes, until
There stares at him out of its own profusion
   That other awakened from himself and slowly
Across the space consenting recognition.

The Peak

Descending, each time we came to where
    The snail–shell road–bend turned
Back circling on itself, we faced
    Into the peak once more. Ice
Had scooped and scraped the rock
    That climbed up to it, rivered
By waters no foot had walked beside.
    The mountain–head possessed a face
Of snow – blown into profile by the winds
    Travelling across it, blindly duning there
This human shape. The peak beyond
    Rose scoured by those same currents
And blown clear: its seamed rock
    Worn by no human wrinkles, stood
At a frontier. Rounding the mountain, we
    Stood with it: the descent, the repetition
As that farness fronted us yet again
    Might have been a dream or a damnation,
But the lowlands opened to receive us,
    Brought us the first sun free of mountain shadow
And the demarcation of ploughland, vineyard, meadow.
    From above the snow–line, and above the snow,
Something was tracking us, measuring our return
    Past the stone certitude of barn on barn.

Netherlands

The train is taking us through a Mondrian –
    The one he failed to paint. Cows
Keep moving along the lines
    Of dyke and drain, the glinting parallels
And the right–angles of a land hand–made.
    True: curvature is no feature of this view,
Yet why did the sky never cause him to digress
    With its mile–high cloud mountains
Pillowed and piled over hill–lessness?
    Flying between the two, go heron and gull

Hunters, haunters of every channel.
There are no verges unplanted, no acres spare:
Water continues accompanying our track,
Cows graze up to the factory windows and we are there.

Anniversary

for Beatrice

Over our roof the planes climb west.
I caught today far out in space
A jet gone inching up the stratosphere
Vertically from a stand of trees,
Over, then down to disappear
Nose-diving the horizon. On high
An arc of vapour scored the shape
One could take the planet's improbable measure by;
Then, as it began to fray and fade
Bits of the bridge came floating down the sky
Combed by the wind. Yet out of view
That arc went rounding on and on
And, half a world away, took also you
Under its wing, reminding this spring day
What day it was by writing it overhead
In a script that only April and you can read.

In Memory of George Oppen

We were talking of O'Hara.
'Difficult', you said
'to imagine a good death – *he died
quietly in bed*, in place of:
*he was run down
by a drunk.*' And now, your own.
First, the long unskeining year by year
of memory and mind. You 'seemed

to be happy' is all I hear.
A lost self does not hide:
what seemed happy was not you
who died before you died. And yet
out of nonentity, where did the words
spring from when
towards the end you told
your sister, 'I don't know
if you have anything to say
but let's take out all the adjectives
and we'll find out' – the way,
lucidly unceremonious,
you spoke to her in life and us.

In Oklahoma

Driving to Anadarko was like flight,
Gliding and grazing the surfaces of land
That flowed away from one secretively,
Yet seemed – all sparsely-treed immensity –
To have nothing to hide. Only the red
Declared itself among the leeched-out shades,
Rose into the buttes, seeped through the plain,
And left, in standing pools, one wine-dark stain.
The trees, with their survivors' look, the grasses
Yellowing into March refused their space
Those colours that would quicken to the ring
Of the horizon each declivity
And flood all in the sap and flare of spring.
The wideness waited. Sun kept clouded back.
An armadillo, crushed beside the road,
Dried out to a plaque of faded blood.
Here, fundamentalists have pitched their spires
Lower than that arbiter of wrath to come –
The tower of the tornado siren
Latticed in iron against a doubtful sky.

Anadarko is an Indian site. Near here the Tonkawa Hills Massacre took place in 1864.

Interpretations

Distinctive, those
concretions known
in Oklahoma as 'rose
rocks' – an allusion
to their red-brown sand-
colour and
similarity to a rose
in full bloom. Petals?
Clusters of barite
crystals are what they are –
the rose-shape made
by the growth of barium
as a divergent cluster
of blade on blade.
The rosettes fed
on an ancient red
sandstone – the host
rock whose colour
they acquired as they
lost their own:
quartz sand-grains
bonded together to become
$BaSO_4$
and await the rigours and the rains
of two million and more
years to petrify then expose
the rose rock or barite rose
in positive relief.
To the Indian eye
those years brought forth
such blood-bonded
and bunched tears as show
a grief of dispossession
no rocks or rock rose
forming could foreknow.

At Chimayó

The sanctuary was begun in the New Mexico of 1813 by one Don Bernardo Abeyta. It is a low-lying church of cracked adobe adjoining the chapel of the Santo Niño Perdido, the Lost Child. In capital letters, pinned to the door, hangs a warning:

NO FOOD
DRINK OR
PETS INSIDE
THE CHURCH

This, as we discover, is a place of notices, messages and names. Particularly names: the givers of ex-votos have inscribed theirs; those who believe it was this place brought about a cure for themselves or their relations, have written signed letters to say so and these are duly exhibited within; the saints are labelled for us – among them, the less familiar San Calletano and San Martín de Porres. Christ is not simply Christ, but Nuestro Señor de Esquipulas.

As we go in through the vestibule the custodian is saying to a travelling salesman that, yes, she will take two dozen. We do not know whether she is speaking of the ex-voto images that are for sale, or the layettes for expectant mothers, blessed on behalf of the Santo Niño. Not only is this place associated with the Santo Niño but with healing, and beside the altar of the Niño there is a hole in the floor from which the miraculous earth is scooped up as a medicament.

We push open the door into the church. It bears another notice, complete with Spanish accent and intonation:

DONT LIVE THIS DOOR. OPEN.
PLEASE

A cloying smell of melting wax from the candles inside. The great vigas overhead and the rough, sturdy walls compact the silence. There is a gaiety about the images: a sculpted Christ wears bright moccasins, a painted St Michael dances on the dragon he has overcome.

The chapel of the Niño also has its notice:

HELP US
KEEP A
CLEAN SCENE

– for many pilgrims come here and perhaps the excluded food, drink and pets somehow find their way inside. After all, what could be more rational, if one has a sick pet, than to bring it in to the source of healing? There are pilgrims here now. They file intently past the bright-red carving of San Rafael holding his fish, into the pósito – the room where the healing earth lies, and where a crucified Christ hangs from his cross wearing a baby-dress of turquoise-coloured rayon decorated with nylon lace and plastic roses. Innocence of taste possesses its own fecundity to which these crowded walls bear witness, covered, as they are, with letters of thanks, photographs, crutches, Leonardo's *Last Supper* in several reproductions, a Raphael Madonna, pictures of Christ from paint-by-numbers sets, an airforce uniform (a sergeant's), keys, a penned description of the sanctuary, beginning, 'In a valley protected by wild berrytrees', a poem – 'The twinkle of a stary stary night' – by G. Mendosa of Las Cruces, a framed portrait of the black-faced Guadalupe Virgin which also contains those of the donors in passport-size snapshots. In the midst of all this sits the effigy of the Santo Niño de Atocha in his wooden stall, cloaked in green and white, his cherubic but sallow face shadowed by a cockaded hat of seventeenth-century cut. There is something dandyish about his attire, but the rope of turquoise beads he wears round his neck has been broken. Someone has cobbled it together with a plastic-coated hairpin. It serves to display a tiny white cross with a minute Christ on it.

In this fecund chaos the messages on the walls carry a sole discordant note, a confession of waste. It is written by a prisoner, still in gaol, who admonishes himself with a cross composed out of two words:

G

MOM

D

The others leave crutches, thanks for cures or the pictures they have painted. He is the one sinner to confess his faults, and the thought of them jars his prose into unpredictable clusters of rhyme: 'I've wasted my life and its cost me my family and friends... No longer with a home not even a place to roam and this cell has become my domain. I know that its blame for bringing shame to my name and now I must part with my time.' 'Bringing shame to my name...': among all these Mendozas, Gonzalezes, Medinas, Antonios, Serafins, Geias, he alone guards his anonymity. In this place of names, he is the only one to realize that to use his name would be a sort of blasphemy and that here he must forfeit it.

Driving back through the dusk I find it is his unsigned letter keeps returning to mind, outdoing the presence of those garish saints. And I wonder from what source a feudal word like 'domain' came to him in his cell where, King of Lackland, he is monarch of all he surveys. Perhaps, turning it over on his tongue, he tastes anew each time the lost liberty of these vistas, this unfenceable kingdom of desert and mountains.

The Tax Inspector

at Tlacolula

I had been here before.
I came back
to see the chapel
of hacked saints.
It was shut.
A funeral filled
the body of the church:
small women with vast lilies
heard out the mass: the priest
completing communion
wiped wine
from his lips and from
the gold chalice
which having dried
he disposed of: the event
was closed. The organ
whose punctuations
had accompanied the rite
broke into a waltz
and the women
rose and the *compañeros*
de trabajo of the dead man
shouldered the coffin forth
to daylight. The waltz

seemed right as did
the deathmarch, the woe
of the inconsolable brass
preceding to the *campo santo*
the corpse, the women
and the *compañeros*
who sweated from street to street
under the bier,
swaying it like a boat.
And this was the way –
a banner declaring
what work he and his *compañeros*
had once shared –
the tax inspector,
ferried across on human flesh,
was borne to burial.

At Huexotla

Tall on its mound, el Paupérrimo –
the poorest
church in Mexico
and the smallest.

It was not the sight
but the sound of the place
caused us to quicken our step
across the intervening space

between us and it –
such skeins, scales, swells
came from each bell-tower
though not from bells.

Who would compose
a quartet for flutes? – and yet
that was the music
rose to assail us.

A minute interior:
sun on the gold:
flute-timbre on flute
still unfolded there.

Flanking the altar,
caged birds hung,
the alchemy of light transmuting
gold to song:

for it was the light's
reflection had set
those cages in loud accord
and only night would staunch it.

Machu Picchu

All day, the weight of heat and then
    Evening brings in the thunder-heads:
A moving mountain leads their cavalcade
    Of silent herds, decaying and re-forming,
And the mountain, too, toils, trails
    Across the view of empty upper-sky
A whole high geography: foot-hills
    Hollows, vales and forests follow
The world-in-making of this awakened height
    That seeps up massively and darkly clear,
Through the more – or is it less – than human light,
    Like an inkblot spread-out magnified:
Forest climbs with the piling crag:
    The single bird that dips before it
Seems astray from there and flies to say
    That Machu Picchu has been dispossessed
Even of its houses, its stone shells'
    Pure prospect of a dwelling place
And the storm that is rising will efface the rest.

Winter Journey

I

When you wrote to tell of your arrival,
   It was midnight, you said, and knew
In wishing me *Goodnight* that I
   Would have been long abed. And that was true.
I was dreaming your way for you, my dear,
   Freed of the mist that followed the snow here,
And yet it followed you (within my dream, at least)
   Nor could I close my dreaming eye
To the thought of further snow
   Widening the landscape as it sought
The planes and ledges of your moorland drive.
   I saw a scene climb up around you
That whiteness had marked out and multiplied
   With a thousand touches beyond the green
And calculable expectations summer in such a place
   Might breed in one. My eye took in
Close-to, among the vastnesses you passed unharmed,
   The shapes the frozen haze hung on the furze
Like scattered necklaces the frost had caught
   Half-unthreaded in their fall. It must have been
The firm prints of your midnight pen
   Over my fantasia of snow, told you were safe,
Turning the threats from near and far
   To images of beauty we might share
As we shared my dream that now
   Flowed to the guiding motion of your hand,
As though through the silence of propitious dark
   It had reached out to touch me across sleeping England.

II

Alone in the house, I thought back to our flood
   That left not an inch of it unbaptized
With muddy flux. Fed by the snow-melt,
   The stream goes lapping past its stone flank now,
And the sound beneath all these appearances
   Is of water, close to the source and gathering speed,
Netting the air in notes, letting space show through

As sound-motes cluster and then clear
Down all its course, renewing and re-rhymed
    Further-off from the ear: I listen
And hear out what they have to say
    Of consequence and distance. That night
The wave rose, broke, reminded us
    We cannot choose the shape of things
And must, at the last, lose in this play
    Of passing lights, of fear and trust:
Waiting, as I wait now, I wish you could hear
    The truce that distils note-perfect out of dusk.

III

I must tell you of the moon tonight
    How sharp it shone. You have been gone three days.
Cold burnt back the mist. The planetarium
    Set out in clarity the lesson of the sky –
Half lost to me: I thought how few
    Names of the revolving multitude I knew
As they stood forth to be recognized. I saw
    The plough and bear – were those the Pleiades?
A little certainty and much surmise, what is the worth
    Of such half-recognitions? They must be
For all their revelation of one's ignorance
    Worth something – let me say this at least:
Though bidden by darkness to the feast of light,
    I came as one prepared, and what I could not name
Opening out the immensity flame by flame
    Found me a celebrant in the mass of night,
Where all that one could know or signify
    Seemed poor beside the reaches of those fires,
The moon's high altar glittering up from earth,
    Burning and burgeoning against your return.

IV

I lay the table where, tonight, we eat.
    The sun as it comes indoors out of space
Has left a rainbow irising each glass –
    A refraction, caught then multiplied
From the crystal tied within our window,

Threaded up to transmit the play
And variety day deals us. By night
   The facets take our flames into their jewel
That, constant in itself, burns fuelled by change
   And now that the twilight has begun
Lets through one slivered shaft of reddening sun.
   I uncork the wine. I pile the hearth
With the green quick-burning wood that feeds
   Our winter fires, and kindle it
To quicken your return when dwindling day
   Must yield to the lights that beam you in
And the circle hurry to complete itself where you began,
   The smell of the distance entering with the air,
Your cold cheek warming to the firelight here.

Heron

Metamorphosed
by a god
you could not flow
hunchback into ballerina
as swiftly as the stiff–
legged heron, frozen now
– a pond-side
garden bronze
the flash of fish
will bring to life once more.

That kink
in the neck
all but disappears as he
stretches it to drink
through the needle-fine
now slightly open
beak: they tell
how a heron hunted
can transfix
the falcon with that bill.

An aristocrat?
The moor-hen
waddles demotic
by this mincing stalker who
is weightless like his shadow;
however, you
must not judge
his politics or
his ancestors
by the way he walks.

For who would guess
that he, content
with solitariness
will nest
in the trees alongside
other species,
or that one so studious
of quiet
united with his kind
turns all at once gregarious?

The Harbinger

A peregrine peers in
at a November window:
in air he could see his prey
a hundred feet below

but misses me
in this glazed interior,
looks through it and beyond
to the darkness where

– a sight past seeing –
he might in one
undistracted stare
gaze prey into being:

then he is gone
this sharp-faced harbinger:
there follow
flurries of a fine snow –

an infinitesimal
and delicate feathering,
mazing the space he now
harries his cold-dazed quarry in.

A Rose for Janet

I know
this rose is only
an ink-and-paper rose
but see how it grows and goes
on growing
beneath your eyes:
a rose in flower
has had (almost) its vegetable hour
whilst my
rose of spaces and typography
can reappear at will
(your will)
whenever you repeat
this ceremony of the eye
from the beginning
and thus
learn how
to resurrect a rose
that's instantaneous
perennial
and perfect now

February

In the month-long frost, the waters
    Combing the detritus that clogs a stream,
Leave gleaming in their wake these twists of glass,
    Caught crystals, petal and frozen frond:
At night, if you could fly and sweep
    With the owl's deep stare the valley reaches,
You would see in each water-way
    These barbed garlands glistening back
The light of an oval moon, whose full is failing,
    That must pull awry the brilliant symmetry of day
On freezing day, and gather up at last
    These gauds that distract the owl's encompassing eye.

Mid-March

I hung the saw by its haft from the saw-horse end
Pointing away from me into the wind
So that the blade should injure no one: the current
Running against the saw-teeth headlong, sent
A thin cry up, half-way to music, a high
Metallic song and severing of air from air,
A prelude to the night's frost, as it were.
The in-between season vibrated from those notes.
For weeks of immoveable snow only a gong could float
The appropriate brooding major across the land
To summon the storms in. This wirey band
Of reverberations vanished skywards, or perhaps
The March moon's crescent of peel is a snapped-
Off fragment of one of them solidified
On the freezing blue of a darkened sky.

From Porlock

Winding on up by the public way
    The roar of descending water in his ears

From the torrent that runs counter to his climb,
   This person does not pause to investigate
The sheen, the shimmer at the edge
   Of visibility, or the sway and glint
Off the new mintings of metallic sea
   Down back below him. His eye
Is elsewhere than the spindly trees
   Wooding the gullies, writhen by their growth
Into such shapes as (judging by that look)
   Might figure forth his mind into a book,
Its script all knots and tilting stems
   Huddled within sheer margins. That wood
Of his can never emerge as trees
   But logged and ledgered. His mind
Is on business that it leans towards
   Though leans less now that the summit
And the moor itself have both been breasted
   And the soundshape of the skylarks' kingdom
Is ringing above him – a dome
   It would daze the eye to climb up into
But not the ear. His ear is listening
   Through and through the house whose door
He hammers at. His knock gone probing into every room,
   He has the dream by the root, he has it out,
Has now what, unknowing, he came for,
   And the larks suspended in their dome behind him,
Hears the steps of the dreamer approaching across the floor.

The Well

for Norman Nicholson

We loosen the coping-stone that has sealed for years
   The mid-field well. We slide-off this roof
That has taken root. We cannot tell
   How the single, pale tendril of ivy
Has trailed inside nor where
   In the dark it ends. Past the dark
A small, clear mirror sends
   Our images back to us, the trees

Framing the roundel that we make,
    A circling frieze that answers to the form
Of this tunnel, coiled cool in brick.
    We let down the plumbline we have improvised
Out of twine and a stone, and as it arrives,
    Sounding and sounding past round on round of wall,
Our images liquidly multiply, flow out
    And past all bounds to drown in the dazzle
As a laugh of light runs echoing up from below.

Coombe

The secrecy of this coombe is weighted through
    With the pressures of the land that does not show.
Over its ridge – the massing of the moors,
    The withstanding cliff and the inland sweep
And drop whose encompassing granite hand
    Extends us the deep lines of its palm
Through softer soils that a river
    Silvers and darkens between. Climb
To the crest and the river has lost itself
    Down in the leafed-round dip and now
Dartmoor is shouldering up against the sky
    Its stone-age pastures and the silences
It kept from the Romans with. In a buzzard's eye
    It might all lie one map, but we
Take in our territory by inches then by bursts,
    More like that heron who stands, advances, stands
Firm in the sliding Torridge that divides
    The sheer of the woodslope from the packed cornland.

Hearing the Ways

Stream beds are pouring
a week's rain through –
hill-race into hollow,
mill-race out of view.

Under a cleared sky
you can hear the ways
the waters are steering
and measure out by

the changes of tone
their purchase on place,
catch the live note off stone
in the plunge of arrival.

The closed eye can explore
the shapes of the vale
as sure as the Braille
beneath a blind finger.

In all its roused cells
the whole mind unlocks
whenever eye listens,
wherever ear looks.

What Next?

As the week-long rain
washed at the slope
the land began
to slip jerkily
down – not all at once
but like the several
frames of an unsteady
film that then
came right
unexpectedly, to go on
pouring forth its smooth
successive images
of rain, mud, rain
until the film again
(a montage unintended)
cut and the whole

slope was coming away
and the image
of a tidal wave of clay
in which there hung
a crumbling island with the trees
still upright on it
buried the road and left us
under our oilskins
high and dry
to retreat into
a perplexed nervous domesticity
and ask ourselves
as we regained our hill-top house
what next...?

The Night Farm

It seemed like a city hidden in the hill,
And this the first house with its flaring panes –
A forge, it might be, from which the fire pulsed out
Above the steep descent of streets whose veins
Of light wound down into the hill heart.
But the beams that had brought this hidden town
To birth in thought were also telling
Of the ardent geometry of dwelling
And the purity of the dark from which they shone.

The Hawthorn in Trent Vale

After fifty years, the hawthorn hedge
    That ran through the new estate
Still divides the garden ends, resists
    With wounds to wrist and elbow every move
To fell it or constrain. This ghost
    From a farm now gone, remains to haunt

And prick the sleep of gardeners dreaming ill
  Of the one unaccommodating dendrophil
Who has tenderly let his portion swell into tree entire,
  Green fire and blossom fed
From the darkness under bed and masonry.

The Way Through

How deep is the sea-cave runs beneath the cliff?
  Less deep than the reflection on its floor:
For the sky comes into the cave to occupy
  A rock pool – sea that does not reflect the sea –
And this image of the whiteness of the sky
  Tinged by the pale green of the roof, the walls,
Reads like a gap in the floor of rock
  That you could fall through. The image refuses to believe
You are more solid than this downward way,
  This crevice that speaks of falling day by day by day
Through a space which does not yet exist,
  Abiding the note that will shatter glass and rock
As Dies Irae widens the last crevasse.

Night Ferry

Where does the ripple in the sky begin?
Behind the mountains holding the waters in.
You'd think the ripple on the water spread
Through rock and pine, vibrating overhead
In one continuous circling-out of power,
From whitening wake through darkness to the stir
Of cloud that, wave on wave, drinks up the last
Suffusions of the sunlight without haste.
Then night is on it all. The parallels –
Two fraying lines the eyes can scarcely tell –
Narrow in foam towards a far pulsation

That shapes the wharf; the tiny constellation
Our stern is thrusting from us. Now we go
Darkness on either side and dark below,
Into the grasp of the expanse and deep;
Yet summit snows still glow beyond the sleep
Of other tints – the strait and shore, one shade –
Holding the space above us open, blade
On jagged blade, and cut against the sky
A frontier for us. Dark must liquefy
Even that height and as the peaks go down
The last reflected light fade, founder, drown.
Air seems coldest then, catching the breath away
In one extinction of the blood and day
As the north brings down the ether from each peak unseen,
Driving the watcher on the deck within.
We crouch in the body's half-way house, and yet
Our travelling lights caught up into the net
The waters cast around us, swaying shoals
Bulge at the interlacings, dolphin schools
Of light break from the water-mesh they make
And ride up along the sides from prow to wake.
Cold holds the boat. One thin wall keeps us dry.
Little unseams dark pines from dark of sky
And we hang in the balance of fathoms, chart and stars
Where mountains on mountains stand round us and only the

water stirs.

Ararat

We shall sleep-out together through the dark
The earth's slow voyage across centuries
Towards whatever Ararat its ark
Is steering for. Our atoms then will feel
The jarring and arrival of that keel
In timelessness, and rise through galaxies,
Motes starred by the first and final light to show
Whether those shores are habitable or no.

ANNUNCIATIONS

1989

Annunciation

The cat took fright
at the flashing wing of sunlight
as the thing
entered the kitchen, angel of appearances,
and lingered there.

What was it the sun
had sent to say
by his messenger, this solvent ray,
that charged and changed
all it looked at, narrowing even the eye of a cat?

Utensils caught a shine
that could not be used, utility
unsaid by this invasion
from outer space, this gratuitous occasion
of unchaptered gospel.

'I shall return,' the appearance promised,
'I shall not wait for the last
day – every day
is fortunate even when you catch
my ray only as a gliding ghost.

What I foretell
is the unaccountable birth each time
my lord the light, a cat and you
share this domestic miracle:
it asks the name anew

of each thing named
when an earlier, shining dispensation
reached down into mist
and found the solidity
these windows and these walls surround,

and where each cup,
dish, hook and nail
now gathers and guards the sheen
drop by drop
still spilling-over
out of the grail of origin.'

The Blade

I looked to the west:
I saw it thrust
a single blade
between the shadows:
a lean stiletto-shard
tapering to its tip
yellowed along greensward,
lit on a roof that lay
mid-way across its path
and then outran it:
it was so keen,
it seemed to go
right through and cut
in two the land
it was lancing. Then
as I stood,
the shaft shifted,
fading across grass,
withdrew as visibly as the sand
down the throat of an hour-glass:
you could see time
trickle out, a grainy
lesion, and the green
filter back to fill
the crack in creation.

Variation

And there is nothing left remarkable
Beneath the visiting moon.
            Antony and Cleopatra, 4.xiii

What is left remarkable beneath the visiting moon
  Is the way the horizon discovers itself to be
The frontier of a country unseen till this:
  Soon the light will focus the whole of it

Under one steadying beam, but now in rising
   Still has to clear the brow of a hill
To unroll the unmapped differences here,
   Where the floor of the valley refuses to appear
Uncoped by the shadow of its flank: it is the speed
   That accompanies this deed of climbing and revealing
Marks the ascent: you can measure out the pace
   Of the unpausing visitant between tree and tree,
Setting each trunk alight, then hurrying on
   To shine back down over the entire wood
It has ignited to flicker in white. Free
   From the obstructions it has come burning through
It has the whole of the night sky to review
   The world below it, seeming to slow
And even to dream its way. It does not arrive alone
   But carries the memory of that spread of space
And of the aeons across which it has shone till now
   From the beginning. This is the illumination it pours
Into the shadows and the watcher's mind,
   As it touches on planes of roofs it could not foresee
Shaping and sharing its light when it set out
   In a rain of disintegrating comets, of space creating.

In New Mexico

Where had the clouds come from? A half-hour since
   There was none, then one, the size
Of a man's hand that unclenched, spread, grew
   In no time into an archipelago on blue –
Blue that had begun with only an eagle in it
   And, even now, offered its unfilled miles
But not for long. The inter-breedings,
   The feathery proliferations of cloud-boats
Careless of anchorage, set out in flotilla
   Over this dry sea-bed they pied with their shadows
Until they covered the entire sea above.
   In the spaces between, you saw through
To an upper blue where whole webs

Of thread billowed and floated free,
As if ready to be wound down and repair
    The least signs of thinning away there
Of what was already more than enough:
    Throughout the vagrant disorder of the sky
Excess was to be the order of the day.
    By afternoon, scarcely the rocks held their own:
The ground was no more than a screen
    Onto which the heavens could project themselves
And alter it all at will. True,
    You could pick up a stone and feel
That was a tight world still, but the white
    Seed of the cottonwood as the breeze that was shaping the cloud
Took hold of the tree and shook it,
    Was drifting across the sand like shreds of sky.

Above the Rio Grande

for Claude-Marie Senninger

The light, in its daylong play, refuses
    The mountains' certainty that they
Will never change – range on range of them
    In an illumination that looks like snow.
On this afternoon when the clouds are one impending grey
    Above the Rio Grande, the light will not obey
Either the clouds' or the rocks' command
    To keep its distance from them. It shifts and shows
Even the cloudshadows how to transform
    The very stones by opening over them
Dark wings that cradle and crease their solidity –
    As if to say: I gather up the rocks
Out of their world of things that are merely things,
    I call dark wings to be bearers of light
As they sail off the shapes they pall
    And, in their wake, leave this brightening snowfall
That melts and is renewed. Yet if the light
    Washes the rocks away, the rocks remain

To tell what it is, and only so
    Can they both flow and stay, and the mind
That floating thing, steady to know itself
    In all the exceedings of its certainty,
As here, beneath the expanses deepening
    Through the cloud-rock ranges of evening sky.

The Santa Fe Railroad

The tri-toned whistle of the night train
    Starts up a blues that goes no further
Than this one repeated phrase, and yet it goes
    Far enough. The desert has no need
To declare itself by fanfare. It is itself indeed
    As you and I might be only in Eden.
And so the three tones – flattened on the final note –
    Float out over so much of space
There is no more to say except: these notes
    Express enough of possibility and of sadness, too,
To tell the extent and loneliness of the continent.
    Is that not so? – I ask Adelicia, who replies
When you catch the trainsounds here, it's going to rain.

Parking Lot

Rain has filled all the streets
    With mirrors: the desert drank them;
The asphalt, mercury to their flickerings,
    Confronts the city with itself in fragments –
PARKING reading as ARK reversed
    (I took it for Russian). A slice of building
Has got in on the reflection of a car
    Disintegrating and reassembling between raindrops:
A piece of tree dances across the wrinkling image.
    Parked, I see half a man

Float by, and hear from the missing portion
    A throat being cleared and then
He walks away into his own entirety
    As I look up from the pool to where
He is passing the tree. It has pieced itself together now
    Beside a yellow fire hydrant
Into an appreciative maple, open-leaved
    To the wet spring morning, the yellow
Dwarf that accompanies it, the sole thing
    Small enough to be mirrored there whole.

Ailanthus

'Ladders to heaven' is the Indian name
for these trees that in the heat
surreptitiously root themselves and grow
where nobody sees them –
as this one, live, lithe, grey,
out of the woodpile. Though its boughs
are supple and almost white,
it is not quite a willow.
Attacked, hacked back, it renews
and grows again up against the house
fingering the flank of the adobe wall
in each breath of wind.
'Rank' is the word
the poet chose for its odour,
but it is neither prized nor praised
for that. No need to climb
the ladder: the heaven
it leads to
lies downwards out of the sun
and under the cool liquidity of its shade.

Catalpa

A hill of leaves,
the tree three days ago
stood bare of bloom.
White torches flared
below the height they were to climb
and light from foot to crown
and did. It was the close of May
when roses overblown already
burned-on still,
but now another fire
struck up the tree:
more foam than flame,
spray after spray
riding the tide of wide and deep-green leaves,
this risen sea of flowers
had flooded every branch till all
the tree was one swaying festival.

Acoma: The Round-Up

I took the cliff-path down
– hand-holds and steps of rock –
and climbed to the plain
from the mesa top.

Singing (I thought it was)
wound on up the stair
in bursts of resonance
through the stony fissure.

It was the cattle
they were herding together,
closing the circle in,
rider by rider;

then driving them on
to await in the shade

of the cottonwood trees
those bringing the strays.

So the herdsmen sit
with scarcely a word,
diffusing a calm that
seems to flow through the herd.

And the only sound
is the metal whir
from the bladed wheel
that raises the water,

as the breeze spins it round
and cools all the air
under the leaves
where the gathered beasts are.

Here and There

There creeks had dried to saltstains in their beds,
To grains of the surrounding desert: veils
Of dust wove in a red transparency
Along the currents of the restless air,
Mile-wide chimeras changing dust to fire.
Now, more than mountains shut us from that scene
Our sun is westering towards, and yet we share
In a world imagined that is really there,
That reaches for our thoughts across the space
And time that free us, our imaginings
No more or less than links in that one chain,
Plains, peaks and seas, the tideline, estuaries
All stored within the mind's bright satellite
As it comes curving homeward. Here, we ride
On the muscularity and shift of tides
We can no longer see – the repetition
Of rippled dunes of sand, sustained and lit
Beyond our gaze, beyond this one day's lapse
Bright at the brink, and still suffusing night
With the waves on waves of its continuing fire.

The Plaza

People are the plot
and what they do here –
which is mostly sit
or walk through. The afternoon sun
brings out the hornets:
they dispute with no one, they too
are enjoying their ease
along the wet brink of the fountain,
imbibing peace and water
until a child arrives,
takes off his shoe
and proceeds methodically
to slaughter them. He has the face
and the ferocious concentration
of one of those Aztec gods
who must be fed on blood.
His mother drags him away, half-shod,
and then puts back the shoe
over a dusty sock.
Some feet go bare, some sandalled,
like these Indians who march through
– four of them – carrying a bed
as if they intended to sleep here.
Their progress is more brisk
than that of the ants at our feet
who are removing – some
by its feelers, some
supporting it on their backs –
a dead moth
as large as a bird.
As the shadows densen
in the gazebo-shaped bandstand
the band are beginning to congregate.
The air would be tropical
but for the breath of the sierra:
it grows opulent on the odour
of jacaranda and the turpentine
of the shoeshine boys
busy at ground-level,

the squeak of their rags on leather
like an angry, repeated bird-sound.
The conductor rises,
flicks his score with his baton –
moths are circling the bandstand light –
and sits down after each item.
The light falls onto the pancakes
of the flat military hats
that tilt and nod
as the musicians under them
converse with one another – then,
the tap of the baton. It must be
the presence of so many flowers enriches the brass:
tangos take on a tragic air,
but the opaque scent
makes the modulation into waltz-time seem
an invitation – not to the waltz merely –
but to the thought that there may be
the choice (at least for the hour)
of dying like Carmen
then rising like a flower.
A man goes by, carrying a fish
that is half his length
wrapped in a sheet of plastic
but nobody sees him. And nobody hears
the child in a torn dress
selling artificial flowers,
mouthing softly in English, 'Flowerrs'.
High heels, bare feet
around the tin cupola of the bandstand
patrol to the beat of the band:
this is the democracy
of the tierra templada – a contradiction
in a people who have inherited
so much punctilio, and yet
in all the to-and-fro
there is no frontier set:
the shopkeepers, the governor's sons,
the man who is selling balloons
in the shape of octopuses, bandannaed heads
above shawled and suckled children
keep common space

with a trio of deaf mutes
talking together in signs,
all drawn to the stir
of this rhythmic pulse
they cannot hear. The musicians
are packing away their instruments:
the strollers have not said out their say
and continue to process
under the centennial trees.
A moon has worked itself free
of the excluding boughs
above the square, and stands
unmistily mid-sky, a precisionist.
The ants must have devoured their prey by this.
As for the fish… three surly Oaxaqueños
are cutting and cooking it
to feed a party of French-speaking Swiss
at the Hotel Calesa Real.
The hornets that failed to return
stain the fountain's edge,
the waters washing and washing away at them,
continuing throughout the night
their whisperings of ablution
where no one stirs,
to the shut flowerheads and the profuse stars.

Oaxaca

In the Emperor's Garden

It began
With Monsieur de la Borde in a white wig.
His aim was to make this garden in the south
Perform in miniature with the same
Blithe, musical display as does Versailles
Or (say) the Luxembourg. But Mexican at heart,
Although it started with this clear intention,
The urgent earth at once deterred it,

The situation – a steep hillside –, the flora
  Of tropical exuberance. The masons tried
With walls, summerhouses and cascades
  To abide by that intention, but their touch
So lay on each pond and fountain you are forced to say
  One thing: This is not French. It hangs
Precipitously above a deep ravine
  When it should have been level. The mangoes,
The sapotes and the Indian laurel, all
  Outgrew the proportions of the place,
Interlaced and roofed out the sky
  With an opaque and sombre canopy:
They are not, as they were intended to be,
  Decorative features of the garden: they
Are the garden itself where one cannot see
  The trees for the forest. Ducks and geese
Lead a lonely, dignified existence here,
  On waters beneath impermeable shade,
Surrounded by arbours of rose and jasmine
  And fountains that for a century have not played.
Hispanicized José de la Borda
  Was long since dead when the Emperor arrived.
The country already slipping out of his hands,
  He planted gardens and bandstands in every town
And there they took. He dreamed
  While the opposition massed and the army fled,
Of extending his empire even now,
  And the trees nodded their absent-minded accord
Above the borders of el Jardin de la Borda.
  A tangle of coffee trees replaced the beds of flowers
Where the Emperor and his Empress strayed alone
  In the company of waters, leaves and stone,
As the retaining walls bequeathed their symmetry
  To the volcanic, shifting soil, their masonry
Silently easing its spoils into the abyss beneath.

The garden at Cuernavaca was a favourite haunt of the Emperor Maximilian (1832–67).
Installed and then deserted by Napoleon III, Maximilian was shot by the republican
opposition.

Hudson River School

for Dorothy and Bill

We drove to the river to see if the shad were rising
Down vistas the painters once flooded with Claudian gold:
The uncompleted spring was still dividing
Shadow-pied acres between the sun and cloud.

As the heat flushed through, you could feel the power of summer
Waiting to overtake the spring only half-begun:
'Where are the fishers?' we asked a woman there,
'You'll see them,' she said, 'once the shad are beginning to run.'

They were not running today here, and the lines
Casting infrequently out from coverts along the shore,
Were merely the first and desultory signs
Of what must turn fever and fervour as more and more

Shad thronged the channels – shad that once filled the fords
In such abundance, you could not ride through
Without treading on them. They have outlasted the herds
Of buffalo, the pigeon flocks that even the painters knew

Only by hearsay, for their retrospective gold
Was painting a loss already. We turned to climb
Out of the valley: Van Winkle's mountains showed
Heaped massively up along the horizon line:

As the hills rose around us we began to see –
Only a few at first, then flare on flare
The blossoms that blew from the shadbush, tree on tree,
Whitening the crests in the currents of the air:

The shadblow that comes when the fish are coming
– Spring brings a yearly proof the legend is true –
Told plainly that plenitude could not be long
In reaching the valley to foison the river anew.

Along the Mohawk

The child floats out his Indian cry
Across the river. Where did the Mohawks go to?
It arrives with the breath of mudflats as we pass by
Down the disused railroad's asphalted avenue.

What is it the fishers who crouch at the river bends
Hope to hook from this discoloured water?
A rabbit, scenting our approach, pretends
As it freezes in the brush, to exist no more.

You can hear the swish of the cars beyond
The far-bank trees: the even wavelets sway
Up to muddy margins: a docile pond
The river appears, no longer a waterway –

Way of the Algonquin as they came down,
Silently scaled the unmanned stockade,
Dropped into the streets and razed the town,
And the cries of victor and victim carried

Up the river reaches and along these shores
To where a rabbit crouches against invaders
And a railroad, silenced by the swish of cars,
Is the pathway fishers follow across this glade.

Pines

The pines are the colour of the day. They take in
    From the changes of sky and from the bay
Each prevailing, passing shade – thus blue
    Becomes the colour of trees – as true as
And no more to be gainsaid
    Than that hint of red the light is proffering
Between the trunks, only to deny it:
    Sun now burns the whole forest black
With shadow, up to the very crow's nest

Of each masted pine-tree: there
Such birds as range and turn in the setting light
Rise like the spirits of trees estranged
That have yielded themselves to a single certain shade
And, as if by a welling from within,
Darken towards the darkness night has made.

In the Steps of Emily Carr

When she got there
The place had disappeared: only a line
Of totems straggled along the bayside
Tipped from the true by winds that patterned through
The breast-high grass the ruins sat in.
She began putting the place together
In careful paint – and then the cats,
An army of them out of every quarter
Of the dank, forsaken clearing, crept
Closer and closer in, yellow-eyed and lean,
Purring, pleading to be taken back
Into the circle of recognitions they had known
Before the dominion of the nettle and the rank
Ferocity of sea-grass, bushes overgrown
And forest dense behind them with the silence
That inhabited it. She left them
Doleful at the very water's edge,
The sole attendants of the wooden goddess
Who still stood, waist-deep in strenuous growth
Amid the odours of rot and humus. They had tasted
The ineradicable sweetness of a human good.

Emily Carr, Canadian painter (1871–1945)

North with Lawren Harris

Here is the glacier of no return. Ice
   Opens into fields and furrows, dry
And hard, and scarcely with a fissure in it –
   A single causeway across silence,
Paved from side to side with white,
   A marble thoroughfare between the tombs
Of a city buried and set round
   With cliffs, that seem as insubstantial
As the blue that bounds them. The scene
   Looms so removed not merely from the presences of men
But from their thoughts, so treelessly complete
   It seems a world no man has known.
Even the spirits that congealed these slopes
   Have perished long since here –
White archangels that heaped them up for tombs,
   Stretched in their shrouds of brilliant hoar.
Too many winters tempered what you drew and saw.

Lawren Harris, Canadian painter (1885–1970)

Far Point

The road ends here. If your way
lies north, then you must take
to the forest or the bay. A café
which is a poolroom which is a bar
serves clams and beer;
the woman who brings them in,
a cheerful exile here,
counts out coins
'Eins, zwei, drei…
with the queen's head on them.
'Look!' I hear her say: a skiff
with an outboard goes past the window.
It's from the island (a strip of sand
with pines and houses on it) and a deer

is swimming in its wake. 'It belongs
to the people in the boat. They should mark it.
I knew a couple who tamed a seal.
It would swim behind *them*, too,
then one day somebody shot it.'
'How would you mark a seal?' I say...
'It's easy to mark a deer.
You know how he found it?
It was being born. Out in the woods.
He couldn't resist touching the fur
so the mother abandoned it –
it was the smell of a man on it frightened her.'
The man opens the door:
a group of Indians are playing pool,
the usual clientele on the bar stools.
They look like lumberjacks. Americans,
they came north to stay out of the army
and never went back. Now they are grey.
He joins them and the deer
paces the veranda and tries
with its great deer's eyes
to look through
the deceptions of the long window
and find where he is.
The pool-players, backs to the light,
stand facing away
from centuries of clambake, potlatch
and tribal ferocities
down a totem-guarded coast.
The poles rotted and the seeds,
dropping inside their crevices,
turned them back into trees.
The cue's click, click
rehearses its softly merciless music
ticking away the increment
of unwanted time. We return
to the car, past fragile shacks
whose cracked white paint
the sea air is picking apart.
We discover the deer once more
that gazes right through us,
then catching sight of a pair of dogs

arcs off to play with them,
perhaps thinks it's a dog.
Across the blue-grey strait,
the ragged ideograms of firs
in a rising and falling fog:
clouds are what we appear to contemplate
above them, then the mist
stirs, sails off
and we see it is summits
we are peering at,
that go on unveiling themselves
as if they were being created.

Algoma

(Northern Ontario)

Each day advanced the passing of the leaves:
The maples first – so much of richness there,
Colour could not have held beyond that pitch,
Yet fallen, frosted, when October sun
Sets them alight once more, their thousands burn
At first intensity. The yellow leaves
Followed the scarlet fast and left all bare
Except the spruces whose interior dark
Densens their louring greens against the light.
The Dipper measures out sky spaces now,
Capella, unencumbered, pricks the eye
Where leaves on leaves had stalled it night on night,
And the first flakes thickening down the wind
Solidify the dark, then hide the sky:
Nobody owns these lands with only the pole behind.

Lines Written in the Bay of Lerici

These giant butterflies feel out the wind
  And circle one another, swaying so safely round
No craft is spilt or split: they lift
  Their wingfuls of air and lifted by it
Bear their own burdens lightly, true
  To the coast curves as the hulls pursue
This swerving waltz of wake lines:
  The salient points, the salient sails
Reassembling, finding new spaces for themselves,
  The sea is a blue page to the signs
They write out on it. Like lizard tails
  (In shape, not shade – in rhyme, not reason),
The veering of these trails! – and deft as lizards
  That lighten across the walls of this high garden,
Where our feet on the sloping ground of a terraced hill,
  Teach us to tell the pitch and scope
Of a score of sails, tacking and steadying
  There below on a bay cupped-in
From the full breath of the September Apennine
  That autumn is whitening, wintering already.

The Labyrinth

for Astrid

Generations labyrinthed this slope – wall
  On low wall, then pergolas of vines
To roof them in. Two workmen
  Pensively complete a further parapet
And they, as we wind up past,
  Give us good day. At our return we find
One of the pair a level higher.
  He greets us yet once more and vanishes –
Only to reappear below us carrying with care
  The single brick that he was looking for,
Exiting by a sidepath to press home

The one piece missing that (once mortared-in)
Will answer to the picture in his mind
    Perhaps, until all fits –
A provisional offering to the god of limits.

Carrara Revisited

Only in flight could you gather at a glance
So much of space and depth as from this height;
Yet flight would blur the unbroken separation
Of fragile sounds from solid soundlessness –
The chime of metal against distant stone,
The crumple and the crumble of devastation
Those quarries filter up at us. Our steps,
As they echo on this marble mountain,
Make us seem gods whom that activity
Teems to placate. But not for long. The hawk
Stretched on the air is more a god than we,
And sees us from above as our eyes see
The minute and marble-heavy trucks that sway
Slowly across the sheernesses beneath us, bend on bend,
Specks on an endlessly descending causeway.

The House in the Quarry

What is it doing there, this house in the quarry?
    On the scrap of a height it stands its ground:
The cut-away cliffs rise round it
    And the dust lies heavy along its sills.
Still lived in? It must be, with the care
    They have taken to train its vine
Whose dusty pergola keeps back the blaze
    From a square of garden. Can it be melons
They are growing, a table someone has set out there
    As though, come evening, you might even sit at it

Drinking wine? What dusty grapes
    Will those writhen vine-stocks show for the rain
To cleanse in autumn? And will they taste then
    Of the lime-dust of this towering waste,
Or have transmuted it to some sweetness unforeseen
    That original cleanliness could never reach
Rounding to insipidity? All things
    Seem possible in this unreal light –
The poem still to be quarried here,
    The house itself lit up to repossess
Its stolen site, as the evening matches
    Quiet to the slowly receding thunder of the last
Of the lorries trundling the unshaped marble down and past.

At the Autumn Equinox

for Giuseppe Conte

Wild boars come down by night
    Sweet-toothed to squander a harvest
In the vines, tearing apart
    The careful terraces whose clinging twines
Thicken out to trunks and seem
    To hold up the pergolas they embrace.
Make fast the gate. Under a late moon
    That left the whole scene wild and clear,
I came on twenty beasts, uprooting, browsing
    Here these ledges let into the hillside.
They had undone and taken back again
    Into their nomad scavengers' domain
All we had shaped for use, and laid it waste
    In a night's carouse. Which story is true?
Those who are not hunters say that hunters brought
    The beasts to this place, to multiply for sport
And that they bred here, spread. Or should one credit
    The tale told of that legendary winter
A century since, which drove them in starving bands
    Out from the frozen heartlands of the north?

Ice had scabbed every plane and pine,
    Tubers and roots lay slabbed beneath the ground
That nothing alive or growing showed above
    To give promise of subsistence. They drove on still
Until they found thickets greening up through snow
    And ate the frozen berries from them. Then
Down to the lowland orchards and the fields
    Where crops rooted and ripened. Or should one
Go back to beginnings and to when
    No men had terraced out these slopes? Trees
Taller than the oaks infested then
    These rocks now barren, their lianas
Reaching to the shore – the shore whose miles
    On miles of sand saw the first approach
As swarms swam inland from the isles beyond
    And took possession. Are these
The remnant of that horde, forsaking forests
    And scenting the orchards in their wake? I could hear them
Crunch and crush a whole harvest
    From the vines while the moon looked on.
A mouse can ride on a boar's back,
    Nest in its fur, gnaw through the hide and fat
And not disturb it, so obtuse is their sense of touch –
    But not of sight or smell. I stood
Downwind and waited. It takes five dogs
    To hunt a boar. I had no gun
Nor, come to that, the art to use one:
    I was man alone: I had no need
Of legends to assure me how strange they were –
    A sufficiency of fear confessed their otherness.
Stay still I heard the heartbeats say:
    I could see all too clear
In the hallucinatory moonlight what was there.
    Day led them on. Next morning found
These foragers on ground less certain
    Than dug soil or the gravel-beds
Of dried-up torrents. Asphalt
    Confused their travelling itch, bemused
And drew them towards the human outskirts.
    They clattered across its too-smooth surfaces –
Too smooth, yet too hard for those snouts
    To root at, or tusks to tear out

The rootage under it. Its colour and its smell,
    The too-sharp sunlight, the too-tepid air
Stupified the entire band: water
    That they could swim, snow that had buried
All sustenance from them, worried them far less
    Than this man-made ribbon luring them on
Helpless into the shadow of habitation.
    The first building at the entrance to the valley
Had *Carabinieri* written across its wall:
    Challenged, the machine-gunned law
Saw to it with one raking volley
    And brought the procession to the ground,
Then sprayed it again, to put beyond all doubt
    That this twitching confusion was mostly dead
And that the survivors should not break out
    Tusked and purposeful to defend themselves.
Blood on the road. A crowd, curious
    To view the end of this casual hecatomb
And lingeringly inspect what a bullet can do.
    It was like the conclusion of all battles.
Who was to be pitied and who praised?
    Above the voices, the air hung
Silent, cleared, by the shots, of birdsong
    And as torn into, it seemed, as the flesh below.
Quietly now, at the edges of the crowd,
    Hunters looked the disdain they felt
For so unclean a finish, and admired
    The form those backs, subdued, still have,
Lithe as the undulation of a wave. The enemy
    They had seen eviscerate a dog with a single blow
Brought into the thoughts of these hunters now
    Only their poachers' bitterness at flesh foregone
As their impatience waited to seize on the open season,
    The autumn equinox reddening through the trees.

Oxen

There are no oxen now in Tuscany.
Once, from any hill-top, you might see
The teams out ploughing, the tilled fields stretch away
Wherever those bowed heads had chamfered round
The swelling contour. The first I ever saw
Strode over ground in such good heart their ease
Was the measure of its tilth. The ploughman knew
His place – behind his beasts, and at the head
Of all the centuries that shaped these hills.
Once, *Belle bestie*, I murmured to myself,
Passing a stall that opened on the road
And catching sight of oxen couched inside.
Belle bestie a voice replied, and I
Was ushered in to touch and to admire
The satin flanks, the presence on the straw.
I recognized the smell, recalled the warmth
Of beasts that rustled all one winter night
In the next room: the stars across Romagna
Pinned out the blackness of the freezing sky
Above a plain that sweat of ox and man
Had brought into fruition. Once I saw
An ox slain in an abattoir. The blood
That flushed the floor was dark and copious –
More than enough to hold the gods at bay
Or bring the dead to speech. The dead spoke then
As every deft stroke of the butcher's men
Revealed an art that was not of a day.
The toughest ground that ever oxen broke
Was by Sant' Antimo. I watched the dust
Turn their slaverings brown and choke the man
Who jolted in their wake and cursed the stones
That cropped out everywhere, unslakeable
The thirst that parched him. He would have been the first
To welcome in the aid that brought his end,
These cheerful tractors turning up the land
Across all Tuscany. No bond of sweat
Cements them to his generations: careless blades
Advancing to the horizon as the clods yield,
Bury both beast and man in one wide field.

The Butterflies

They cover the tree and twitch their coloured capes,
    On thin legs, stalking delicately across
The blossoms breathing nectar at them;
    Hang upside-down like bats,
Like wobbling fans, stepping, tipping,
    Tipsily absorbed in what they seek and suck.
There is a bark-like darkness
    Of patterned wrinklings as though of wood
As wings shut against each other.
    Folded upon itself, a black
Cut-out has quit the dance;
    One opens, closes from splendour into drab,
Intent antennae preceding its advance
    Over a floor of flowers. Their skeletons
Are all outside – fine nervures
    Tracing the fourfold wings like leaves;
Their mouths are for biting with – they breathe
    Through stigmata that only a lens can reach:
The faceted eyes, a multiplying glass
    Whose intricacies only a glass can teach,
See us as shadows if they see at all.
    It is the beauty of wings that reconciles us
To these spindles, angles, these inhuman heads
    Dipping and dipping as they sip.
The dancer's tread, the turn, the pirouette
    Come of a choreography not ours,
Velvets shaken out over flowers on flowers
    That under a thousand (can they be felt as) feet
Dreamlessly nod in vegetative sleep.

Chronochromie

The thrushes are singing their morning plainchant,
    Colouring time – rehearsing once again
In flood and droplet, cascade and chime
    Those centuries before our coming here

To measure and to minute out
    All to our purposes. Now we go
Back with the birds to before we were.
    We cannot stay long. Only the angels
Could listen out that song
    Through the millennia of our silence. Yet angels
And other feathered things have in common
    Merely their wings, for thrushes
Both sing and stab. And we alone
    Who invented angels, but not the birds,
Hear brink and beginning in their wordless words –
    Hear space begetting time once more
In the falls and flourish of that coloratura.

Ruskin Remembered

What is it tunes a Scottish stream so fine?
Concurrence of the rock and of the rain.
Much rain must fall, and yet not of a sort
That tears the hills down, carries them off in sport.
The rocks must break irregularly, jagged –
Our Yorkshire shales, carpenter-like, form merely
Tables and shelves for rain to drip and leap
Down from; the rocks of Cumberland and Wales
Are of too bold a cut and so keep back
Those chords their streams should multiply and mingle.
But there must be hard pebbles too – within
The loosely breaking rock, to strew a shingle
Along the level shore – white, for the brown
Water in rippling threads to wander through
In amber gradations to the brink, the ear
Filled with the link on link of travelling sound,
Like heard divisions, crisp above a ground,
Defining a contentment that suffices –
As walking to unblent music, such as this.

A Ruskinian Fable Retold:
Courtesy

– or however you'd denote
the behaviour of this quartz,
living side by side
with the seemingly more modest
green and slender
mineral called 'epidote':
they can't go on
growing together now
much longer: the quartz
five times as thick
is twenty times the stronger.
Sensing, at the very crown
and self-built summit
of its own existence,
the presence of its weak
persistent neighbour,
it pauses there and lets
the pale-green film
of epidote grow past
to occupy the space
beyond it. The cost
of this well-bred hesitation?
Its own crystal life.
No: 'courtesy'
is not the word: courtesy
is closer to common sense
than immolation.

Bluebells

Bluebells! we say seeing the purple tide
   Overflow from the wood to meet us.
If we could fly above them, we could read
   The sprawled, imperial hieroglyph of this spread

Above whatever nutriment of earth has fed
    Their fresh advance. The scent
Drenches the summer air it cools
    With the fullness of their presence: they
Swarm down the woodbank, a flower army.
    If the angelic orders were visible in time,
Then these might glow as the iridescent shadow
    Of such splendour. If they are blue –
Silent the bell-mouths crowding on each stem –
    It is only our words so call and colour them.

Harvest

for Paula and Fred

After the hay was baled and stacked in henges,
We walked through the circles in the moonlit field:
The moon was hidden from us by the ranges
Of hills that enclosed the meadows hay had filled.

But its light lay one suffusing undertone
That drew out the day and changed the pace of time:
It slowed to the pulse of our passing feet upon
Gleanings the baler had left on the ground to rhyme

With the colour of the silhouettes that arose,
Dark like the guardians of a frontier strayed across,
Into this in-between of time composed –
Sentries of Avalon, these megaliths of grass.

Yet it was time that brought us to this place,
Time that had ripened the grasses harvested here:
Time will tell us tomorrow that we paced
Last night in a field that is no longer there.

And yet it was. And time, the literalist,
The sense and the scent of it woven in time's changes,
Cannot put by that sweetness, that persistence
After the hay was baled and stacked in henges.

The Garden

for the same

                        And now they say
   Gardens are merely the expression of a class
Masterful enough to enamel away
   All signs of the labour that produced them.
This crass reading forgets that imagination
   Outgoes itself, outgrows aim
And origin; forgets that art
   Does not offer the sweat of parturition
As proof of its sincerity. The guide-book, too,
   Dislikes this garden we are descending through
On a wet day in Gloucestershire. It speaks
   Accurately enough of windings and of water,
Half-lost pavilion, mossy cascade,
   But is afraid 'the style is thin'. One must smile
At the irritability of critics, who
   Impotent to produce, secrete over what they see
Their dislike or semi-assent, then blame
   The thing they have tamed for being tame.
But today, see only how
   Laden in leaves, the branchwork canopy –
Bough on bough, rearing a dense
   Mobile architecture – shudders beneath its finery
In cool July. Heat, no doubt,
   Would flesh out the secret of this garden where
(Or so it's said) the man who imagined it
   Could wind down to find
His gypsy inamorata waiting there
   By the hidden lake.
                    There are three lakes here
And a fluttering curtain of rain that falls
   Differently in each. The first
Lies open to the farmland and it takes
   The full gust and disordering of the weather
Across its surface. The second –
   We have descended further now
Bending our way in under each low bough –
   Shelters between the hills' high shoulders,

And so the green, smooth plain of water
    Lies taut under the nail-points of the rain.
We must enter next a key-hole door
    Into darkness: through a rough window-slit
We catch a runnel wrinkling over stone,
    And the pool that stretches to receive it
So fills the aperture we can not take in
    Its true extent: we are all eye –
Which is not eye enough to outdo
    The dark we are trying to gaze out through.
A twist in the tunnel: light! We are delivered
    And now we can freely move
Beneath a pergola 'in the precise arch'
    (I quote to show the disapproval I disapprove)
'Of a railway terminus'. This is no end
    However, but the start of the final lake.
You can see the rain withdraw across
    This widest of the waters, the transparent scrim
Suddenly towed aside, and calm
    Flowing up to its receding hem:
Fish in the cloudy depths might well be swimming
    Through sky such as threatens us still.
We have the hill to re-ascend, and do,
    Up to the formal garden at its summit:
The statuary, the espaliered avenue
    Ignore the twisting path. The descent
To the hidden lake now hoards from sight
    The walks and walls, the subterranean door
Into an imaginary place that time
    Turned real. The imagination hovers here
Half rebuked, with its Doric and Chinese;
    Nor can a planned secretiveness outdo
The cool green of that chamber
    Shut from view beneath the gloom
Of the copper beech. Its tent conceals
    Not darkness, but an inner room,
An emerald cell of leaves whose light
    Seems self-sustaining, and its floor
A ground for the reconciling of our dreams
    With what is there.
                            So here we stand,
We two, and two from another land,

To meditate the gift we did not ask –
The work of seasons and of hands unseen
    Tempering time. What has not disappeared
Is a design that grew – ultimately to include
    (Beside plants of oriental and American species)
Us four, in its playful image of infinity,
    The whole of it assembled with a view
To generations beyond the planter's: there is nothing here
    We shall ever own, nothing that he owns now,
In those reflections of summer trees on water,
    This composure awaiting the rain and snow.

Letter to Uehata

Since I returned, the trees have a Japanese look,
    And bare in their wintry sinuousness seem
To retrace in air the windings of those paths
    That followed so faithfully the swelling ground,
Then lost for an instant, came back into view
    With the trees they wound on through, reflected
(Borrowed, as you would say) by some pool.
    That landscape was arranged – to reflect
And reflect again the grain and grandeur
    Of the world we see, and that the centuries
Have unrolled to now, as if time
    Were itself the paradigm of a path
That has brought me to where I can read
    In the bareness of the trees a double scene –
Where I am now and where we both were then.

Apples Painted

for Olivia

He presses the brush-tip. What he wants
    Is weight such as the blind might feel
Cupping these roundnesses. The ooze
    Takes a shapely turn as thought
Steadies it into touch – touch
    That is the mind moving, enlightened carnality.
He must find them out anew, the shapes
    And the spaces in between them – all that dropped from view
As the bitten apple staled on unseen.
    All this he must do with a brush? All this
With a brush, a touch, a thought –
    Till the time-filled forms are ripening in their places,
And he sees the painted fruit still loading the tree,
    And the gate stands open in complicity at his return
To a garden beneath the apple boughs' tremulous sway.

Winter

There is no light left. And yet
    A glow light covers and colours
The ground beneath the trees: it is leaves
    Have fallen from the beech – the same red
As the earth that shows between them, smouldering
    On shining trunks, a fire
The mirror-surfaces of rain redouble
    In unlit air. Mirror on mirror
Hands it on into the wood, raises
    The light of this ground-level brazier
Half way up the boles and into our eyes
    In a punctual sunset, where we had looked
For darkness underneath the night-wide
    Moss-fattening down-drift of the wet.

The Cycle

So fine the snow
You must look to the blackness of the trees to show
The shaping of its grain against the wind.
    The sky is as white as that descent,
The ground, too, hides what it receives
    Transforming to a blent and cleanlier white
The hanging threat vouching for more and more.
    The house is going under as the drift
Climbs walls and door and, sieving through,
    Gathers finely in a threshold line.
It appears to mean that we – the ones who've seen
    A flood seeping across that limit –
Stand guarding a frontier, the incursion
    Refusing to disband until it must, and then
Grudgingly reveal the green the spring
    Thrusts back at us, the cycle rebegun.

Two Poems for Fay Godwin

I *Leaping Lurcher*

More flag than dog –
more pennant than drapeau –
see it stretch mid-air
to clear the topmost
barbs of a fence-wire,
and hang for the infinitesimal
flick a shutter takes
to imprison it and show
(what did not quite occur)
the poised, heraldic flight
caught flat as a weathervane
to be unwrought by time,
metal to muscle, forefeet
prepared already
to take the fall
they must prevent
and steady into movement

A phalanx of sheep,
the sun behind them,
defended the further shore:
shadows sloping towards us,
their heads and shoulders
cast across grass
a battlement in silhouette
that ceased at the water: the real
heads (a wholesale decapitation)
overshot this shadowy parapet to reappear
in reflection, upside-down and yet
as alert to our intentions
as those heads-on-shoulders
awaiting our first move:
I opened both eyes,
clapped my hands
and the snapshot
fell apart bleating.

Felix Randal

or the Black Economy

The farrier comes with his forge. He shoes
  For cash only. The ash of a portable fire
Leaves no trace in the account books of the nation,
  The acridity of singeing hooves prompts no enquiry
And the sounds of the hammer are swallowed by the air
  As scavenging farm dogs gobble the parings.
The collapsible forge ballasts his swaying van:
  Unpursued by conscience or by priest – Felix is gone.

Music and the Poet's Cat

Your ears resented the discords,
the scream of the woodwind
in *Tapiola* before the whirlwind
spreads through the orchestra
diminishing those centuries
of chorales and firm persuasions.
Now that you are gone,
run into marl and waterdrops
beneath your stone,
once more I listen
and my ears take in
those selfsame notes
across this rent
in time and I
resent both it and them.

Ode to Dmitri Shostakovich

I

To what far room of never-to-return
The raw brass singles out and calls us –
A tale too often told, one old already
Long before the pen of Mandelstam
Entangled itself in the Georgian's moustaches.
Those feelers found him out, and you survived
To play the fool and to applaud the play
That you must act in. Notes told less than words
And now tell more, each vast adagio dense
With the private meaning of its public sorrow.

II

You stole the Fate Motif from Wagner's *Ring*
(Great artists steal and minor merely borrow) –
Fate had declared itself as daily fact:
This day might be the allotted span. Tomorrow...?

Stalin was dead. But not his heirs, and not
The memory imprinted in the nerves, the heart.
Light-eared, light-fingered, you had earned your share
Of that absurd prestissimo from *William Tell*,
To accompany an endlessly running man
In one of the silent comedies of nightmare.

III

Inscribing score on score with your motto theme –
Mnemonic of survival, notes for a name –
'I am still here,' you signal, yet once more,
And now that you no longer are, the same
Chime recurring takes on the whole of time
Out of a permanence few of us can have.
In the photograph you pass smiling to the grave.

Moonrise

I cannot tell you the history of the moon,
Nor what they found contained within its dust.
All I can say, this December afternoon,
Is that it rises early as the last
Of the crows are spying out a way
In semi-darkness to a darkened nest,
Its phosphor burning back our knowledge to
The sense that we are here, that it is now.
Against the east, the tautness of its bow
Is aiming outwards at futurity
And that will soon arrive, but let it be:
The birds are black on the illuminated sky
And high enough to read the darkness here
By this risen light that is bringing tides to bear.

Orion over Farne

for John Casken

The growling of the constellations, you said –
   A more ferocious music of the spheres
Where, above Farne, the Scorpion tears
   Orion still, teaches him hunt elsewhere,
But hunt he will – and here
   Over the breathing body of the sea,
Heard through the darkness and the star-rimed air
   To the sharp percussions of the tide on scree.
Close to, a poet feeds this frosty soil
   Where the November constellation sets
As storms on storms begin, as the spoils
   Of another year are scattered and constellation
On hunted constellation grinds and growls.

Chance

I saw it as driving snow, the spume,
   Then, as the waves hit rock
Foam-motes took off like tiny birds
   Drawn downwind in their thousands
Coiled in its vortices. They settled
   Along ledges and then fell back,
Condensed on the instant at the touch of stone
   And slid off, slicking the rock-sides
As they went. The tide went, too,
   Dragging the clicking pebbles with it
In a cast of chattering dice. What do they tell
   These occurrences, these resemblances that speak to you
With no human voice? What they told then
   Was that the energies pouring through space and time,
Spun into snow-lace, suspended into flight,
   Had waited on our chance appearance here,
To take their measure, to re-murmur in human sounds
   The nearing roar of this story of far beginnings
As it shapes out and resounds itself along the shore.

The Headland

A silence lies over the headland like a death
    That has left in the air an echo of the stir
That it has checked – you hear it in the breathing of the sea
    Lipping at the pebbles continuously
Below the cliff, as if it could not articulate
    The word it wanted to deliver, yet bringing to bear
All of the forces it takes to shape one word:
    Unseizably it rehearses an after-life
(The only one certainly there) like that of verse
    That holds its shell to the ear of a living man,
Reminding him that he will be outlasted
    By the scansion in its waves, beating a shore
That is the beginning of the voyage out
    Towards the continuing sunsets, on and on
Cast back across the façades of the shoreline town.

For a Godchild

Given a godchild,
I must find a god
worthy of her. Dante
refused – in courtesy
(he said) to the god
he venerated, to wipe
a sinner's eyes in hell:
I must tell her of that
one day, and see
that she ponders well
what she takes to be
the dues of deity –
and learn that a god
who harbours anger where
thirst has no slaking,
eyes no ease,
is either of her own
or others' making.

THE DOOR IN THE WALL

1992

The Operation

A cold spring morning sees
   The man who has come to trim trees
In the valley wood, up against a sky
   That looks down, through and into
A cat's cradle of twigs and branches.
   The man paces this swaying cage,
Giving thought to the size and shape
   Of what he must do, exploring
Floor by floor each pliant storey
   Threatened by rot and over-crowding:
He weighs by eye what high limbs
   Stand to fall, when winter squalls
Rake the valley, and rounds out
   His loppings to please the tidy mind
Of the owner of these trees. Then
   Into action: standing there
Forks apart, spanning half a branch,
   He power-saws the other half off
And scaling a stair of boughs, repeats
   At each rung his noisy squaring.
But what finesse – raucousness apart
   As the blade combusts – in the way that he
Slices the slender outgrowths from the tree,
   Works at it with a dabbing motion,
Then leans back, inspects and jabs again –
   Painting not pruning: he is as much
Making a tree as taking a tree apart,
   Walking a world of his own creation.
He darts with his saw, having at what he sees
   Like a slightly clumsy fencer. No –
'Clumsy' cannot be just. Who'd dare
   Fence on a beech bough, trust
To sprung pliancy fifty feet and more
   In air? A voice-over – caught
Between bursts from the ignited saw,
   Prompting *More to the right, more*
To the road side – proceeds from the critic
   (The artist heeds him, too) who lies
Stretched across the cab-roof of a truck

Sizing up the shape of the new
Treescape after the morning's abbreviations:
   That'll do. The expert in metamorphoses
Restrains his saw, and leans
   Down into the twiggery to extricate
Boughs that have lodged in there,
   Tosses them to the ground with a crackling roar.
The painter and the fencer now disappear:
   He has one more image to dance
In and out of, and clings to his rope
   As a 'Me Tarzan' swing returns him
To the top of his ladder: he trots down,
   Hopping earthwards from five feet up
And walks horizontally away – primate
   Into man – to put a distance between
Himself and what he has done, and to survey it:
   The hard hat he appeared to be wearing
Turns out to be his own red hair.
   Then the corpse on the cab-roof
Suddenly resurrects: *Not bad*.
   His eyes – he is grounded, too – take in
The fallen logs they must soon begin
   Piling aboard and the litter along the road
To be gathered and fired, before moving on
   Down the freshly tarred approaches. Evening:
And the procession of their fires dies back
   To heaps of glowing ash, and a low haze
Starts climbing throughout the trees,
   Altering, as it flows into the twilight,
The million burin strokes of branches
   To soft charcoal lines, the incense
Leaving the senses open to the night.

The Clearance

They have fired the brush in the half-felled wood:
   Extinguishing piles still smoke on, blue;
Beacons of briars and ivy blazing through,
   Crest the detritus. A glitter

And, suddenly red, a starburst breaks
   As the wind takes hold, and the burnings
And the glows go spreading uphill
   Into the wood-heart. The cut logs
Tell, in their greenness, of how wet
   The wood was, that now lets in
The hilltop horizon and the sky.
   Fresh plantings will branch out there,
Feel the embrace of entering air –
   Spaced to receive our climbing glance
That can survey all of the falling stream
   Woodland had hidden away, a white
Rope the water lets down
   Sounding closer and closer against the ear,
A keen, clear flight to the feet of whoever is standing here.

Siena in Sixty-Eight

The town band, swaying dreamily on its feet,
   Under the portraits of Gramsci and Ho,
Play 'Selections from *Norma*', and the moon,
   Casta diva, mounts up to show
How high the sky is over harvested Tuscany,
   Over this communist conviviality within the wall
Of a fortress that defends nothing at all.

History turns to statues, to fancy dress
   And the stylishness of Guevara in his bonnet. Here,
Red-bloused, forgetful sales girls
   For the revolution, flirt with the males
At a bookstore under an awning of red:
   Lenin, Che, Debray and Mao –
The unbought titles, pristinely serried.

'Realism and sobriety', one might write of the art show:
   In *No to Repression*, a procession of women
With raised fists, shouts No, No, No.
   And between *American Bombers* and *Black Boy Cleaning Shoes*,

Somebody, unteachably out of step,
    Has gouged intently into paint
The stigmata of St Francis in *Miracle of the Saint*.

Consciences drowse this summer night
    Warmed by the after-glow. Fragrance of cooking
Weighs on the sense already fed by it,
    The wild boar turning and turning on its spit;
And the air too greasily replete to lift the red flag,
    The morning headlines grow fainter in the dusk:
'Where is Dubček?' 'Tanks on the streets of Prague.'

Paris in Sixty-Nine

for Octavio Paz

'I love', I heard you say,
    'To walk in the morning.' We were walking,
Spring light sharpening each vista,
    Under the symmetrical, freshly-leafing trees,
By boulevard, bridge and quays the Douanier
    Had painted into his golden age
Of a Tour Eiffel perpetually new.
    I replied: 'I trust the thoughts that come to me
When walking. Do you, too, *work* when walking?'
    'Work when I am working…?' My error
(Traffic was too loud to fight with words)
    Came clear to me at last – for I
Am far too fast imagining that my friends
    Prefer, like me, the stir of street or landscape
To four walls to work in. Sunlight
    Had begun, after a night of frost, to warm
The April air to temperate perfection,
    In which the mathematics of sharp shade
Would have gratified Le Nôtre, 'auteur de ce jardin':
    His bust surveyed it: in the pavilion there
The subtler geometries of Cézanne. Refaire
    Poussin après la nature! – he and the auteur

Might have seen eye to eye, perhaps,
　　But for the straight lines and the grandeur.
All was not easy here. Gendarmerie
　　Clustered at corners, still unrelenting
After the late events, although the theatre
　　Deserted by its actors now, lay silent
But for the sloganned walls. 'De Gaulle', I said,
　　'Is an unpleasant man.' 'But a great one,'
You replied, to my surprise, for you
　　Believed when the students had their Day
It was a sign that linearity
　　Was coming to its close, and time
Was circling back to recurrence and fiesta.
　　Before the walker the horizon slips from sight.
What matters in the end (it never comes)
　　Is what is seen along the way.
Our feet now found confronting us
　　The equestrian bulk ('Paris vaut une messe!')
Of Henri Quatre in the Place Dauphine,
　　Horsed on the spot that Breton called
'The sex of Paris', legs of roadways
　　Straddling out from it. Was it the image
Drew him to that statue, or had he
　　(Eros apart) a taste for monarchy?
'Pope of surrealism' is unfair, no doubt,
　　And yet, it comprehends the way he chose
To issue edicts, excommunicate his friends.
　　I saw his face look out from yours –
Or so it seemed – the day that I declined
　　To dine in company, which led you on to say:
'Always the Englishman, you want to found
　　Another church.' So, always the Englishman,
I compromised and came – Paris vaut une messe.
　　For it was Paris held us on its palm,
Paris I was refusing as well as you
　　And should have said no to neither:
Paris looked in on all we were to say and do,
　　And every afternoon concluded with
That secular and urban miracle
　　When the lights come on, not one by one,
But all at once, and the idea and actuality
　　Of the place imprinted themselves on dusk,

Opening spaces undeclared by day.
  All the recurrences of that constellation
Never reunited us by that river.
  Yet, time finding us once more together
On English soil, has set us talking,
  So let me renew my unrequited question
From twenty years ago: 'Do you, Octavio,
  Work when you are walking...?'

In a Cambridge Garden

to the same

Another town and time – and little left of it
  Before you were to go. Castles in Spain
Stood solid to receive your royal progress
  While Wren detained us. Beyond his colonnade
Arched and shaded, as if Italian paviours
  Had laid the flags we echoed on – our way
Led us to lawns whose midday shadows
  Seemed cast from trees as massive
I was about to say, as those that grow
  In Mexico itself – but no: this plane,
This copper beech, both take their scale
  From their own setting, and could stand
Nowhere but here, their power contained
  Beside a wall in England. Had you stayed on
Twenty years ago, had I gone
  To live in the house at Nine Mile Swamp,
My children would have been Americans, and you
  An exotic in this Cambridge garden. Now
These inquests on past possibilities
  Serve merely to say that we
Were right to choose the differing parsimonies
  Of the places we belonged to. I thought
That I could teach my countrymen to see
  The changing English light, like water
That drips off a gunwhale driving through the sea,

Showing the way the whole world
Dipping through space and cloud and sun,
　　Surges across the day as it travels on
Turning. In short, I stayed. Your life,
　　Pitted against the rigid summa
Of Thomists turned politicians, grew
　　More public every year, and mine
In its privacy, more sociable, perhaps,
　　Than one that contemplates that upstate view
Over uninhabited acres blank with snow.
　　What would you have missed the most?
First, I know, would have come colour.
　　We cannot pretend our island exhalations
Do not douse the harshness of that clarity
　　That burns back in ochres, oranges and reds
Off Mexican walls. The ground beneath them
　　Wears a brown Franciscan serge –
Not drab, because seen at first intensity
　　Under such a light. Some, I suppose,
– Not you – might find the colours of a place
　　Small reason for living there –
It took an Englishman (John Locke),
　　Meagre and precise, to call them 'secondary'.
And here, fanaticism and moderation meet –
　　I think when Mercader killed Trotsky,
The colours of that garden in Coyoacan
　　Counted for little: he hurried through
Drawn by the thought of what it was he'd do,
　　Senses sheered back to its accomplishment.
So you returned. To the monoxide monotony
　　That taints the trees of Mixcoac –
'There *are* no gardens,' as you said, 'except
　　For those we carry with us.' Now we, too,
Must hurry through the hospitality
　　Of this one, ready for the car
(The gates are opening) that awaits you
　　(And the street looks in.) And so we coincide
Against distance, wind and tide, meet
　　And translate our worlds to one another,
Greet in verse. A poem is itself
　　A sort of garden – we are waving our farewells –
Seasonable at all times as we bring

Our changing seasons to it – we are losing sight
Of the speeding car that is launched and one
   With the traffic now and the mid-May sun.

Tübingen

Today the sun
constructed a sort of ecological clock:
it brings out a shadow
beside each bush –
a dark arrow to indicate
the direction of the flock
that browses the volcanic hill
(it is unsafe for building): up
they climb each morning –
out of the roofs, it seems,
of the surrounding houses.
The shepherd has gone on ahead,
his shadow walking beside him
with his dog. Then one forgets
dog, shepherd and flock
until next morning and the clock
is in motion once more.
But where are the sheep? I see
only shepherd, shadow and dog
striding towards the horizon summit
and the Bismarck Tower that crowns it
bristling with aerials. Dog and man
are like the attendants of some god or goddess –
a suburban Aurora
who has failed to rise. Perhaps the flock
lies nodding beside her. From the street side
none of these hill-top goings on
are visible. *Mensch in Not*
one reads on the beggar's sign:
he is young indeed
for a beggar – there must be more
than meets the eye to this *Man in Need.*

If you sit for long
on the steps of the Stiftskirche
you will be asked
'Do you want drugs?' I ask
myself, 'What is a *Stift*?' –
I must buy a dictionary.
When I return to my rear window
I see with elation
the whole flock up there:
the shepherd comes down
to speak to a friend
at the field's edge and the sheep
descend behind him, as if they too
might share in their conversation.
A *Stift* turns out to be
a seminary – there is one here
that Hölderlin attended
who went mad waiting
for the deities of Greece to reappear
on the steps of the Stiftskirche.
I thought of Endymion tonight.
Under a not-quite full moon
the shepherd stood on his hill top
and watched the dog
herd all of his sheep down
in one fleecy sweep.
A bat flickered past.
The sheep continued to flow
then vanish under the roofscape
until the last had disappeared
along with the dog: it is the turn now
of the man to follow
which he does. It was not a bat
but a swallow out late
that dips and returns again and again
in front of a hill where only the moon remains.
I wanted to know
where it was that a flock goes to
regularly at ten o'clock
of a fine June evening, and so
set off uphill one Sunday
(the sheep had failed to appear)

to find what the rooftops were hiding there.
The flock lay huddled together
fenced round by a netted fold
and the dog, now at leisure,
came boldly snuffling up
to the bench I was watching from
and left a wet stain
on its iron leg. A tiny man
with a Punch nose and unshaven chin
a white stubble covered
dismounted from his Honda and began
to collect with care
all the sheeps' dung he could find
as though each piece
were a rare mushroom.
At last Endymion
arrives to inspect the pen.
'You must be content
up here,' I say. Surprised,
'I am more content', he replies
'than I would be down there,
but I am not content.'
The man who grazes and the man
who gazes at him, eye
each other. 'Why are you not content?'
'People dislike sheep. They dislike
the sheep-smell and their dislike –
well, it settles on me. That's why.'
The minute man
with the unshaven chin
has packed the dung
inside an enormous wicker basket
to which he attaches himself, then
mounts his machine
and winds towards the town
with a shut-off engine, as though
he preferred not to break
the silence he is freewheeling through.

Blaubeuren

And now the season climbs in conflagration
   Up to the summits. The thick leaves
Glow on either side of the descent
   A fire-ride carves between the trees –
A blue, unsoundable abyss. The sun
   Is pushing upwards, firing into incandescence
Lingering vapours. The tufted pinetips
   Begin to define the hilltop where a cross –
Too blatant to beckon a heart towards it –
   Stands stolid and ghostly, a dogmatic
Concrete post hardening out of mist,
   And, grey to gold, touch by touch,
The wood mass – beams breaking in –
   Visibly looms above the town. Below
Floats back a climbing bell-chime
   Out of the theological centuries: that, too,
Caught up into the burning vibrancy,
   Seems yet another surface for refraction,
Fragmenting into audible tips of flame.
   The beacon of the day – the mist has burned away now –
Blazes towards the death and resurrection
   Of the year. To be outlived by this,
By the recurrences and the generations, as today
   Has lived beyond the century of Dürer –
His rocks stand jutting from the foliage here –
   Is to say: I have lived
Between the red blaze and the white,
   I have taken the sacrament of the leaf
That spells my death, and I have asked to be,
   Breathing it in at every pore of sense,
Servant to all I see riding this wave
   Of fire and air – the circling hawk,
The leaves… no, they are butterflies
   That love the ash like leaves and then
Come dancing down from it, all lightness
   And away. Lord, make us light enough
To bear the message of this fine flame
   Rising off rooted things, and render it
Back to the earth beneath them, turning earth
   Itself, while the light still holds,

To a steady burning, a clarity
　　Bordering the blue, deep fold of shadow:
Cars, weaving the woodslope road,
　　Glitter like needles through the layered leaves.

Campos de Castilla

i.m. Antonio Machado

The storks, back on their bell-towers here,
　　Tell winter is at an end. This year
They stayed, but the December sun,
　　Flashed off their white, cannot persuade
The months away, stretching between
　　The pastel of this frost, its mist of melting,
And the return of green to what appears
　　All desert now. The holm oaks
And the vinestocks rear dun presences;
　　Fields, fallow to the eye, lie tilled
And quiet above the corn that soon will fill them –
　　Soon, that is, in the scope of the wheeling seasons
And of storks, their longevity before them,
　　Citadelled on twig-pile summits above Castile.

Alcalá de Henares – Toledo

The Door in the Wall

i.m. Jorge Guillén

Under the door in the wall
the slit of sun
pours out at the threshold
such an illumination,

one begins to picture
the garden in there,
making the wrinkled step
seem shadowy, bare;

but within the shadows
an underfoot world puts forth
in points of light
its facets of worth –

surfaces of such depth
you have only to eye them,
to find you are travelling
a constellation by them;

and the sun that whitens
every lightward plane
leaks up the stone jamb,
reappears again

where the flickering tangle
of thick leaves covers
the top of the wall and
ivy piles over.

So the garden in there
cannot mean merely
an ornamental perfection
when the gardener lets be

this climbing parasite
within whose folds
birds find a shelter
against rain and cold.

But let be the garden, too,
as you tread and travel
this broken pathway
where the sun does not dazzle

but claims company with
all these half-hidden things
and raising their gaze
does not ask of them wings –

fissures and grained dirt,
shucked shells and pebble,
a sprinkle of shatterings,
a grist of gravel

where the print and seal
the travelling foot has set
declares, Jorge Guillén,
the integrity of the planet.

At Bob Lucid's Place

There was enough of summer
in the autumn
to fill the entire afternoon
with sunlit colour,

and there was enough
of silence in the room
to lighten the burden of the city
as it filtered in

through curtains the air kept shifting,
raising among the leaves
of a magazine
tiny tidal sounds

as it breathed them open
and shut them again:
this pulse kept clear
a fluctuating frontier

between the room
and the traffic of feet
and cars negotiating
the intersection on the street

that awaited us,
the shadows of passers-by
advancing eagerly out of a sun
casting them forward from its blaze on the horizon.

At Hanratty's

I catch the flare of fire
at the kitchen door,
out of which emerges
a sweating ballet
of waiters and waitresses.
Do waiters, as Sartre wrote,
act quote waiting unquote? Here,
since half of them
are actors between shows,
the question grows more intricate.
That woman who is acting 'crying'
behind her quivering napkin,
down to the requisite *Boohoo*
(enunciated a little too clearly
to be quite true, however)
lowers her linen guard
to reveal – not the anticipated grin –
but a wet face, and feelings
that are painfully genuine. But do
waiters act? I think Derán does.
She is surprised that I
can recall her unusual name, and so
wants to hear from me what else I know.
She has a way of whirling past
like a small dervish, and indeed,
Turkish by descent, 'my parents'
she explains 'are Kurdies'.
Is this plural all her own,
or an affectionate diminutive
or – she is moving fast –
was it 'Kirghiz' she said?
I ask myself
what Turkish girl would wear
that unkempt head
of electric hair without curl
or unaffectedly try on
such innocent familiarity?
She acts like an American.
That stolid waiter
scarcely acts at all, I think:

we try his patience
by not ordering 'yet', and then
desert his table
(too close to the entrance): he remains
patient and willing
to lend an ear as he passes
to the lady in glasses who
wants to know 'where...' –
I cannot hear the rest
and neither can he
but, pivoting on one foot,
bends over closer
to seize her syllables.
Perhaps he, too, –
who knows? – was one of those
who grow into a patience they begin
by merely feigning.
The woman of tears
is leaving, her three
friends steering her by,
supporting her now silent distress
(I glimpse a dry face and eye)
to the door we must follow them through
out and on
into the stir of this street
of nationalities learning parts
that are new to them – of Juans
who would prefer
to be called John.

New York

Ode to San Francisco

'I write to you',
                    he explains,
'in blood,
             four of my friends
having died of late.'
                         He does not state
the cause.

                    It is strange
to live in a city where
                              one third of the males
may die of the same malady:
                              an ecclesiastic
of the cathedral is dying:
                              what he calls
'a caring relationship'
                              has brought him to it.
The writer of travelogues
                              is dying:
he continues to speak
                    of a tropical infection.
The shape on the side-walk
                              that cannot sit erect
against the sunlit wall
                    but falls forward
is dying –
              the placard beside the begging cup
is there to identify
                    the nature of his sickness.
The city
         has an air of medieval fatality.
I once thought it gay
                    (that damaged word),
then suddenly
              the bright towers
took on
         a look of such duplicity
I saw that the ocean
                    was too weak
ever to cleanse it,
                    although the home
of Venus herself –
                    though not of her son Eros.
Hesiod
       calls him the son of Chaos
but that was before
                    succeeding generations
spoke of him
              as that 'mischievous child'
Cupid
       thinking him half a joke.

Porto Venere

The older man
is bewitched by the boy
he is travelling with
across the bay:

the boy wears a hat with a brim
as a girl might
coquettishly, and is more
than beautiful to him.

This love has no context
except the day,
the ferry between two ports –
and then?

A walk in the sun
till the next boat comes
to return them where
the far shore glints in the marine sunglare

and the muscular waters
continue to lie –
heaving them to the harbour –
of an inexhaustible physicality

which the severing sea
and the rage of the goddess
who gave her name to this anchorage
keep to themselves forever.

September Swamp

The name of the bird that punctuates this swamp
   With its swamp-bird cries
I do not know: that it belongs here
   With that songless song – one
Unhurried, repeated note – is clear
   From the cicadas' dense, unchanging raga,
From the way the water, that scarcely stirs,

Is seeping invisibly beneath the green
That mantles a slow and certain course
    To the Susquehanna. The leaves that fall
On to this surface will never flow so far:
    All movement is below, save for the blue
Crackle of the dragonflies through static air,
    And turtles like the resurrecting dead, that raise
A serpentine neck and head, and then
    Ease free the whole armoured body,
Sloughing the weed aside, to climb
    A half-sunken log and taste
The luxury of light. They
    Are the consciousness of this place, its satisfaction,
Between the dragonflies' swift, aerial transaction
    And the unsunned fecundity that first gave rise
To swampsong, turtle and to dragonflies;
    That, under the weight of the September heat,
Is urging its furtive current towards open sea.

The House on the Susquehanna

A cat stalks by, treading
    From tie to tie of the railroad track
That runs between house and river.
    It is listening to the grass and does not see
The silent immensity of still water
    That flows with no more show of movement
Than the swamps that feed it – yet
    Can take possession of house and town
In one rising sweep. You can tell
    The current by the slight swell at the tips
Of the reflected trees – it scarcely ruffles
    Their riding image. The gleam on the surface
Might almost rekindle that dream
    Of pantistocracy in this spacious place
The dreamers never saw. The house
    On the shore is foursquare and of brick.
In the flailing grass, the cat has its mouse.

*Pantistocracy: this utopian community on the Susquehanna, where all should rule equally,
was the dream of Coleridge and Southey.*

North

It feels like the sea at first.
The raked tails of the planes
resemble the sails of yachts,
and one of these
sticking out from its hangar
is a trapped fish.
AIR NORTH it says
on our fuselage, the stem
on the right hand of the N
sprouting an arrow, and the plane
swings up and out to follow
the sign of that vane, converting
figure to actuality –
up into northair where
below, roads slim, turn
tentative in their approaches
to a landmass they can neither
enfold nor cross: forest:
a lake in the shape
of yet another fish
(how many fish
does that fish hold?)
and the metal of barn roofs,
silos, sending back
sun-morse, flickering
messages of habitation. Traffic
has thinned on the highways now:
an untidy settlement,
like a thousand, thrown-away
butts of cigarettes, a few,
symmetrical, and the rest
at ugly tangents to one another:
but this fades, too,
into the distances and more
lakes show through the twilight.
The pilot and co-pilot fit
(only a few feet ahead of us)
into a tiny cockpit:
one of them produces and then

spreads wide a map
so that it fills their entire
space: he seems to be checking
points on this
against points on the ground,
but is confused
by the twilight, till he has found
a hand-torch
which he focuses with care
onto the overlapping sheet and (yes)
we are there, almost, and begin
our descent now: down
into Chinese landscapes
of mist and pine, and we try
to read the reality
from the uncertainty of what we see
(is it a snowy contour
or the edges of moving tide
keeps riding in at the spot
where the mountains can hide no longer
the level land?). The wind
that plumps out the air-sock
on the landing field
is the measure of that cold
which strikes through the opening door,
then enfolds us entirely: night
and ahead the unending road,
sharpness of pine-scent, dead
skunk that clings to the tyre-treads
of the waiting car:
it beams us on, into the beginning
of yet more distances until,
downhill out of darkness,
we arrive suddenly at our destination,
drive in among the illumination
of wide-set streets, the town
lights at last of the clapboard north.

Geese Going South

Planing in, on the autumn gusts,
   Fleeing the inclement north, they sound
More like a hunting pack, hound
   Answering hound, than fugitives from the cold:
Flocks, skeining the air-lanes
   In stately buoyancy even seem
To dance, but one's weightless dream
   Of what they feel or are, must yield
The nearer they approach. I sense the weariness
   Of wings that bring them circling down
Onto this cut corn-field
   That offers small sustenance but rest
Among its husks and straw. Rest –
   Yet they continue calling from extended throats
As they did in flight, expending still
   Energies that they will not stint
Crying to one another – is it? – encouragement.
   I break cover for a clearer sight, but they
Instantly perceive this senseless foray
   No hunter would attempt: a thousand birds
At the snap and spread of a great fan,
   A winnowing of wings, rise up
Yelping in unison, weariness turned to power,
   And tower away to a further field
Where others are arriving. I leave them there
   On the high ridge snow will soon possess.
A moon that was rising as the birds came down
   Watches me through the trees. I too descend
Towards the firefly town lights of the valley.
   What does a goose, I ask myself,
Dream of among its kind, or are they all
   Of a single mind where moonlight shows
The flight-lanes they still strain towards
   Even in sleep? ... In sleep
The town beside these transient neighbours
   Scarcely dreams of their nocturnal presence
Awaiting dawn, the serpentine stirrings
   And restless moon-glossed wings,
Numb at arrival, aching to be gone.

Hamilton, USA

Upstate

Climbing across a mountain meadow,
    I was walking – I soon saw –
On no more than a word: 'meadow',
    With all its English aftertaste
Of luscious pasture, of spring flowers,
    Could conceal no longer now
The fact that I was bleeding: barbed stalks
    Had scored my ankles, grasses
Grudged me footroom. I should have come
    Booted and armoured against harm.
At the summit, once thorns had thinned,
    I lay outstretched and submitted to the charm
Of seeing only sky: the golden-rod
    Blotted the distances, thickly nodding
Across my eye-line. Sunbursts:
    And – between – the flickering blade of air
Declared the wind that was tossing the flowers
    And kept the blue so clear today,
Came straight from Canada. You could take
    The measure of arriving autumn here
In the cool, brisk stir that bent
    The woodland larches. Snow
Was invading my mind already as the chill
    Struck into summer. When I came downhill
I took to the wood. It was thicketed.
    Soon, my foot found out what seemed
A wandering border of small stones,
    Their order, or what was left of it,
A human order. Time here
    Rifts as sudden as the weather
In its displacements. They who had ploughed
    Or pastured their beasts where now
Thorn has undone endeavour, lay
    Under this scattering of headstones – some,
As I knelt down, I saw, engraved
    With date and name. History on these hills
Means yesterday, means barns
    And houses that have disappeared already
From the cleared spaces. A graveyard

In a wood, a brambled meadow – blood
Redefines the word – where growth renews
  Between the asphalt highroads and in view
Of the one constant that I hold in common
  With those who died and those who rode away –
The wide circuit of a mountainous horizon.

The Stair

The limbs of the giant spruce that leans
  So close to the house, have formed
A kind of stair, a walk-way
  Up to the summit. The squirrel that lives here
Scorns to descend it step by step,
  But with an insane bravado runs
To a branch end, then drops
  Accurately off and, six flights down,
Arrives upright, pine-cone in hand,
  To remain there, tear at and eat it:
Perfectly secure, he is perfectly sane.
  Today, comes snow. We should accept
The long-standing invitation
  To climb those now carpeted treads,
But snow and commonsense say no –
  Such analogues are not to be acted on.
And yet we inhabit our images: squirrel
  Can even seem a god of heights,
The tree his spruce fane. The animal
  Is asleep, and if he were not, he would be
Unconscious of the place devised which we
  Take into our minds and so ascend
The real by way of the imaginary tree:
  Both lean to the house together,
And, even without their deity, can teach
  These wooden walls that this house is a tree house:
We live in a place always just out of reach.

The Trees

The sunset light is singeing the horizon
    Above leafless woods, the freeze
Setting its seal on all the tilted
    Surfaces of the land, on roofs and road,
Till only the trees still stand out there
    In this after-midnight snow, ledge
On ledge of the pines weighed down,
    Fingers of fir shaped into distinctness
By the accumulating white. In the dark
    Of starless dawn, the first plough
Goes through, and early cars
    Armoured in ice, come crunching out
Over frost, their careful beams
    Brushing the trunks whose ancestors supplied
These clapboard walls outfacing still
    Deepening December and the chill to come.

Fire

About ship! Sweat in the south...
            Basil Bunting

'It will end in fire,' is what the sun
    Above Mayagüez repeats to the ocean,
And each wave re-tongues it west
    To Cuba and Mexico. The royal palm
Does not hunger and anger for apocalypse,
    But outgrows its own green crown,
Re-tips itself with that lance of green
    That bears a hawk, its beak
As sharp as the point it rides on
    Eyeing back glare. Light,
That is the servant of surfaces, must filter
    To feed its opposite – dark soil
Out of which frangipani and cinnamon
    (Crumple the leaf and you will catch the spice)

And all the growths you cannot name
   Hiding in one another's shade,
Cautiously approach that naked flame.
   But it is westering. The roosting pelican
Sits preening in his tree, prepares
   For the coming cool – foretaste
Of the freshness he must feel tomorrow
   As he dives for fish on fish, and sea
Opens its Eden to him, fire deferred
   In the wide transparency he plummets through.

Puerto Rico

December

They are decorating their concrete houses
against the coming season,
the fishermen and the fishermen's families.
Paint-pot in hand, or trailing a festoon
of fairy-lights along the roof,
they pause to say: *Buenas tardes.*
So little space
between them and the hurricane
if it should come this way off the ocean,
except for the single track we have taken.
It divides them from that sea
they cross with so little fear, boat tilted
by the rearward weight
of its outboard, prow
raised above the water
like a horse's neck,
one at the tiller and one
crouched in the scuppers
like the horse's rider.
At the pescadería
they are beaching their craft,
freezing the last of the catch
before the dark comes down.

The fishermen's chapel
has unglazed windows,
and their children, catechized
to the beat of the unbelieving sea,
are watched by the virgin from her boat of flowers,
a sliding pane
drawn between her and them
to keep her from rain and seaspray.
The day's end
stays friendly:
the grizzled fisherman who might almost be
one of the Galileans, asks
where it is we hail from,
and, told, tells us that he
— *o mi padre* —
comes from Corsica. The pelican flock —
natives to this place —,
so streamlined in flight,
look drably disreputable,
hunched half asleep already on their nesting tree.

Haçienda

What I like is when
men take a thing —
this river, say —
and, in the succinctest way,
use and transform it:
at the fall's head here
they have diverted
part of the flow:
a channel now
receives and passes on
through its downhill slot
all of the directed
force that is not
there in untaught nature:
the compacted stream

angles out three ways – one
turns a turbine
to refine the coffee bean;
two flows through
to a grist mill; three
concentrates into
a swirling rush to fill
the open-air jacuzzi
of planter and family –
then, each rill
released from its man-made
duty shoots out and on
back to its bed
at the foot of the fall,
re-joining itself again to spread
under palm and plantain
across the valley floor,
once more a river.

The Autograph Tree

on whose leaves
you can write your name –
or not, if you prefer
to admire the integrity
of the smooth green skin
that can withstand
salt spray and the Caribbean wind.
Privateers used them
as playing cards,
and the penknife
of the passionate engraver
keeps reminding them
Pedro loves Maria,
the ovate heart
that he incises
echoing the leafshape
at an uncertain angle.

Among flaring neighbours,
rises the flower –
a modestly paper-white affair,
as starkly there as the page
no one has written on.

Crossing Aguadilla

Crossing Aguadilla, we get stalled in traffic.
Only patience will see us through: everyone is in town.
How is it these excitable Caribbeans can stay so patient?
Their sense of time must be quite different from our own.
On our way in, the road was already barred
by a procession. A girl with a hard voice
made scratchily severe by amplification, was reading to the walkers
through a microphone passages of scriptural exhortation,
and penitents kept falling on their knees in the dust of the roadway.
Now we are caught between cars, and a blue dragonfly
brightly enamelled as if with car paint
dodges among the scarcely moving cavalcade, and then
floats off to vanish against sea as blue as itself.
Nothing to do but sit here with open windows
that let in the heat and the salsa music,
or roll slowly forward
past the Charismatic Church, the Miracle Pharmacy,
the patch of park where a tiny train
(el tren infantil) with children in it
is going round and round its circular track.
The feather dusters of the sugar-cane blossoms
wave to us from beyond the houses in open country,
but we cannot get there yet out of our half-pleasant purgatory.
We drift in low gear translating the signs –
there is a street here called Absence and another
Happy Days. Next to a McDonald's
large letters say: Jesus is Coming
Prepare yourself. Those for whom these words are meant
continue shopping, as imperturbably intent
as the driver of el tren infantil
that goes on stolidly circling and circling as if for ever.

San Juan

Coming here is like returning to Europe.
The cathedral, marooned among the parked cars,
dates back to Drake who tried
and failed to take the place. Cumberland brought a fleet
and stormed the handsome fort: plague caught him there,
unclosed his grip. Came the Dutch –
these walls withstood them: their masonry is still good.
Down a vista outside of architectural history,
cars file beneath palms to the airport
(the hurricane that leaned on them last week
has left them splayed, or merely brushless broomsticks),
and the ground-crew are standing around our plane,
their shadows projected in front of them
towards this machine that is concentrating their attention.
The flock of egrets beside the runway do not move
as the engines spark into life: they have heard it all before:
if they wished – and they do not – they, too, could be
hanging in the blue above the unseen sharks, or inland,
above roads themselves sinuously in flight
and hardly to be followed out by eye,
hidden by hills as green as England.

From Gloucestershire

a letter to Les Murray

I thought of you and of your farm down under –
They were shearing sheep here in the valley field.
Three men. They'd brought their women with them.
The men seemed roughish and the women wild.

I thought of your place once more when I heard them speak.
'Australian?' I said. 'New Zealand,' one replied.
God, how quickly they could strip a sheep
And turn it loose from the fleece it hid inside.

And all sought out their lambs, almost the same
In size, now they had shuffled off that wool,
Stick-legged, kicking jerkily out of it,
Strange in their nakedness, their udders full.

The women folded the fleeces, each as deft
As the sweating shearsmen underneath the trees.
Nuclear Free I read on one of their shirts:
Not joking now, they were civilized in their ease.

At the end of the day one of the men resumed,
'You always get wrong our accents over here.'
'How did you come?' 'Plane to Los Angeles.
Arizona... Las Vegas... half America.'

Shearsmen and poets travel far these days –
Think of the miles we'd covered when we met
Where dry Judaea spreads for the Bedouin
A sparser pasture than our English wet.

The field now is empty of sheep, the migrants gone.
Homebound, they must circle the world again,
Itself a traveller through space and season,
Trailing the wool wisp vapour of their jetplane.

Sight and Sound

A floating crane
is unloading boulders
from the boat beside it
and transferring them to the tip
of the harbour bar, extending it
in a protective arm far out
into the bay. The crash
of each stone
brings a flash of white
up out of the blue
and a ripple that still has not ceased

to spread before the next
wedding of stone and water
on a risen sea-bed.
The progress –
boulder from boat to sea –
fills a precise three
minutes and then the crane
that has swivelled and swung,
reached into the load and come
back clutching the stone of its choice,
will repeat the arc again
gracefully as before.
Seen from here
the whole operation is silent
(which clearly it cannot be)
and when the load has gone
and both crane and boat set out to sea,
they depart in a majestic, mute cortège
until, suddenly free
of all obstruction
the distance and the air transmit
the engine-beat,
the unhurried pulse of this retreat across the bay,
a single wake cut white behind it.

A Glade

of hawthorn trees,
          laid bare
on the seaward side
          by the constant
flow of sea air,
          clung to the cliff:
on the one hand
          minute, burnt leaves –
whole leafless branches
          knotted together
by the grey-green lichen

                              that encased them;
on the other –
                    red and flourishing –
berries the birds
                    fed from gratefully:
what gave the mind
                              pause in that place
and cause
          to dwell on,
was the way
              the force
of the air had pressed
                              dead boughs
and living into one
                         close intertexture
that roofed in
               a moss-floored room,
a sanctum
             suspended for as long
as the cliff held
                    that was losing ground
already
          to the sea beneath.

The Choice

Between a field of barley and the sea,
Which would you choose to own ten acres of
In substance and in sound? The groundswell pours
Its repetitions in at open doors
Of sense, and shares the threshold with the dry
Sea-whisper of a million beards of barley.
This shimmering estate through which the same
Rumour is running as disturbs the grain,
Dark as the soil and deeper than the roots,
Offers you ownerless rows on rows whose fruits
Are all that happens between sight and sunlight,
Between blue and white. Which will you choose?

On the Shannon

for John Scattergood

Gulls, working their way upstream,
   Turn suddenly dazzling as the sun
Brings the colour of the gorse to life
   On the plain behind them. Here
Where the river loops lazily past
   The walls of Clonmacnóis, two towers
Confront them, from whose crevices
   The nesting jackdaws call, call
Their dark ungainly cries. It is they
   Should be the marauders following the way
The first attackers came and blackened
   The place with fire. That was before
The giant kicked down the castle
   Past whose fragments the gulls fly in,
As white as the spirits of those monks would be
   Risen and returning here to see
Their ruins occupied, hearing beyond these cries
   The silence that first drew them to the spot
Solid throughout the sky, and far below,
   The hardly audible waters still bending by.

In a Cornish Church

Lady of alabaster,
you hold in your skirtfolds
your dead children,
and you wait
for that great day
whose explanation
will be clear;
and why so many of you came
only to die here,
leaving no memory
except this unnamed stone

will then appear
perhaps. Till when
you in your whiteness
will abide
as patient as the ammonite
coiled in the cliff,
as if you waited
to reclaim from silence
your living children and your name.

Response to Hopkins

What by your measure is the heaven of desire...?

Camomile sweetens the cliff-top grass:
   Below, vivid uncertainties disturb
The massing of these waters: you would not think
   That the tide was receding where they beat,
As the wind piling wave on wave
   Pulls against the insistence of the moon.
And do they belong to the sea or to the sky
   These purples and these greens? The water
Washing its predilections from the eye,
   Carries such light in it, that when the hawks
Red-brown flash by, their colour
   Lightens at the reflection from beneath. Above,
All kinds of cloud – cumulus climbing,
   Fair weather dapple and horizon mist,
Fill up the air-lanes all the way
   Inland to Dartmoor. Their shadows
Move on the waste, hastening across,
   Masking each sunburst and so transform
Space to an inland sea awaiting storm.
   What by my measure is the heaven of desire?
This inconstant constancy – earth, water, fire.

Hartland Cliff

What did we walk into
above that sea?
Our talk persuaded time, perhaps,
that there might be

exceptions to time,
if not to tide
across the bay we lay beside
that dry July.

The oyster-catchers
with raised wings there
balancing on the rocks, ignored
all the airy lures of elsewhere.

And we watched them hover
and poise, sub-theme
and accompaniment
to the waking dream

we had walked into:
I cannot say
whether we stopped the turning world:
time flowing, yet not away,

was at the full along that coast and we
had at our feet
a double sea –
not quite a poem, yet

only the turns of verse
could contain and then let go
the accumulation of that flow
to the shift of light

late afternoon brings
– to the reshaping of the waters
by a moon unseen,
to the sheen and spread of wings.

Song

To enter the real,
how far
must we feel beyond
the world in which we already are?

It is all here
but we are not. If we could see
and hear only half
the flawed symphony,

we might cease
nervously to infer
the intentions of
an unimaginable author

and stand,
senses and tongues unbound,
in the spaces of that land
our fathers brought us to,

where, what will be well
or not well,
only time
or time's undoing can tell.

Second Song

On each receding bush,
the stipple of snow today
has posted into the distance
this silent company

on the alert for openings
which yesterday were not there,
tracking through field and covert
into the fullness here;

and not on bushes only,
but on stump, root, stone —
why is it a change of weather merely
finds directions where there were none? —

so that each Roman road,
on entering the maze,
crosses the hills in confusion
at the infinity of ways

only a little snow
has chalked in everywhere,
as if a whole landscape might be unrolled
out of the atmosphere.

February

February is the mad month for the fox, the wind
Carries its call now the animal grows blind
With the lust that is hollowing its side,
And darkness darkens the hoarse note of that need.
Daylight comes to our solitary window:
Waking, you see how many creatures go
By night on errands as urgent as those calls,
With all the restless encirclings round our walls
Writ large on the brilliant emptiness out there,
Imprinting the snow of a populous thoroughfare.

The Broom

the new wife's tale

I listened hard. I do not believe in ghosts.
    The house was changing. Indeed, I never saw
Such thorough renovation. 'You do not know',
    She said, 'how many ghosts there were

Needed to be laid. The dead
   Don't bury their dead: only the living
Can do that for them – they go on breeding.
   In room after room she multiplied herself
And lay in wait. For him, not me.
   Yet one bright day I entered my own kitchen,
Or almost did – inside the door
   The sight of a broom scratched to and fro.
It was the sound – dry, rasping
   Across the quarries – first made me see it,
Stopped me. It was familiar enough, a stark
   Discordant blue I'd never cared for.
I hurried through expecting the cleaning woman.
   Nobody there, of course... It was things
She seemed to cling to – a clock, a chair,
   Now this (it was she had bought it)
Left leaning against the wall, but then I saw –
   Whatever it was she'd meant by it – that I
Must sweep the place clean
   Of all she was re-living or imagining.' Determination
Flawed lines in her young face. I do not believe
   In ghosts, except for the one she saw almost.

On a Passage from Hardy's Life

You were a poet who put on the manners of ghosts,
Thinking of life not as passing away but past,
Taking the ghost view of surrounding things,
A spectre who, making his calls in the mornings,
Found satisfaction in his lack of solidity
Before he had entered into true non-entity.
Even in paradise, what you would wish for,
Would be to lie out in the changing weathers here,
And feel them flush through the earth and through you,
Side by side with those you had known, who never quite knew you,
Dreaming a limbo away of loam, of bone,
One Stygian current buoying up gravestone on gravestone.

A Note Left on Finding Two People Asleep

There is a point between our houses where
Comes a sudden lightening of the air
In the dog-days, a breeze that gratefully flows
As an earnest of refreshing company,
When we shall sit beneath your trees and hear
The musical trickle of the stream descend
From pool to pool, imagining the theme,
The 'little phrase' in the sonata of Vinteuil
To have been like that – first stated there
Where the breeze breaks in, to be repeated by
The voices in your sleep, the falling water
And the turning leaves of the long books of July.

Before the Concert

If I could lay hold
on this glass of water and the stable
transparency of its contents
that contain an image of the table

on which it stands – under the glass
a draped, red cloth –
then I should possess not only
that coolness and that red, but both

of the foreshortened lutes
waiting to make music there,
under a curving window
on either side of the reflected score,

but the lutenist
(whose throat is sore today)
lowers a Brobdingnagian hand
and takes away

this universe, and I
watch it wash and disappear
over the threshold of his dryness,
until it's clear –

those minute instruments,
their world quicksilvering into water
under a melting window –
that is a room I shall never enter.

The Prisoner

This prismatic
green-glass
stopper
of a bottle
long destroyed
stands in the light
from our window where
it has taken up
the grey-white
shell shard
sharing the ledge
beside it: this,
which you might suppose
unchangeable and hard,
it transforms into
the image of a man who
sits there in a hat
– in this vitreous prison
a tight fit –
with one arm
(his left) bent
sideways to accommodate it
better: the top
of the inverted stopper
(now its base)
raises him up

in miniature majesty
on a sort of dais:
the awkward angularity
of the arm and the confinement
of the head confess
such a discomfort
and rigidity, it seems
as if this monarch of littleness
were only waiting
for someone to
remove the shard and thus
permit him to break out of his dream –
and this he does
the instant that I do.

On a Collage of Marie José Paz

A scrap in this house
of patches, a landscape
photograph opens
a window on a tree. Where

are we? She
has cleared a space
out of elements
neither here nor there.

By the stair of sight,
from the side we cannot see,
I climb down into it,
all at once free

in this tiny confine
I can compare
only to the atmosphere we breathe
in a poem's stanza –

stanza, indeed,
this image that makes room for
entrance, this interior
turned inside out

towards the eye
and the eye's body, the clear
pane of air,
the being here.

On a Glass Engraving by Peter David

At first sight,
there is nothing to see —
only when he has set
the goblet turning
in its lit cabinet
does the stippled surface
become depth, the image
solidify: his diamond,
among jungle densities
of a summer day,
discovers a tiger,
whose level look
takes us for its prey,
and walls, leaves,
water, all
now burn
from the shadows
above the swirl
of a still, vitreous
whirlpool, where the bowl
arrives at its base and stem:
this glassy water
seems like the pool of origin
at which his dark forms
drink in their light,
but that illumination

flows from the wrist and firm
hand of this zoologist
trained to measure
the minute. His microscope
opens two ways –
the world and the mind's eye
curving together
round this speckled frieze.

Portraits of Hands: Hals

Could one guess
the face from the hand? –
this one that grasps, and that
which languishes
lapped in its glove.
It is the well-articulated skeleton
shows in this dandy's
dangling fingers.
An unseen hand
is in hiding
within the snouted crown
of a hat the other hand,
spaced to its swell,
spreads out fingers over. These
old woman's knuckled hands
lie layered
one above the other,
a single finger ringed.
That hand,
about to flow away in paint,
steadies suddenly
grasping the arm of a chair.
The pinch-of-snuff
finger and thumb take hold
of a circular hat-brim.
The hand on hip
of the I beyond all fellowship

beside the clasped
hands of the husband and his bride.
And they accuse this brush
of 'show', but what can they
surmise of a variety whose eyes
deny it daily?

On a Dutch Picture

This realist knew there are no such clouds
   As those that ply the painted heights
Of his flatland sky. He had seen
   All kinds, no doubt, containing
Every sort of weather, and waiting for a word
   Out of the sea, to say at last
Which of the weathers it was to be.
   He might well have shown the moment
When cloud-bars in evening sky
   Seem to be moveless, were it not
For the still mass of a single tree
   They are drifting towards. But he preferred
To fill his upper air with shapes
   Wholly imaginary, that scale the canvas space
Like his tentative painter's mind
   Finding its way, feeling how far
He has left behind the land down there,
   Hoveringly revealing what is real
In its green extension towards light that catches
   On the steel of sea where it edges against the polder.

The Discovery

The summer the stream
dried up we tried
following its bed
deep between the high
tree-shut-in banks
almost a tunnel:
no one had walked
that way before
nor could they
now the water reoccupies
the course we clambered:
our cries at finding
stones shaped to our delight
echoed and re-
echoed chambered
in earth and leaves:
if no one
followed us into
the dusty shingle then
we were the first
and last men on the moon

Lunar

There is no water on the moon, no sound of it:
  Valleys of deafness, giant crania
Split and upended to contain the glare
  Of white-cold light reflected.
Untouchable and untouching, in weighted gear,
  Those who walked here have left behind
The tread of bootprints going nowhere:
  Wind cannot ruffle or weather stain
The flag they planted in this desert whiteness,
  The star-ray that catches the unmoving ensign
Iridescing with the colours of a world away.

The Morning Moon

The morning moon
that I failed to see
appeared to stop (you tell me)
above the house-top,

as if it were itself
the sole luminary of day,
shining after frost
out of a cloud-clear sky:

in my picture of the scene
the sun is lost to me,
with this high visitant
in the zenith of the mind's eye.

Mapped, without motion,
so starkly near, so far,
that which I never saw hangs
as still as the pole star.

Picking Mushrooms by Moonlight

Strange how these tiny moons across the meadows,
Wax with the moon itself out of the shadows.
Harvest is over, yet this scattered crop,
Solidifying moonlight, drop by drop,
Answers to the urging of that O,
And so do we, exclaiming as we go,
With rounded lips translating shape to sound,
At finding so much treasure on the ground
Marked out by light. We stoop and gather there
These lunar fruits of the advancing year:
So late in time, yet timely at this date,
They show what forces linger and outwait
Each change of season, rhyme made visible
And felt on the fingertips at every pull.

JUBILATION
1995

For a Granddaughter

1 On the Terrace

Blest the infant Babe...

Four of the generations are taking tea,
Except that one of them is taking milk:
It is an English, autumnal afternoon,
The texture of the air half serge, half silk.

It is an English, autumnal afternoon,
And all four of the seasons are sitting here,
Except that one of them lies interfused
With the flesh that feeds, the arm that cradles her.

The seasons are talking in a fugue of voices,
Except that she is trying out the sounds
Through which her tongue must learn to reach the words
To speak with the world which summons and surrounds

Her kindling senses: the circumference
Of many circles draws her from her warm
Dark continuity with all things close,
To know more than the flesh, the food, the arm –

That circle within the talking circle here,
By the old house, its stone-flagged passageway,
Within the circle of the lawn, the flowers, the trees,
The young attention widening where they sway.

2 To Be Read Later On

Poets, my dear, are much the same as you:
Watching whatever shapes come into view,
They try a murmur, a melodious sound
To suit the sense of what it is they've found
And go on finding, as they write and pause,
Their aim as much the wonder as the cause.
I watched today what would have pleased you, too –

The shadows on the curtains where they blew
In at the window, shadows that showed how
(The frame quite rigid, yet the lines one flow)
Wrought metal can turn molten in the sun
Leaping along the muslins as they run,
A whirl of lattices, a flying net,
The whole breath of the day caught up in it.
Mallarmé (a poet you must read)
Wrote of une dentelle abolie – indeed
The sun writes on a curtain and erases
(In going out) those lines that are its phrases.
Whether the conflict is a birth aborted,
A Work unconsummated he had courted
(You'll spot the allusion when you read his verse
Or hear how Boulez makes the terse more terse),
For us that flowing through the window space
Could only fill more full the blowing lace,
As if our futures – yes, both mine and yours –
Were breathed towards us off the Severn's shores,
And when you lift this poem to your ear
One day, it is that breath of ocean you will hear.

3   Jessica Learned to Kiss

Jessica learned to kiss,
Yet never would
Kiss me. This

Withholding of a kiss
Seemed to be
Part of her glee
At parting.

Or was she
Wise enough to see
That to defer
Made time doubt
Its hold on her
And me?

At all events
Only this week,
Perhaps disenchanted
With philosophic teasing,
A kiss she planted
On my cheek.

4   *After Hugo*

Jeanne songeait...

She was dreaming, sitting on the grass:
Her cheek was pink, her gaze was grave:
'Is there anything you would like to have?'
(I try to anticipate her least desire
To find what it is that sets her thoughts on fire.)
'Some animals,' she said – just that, no more:
I showed her an ant in the grass – 'There you are!'
But her imagination was left half-fed:
'No. Real animals are big,' she said.
Children dream of the vast, the ocean draws,
Cradles and calms them on the shore
With its rough music; its shadowiness
Will wholly captivate a child's mind,
And so will the terrifying flight of the sea-wind.
They love to be terrified, need wonder, feel no distress.
'I have no handy elephant,' I replied,
'So would you like something else? – just say what.'
Pointing a small finger at the sky, she answered 'That!'
Evening would be overtaking the world soon –
I saw climbing up above the horizon an immense moon.

5   *Pavane for a Live Infanta*

How would you like to wear
a yellow dress
such as this
in Velázquez's picture?
Your brocade
will make you feel at first

a little staid
perhaps, and so
you must learn
to dance the pavane, a slow
dance in which
your skirts will sail
over the sea-floor
of this giant palace
as noiselessly
as a painted ship.
The painter pauses:
he knows that he
can render only
your presence here
but not your movement.
Your favourite dog
has the air
of sitting for his portrait,
but has fallen asleep,
which only goes to show
how peaceful and how slow
a pavane can be,
and how skilfully
you dance it, gliding
past his nose
unespied. Your meninas
– your waiting maids –
cluster round
to slow more and more
your pace: they
and your dwarves
Maribarbola and Nicolás
think that your gait must grow
ever more sedate,
so that the artist can
at last proceed
to contemplate
you of the pavane
in utter stillness.

6   *To My Daughter*

'Families', I said, conscious that I could not find
    The adequate epithet, 'are nice.'
'Nice families', you replied, adding
    To the faded adjective a tiny spice,
'Are nice.' What I had meant was this:
    How far we (a wandering family) have come
Since that day I backpacked you down
    Into an Arizona canyon with its river
Idling below us, broad and slow;
    Next, it was the steady Susquehanna;
Now swifter currents of the Severn show
    That time is never at a stand, although the daughter
You are leading by the hand, to me
    Seems that same child cradled in Arizona.
No – you are right –: *nice* will never do:
    But it is only families can review
Time in this way – the ties of blood
    Rooting us in place, not like the unmoving trees,
And yet, as subject to earth, water, time
    As they, our stay and story linked in rhyme.

Against Travel

These days are best when one goes nowhere,
The house a reservoir of quiet change,
The creak of furniture, the window panes
Brushed by the half-rhymes of activities
That do not quite declare what thing it was
Gave rise to them outside. The colours, even,
Accord with the tenor of the day – yes, 'grey'
You will hear reported of the weather,
But what a grey, in which the tinges hover,
About to catch, although they still hold back
The blaze that's in them should the sun appear,
And yet it does not. Then the window pane
With a tremor of glass acknowledges
The distant boom of a departing plane.

The Cypresses

The cypresses are hesitating whether to move,
as though they could advance uphill if only they wished.
Then they go completely still; they are shamming dead –
they feel something is about to occur
and they want to be unnoticed by it.
Suddenly, we learn what it is:
the lake below, having lain in a Götterdämmerung light all
                                                    afternoon,
disappears beneath cloud and rain. Now
the cypresses are losing their composure, but only a little.
They do not toss to the Byronic thunder music –
their foliage is too compact for that;
the brushed-up look of this leafy chevelure
has an electrical restraint about it.
Only a stirring at their very tips gives them away,
though the two just outside the window
begin conferring together, then one of them
perceptibly shudders through its entire length: rain
has arrived here too and the full force of it takes them
and – yes – twists and pummels and pushes them out of the true –
they who were the only plumblines on this uneven slope,
and the sense of the vertical goes out in a blackness
that might have been drained from them. The rain and the
                                                    lightning
show that the unsubjective south does not start here: you are free
to read into this sunless ferocity
the presence of a tortuous god who hides his intentions
in smoke, and hints at them with explosions of light
right down to the bottom of this seething pit. Then the rain
climbs off, the trees come into focus once more
momentarily clear, and through the gaps in the foliage
you can see the lake again across which a ferry is passing:
it enters a gap and leaves it (it takes
five seconds for a craft to sail through a cypress tree).
Even the gulls are in circulation once more,
going round and round, stark white above the still-dark lake.
The cypresses overcome their uncertainty – this time
they are not going to be recognized – and emerge in disguise:
their clumps and companies have evidently

turned into a convocation of tall, thin clerics
poised at the foot of the incline on their way to a shrine
somewhere up at the summit. The pair of trees nearer at hand –
a tall one beside a smaller – are a mother and child,
the mother gigantic and the child likely to take after her,
though keeping its distance while listening intently upwards.
Thunder still resounds through the mountains
and the convocation has not yet moved away.
The ferry boat is re-establishing the timetable of the everyday:
Bellagio, Menaggio, Varenna, Bellano…
The shrine is catching the last light now
or is it merely an outcrop of white rock just by the peak
needing no further miracle or shaping story
to be what it is?

Lago di Como

Sun must first filter through a haze
    That eats whole mountains here. How lonely
Those mountains would be without our presence.
    For only we can tell back to them their surfaces,
Their whites which absorb so many shades,
    Those surfaces accepting so much shadow
Into their clefts and crevices, yet marbling with light
    The lake beneath them, so that mountains stand
On columns that cross the waters, columns
    That undulate in flakes of white and gold.
This is the story told back to the mountains
    And, as evening begins, must be re-told,
To these summits taken by white fire
    From a sun that is already going, has not yet
Gone down behind the further shore whose crags
    Are climbing blackly upwards into silhouette.

Varenna

Waiting for the ferry
we watch the late sun
gilding inordinately
the lakeside town

and the lake itself,
as if to insist that we
need look no further:
immanence is mystery

where the column of sundown
reflects in a vertical
tall encroachment
like flickering oil,

shoots into the harbour
flames that wrestle and dance
through each undulation
of the travelling substance,

till a peak comes between
and the fire-threads fray
and the darkening water
ferries night through the bay.

Asolo

for Rosa Scapin

Fountains of limestone, limestone colonnades
   Reverberating like wells, porticoes of shade
And against the sky the dark of cypresses:
   Browning brought them back from Tuscany
To stand against the sunset. Terraces
   Could not mark the gradation of a hill
More exactly than their ranks, and when the sun
   Climbs down behind them, one
By one they offer it their stair
   To steady its descent then disappear.

To Vasko Popa in Rome

'Rome I dislike,' you said in French,
　'With its imperial pretensions.' You
Were the least imperious of men, in verse
　And person. We met only once again
And it was clear your days were near their end,
　Your life and death feeding on cigarette
On cigarette. 'Like a prince in exile,'
　Someone said, but that seemed fanciful for a man
Indifferent to empire. You were in exile from yourself,
　From that puzzled ebullience, watchful irony,
Balanced, it seemed almost bodily –
　For you were then a man of ample flesh –
Between Gallic precision, Italian largesse,
　As our conversation veered from tongue to tongue
In search of words adequate to express
　Our sense of the occasion. As to princeliness, I recall
Hearing you muse, 'Hughes, they say,'
　(Crossing the Borghese park near midnight)
'Lives like a prince.' 'That's true,'
　Was my reply, 'if generosity's what they intend,
And if you are his guest or friend, it's you
　Who live like one.' Pacing on,
Complaining of the melancholy great cities breed,
　As if all generosity must feed that, too,
You drew your gloom from a reserve of riches
　That soon must fail. In Rome, today,
I almost persuade myself you would agree
　That the bounty of the place exceeds pretension,
Bursting on one, as when the roar
　Of the Trevi fountain rounds the corner of its square;
And that these levels of wrought stone and water –
　Metamorphosis over an ungiving ground –
Are one more form of poetry, and we
　Guests of the imagination here. The imagination
Proposes what it does not need to prove
　And, when all's said and done, what cannot be:
Now we shall never pace this square together
　Through the Roman sunlight and the autumn air.

San Carlo ai Catinari

An angel orchestra
have just fluttered down
in stone and settled on the rim
of the dome to hymn
Saint Cecilia.

I admire this scene
so far above my head
for its solidity: these
are no shadowy presences
but flesh and stone inter-inanimated.

If we were angels
we could no doubt hear
their silent music
fleshed in the substance
of another sphere –

A sphere that sense
enters but rarely and when it does,
gathers more palpable evidence
of what it is
so delights it here.

For what could heaven imply
but the increase and care
of each tuned faculty
turning to attend and praise,
imaged in that high consort there.

Roman Fugue

Beyond the window
from their rooftop terrace
the backs of three
statuary busts
gazing apparently

towards a striped awning
builders have draped
before their operation
on a pilastered
and arched façade: half
a builder – cut in two
by that sheet or screen –
walks an unseen plank
intently searching
for something just out of view
ignored by the procession
above his head
of small clouds crossing the Roman blue
in contrary motion.

Gutenberg and the Grapes

for Bill Murphy

Watching them turn the screw
tighter, tighter
above the press
he knew at last
what it was
he was looking for:
it must have been
the winey air
had opened his senses
and imprinted the secret there
as the great block
bit into pulp below
and the wine-clock clink
of the machine
ticked towards a time
beyond him like the strokes
on an anvil: the copiousness
of the grape was filling
the cask before his eyes:
wine had gone to press.

Horizons

for Bruna Dell'Agnese

'That imaginary, uncrossable line we call
    Horizon': it is, of course, illusion
Like so much else, and yet our eyes
    In their myopia surprise the truth. I stand
Where a hill above the cliff takes in
    Not one but two horizons – land
And, as if the deluge hung in momentary abeyance,
    The blue curvature of the sea above it,
Impending with its weight of liquid acres.
    But, no, what we carry from the scene
Is less the image's apocalyptic threat
    Than that parallel measure, as intangible
And clear a presence as the spanning rainbow,
    That goes on telling us the world is there
And what shape it has, the bow itself
    Nothing but sunlight, water, air.
That imaginary, uncrossable line
    Confronts us with as fine a demarcation
As the sailing, selvedged clouds
    Balancing along the wind and above the sea
Their changing images true and imaginary.

Valestrieri

for Astrid Donadini

The bridal veils of the olive trees, you said,
    Seeing the white nets spread
Underneath the boughs. But these
    Slung higher to catch the crop
In its fall are the hammocks of the autumn voyage
    Into winter, swung in the after-gale
That follows the first bright cold
    Cutting mist, bringing back sun

Into the orchards here. They have cleared the ground
    Of its brush where the nets must lie –
There is to be no waste – and all is readied
    For the slow maturing of berries still green.
But the echo of volleys through the colder air
    Bursts from the presence of huntsmen there, unseen,
Lying low claiming consummation now
    In the pattering ricochet of aim on spendthrift aim.

Down from Colonnata

A mist keeps pushing between the peaks
    Of the serrated mountains, like the dust
Off marble from the workings underneath:
    Down from Colonnata you can hear
The quarrymen calling through the caves
    Above the reverberation of their gear
Eating through limestone. We are moving
    And so is the sun: at each angle
Of the descending road, the low light
    Meeting our eyes, surprises them whenever
It reappears striking a more vivid white
    From the crests behind us. Down
And on: the distance flashes up at us
    The flowing mercury of the sea below
That we, passing Carrara, lose
    Until it shows once more backing the plain.
But the sun has outdistanced us already,
    And reaching the level water, dipped
Beneath it, leaving a spread sheen
    Under the final height dividing us,
And across the liquid radiance there,
    A palpitation of even, marble light.

A Retrospect: 1951–91

We go down by the deserted mule-track:
    Myrtle berries and purple daisies overhang
This unused pathway of cracked stones
    The walls wind round with. It leads
Between netted olive trees and enters
    La Serra from above, down past the house
Its poet was born in, that will one day –
    This is a country of inscriptions – bear
Let into its wall, a crisp-cut *lapide*.
    You could still hear his mother tongue
(His mother's tongue) if only you
    Could speak it and could call out to
That woman who descends in front of us,
    Her kindling carried on her head as when
We first came here to streets that have withstood
    Corsair and scimitar. A poor place then,
But its stone severity hospitable
    With wine and conversation round a fire
That stung the eyes with woodsmoke. She
    That solid apparition, has disappeared
Along her alley, as we turn to cross the square,
    Into a rawness blowing off the bay
That tells how the season and the world
    Are travelling to where these forty years began
In a tumultuous autumn of seastorm, cold and rain.

The poet in line 7 is Paolo Bertolani, author of the dialect poems 'Seina'.

Portuguese Pieces

for Gualter and Ana Maria Cunha

1 *Alto Minho*

Não, não é nesse lago entre rochedos...
Pessoa

Bees move between the rosemary and the rose.
The oranges are waiting to be picked.
The coigns of granite by the threshing floor,
The inscription of the runic mason's mark
Ask to be clarified by the hidden sun.
(Later, it will break along the river
To show where the waters of the floodtide reached
And stained with mud the lower leaves of trees
The colour of stone, a petrine fringe reflecting
In the calm beneath...)
Here, bread and reality are reconciled
By the excellence of maize, the spread hunks.
We are eating honey in a granite house.

Quinta do Baganheiro

2 *Ponte de Lima*

Lima was *limes*, limit –
beyond the river, only the mountains.
On its bank, the alameda of tall plane trees, now,
and ghostly washing
that catches the final light, the flow
of still-warm air. The blade
of the river is broken
by the housetops and the trunks
that rise between the eye and it
on the brink of the unimaginable,
its sinuosities unclear.
Was it *limes* or *limen*, limit or threshold?
They called it Lethe, the Romans, and bridged it.
Their bridge is still here.

3 *Soajo*

A glitter of particles
embedded in bedrock –
no asphalt here: a jigsaw of granite
paves the village square.
Granite curves the well-kerb,
granite guards the grain:
from a dais of staddlestones
looms a mausoleum for maize
that rings the hill-top
with tombs for a dynasty of kings.

4 *Swallows*

Swallows outshout
the turbulent street:
swallows are messengers
where the day and night meet,
bringing news
from gods older than those
who pose in the gold interiors,
on the tiled cloister wall;
and a swallow it was
that arrowed past
threatening to graze you,
but delivered itself instead,
disappeared into
the dark slot above
a lintelled doorhead.

5 *Oporto: St John's Eve*

At this pagan festival of St John,
Churchkeys click in the shut lock.
Gilt and silver glint from the resonant dark.
Their surfaces are playing with the fire
Youth is leaping through outside.
The iron parapet
Sways with the crowd's weight

Above the river. In hillslope spate
Sheer saturnalia flows.
Are those salutations blessings or hammer blows?
The midnight churches are looking the other way,
Like the public plinths
Where sculpted deeds are done,
And the bedraggled Eagle still cedes to Wellington.

6   *In Lisbon*

At the Versailles
The waiter talks of his pride in the place,
With its ornate soffits, mirrors, glistening wood.
Once, he had gone to look upon the face
Of the real Versailles
To see how the two compared, and found
The ceilings in the apartments of the Pompadour
Were just like these... Pessoa, all around,
Demolitions are dragging your city down,
And cranes constructing the blank bank architecture
The future will know us by. At the Versailles
We reconsider the Pompadour and find
Only by style will you engage the affections of the mind.

7   *Tagus, Farewell*

It is a very filtered light
    Permits this fine gradation of the fields
From the passing train. It is the cloud decides
    The softness of these shades of green. This
Is an English summer scene renewed
    To eyes returning from Iberia's blaze
On glittering granite: Tagus, farewell.
    When Wyatt came, with spur and sail,
Back into Kent and Christendom, and found
    Thames like a bent moon-bow,
The river running through English ground
    Exposed 'her lusty side', mistress
Or doubtful bride. So she remains
    In this same world of whim, of trade and trains.

But the light deals no deceit that sees
    The same month ripening now that brought
Wyatt to England and unease, a mind in woe,
    Closed to the sweet complexities of weather.

Zipangu

for Yoshiko Asano

1   *The Pines at Hakone*

The pine trees will not converse with foreigners. Their aim
is to hide everything that lies beneath their crisp, dense foliage
or at their feet – those ferns, for instance, that reproduce
the pine pattern on every leaf and lie low
the air scarcely stirring them. They have learned
to keep secrets by studying the tall trunks that surround them
and that might still be living in the Edo period.
Touched by the breeze, they rock on their pliant roots
and shift slightly their green vestments, beginning to oscillate,
to lean from side to side, even to bow –
though not deeply as is customary with this people –,
as if good manners were all they had on their minds
and they had spent a long time considering the question
without coming to any conclusion. The tiny agitations of the wood
are on the surface only, and they soon resolve themselves
into the general unison of branches, heaving, subsiding.
Today the clouds are as secretive as those branches
and they refuse to reveal the summit or the sides
of Fujiyama. You sense it there, but you cannot see
its bulk or its snow-streaks that Japanese art
has made so famous. (Hiroshige was here
but on a clearer morning.) Days later
and back in the capital, I watch the carp
in the pond of the Yasukuni shrine. These fish
in their extrovert muscularity, their passion for food
are all the trees are not; they steer themselves unerringly
with a blunt muscular force, their whiskered circular mouths

forming the O which means *give*, rolling over
on one another's backs, to get what is given, and arriving
with the massive bodily impetus
of legless sumo wrestlers ruddered by flickering tails.
But this is a military shrine, its gate a tall ideogram
topped by a bar like a gigantic gun-barrel
and the mere good manners of trees do not serve here
to distract the visitor from what he wishes to understand.
Though when he rises to go, the lit lanterns,
as if disguise were after all the mark of this nation,
throw through the branches a light of festivity, a carnival glow,
their object solely to beautify the spot
and make us forget what stern ghosts linger here.

2 *Heron*

The river crosses the city over a series of falls:
at each of the falls, waiting for fish
a small white heron – sometimes
a whole group of them, all
at a respectful distance from one another.
Perhaps they have fished the river too long –
they seldom visibly produce anything from it.
Perhaps their decorative tininess is the result
merely of malnutrition. They are indifferent to traffic
flowing by on either side, and to strollers
who pause to see what they might catch.
They watch the water with such an exemplary patience,
they seem to be leftovers from a time
when the world was filled with moral admonitions
and everything had been put there to mean something.
We, however, fail to take the lesson to heart
and continue to worry over their inadequate diet.
As evening arrives, the light on the buildings
goes golden, an Italian light, and the mountains
darken and press forward to stand protectively
round the city. Midnight
and below the roadway, in the glare of passing cars,
huddle the heron, roosting with one leg raised, and bent
even in sleep, towards the flash, the fish, the disappointment.

Kyoto

3 Shugakuin Garden

The variegated tremor
of the reflected foliage
brings autumn to the ponds:

the rising fish
create circles within circles,
pools within pools:

under garden branches
there is every sort of water
to be seen and listened to

as it talks its way downhill
through the leat of its channel
out into the rice beyond:

you will find no frontier
between the garden and the field,
between utility and beauty here.

4 Yamadera

You go by the local line:
schoolchildren keep getting off the train,
returning to those villages
beneath vertical mountains.
Kumagane: conical hills
beyond the little station;
Sakunami: the sky is darkening
and so are the trees;
it will rain soon – in time
for our arrival
by this narrow way
to the deep north,
though 'deep', they say,
is a mistranslation

'Yamadera': the title of Bashō's travel book, 'The Narrow Way to the Deep North', is the
translation (or invention) of Nobuyuki Yuasa (Penguin Books, 1965).

of the title of Bashō's book,
and 'far' would be more accurate
'though less poetic,' they add.
The river in the ravine,
this intimate progress between sheer slopes,
what must it have been
for a traveller
on foot and horse-back?
Our rail-track way
is a smooth ascent
through turning maples
into cooling autumn air,
the faint aroma of snow in it.
It was here he wrote –
but would not write today –
the shriek of the cicada
penetrates
the heart of the rock.
He came, then, in heat.
The climb up the mountain face
which is the temple
must have cost him sweat,
his feet on the thousand steps
that lead past the door of each shrine
up to the look-out where
you can take in the entire valley,
echoing, this afternoon,
with shot on shot
from a whole army
of automatic scarecrows.
The rain arrives, but does not stay,
from a grey cloud
darkening half the sky
and disappearing. On the way down
we see once again
what arrested our upward climb –
stones to the miscarried,
and prayer-wheels
to wish the unborn
a reincarnation in a human form.
And so we depart
in the light that saw his arrival –

that of late afternoon,
to wait for the train
in this still distant corner. Clearly
the poetry of 'deep'
is more accurate
than mere accuracy –
a journey to the interior
is what it must have felt like then.
They say he came as a spy
(the villages are passing in reverse order now),
that there was more to it than met the eye,
calling on abbots and warriors,
to sniff out plots before they occurred.
There is no doubt, some say,
others that it is absurd
to speculate now. And so
we leave Bashō to disappear,
deeper and deeper,
while we cross the angular paddies
towards the shapeless cities,
the mountains already drawing apart
on either side of the wide plain
into two great parallels
echoing the track of our train,
our own narrow way south.

5   *Epilogue*

This advanced frontier
of Asia, this chain
of volcanoes, arcadian,
alpine, weird,
its ravines noisy with waterfalls,
its countless rivers
too impetuous for navigation,
ports few and coast foam-fringed –
the tree-fern, bamboo,
banana and palm grow here
side by side
with pine, oak, beech and conifer.
Wild animals are not numerous

and no true wolf exists
(the domestic dog
is wolf-like but ill-conditioned).
The lobster stands for longevity
and all history before 500
must be classed as legendary.
This is the place
Marco Polo never visited
but, jailed by the Genovese,
rehearsed its wonders
in bad French
to a Pisan fellow prisoner
calling it
Zipangu.

Interior

Approaching the house,
he lingers at the door;
it is the thing he sees inside
delays him there:

the drawing-room
seems to essentialize
asters, dahlias and golden-rod;
the red-gold sunlight lies

in puddles across the floor,
turns the blue of the carpet
more blue yet and leaves
a hazy aureole round each chair:

the colours of autumn
within four walls burn
more richly than maples, asters
fanfaring his return

to this domestic fire
carried indoors from outside:
here is a hearth rekindled
from the whole red tide

by the reconnaissant hand
that hesitating must pause
before it places its final flower,
stands back from it and withdraws.

Snapshot

for Yoshikazu Uehata

Your camera
has caught it all, the lit
angle where ceiling and wall
create their corner, the flame
in the grate, the light
down the window frame
and along the hair
of the girl seated there, her face
not quite in focus – that
is as it should be, too,
for, once seen, Eden
is in flight from you, and yet
you have set it down complete
with the asymmetries
of journal, cushion, cup,
all we might then have missed
in that gone moment when
we were living it.

The Improvement

The hallway once
Ran straight through the house, and you could see
Entrance to exit in one sweep
Of the eye across a cobbled floor –
Unexplored, the territory of the rooms
To either side. One day
It was resolved to block that shaft
With a vestibule, and to curb its tendency
With a further jut of wall halfway.
Do I like the changes? A ghost
Could not pass straight through
Without confusion now. What ghost, you say?
The ghost that is my memory which quickens still
At the thought of the long passage lit
From door to door, the clean
Flight of the senses through it, like a wife
Running to meet her man, like a bird's flight, a life.

To a Yorkshireman in Devon

for Donald Davie's 70th birthday

Eden was never Abyssinian –
In spite of Milton and received opinion.
He chose, at last, the paradise within.
'Within', without the rest of it, sounds thin –
Even to one like me who, as you say,
Has gilded rural scenes inordinately:
I could not live only on leaves and grass
For all my equanimity, but let that pass.
Gurney thanked God for Gloucestershire. You see
At once how a mere county boundary
Could not explain the intentions of the Lord.
And yet, is it, Donald, utterly absurd
Like Edward Thomas to accept a war
Convinced it was Eden you were fighting for? –

That Eden Gurney found on midnight walks
Glimmering along boughs, up nettle stalks,
Through constellations that the Romans knew
Standing in that same damp of Cotswold dew
On sentry go. And Gurney's thanks began
With the Georgic feelings of the Englishman
For land that is worked. And so his Eden means
The practicality of rural scenes
Besides the poetry of place – divine
And human, not too rigorous a line
Severing the two creations. I,
A gardener beneath our doubtful sky
Hoeing my beans – no, not nine rows like Yeats
(His were the kind one neither plants nor eats) –
See you beside your lawn of camomile
(In thought, that is – visions are not my style),
With pipe and books and mollifying glass,
Challenge the ill-kempt verse that tries to pass
The approbation of your level gaze,
Though not so partial that you cannot praise
Writers whose premisses dispute your own,
Oppen and Olson, Niedecker and Dorn –
Gurney himself whom we rejoice to see
With Bunting at our island's apogee.
So if I must decide on qualities
That show you as you are, it's my surprise
At where you'll lead us next that makes my task
So difficult a judgment, when I ask
What are the limits within such a mind
That's principled, yet never is inclined
To set up and defend impossible frontiers,
Brooding on words and meanings these long years;
And now your great climacteric's wide south,
A region to delight and nourish us both,
Offers beneath the shadow of the moor
The Sabine promise of your open door.

Crossing the Moor

for Fred and Paula

Crossing the moor, the prehistoric stones
    Keep to their circles and their avenues, imprint
On earth a planetary map that we
    Can read no longer. We enter
The fractured ring; the veering weather
    Entering with us, brings out the glitter
From the grey: sunlight has made
    Malleable the solidities and so has shade
As the monoliths darken beneath cloud;
    Then a tongue of flame, flickering through the air
Leaves its glancing brightness everywhere
    Setting light to stone. The great
Clock of circle and avenue still
    Measures for us, chartless as we are,
Weather, space and time – the mobile features
    Continually re-forming of that face
The universe turns towards us where
    We cross by the sea-lanes of the open moor.

Hay Tor

The moor is starred with yellow tormentil
    In a rune of stones, as though some citadel,
Detonated here, had strewn the hill
    With fragments, and sheered away
From words to soundlessness – stone patiences
    Outwaiting time. Circles and avenues remain
To measure the naked ground, that then
    Were the forest markers, maps of processionals:
Landlocked among leafage, men
    Sought for the open circle and were led
Between trunks and growth where now
    Under a bare sky gorse and heather
Climb through the debris ivy holds together,

And the constellations of the tormentil
Channel a wind, blowing as it lists,
   Through the breathing spaces where gone villages
Felt the stir of foliage fingering their stone.

Jubilación

a letter to Juan Malpartida

You ask me what I'm doing, now I'm free –
Books, music and our garden occupy me.
All these pursuits I share (with whom you know)
For Eden always was a place for two.
But nothing is more boring than to hear
Of someone's paradise when you're not there.
Let me assure you, robbers, rain and rot
Are of a trinity that haunt this spot
So far from town, so close to naked nature,
Both vegetable and the human creature.
Having said that, now let me give a sample
Of how we make short northern days more ample.
We rise at dawn, breakfast, then walk a mile,
Greeting the early poachers with a smile
(For what is poetry itself but poaching –
Lying in wait to see what game will spring?).
Once back, we turn to music and we play
The two-piano version of some ballet,
Sacre du Printemps or Debussy's *Faune*,
On what we used to call the gramophone,
To keep the active blood still briskly moving
Until we go from dancing to improving
The muscles of the mind – 'in different voices'
Reading a stretch of Proust, a tale of Joyce's.
And so to verse. Today, the game lies low,
And Brenda, passing, pauses at the window,

Jubilación: the Spanish for 'retirement'.

Raps on the pane, beckons me outside. She
Thinks, though we can't plant yet, we still can tidy,
Clear the detritus from the frosty ground
With freezing fingers, and construct a mound
Of weeds and wood, then coax it to a red
And roaring blaze – potash for each bed,
As Virgil of *The Georgics* might have said.
I signal back my depth of inspiration,
The piece I'm finishing for *Poetry Nation*
(What nation, as a nation, ever cared
A bad peseta or a dry goose turd
For poetry?). Our Shelley's right, of course,
You can't spur on a spavined Pegasus
Or, as he puts it, 'There's no man can say
I must, I will, I shall write poetry.' –
Or he can say it and no verse appear.
As you now see (or would if you were here)
The winter sunlight sends its invitation
To shelve these mysteries of inspiration
And breathe the air – daybreak at noon, it seems,
The swift de-misting of these British beams
(Our watercolour school was full of such
Transient effects – we took them from the Dutch).
Strange how this wooded valley, like a book
Open beneath the light, repays your look
With sentences, whole passages and pages
Where space, not words, 's the medium that assuages
The thirsty eye, syntactically solid,
Unlike the smog-smudged acres of Madrid
Boiling in sun and oil. You must excuse
These loose effusions of the patriot muse.
Not everybody's smitten with this spot –
When Chatwin lived here, he declared he was not,
His cool, blue eye alighting only on
Far distant vistas Patagonian,
Untrammelled in the ties of local life,
Lost to the county, to both friends and wife.
We'd walk together, talking distant parts –
He thought we all were nomads in our hearts.
Perhaps we are, but I prefer to go
And to return, a company of two.
Hence jubilation at my *jubilación*

That we, together, leave behind our *nación*
And visit yours – or, just look up, you'll see
The vapour trails above us, westerly
The high direction of their subtle line,
Spun between Severn and Hudson, and a sign
That we shall soon be passing at that height
And, if the weather's clear, catch our last sight
Of Gloucestershire beneath us as we go.
But I must use 'la pelle et le râteau'
(Things that were images for Baudelaire),
And with the backache, spade and rake, prepare
The soil to plant our crops in on returning.
So I must pause from versing and start burning,
To anticipate the time we're once more here
In the great cycle of the ceaseless year.

Durham in March

You can take it in at a glance
    This climbing town above its river,
Backed by the arches of a viaduct
    That ushers you in, prince of the place
It seems – prince-bishop, rather,
    Its castle and its coinage in your grasp.
For three cold days, your eyes
    Will rule over gulls and weirs,
Ramparts pierced by your posterns,
    The trinity of towers. Then time
Brings round the abdication of these powers.
    The train is moving. Below the parapet
Roofs and terraces, contouring-out the drop,
    Hold up their image, clear as on a coin,
Of a town compacted. Place, once more,
    Has outrun your words, your links of sound
Echoing back a sisterhood of shapes,
    Driven apart now by the growing space
Between you and them where they attend
    On the weathers that mark-off your three-day reign.

Near Bickering

The seam that runs sinewing England
    Crops out here. I recognize
The colour of home, the Cotswold colour,
    Across these high wolds of the north,
In the free-stone barrier that divides
    Lawn from corn-field. An apple
Lies like a tiny boulder in the grass
    Bruised by its fall, and brown as stone;
Corn of the selfsame colour does not yield
    To the push of air. It is Yorkshire August here,
Cool even in the sun, and calm,
    So that only the thistledown can show
Where the air currents move, and drifts
    Earthwards with silk-thread tentacles
Reaching for rootage as they brush the ground,
    Aerial gleams through so much petrifaction,
First silent sorties in this truce with stone.

Autumn

        Neither pink nor brown,
    You cannot take it down in ink
The colour of fallen leaves – a brush
    Might match it, or music even
In an upward scale of infinite intervals
    With a change of key where a hill
Meets heaven and all the degrees
    Of autumn on ground, slope, trees
Clash suddenly with – no adjective
    Can define the blue that brightens
Through the whole sky and, in the chemistry of sight,
    Changes this glow that crackles at our feet
By being its antithesis: far, cold,
    Never to be trodden, that is where
Comparison ceases and we breathe the atmosphere.

Weather Report

for Brian Cox

First snow comes in on lorries from the north,
    Whitens their loads – an earnest of that threat
Cromarty, Mull, Fair Isle and Fastnet
    Have weathered already. It has passed
Down the Pennine chain and choked Shap Fell;
    The Snake is lost and every moor
In Derbyshire under a deep, advancing pile.
    It covers the county, dwindling south,
But the wind that carries it, overshoots
    The frontier snow has mapped. It is the wind
Seems to be blowing the sunlight out
    As it roams the length of the whole land,
Freezing the fingers of tillers and of trees,
    Until it curls back the tides off Cornwall
Telling the snowless shires they too must freeze,
    In this turbulence that began as Swedish air
And has turned in the translated atmosphere
    To the weather of the one nation we suddenly are.

Cosmology

Where is the unseen spider that lets down
    This snow-web from the meshes of whose cold
Birds, stung out of stupor, suddenly unfold
    Into flight? The hungry huntsmen crows
Dismember the unmoving, beak them off bushes,
    Haling them up to their tree-high end.
There, strung with sinews of white the boughs
    Twist into a wickerwork from which a snow
Of feathers flows down as the shrieking ceases.
    The sun emerges now to show it all plain
And dazzle us with the same questions still.
    We pursue them anew with legendary solutions
Each dawn disowns, then leaves us standing here
    Rich orphans among an inheritance of snows, of stones,
Feeling the warmth ebb back into the year.

December

Frost followed frost, each colder
    Whiter than the one before. The crystals'
Sparkling salt, it seemed, had changed
    The nature of the things it clung to:
You walked in a world that well might break
    Into glassy chimes, gamelans of the cold,
As whole hillsides, struck by the light,
    Stood out revealed, trees ranked in white,
Their detail microscopically incised, unreal,
    Sun full on their fragile armour that soon would
Melt off them in a single afternoon.

The Track of the Deer

        ...The track of the deer
That strayed last night into the garden,
Stops beneath the fruitless apple tree,
Shaped out and shimmering with that frost
You can feel here at the edge of all imaginings:
The departed deer glimmers with the presence
Of sensed, substantial and yet absent things.

To a Photographer

for Justine

The house in the paperweight is covered with snow:
The camera caught it in the boughs' embrasure,
And all is a circular window where the glass
Is keeping from time this moment of winter leisure –

Before the snowplough has opened the road again,
And the white on the roof has started to slide away.
The limewash lit by the sunlight seems a glow from within,
Like the pleasure of bodily warmth on a winter's day.

I can take up that day in my hand once more,
Now the springtime has altered this scene of your art,
But must wait out the year to breathe in its cool and find
How your image, like air, has entered and tempered each part.

The Shadow

The sun flung out at the foot of the tree
A perfect shadow on snow: we found that we
Were suddenly walking through this replica,
The arteries of this map of winter
Offering a hundred pathways up the hill
Too intricate to follow. We stood still
Among the complications of summit branches
Of a mid-field tree far from all other trees.
Or was it roots were opening through the white
An underworld thoroughfare towards daylight?
There stretched the silence of that dark frontier,
Ignoring the stir of the branches where
A wind was disturbing their quiet and
Rippled the floating shadow without sound
Like a current from beneath, as we strode through
And on into a world of untrodden snow,
The shadow all at once gone out as the sun withdrew.

Walks

The walks of our age
are like the walks of our youth:
we turned then page on page
of a legible half-truth

where what was written
was trees, contours, pathways –
and what arose as we read them
half conversation, half praise –

and the canals, walls, fields
outside of the town
extended geographies
that were and were not our own

to the foot of the rocks
whose naked strata threw
their stone gaze down at us –
a look that we could not look through.

That gaze is on us now:
a more relenting scene
returns our words to us,
tells us that what we mean

cannot contain
half the dazzle and height
surrounding us here:
words put to flight,

the silence outweighs them
yet still leans to this page
to overhear what we talk of
in the walks of our age.

Transaction at Mallards Pike

for Richard Verrall

The trunks of the spruce at Mallards Pike
    Float their reflections out across the lake
Into its depths. This columned church,
    This underwater shrine, sways in the wind;

Its dark recession might well be a mine
   Like those on either shore, but here
It is the light transforms itself to ore
   Not to be sold: the sliding darks
Yield up no miner's harvest of black gold
   To be weighed and traded afterwards.
Even the swimmer through that foundered nave
   Is robbed of the wealth of it we have
In our dealings with a sun and surface that
   Offers itself as mirror to the trees,
Then jostles their rigid tallnesses to a play
   Caught only here between the wood and light –
Walkers on water dark alone can drown,
   Weightlessly undulated between dawn and sundown.

Forest of Dean

The Song of Adam

It was the song of Adam
the devil envied most,
and the song of Adam
that Adam lost,

and could catch only
the attenuated echo
as he wove an accompaniment
to that remembered flow,

as if he might restore
from the tune in his head
the variable, self-sustained
unfaltering aria, fed

from the steady spate
and the hidden source
Adam and devil can only hear
as one leaden curse.

To a Christian Concerning Ivor Gurney

You will have much to explain to your God on the final day,
And he, also, will have much to explain to you –
Why (say) the mind of Gurney, whose preludes I am listening to,
Should, through so many years, have to waste away
Into inconsequence – composer, poet who dreamed that our land
Would greet in him an heir of Jonson and Dowland;
But its mind was elsewhere, and so was that of your Lord,
Assigning this soldier his physical composition –
That blood, those chromosomes that drew him to the absurd
Disordering of notes, to the garrulity of the word,
Instead of the forms that already his youthful passion
Had prepared for the ordering of both self and nation.

9 a.m.

For a long time
There is sunlight in the sky, but in the streets no light;
Then it arrives and walkers going by
Are joined to their shadows. Overhead
On a tall building a flag
Twists shadowless in the morning air:
Why so, when there are shadows everywhere?
I see a running man, dwarfed
By his shadow-legs; a man whose shadow-stick
Trails a long stilt to far-off shadow-feet;
A pigeon flies down to land
On its inverted cut-out, and the cars
Carry for a moment the shadow-shaft
Of the lamps they are passing under. Now,
Screened far above me on a single
Facet of sky-high wall, I see
The shadow-flag an hour will efface,
Passing its serpentine black rag
From side to side across a surface
Of resplendent concrete it is energetically cleansing.

Knowledge

I want the knowledge of afternoon as it recedes
    Up to the very edge of disappearance;
And of all the space I see it passing through,
    And all of the time it takes for light
To linger out its slow retreat from sight –
    Tree after tree, roof after roof –
And sensing them present there, to feel
    All that the charged recesses of the dark conceal.

On the Late Plane

The city is spreading its nets to catch the eye
    Of flight after flight crossing this night sky –
Nets of illumination that distance turns filigree,
    The fine-spun logic of an arterial geometry
Webbing outwards and on from each settled spot
    To reach to wherever the light still is not –
To pockets of dark where mountain sheernesses
    Ink-out the gossamer glow with their million fir trees.
Here is a star-map brought to the ground, a beauty
    Bestowed on the innumerable roadsides that by day
Harbour no hint of this transfiguration where
    They draw down the gaze of the night-sky traveller.

THE VINEYARD ABOVE THE SEA

1999

Verse

The pause at the turn, however infinitesimal,
    Is there to ensure we do not run ahead
Of the heartbeat, the knowledge in the blood
    That will not be hurried beyond a present good
Before it has fed on it. Where are you going
    And towards what beyond, asks the pulsation
To which everything is bound: time to return
    To the paced-out path for those who raced it.

A Festivity

for Fred Siegel

Late afternoon and a rumble of planes,
    Flight-lanes imprinted on the sky
In crumbling chalk, decaying arabesques;
    Or leaning a Jacob's ladder up between
One mid-air plateau and the next above it.
    Pluming away, they start to congregate
With that which they most resemble now –
    The passing nebulous cloud company
That crowd before a disappearing sun
    And still are on display, once it has gone,
In the light it has left them, a yellow band
    Like the sand of some celestial beach
Which is gradually becoming sea, and they
    A blackening armada trailing smoke.
Dark shipshapes, spectres of voyaging,
    Keep moving on like the planes themselves
That are creating, as they go, their own unspooling
    Tickertaped west, leaving us ours,
An abandoned festivity to be completed
    Elsewhere, a few wraiths suspended wavering,
Catching the red rising from below,
    Above an embered twilight that in cold
And dark is alchemizing to an airy streak of sunset gold.

Mythology

The Greeks must have got it from clouds. Polypheme
   Cranes up bull-necked over the horizon
And scans sky above the valley. The shape
   That threatens him, all muscles, moving domes,
Body or city rising compact,
   Must be a god in the making – higher
Than him in fact. He goes on growing
   Gazing: the vertical white nude
Grows, too, and spreads its snows
   Overhead, as if it would outdo
Any aggressor from below. He pauses, now.
   His one eye must clearly have seen
How the immaculate upward drift is beginning
   To fray from its perfect outline
And slowly grey against the blue behind it,
   Letting it through unawares as it stretches and thins,
Scarcely distinguishable at the edges
   From that azure suffusion that seeps in
Little by little, drinking the god whole.
   Olympus is overthrown. Its battlements
Are coming down. An anchorless ship,
   It is changing into the mist surrounding it,
And the thunder sounds its undoing wide
   As it gigantically, visibly drowns
And watching Polypheme crouches there satisfied.

In Abruzzo

The stretched-out sleepers, limestone sentinels
   Who have forgotten what camp it is
They are defending, do not realize
   That other eyes are overlooking their shoulders –
The Great Rock, the range of the Maiella –
   Heaped-up, crowding one another back
In this history of shift and slide, of sudden

Fissuring along the mountainside
Into the worked stone world of dwelling
    (You might seize on the wrought iron
Of its balconies as the façade folds open
    And crumbles down). Today the distances
Are at truce, nothing toeing loose
    The long negotiation between flesh and stone:
Beneath ramparts, the awning stripes
    Of a market give back the light,
And voices, climbing up from below
    Tell human time and not the cold
Chronology of looming strata. But the slow
    Ranges of silently invading cloud
This July day of mountain autumn
    Begin to unsay the promises of sun
That opens a path through the pale reaped hayfields,
    Warming this parapet we are leaning on.

Trebiano

I live in a small city, and I prefer to dwell there
that it may not become smaller still.

Plutarch

I

These outposts were the centres once.
    The bulwarks of the ruined fort contain
The village cistern. What you find
    Are veering streets stacked above a plain
So wide that you scan its flat immensity
    For sails. You can hear more than you see
Down there, the clang and ricochet
    Of the place to which activity has fled
Flung up at you, and to be heard
    Even in the gullies between the dwellings
And against the walls of the bishop's house
    From which its inhabitant departed
Centuries since. What Trebiano lacks
    Is its Plutarch perhaps to come – the single

Mind that will expand the circuit of that site
    On which the hill-top houses stand
Sending down pin-prick morse
    From shuttered windows into Ligurian night.

II
Hawks
Inhabit the gaps in castle masonry.
Stones that hold down the rooftiles here
    Come from its crumbled wall whose ivy
Forces a slow and silent entry
    Gripping and grinding the stone's precariousness.
Imprinting themselves on the summit silences,
    Rumours of cars crossing the valley floor.
A fig-tree has fastened itself to the threshold where
    A wind is rising with tidal sounds through the leaves.
Thwack of the returning hawk that lands in its lair.

III
Bent above distances at this high window,
    Crow's nest that does not sway surveying change:
The plain of the Magra crossed, re-crossed by rain
    Yields for an instant to a far suggestion
Of sun that coldly catches the blades –
    Two sickle-shapes where the river curves
Then curves again winding to the Tyrrhenian
    Which shows, a sliver of sea, blotted by hills
(The eye drawn right) that mass, ripple and then fall
    In leisurely sloping folds of green
To where the land ends and the Ligurian sea
    Extends water once more in horizontal calm.
The linear glint goes out as the rain
    Shadows it over, the two half-moon blades
Darken beneath the flying fringes
    That advance below and have already reached
The dorsal roof-ridges of this village,
    Tile locked on tile, like the bones
Of an extinct species. Rain
    Glitters and slides into gutters polishing
The cheerless ancient houses that cling

In two parallel streets to a hillside
More precipice than slope. We are that continuing race
   Defying the attempts of earth itself
To have done and huddle us off it. We
   Persist like the returning light that, overcome,
Reaches out to touch the surfaces it had lost,
   As if it were resurrected from under a sea
Off a phosphorescence as marine-sharp, nacreous,
   As that which enamels these now shimmering roofs.

The Vineyard Above the Sea

This frontal hill falls sheer to water,
   Rugged forehead whose rhythmic folds
Are of stone, not flesh – walls
   That hold up the soil and the vines between,
Whose final fruit, essence and asperity,
   Is wine like daylight, tasting of the sea.
I lift a glass of it towards the sun
   Catching, within, the forms essentialized
Of these cliff-edge vine-rows –
   Cables hoisting a harvest to the summit –
And beyond the ripple of rock-shoulders
   Bearing the load of grapes and stone,
The town itself – almost a woman's name –
   Corniglia, as tight-gripped to its headland
As to their heights these walls, floating
   Along the contours like the recollection
Of a subsided ocean that has left behind
   The print of waves. Windows, doors
In the heaped façades cast a maternal glance
   Over a geology festooned, transformed,
Where through the centuries it hunched a way
   Towards these cube-crystals of the houses,
This saline precipice, this glass of light.

Fonte Gaia

Children beg *monetine*
and fling them – *per la fortuna!* –
into the waters of the fountain.
A pigeon perched on her head,
Sapienza, not Fortuna
governs this flow,
graceful and severe.
Between what they wish for and what they will know
let no malignity interfere,
no waters tainted by coins and excrement
infect and blur the intent
innocence of their trust in luck.

News

The people in the park
are not news:
they only go to prove
what everyone knows –
the sufficiency
of water and a few trees.

The people in the gallery
are not news either:
they are here for more trees
and the permanence of water
of various kinds: everything
from the seastorm to spring rain.

Walking in the street,
we are not news, you and I,
nor is the street itself
in the first morning sun
which travels to us from so far out
sharpening each corner with its recognition.

News
wilting underfoot, news
always about to lose its savour,
the trees arch over the blown sheets
rain is reducing to a transparent blur
as if water with trees were alpha and omega.

Oporto

I

And then the river
overflowed and rose
uphill through
the long canals of streets:
it mistook
the churches for cliffs
and the chapels within
for sea-caves
and covered them
with an armour
of golden molluscs.

II

Is this a queen
or is it the queen
of heaven balancing
her gigantic crown
like the burdens
the peasant women
carry on their heads?

III

Luke, with a quill in hand,
is concentrating:
at his feet, the eagle
brings his inkwell to him

strapped round its neck,
and gazes up towards
the gospel he is penning.

IV

In a glass case
the wrapped dead Christ
in a covering like butchers' muslin
bordered with lace.

V

A female saint,
with a shepherd's crook,
holds on her left hand
an open book,
a dove craning up out of it.

VI

Leaving
I drop coins
into the begging bowl
of cupped
unclean fingers
and though we greet
by touch
our eyes do not meet.

Rua do Carriçal

The inhabitants of Rua do Carriçal,
in their island street –
their urban Innisfree
jammed between two thoroughfares –
live remote from either
psychosis or a nunnery, and yet
someone has written on the wall
Psychotic Lesbian Nuns.

The woman washing her balcony floor
cannot read this scrawl
since it is daubed in English,
but wrings out her rag
in island innocence. Her neighbour
has trained his vines
to an iron trellis and emerges
from the greenery below
watering a miniature garden –
strawberries in plastic tubs, a slim
rectangle of soil in which
cabbage and cala lilies grow
side by side, gigantic roses
looming above lettuces,
striped pumpkin and potatoes.
Besieged by pylons,
a radio-mast, street-
end traffic and the monomaniac note
from a generator,
its parked cars
cluster as close as pumpkins growing,
where, immune from harm,
the pre-Freudian Carriçal exudes
into Lusitanian noon
its convent calm.

The Green Balloon

In Citadel Park,
the stalled balloon refuses
to climb across the trees
and from there take in
the rowers on the lake below,
all pulling away in time
with the accordion music:
the combusting of its gas,
loud as a school of drummers,
seems vanity and excess,
where every child
is attached to its own

floating toy balloon
that effortlessly discovers
the most convenient current
to keep it hovering in air.
Those cooped in their basket on the ground
might well have found out
children and rowers with a single
swoop of the eye up there
and, between the two,
the human pyramid
the club of athletes
is erecting into view,
storey rising on storey
of the firm yet slightly
trembling arms, building
to a summit that a child
ascends. Arriving at the top,
he turns and takes a bow
as applause breaks below him.
The pyramid then undoes itself,
with pauses for more applause,
as the levels come faultlessly apart
and back to earth. But in all this
accumulation and deconstruction,
the balloon at the park gates
still hesitates to rise
more than a few feet, and then
laboriously returns to earth again
like a bounced ball
gigantic in slow motion.
Its hydrocephalic mass,
doubled by a bobbing shadow,
nods at a gesturing statue
that appears to be fending it off.
Its mountainous shade,
dragging beside its own
lighter-than-air, great
inflated, bottle-green bag,
hangs, half shadow
of a doubt, half threat.

Barcelona

Hellas

1 *Kéa*

It begins with its lighthouse, ends with a tapering down –
    No town, no jetty – of rock into water:
In between – houses, a few, set back
    On barren heights, crossed only
By the frayed rope of a wandering wall
    That negotiates slope and drop to disappear
Then finally show itself on top
    Of the highest point. What does it contain?
Here, neither sheep nor crop. Who is it clings
    Still to Kéa in those scattered dwellings?
We are sliding past, watching this apparition
    Fade into the blaze of Aegean noon.

2 *Apollo at Delphi*

Darkness – as if it were the shadow of a cloud
    The wind was hurrying away – slides
Visibly off the plain, already sails
    Up the grey sides of the mountain to the peak
And leaves its high stones naked as Apollo.

3 *Epidauros*

Into the circle of the theatre
at Epidauros, faced
by its absent auditors
ten thousand strong, I launch
through acoustic space
the ship I have most in mind –
Hopkins' *Deutschland* – and can hear
(his verses, thewed
like an Attic ode)
syllabic echoes cut into the atmosphere
climbing on ancient feet
the limestone tiers

where listening cyclamen have pushed their way
between the slabs
up out of Hades.

4   *Fragment*

Water, a faint aural thread,
that once fed the fountain.
After invasion, turmoils, time,
the place, like the poems of Sappho,
all shards, shreds.

The wren, the lizard and the cicada,
left in possession of the ground,
do not try to imagine
what is no longer there nor ask
which god sanctuaried here,
how did his music sound,
who is this headless woman
draped in a stone snake?

5   *Olympia*
in dispraise of ruins

That intelligent lizard
knows more of the place than I do. To him
all this is a city still complete,
its every fissure leads
into sunlit avenue, shadowy retreat.
I approve of his ignorance of archaeology:
I, too, cannot read a ruin with ease.
For him, of course, the question does not arise.
What Greece lacks is buildings that are entire.
Not those drab towns or these chipped remains,
It is architecture that I admire.
A true building builds you up as you look at it.
The pleasures of ruins are not infinite.

6   *Pastoral*

Goats in Arcadia
tintinnabulate still,
emerge from the milking shed
at the field's margin
with a crash of bells
and hurl themselves downhill
in a cavalry charge.

Goatherd regroups them,
not with a dog or threats,
but with low conch sounds
blown out of the hollow
of his cupped hands,

and through the sloping paddock,
in file they follow the man
in shirt, jeans, slouch hat,
unpied piper, reincarnate Pan.

7   *Like Greek Prose*

'Like Greek prose
with its passion for balance and antithesis,
elaborated by every kind of parallelism
including rhyme.' That might well be
a definition for the kind of poetry
that runs the spoken word
hard into the foreseeable and the unforeseen,
into patterns that lie
at the edges of what is stated, rhyme
suddenly knotted and related
to what was apparently done and gone,
and now, in perfected balance, moves
however unsymmetrically, with the dance
of forces, on and below those surfaces
which are the poem. And take this scene.
A Lapith is overcoming a Centaur:
with effort and yet balletic ease it bends
and accommodates it to this frieze, a half-

rhyme in the question and answer of their posture.
That, too, is poetry, that, too, is Greek.

8 *From the Greek*

Distances, Alexander hungered across these.
Words, the commonwealth of Socrates.
Honey, the monomania of bees.

9 *In the Cathedral*

The Archbishop was preaching that Sunday.
My ear could distill
thanatos, thanatos
out of the torrent of the unintelligible.
Whatever his meaning, his tone was clear:
he had not come here to flatter.
When he got down and was distributing the bread,
holding out a hand to be kissed,
I saw what I had missed before –
the painted image
of a small sad god
spread out on his rood
and the congregation
was clutching bits of bread
pausing to kiss the silver ikons
on their way out:
thanatos, thanatos
was sleeping now, the fray
with a vengeful deity over and done,
as the tide of the after-service conversation
rose and spread across the beach of Sunday afternoon.

10   *Melville on the Acropolis*

Not magnitude, not lavishness
But form, the site.

Herman Melville

for Vincent Scully

He scanned the hill-top temple and the spread
      Horizon of both ocean and of land
With a sailor's eye. Not the dark
      Flux of unending sea – the form
Was Doric and the site lay clear,
      The whole of distance swung in a single arc.
The temple was the containing vantage, he
      The temple's eye left hungry by the sea:
Here, depth rode steady, distances
      Must answer to the pull and measure
Of the ruined, sunlit colonnade that still
      Culminated the upward forces of its hill.
The form, the site: one held in the other's bowl –
  Stone against space, space opening onto mountain –
And the mariner balanced precariously whole
      On this stone ship headed towards Hymettos.

11   *Homecoming*

Frost-fur on every gate and fence:
where the sunlight reaches late,
grey shadows beneath beech and oak
across whitened grass;
but a ticking, a trickling of melted drops
from branches onto leaves long down
and sodden now
where, a steadily climbing vapour,
rime filters back into the atmosphere,
into the invisibility
that clothes all gods.

On the Dunes

for Richard Verrall

The dunes are blue in the eye of the sea,
Swayed into changes that might well be
Sea in themselves. For the sea, no wrecks exist.
They are merely the emanations of the mist
That sink into obliviousness to be caressed,
Processed like these sands, till what remains
Are monuments merely to the sea's power,
Sunk palaces through which the fish are free to display
Their malleability and their scales – also like the sea
When the waves agree to be calm like dunes
Building, changing silently, the one real
Challenge to all that equilibrium,
The tilt of the horizon, that is bringing to bear
The only other eye the sea must fear – the sky –
If it is still to retain its halcyon mood,
Its mine of unadulterated blue,
And not negotiate with the colour of the dunes,
When there is sand in the teeth of the wave
And what is real is not to be sluiced away
And the shreds of dead fish and of men
Assert their right to be recognized
For what they were before the omnivorous water
Washed them down with its midnight feast,
And then a congratulatory sun offered
To reduce what was still floating pulverized.
Beyond, the dunes had watched it all
And wait now to reinstate themselves,
And the winds that had torn up the cosmic fence
Resolve on co-existence, sea beside sand, silence.

Shorelines

Here where the certainty of land begins,
The ocean writes and rewrites its margins:
You can read along the rippling of the sand
The script advancing in its cursive hand,
Denying it has ever signed before
The dozen dishonoured treaties of this shore –
The harbours disappearing into silt,
Alexandra's cottage – royal Edward's guilt
Cost her less smart there – level with the tide.
To the hopes of merchant or of monarch's bride
The ocean does not deal long satisfactions,
Deep in its own ungovernable transactions.
White on this inland table lies a shell.
Lift it towards your ear and listen well.
The approaching breath of ocean that you hear
Says that the world won't end in ice or fire,
But lost to the tidal trickeries of water.

Directions

Just when you're sure that you're not getting near,
A tunnel of trees will suddenly appear
To undo doubt. You enter its half-light.
A mile more now and you will be in sight
Of a long, low house – that's ours. The tunnel, first –
A spot authority will one day worst
Because of its lack of 'visibility'
That helps us sense far more than we can see.
My one regret's that you arrive by car
And not by boat; that these few metres are
Asphalt, not winding water – how this road
Would flow in majesty, a river-god,
If that were the case; then, this shuttered shade
Would filter the daylight through the dark it's made
To sparkle off the surface round your prow,
As off the chromium and paintwork now

Heaving into view. Already I
Can hear the gear change, as you leave the high
Ground for the low that we inhabit here,
Beside the dampness of a genuine river.
You have arrived. You need seek no further.

In the Room

The room is submerged under restless waters –
the floating shadows of the birches
swimming in sunlight through the sable shade
where armchairs and a table
have taken root within four walls:
at each fresh onrush of the wind
the tree limbs and the leaves out there
renew their quivering race across a floor
where distance has come indoors
to reclaim the angled confine for the season
dancing it back to space.

The Gift

The allée I call it. It is scarcely that
    For all the gallic geometry of trunks
Facing each other along either side
    Of a straight, receding track. Call it
English and accidental, two hedges
    Outgrowing their purposes, to meet
Overhead in arched and tangled boughs,
    An invitation to pace the shadows
Imagining a verse-line to accommodate
    The play of muscle in the sway of walking,
Linearity plucked at by leaf and light.
    And yet – it is not quite English, either:
You have only to scratch this county and

Up come the oyster shells and tegulae
Of Rome. No need for archaeology to identify
    Roads like these that have lost their way
In the long recessions of empire. Call
    This one an imperial gift that Caesar
Scarcely intended leaving here
    In the far fold of this valley, shaded
By upstart Cotswold post-colonial trees.

Poem

The great cloud-barrier, building
    At sunset above the skyline, hides
The sun itself, lit by a tinge of fire
    Along its topmost reaches – high ground,
A frontier to the land below, an illusion
    That we live bounded by foot-hills,
In touch with mountains soon to appear
    Out of the hills themselves which go on growing
Above us, cancelling the horizon here.
    So we, too, are within reach of summits,
Our valley a scooped-out shelter
    Under their bulk. And this illusion
Holds us like a solid thing, as firm
    As a poem in its imagining step by step
A world into being that is not there –
    Then is, until that fallen fire begins
To penetrate in a glow the vertical mass
    And whole ingots now show through
Suffusing it as the molten fragments
    Drop behind the curvature of space
Leaving the would-be climber of that hill
    Standing earthbound in the chill of evening.
Cries from the first owl, the shrill fox
    Screaming for a mate, soon leave him
In the irrefutable cold, to the world's slow turning
    Beneath the light of a gradually appearing moon.

For Want of Seraphim

A plane (half-heard)
is pulling out a thread
on the blue of afternoon:
the winter sun
embers horizon clouds
that one by one
submit themselves to dark –
a deeper blue
than that on which the thread
is spreading upwards now
catching a glow of gold
from the low hidden orb:
so why should heaven be poor
for want of seraphim where this
thin gold thread
goes on unroving
in mythless apotheosis
above the dead and living?

Measure

Crossing the field
I catch a wandering light
on the road above it –
a car that veers
and disappears and then
like a lantern
swung from side to side,
from dark to light,
shapes out the twisted distances
the road loops through
before taking aim as an arrow might to flow
straight out of darkness:
I watch it go
this lantern of a car
restored to the linear,
to the visible roadbed
and taking the measure of what lies ahead.

Wall

I

The builders of the wall have pitched a tent,
A single sheet to keep them from the rain.
They have an entire field to circumvent
With the woodland next to it, and seen from here
What they are building looks more like a ship:
Effortlessly it might bear them down
Across the Cotswold troughs and to that gate
Where spring awaits them and their voyage ends.
The tin-can rap trails from their radio
To shorten the long way they have to go
Even under sail. Today the ice
Grips stone to stone. A little noonday sun
May gently prise them open later on.
But no one is saying so, or laying bets.
The boat is grounded and the two-man crew
Gaze back on what they do not need to do:
Now comes the wait, the cold, the cigarettes.

II

The two-man crew – look, one of them's a girl,
Her tow hair all the hat she deigns to wear
In the February freeze. Ungauntleted
Her carmined finger-ends claw rigid stone
She turns into a wall. 'Seven years,' she says,
When I ask her how long she has worked like this.
Against the blue, a high transparent moon
Leads in the month above an afternoon
Already darkening. How many years
Went to the making of as many walls
As contour out these valleys, half of them
Ruinous like this one when she started?
Silently the moon computes them all
And adds a gradual shadow to each wall
Including hers. And do her hands at night
Feel for those frosty surfaces the moonlight
Turns diamantine? I think her sleep,
The easy conscience of a youthful body,

Where time so far has seized no hostages,
Is undug limestone, spring-fed, bedded deep.

III

Came snow by night, as silent as a thief,
With slow addition, with solicitude
And definition not to be seen until
The morning dawns on new-found surfaces
The fall has brought to light: facets of a hill
Climb into sight and fill the emptiness
Of space ungauged. The builders gone, the whole
Builds itself back into receding white
Where distances and nearness now unite
In one clear structure quarried into time.
The snow-coped wall winds from its summit down
In each direction, like an ample wing,
Flying and yet feeling for the ground,
A gesture it required four hands to make
That snow and limestone link without a break.

Snowbound

for Jordi and Nuria

Now we have locked the doors against the snow
And feel it falling at each curtained window,
The house walls seem to thicken and resist
That movement into flocculence and mist,
Shapes that take the impression of the winds,
Scarving themselves around the gable-ends,
Or piling white oblivion on the stones
That once were ways, alternatives, directions
Refusing to become what they are now –
The unmapped territories of the falling snow.
But the room looms squarer as the tightening cold
Penetrates the fault-lines of our threshold:
Here, whiteness of the open book withstands

These long advances out of polar lands
To claim all for the north, that cannot find –
A roving presence, pathless, angered, blind –
The grain this hate of harvest would efface,
Our cell of fire beneath the blank of space.

Blackthorn Winter

Pallor of blossom between still-gaunt trees:
The blackthorn's white acetylene is clearing
Spaces for summer and the vast arrival,
Swimming whose floodtide we shall still recall
This first and tentative, this weightless stirring
Of whiteness above the thicket of winter's vestiges.

Drawing Down the Moon

I place on the sill a saucer
that I fill with water:
it rocks with a tidal motion,
as if that porcelain round
contained a small sea:
this threshold ocean
throws into confusion
the image that it seizes
out of the sky – the moon
just risen, and now in pieces
beneath the window: the glass
takes in the image at its source,
a clear shard of newness,
and lets it into the house
from pane to pane
riding slowly past:
when I look again
towards the sill, its dish

of moonlight is recomposing:
it lies still, from side to side
of the ceramic circle
curving across the water,
a sleeping bride:
for the moon's sake
do not wake her,
do not shake the saucer.

Storm Song

Rain, targeting the pool,
a blink, as the first grain of it
hits and disappears
into the bullseye it has made:
a circle expands and vanishes
towards the water's edge:
wheels within wheels
rim round into infinity
as rain patterns its way
through a phantasmagoria of similes –
as light at first as the arrival
of summer insects
just glancing at the gelatinous surface,
but by now as insistent
as hammer blows on the restless
metal of swaying water –
not the predictable clockwork tinkle
from Nibelheim, but an enthusiastic
whispering sound of the many hands
that make light work, that make
light of work, effortless, edenic,
and thrumming towards full melody
as the inevitable downpour
solidifies, sings to itself, expands.

The Tree House

Descending the fieldslope,
suddenly one's eyes
catch sight
of the house on the rise beyond
through the boughs of an oak
where it now appears
to be suspended, all
one hundred tons of stone,
its chimneys smoking
out of a warm interior
into a world that looks right
in the cold sunlight
of late-winter afternoon.
They say the King
came here
three hundred years ago
bringing – she called herself
'the Protestant whore' –
Nell Gwyn.
A likely story,
but if it happened
or did not, whoever
occupied that matrimonial bed
lay at the centre of this same
stone enclosure with its smoke
rising, the oak not yet grown
to extend its royal embrace
and make the whole house its own
as it does today
and raise it – a tree house –
up into the air.

The Blossom

I never told you how
I saw one day
in the stream the way
a foam flower grows,
whirled and gathered on
the spindle of an eddy
to a blossom that increased
as the water wound
round it and around,
concentrically piling
foam petals there
in a spawn of eyes,
a rising, whitening
bundle of bubbles
as the onrush and the air
caught in the water's vortex
and hung suspended –
the only thing that did
with the current pouring on
paying, to overcome the one
snag in its liquid line,
this tribute of a flower
absent as the poet says
from all bouquets.

Listening to Leaves

The timbre of the leaves is changing tone –
No more caressive, its metallic hiss,
But scaled and serpentine, setting aside
The bland assurance as of petals swelling
Into massed, harmonious shape and sound.
Behind the hill of leaves, a crag of cloud
Heaves outward into blue, the chartless heights
Borne down above the field's restriction,
Their colour and their cold one single breath

Preluding the autumn and its sequel.
We balance on a blade between the two
Seasons and their sounds that sense must travel through,
Catching from the current of the leaves
Its cross-ply meshing in the weave of time.

Gibbet

This dangling man left hanging in the trees,
Wearing corduroy, check shirt and sackcloth face,
Who shifts in the current of Atlantic breezes
In the sharpening light, with summer at an end,
Is the scarecrow that the keeper has strung up
From an ash-bough, to protect his fledgling birds,
And jerks into life at every autumn breath,
The guardian of their continuance and their death.

In Winter

The lit-up house is riding like a ship
Anchored below the hill. Owner and owner's wife
Are reading their winter books whose pages fill
Like sails to the breeze of their imaginings –
Different from mine, no doubt, which in the dark
Suppose that by dawn the house might float away,
Leaving its berth as a deserted garden
Surrounded by the neatly labelled saplings
Planted out yesterday. What images
Shake the pheasant already gone to roost
That a late car wakes? Its metallic cry,
A rusty ratchet, grates from the leafless trees
Its stand-and-deliver to all fantasies.

The Sisters

recalling the Westminster Piano Trio: Shostakovich Opus 67

This is not music for the wedding.
The Hasidim are dancing on their graves.
Muted in its highest register,
The cello mourns, and the passacaglia
Paces through one burial the more,
Notes sounding up out of the darkness as
The bare arms circle their instruments
Hacking the downbows, stroke on stroke. How young
They seemed, wielding the weapons of the music,
Burdened by a time they had not lived through,
Yet recognizing the lineaments of its sorrow
And the severe exactness art had called them to.

To Modulate

is to discover not invent,
to find a way
that was already there but lay
just out of earshot
awaiting touch,
the sleeper in the wood
who responds, the path
that opens behind you
and beyond: here is the place
you will return to once again
after the alpine ledges, the hurricane
of notes becoming
snow-motes, rain, refreshment,
when all seemed to be
concluded but drew you on,
your footsteps echoing
footsteps gone,
this undulant heard text
that outgoes its own occasion,

when the next time and the next,
what is and was
rears within the ear
its replenished civitas.

The First Death

in memoriam Bruce Chatwin

The hand that reached out from a painted sleeve
    When you sensed that you were dying, gathered you
Into the picture: clothes, furs, pearls,
    Bronze of a vessel, silver of a dish
From which the grapes were overflowing. Tangible
    The minute whiteness of those pearls, the galaxies
They strung; the velvets, sleeves, the welcome
    Among convivial company; the offered hand,
All those glistening appearances that now
    Were to declare the secret of their surfaces –
Surfaces deep as roots. You told
    How you were led at that first death
Through the Venetian plenitude of a room
    Across which a glance confirmed the presence there
Of windows spilling light on this festivity,
    And running beyond them, a silhouette –
The columns of a balustrade – then sky.
    You were let into the anteroom of your heaven
By the eye, moving and attending, finding good
    Those textures it had grazed on like a food.
The second time you died without remission,
    Leaving no report on the lie of the land
Beyond that parapet's stone sill, beyond the gloss
    On all surfaces, rich and indecipherable.

Another Summer

O'Hara admired
'the warm traffic'
(there was less of it then) –
that is my image of him
passing between
two parked cars
and patting the paintwork of one
in affectionate salutation
as if it were a person he already knew.
That was New York in sixty-three.
Three more to go.
The month was July when we
lose all apprehension
in the warmth of the world,
our awareness elsewhere
than on personal destiny.
But the place awaited and the hour,
Fire Island offering its sands
to the leisurely attentions of the sea
and the warm traffic of another summer.

To Robert Creeley in the Judaean Desert

Descending this hill,
we are mending
a broken chain –
those years since we

(again in a desert
place) first met –
by telling over friends
whose lives have ended,

and finding
what remains of our
once world.
There is no

arithmetic can show
a balance struck
between loss and gain,
between now and then.

How high the sky is
here above this
other wilderness
as it was there.

Then

for Frances Partridge

You would lie down, you said, willingly to oblivion then,
As you do each night, knowing no morning would wake you:
You would let the great wave irremediably take you
And deal as it might with the body's floating skein.

What was the resurrection? A dream never to be known.
And centuries have deceived us with its expectations:
Why did we credit the legend-led generations,
With the truth at hand in the gap of each friend gone?

Yet this it is to die – to no longer hear
The clear notes of the cuckoo intersecting
The woodpecker's trills laughingly inflecting
On evening space in the after-rain June air.

In Memoriam Ángel Crespo

(1926–1995)

All things engender shadow –
the rose, the rose-arch and the meadow
sombre among surrounding trees
newly in leaf: shadow
is a continual flow
in the soliloquy we weave
within ourselves, and this
makes the diamond of the day
unreal when it insists
on permanence: but then it takes
a slow and spreading shade
from the contrasting undertone that makes
each facet seem
to both gleam and darken,
changing like the surface of a stream
whose points of light
advancing, dance
on the ripple
pulling them forward
over sunless depth. Listen
and you can hear
at the root of notes
a darker music giving form
to a music already there
filling the innocent ear
with only half its story.

MacDiarmid

The sweetness of the vituperative man
Took me by storm and by surprise –
I'd scarcely looked for courtesies
From one who'd so resisted kith and clan,
But wronged the man I met. Crossing today
A field of thistles in full-scented flower
I think of his note recalling the event
Of meeting then in England, and the way
He signed it in that sloping, suffering hand
Christopher Grieve, and with the pseudonym
Hugh MacDiarmid bracketed beneath,
As if that, too, were memory for him.

History of a House

for Richard and Eileen

The place is surrounded by dancing pines:
   Even their trunks, distorted by the mistral
Bend to one accord. Cleft like a skull,
   It might have been split by lightning,
This house with its cracked wall. A long
   Black aperture divides it, entering
At roof level and running down
   An entire side. A fanfare
Of Provençal sunlight assails it. Once,
   It had stood firm, bedded on earth
Above the rocks it tried to imitate
   And that mock it now. The sunburst
Serves only to darken its crevices,
   To bring out the blackness in its window eye
Empty of all save shadow and as black
   With vacancy as the crack itself. The pines
In their insouciance do not ask
   Who built it or who lived here;
They dance with the indifference of youth

At the human years consumed inside.
The lap they dance on and have rooted in
    Proof against mishap, they do not hear
The slow tide rising through the house,
    The electric storm of all the energies
Impounded by that wall, as if it were these
    Had burst the masonry from within.
What happened here is lost to any memory
    Younger than the trees. From the ruined face
Haloed with hints, almost a glance
    Escapes, the lineaments of a persistence
Caught in the climbing light,
    History of a house, occulted and refracted
Between the taciturn rocks and the dance of pines.

By Night

Lights from the hillside farm by night
    Open three doors of fire
Across the swollen stream. It is travelling
    Freighted with the weight a season's rain
Unburdens down all the waterways
    That drain this valley. Those doors
Might well be the entrance to some mine:
    How would you lift its liquid gold,
How would you hold time that is travelling, too,
    In every gleam the light is wakening
Over the waters' face, asleep and flowing
    With its dream of flight towards what end
The winter's night awaits it with? Those strips
    Of flame, vibrant with the current bearing them,
Inscribe our sign and presence here
    Who watch these waters jostling to their fate
In the far-off, sharp sea air –
    Air of origin and end: on the gathered spate
Rides a signature of fire holding its own.

SKYWRITING

2003

Skywriting

Three jets are streaking west:
    Trails are beginning to fray already:
The third, the last set out,
    Climbs parallel a March sky
Paying out a ruled white line:
    Skywriting like an incision,
Such surgical precision defines
    The mile between it and the others
Who have disappeared leaving behind
    Only their now ghostly tracks
That still hold to the height and map
    Their direction with a failing clarity:
The sky is higher for their passing
    Where the third plane scans its breadth.
The mere bare blue would never have shown
    That vaultlike curvature overhead,
Already evading the mathematics of the spot,
    As it blooms back, a cool canopy,
A celestial meadow, needing no measure
    But a reconnaissant eye, an ear
Aware suddenly that as they passed
    No sound accompanied arrival or vanishing
So high were their flight paths on a sky
    That has gone on expunging them since,
Leaving a clean page there for chance
    To spread wide its unravelling hieroglyphs.

Mexico: A Sequence

I   Mexico

It begins with the Atlantic from above:
    Far-down glimmerings of white on blue –
Blue that seemed all sky, but is betrayed
    Into revealing itself as sea, faintest
Dawnings of a pattern on the waves, white points

As sharp as stars suddenly created, fading out:
A wave-capped ocean is what we glimpse
   Until blue takes over once again
As we keep trying to put together
   This wide ambiguity of air and water,
Cosmic theatre we cannot act in.
   Canada lies below, an open map,
A lesson in geography for us scholars
   Who imagine the route to Mexico must lie
Due south, not through dogged unfinished winter.
   Roads are crossing that map beside an estuary:
Snow-beached, an island in it
   Rising patterned in snowy lozenges
Like the Inuit diagram of a fish. On shore
   Someone must have surveyed the place
And squared it off, leaving those lines
   As taut as wire to wait out winter
And surface through the snow, demarcations of nowhere.
   Only the lakes, with scratches on their ice
Like the tracks of skaters, seem to know
   Of the possibility of circles, of ellipses. Faced
By such evidence, shall we believe at last
   That this is spring, is south, is Mexico?

II *Tenochtitlán*

Entering the Doric nave, you might have thought
They were about to paint the entire interior,
But that iron corset of scaffolding was there
Literally to keep the cathedral on its feet.

The walls were collapsing, splaying outwards
While its innards were being penetrated
By the tip of Moctezuma's pyramid
Over which it had been built, prising it apart.

We got back to the car and the six-lane thoroughfare
Out beyond Tacubaya where a gigantic Mexican flag
Failed to unfurl. Only the billboards went on storming the sky
Like trees in a tropical forest fighting for light.

At an intersection someone with a clown's white face
Rushed out grasping a stepladder, mounted it
And began to juggle in mid-air a handful of balls.
This was one of the city's more inventive beggars.

A genuine artist, he was too slow in getting down
To claim the money we were holding ready for him
And escaped as the traffic surged only because of that nimbleness
Which gave his unpaid audacity such style.

There is a plan to bring back the lakes and the canals
Of the Aztec city, to irrigate once more the friable earth
And get rid of the cars. The beautiful idea
Hangs in the air like that unfluttering ensign.

At sundown the metropolis grows grateful to the eye
When the lights come on and it is their constellation confronts us,
And the ghosts of the fallen jacaranda blossoms
Drift smokily over the ground the colour of English bluebells.

III *Xochimilco*

With its network of canals and its artificial islands, Xochimilco is the location from which
Cortés in 1519 advanced on Tenochtitlán, the site of Mexico City.

1   ISSTE

Clerks, on holiday,
navigate at leisure
the waters of this moated fortress
time has turned into a pleasure garden.
Bannered above them looms
their sibillant acronym ISSTE –
INSTITUTO DE SEGURIDAD SOCIAL
AL SERVICIO DE LOS TRABAJADORES
DEL ESTADO: ISSTE
which seems in tune
with the sound of water
the pole of the remero lifts
along a shore whose intersecting twigs

hold floating islands together
that have taken root. All
are free today
to sway in unison,
while the two waltzing
so chastely in the narrow bows
seem to dance
almost without movement:
mariachi at the prow
trumpet the excursionists' approach
while in the stern guitars
and a violin thrum a passage through
the diminished empire of these isles
from which the exasperated conquistador
combed out their ancestors.

2   Marimba

The two marimberos confront
their instrument, this
Kaffir piano that the slave trade
brought to these shores: a prelusive
quivering of wooden keys,
a ripple of sound shadows
over the buzz of bass: their steersman
slides them in close beside our boat,
holding them steady there.
What water music will they float out now?
They suggest items like knowledgeable waiters
when one hesitates
toying with the menu – La Zandunga? –
and bring down drumsticks
selecting notes
for this dance of dignity. The elate
vibration takes fire but never conflagrates,
holding a dulcet truce
while in full flow
like the channel we ride on.
Or Las Chiapanecas? –
the beat is no burden
to this swifter sweetness.

The others I forget, recall
only a different kind of note,
the flicker of paper pesos
fluttering thanks and encouragement, as we
enter this causeway crowded with gondoliers
whose accuracy is the guarantee
of our own safe circuit
back to the embarcadero and the quay.

3   Words

Under his awning,
Cernuda visited this spot
He heard only echoes
of extinct wisdom, of abdicated life.
Silent figures held out a flower, a fruit
from their passing boats
and evidently knew the secret of it all
but did not reveal it.
A veiled sky darkened the waters,
the poplars took on a sickly look,
the musicians seemed to have grown old.
Under funereal branches, he saw
the boats of the sellers of flowers
venture out
to pay periodic tribute
to their drowned recollection of the place,
webbed them in words
and relished that bitter satisfaction
flooding tongue and pen.
Today asks no more
to disperse the Klingsor spell and curse
that words can cast over things
than the sweet acridity
drifting across the sense
where a pair of vendors bend
at their brazier roasting maize,
while, on the bank above,

Section 3, 'Words', contains a paraphrase of Cernuda's prose poem, 'Por el Agua'.

a knock-kneed foal
a branch between its teeth,
is chewing on leaves as new-born as itself,
cantering into view
as if it were the smoke-smell
had woken it to life
and the sky behind it and beyond might well
revive those distinctnesses of line and hue
that, once, in the rarified air,
seemed to annihilate distance.

4   Casa de Alvarado

After the fume of the streets, in front of the massive doors of Casa de Alvarado, Mexico itself – always a composite self – becomes palpable once more: the wall, painted dark red and patterned with lozenge shapes of white stucco, is Moorish in style, *mudejar*. Like the doors it has an impregnable look. High above the doors a small, columned shrine, a saint inside, on top of the shrine a cross of that same ox-blood colour on a red ball laced round with a cross of white stucco. At the shrill bell, the doors are opened and one enters a courtyard sunk deep in time, whose shadows are as cool as a well. Pigeons fly down to drink at a circular tiled basin of stone. From the level of the upper patio, a giant magnolia and bougainvilleas hang over. Through the shadowy recess of an archway light falls into a garden beyond, where tiny squirrels with serpentine tails move through the greenery like black weasels. Two eagles are visitors to the trees of this urban Eden.

For years the place was inhabited by an American woman, an archaeologist. They say she was a sun-worshipper, but Lawrence, who visited her here on three occasions, describes her as someone more dryly rational, 'an odd number who could give the even numbers a bad time'. Her black idols, baskets and shields have been long swept away.

But who was Alvarado? They say he was one of Cortés' captains, the same Alvarado the Aztecs thought of as kin to the sun-god because of his red hair and called him Tonatio or Son of the Sun. It was he who performed the famous jump – *el salto de Alvarado* – when, surrounded by Aztec assailants in canoes and on land, he used his lance as a vaulting pole to leap over a canal and escape them.

Whether this is the true Alvarado of Casa de Alvarado, who can say with certainty? The history of the house and its garden must now also include that of Octavio Paz, the poet who came here to die and to seek, he said, reconciliation beneath these trees with their eagles and beside the cool basin frequented by pigeons. The house in Mixcoac, where he spent his childhood, is a convent. This house, where his days were to end, came nearest perhaps to the recollection of its garden and to that other garden in India where he was married beneath a giant neem tree, 'above its shoulders, the sky with its barbarian jewels'. The jewelled sky awaited him above this final garden which has survived the degradation of the City of Mexico, ravished almost as thoroughly as Aztec Tenochtitlán. 'There are no gardens,' he once wrote, 'except those we carry with us.' Here, a flat-topped arch opens in space another space, another time in time, the shade and shape of trees filling with their presences the garden into which this opening invites us. In the quiet of this sculpted clearing, we are standing in the middle of the world's biggest city that keeps moving, without pause or limit, out over the levels of the Valley of Mexico like lava.

A Visit to Don Miguel

I am about to leave
when he tells me: 'Five
of the president's bodyguard
have been shot dead.' 'Strange.
Nothing about it in the press.'
'There won't be. My brother telephoned
with the news. They will never
confess that it happened. You like this house?
It's haunted. One day
our maid saw a ghost in the dining room.
When we rushed in, there was nothing there –
only the smell of a cigar
in a house where nobody smokes. Years ago
there were executions in the garden –
that's where the ghosts come from
through the back wall
where there's no entrance, you see.' I see.
Then he suddenly adds:

'I've been temporarily retired
for political indiscretions.
I shall return to my post next year
provided I remain discreet.' Outside the door,
'Perhaps discretion' – I put it to Roberto
who brought me here – 'is not his strong suit?'
But there is almost pride in the reply,
'Miguel es un gran conversador.'

Waiting for the Bus

at Tlacochahuaya

               Goats
gnawing the prickly pears
with rock-hard jaws
lean between sand and spines
up into the bush. The crossroads
grow festive as we wait:
it is a subdued festivity
when the people of two villages
meet at a crossroads and kiss hands,
gathering into both their own
the hand to be kissed and with warmth
kiss it, saying softly
Qué tal? qué tal? The surprise
is a ritual surprise –
not so that of the two young men
who know each other yet did not know
both were travelling today
and to the same place – *Aah!* –
and having patted each other
they embrace, wandering side by side
absorbed in the fact of friendship.
A man leads three bulls
across the road, but no one
takes this in: they have eyes
only for humanity – the goats
are also invisible to them.

When we entered the village
a man on a burro had saluted us:
You are going to Tlacochahuaya?
We moved on through the *Buenos días*
of others and to the church
where a one-armed Indian
stood at the door and silent
gestured us inside, but this one-armed guide
neither guided nor begged.
Darkness, then the painted walls
covered with an angel army
– more cupids than angels:
the Dominicans had taught their flock
to paint them here
and unthrone Tlaloc (still tongued
in the village name)
and to convert the pagan gods
into saints and demons.
Two small girls followed us
as we left, asking
apologetically almost
for *moni, moni, moni,*
merely murmuring the word.
We regained the crossroads
and the man on the burro, returning,
was it stated or enquired
You have been to Tlacochahuaya?
And now out of the dust
a bus that will carry us back
suddenly arrives and the conductor
reciting *Oaxaca, Oaxaca,*
begins to stow aboard
his restive customers until
they fill the interior
and, giving blow on blow
to the resonant metal of the vehicle,
conveys to the waiting *operador*
it is time to go.

A Fragment from Mexico

Waiting in the sand, this
terracotta shard of a face
smiled on: when we
unearthed that smile
it did not anticipate the mile on mile
it must travel to here.
It is more leer than smile,
that almost lecherous anticipation
awaiting the sacrifice
when the sun-god is fed
on human hearts:
and still it awaits
and will outsmile
even the deaths of all the gods
under the wide grey of this sky.

From the Plane

for Kálmán Ruttkay

Ruskin would have seen a reason for flying
 On a day like this, with cloud shadows
Blown-by below, shaping out the land
 They clamber across – the immense
Body of Europe, with its mountains spread
 Beneath one's feet. One's feet? Why, they and we
Tread twenty thousand feet of space
 Between ourselves and the relief of Chamonix.
Yet from the ground, he could already see
 The hollow in the heart of the aiguille
As smooth and sweeping in its cavity
 As the curve of a vast oyster shell,
The connected movement in those crested masses
 Like that of sea waves, governed by
One under-sweep of tide that ran

Through the whole body of the mountain chain.
Ruskin did not need to fly: his eye
    Flew for and back to him and what we see
At this height, he taught us standing on two feet,
    Among rocks the metallic tines of water
Curve across and down, into the course
    Of the hurrying river that uncoils its force
Tasselling-on to the unseen horizon.

Piazza

In the piazza at Ascoli Piceno
    The people walk on travertine, not asphalt –
Marble that paviours patterned into squares
    Each with its slim, stone borders
In a mathematic of recession. All the generations
    Go their measured way and savour now
The sharp air of a winter Sunday.
    That child, muffled against the cold,
Has discovered the long line of stone
    Slicing the centre of the expanse
And is following it, has to be restrained,
    Pacified, but already he has caught
A border stretching out edgeways,
    Sets off to follow that. One day
He will put it all together, time
    That he does not know exists, teaching him
To eye it all entire, admit
    That these leisurely restrictions are a fiction
That reveals the real, mapping our footfalls,
    Our swung arms, our slow dance here,
For an afternoon the guests of symmetry,
    Treading its stones in this theatre of chance.

In Ferrara

Carp the size of sheep
muscle their course to the surface
as they leap at the scraps of bread
flung their way. The concerted rush
raises a ripple, pushes back
the floating sediment
on this moat of the Estensi
and leaves a clear, clean space for play
over the beer-brown depths,
bellies glittering, disappearing.
It was energy like this
raised those walls, their height
filled with unfurnished emptiness now.
It is night. The street lamps
punctuate the alternation
of a depth-charge force and a dead calm
under this lavish scattering of bread.

The Etruscan Graveyard at Marzabotto

At the dump, the packaged waste
as neat as war-graves
awaits destruction:
the drone of a generator
insists on efficiency, promises
to destroy all traces:
on the spring wind
there is one other sound,
the whisper of discarded cellophane
like the voices of the dead
shiny and shivering with the season.
On the hilltop remain
in a fold of land
graves that are blocks of tufa,
the dark rock splashed

with ring on ring of orange
from the lichen
that thrives on nothing. One might choose
to lie here and be reclaimed by earth,
as clean as the emptiness
within each box of stone
that has no lid, but lies
open to the dateless sky
that has forgotten
how far their race once spread
who, dead, so succinctly occupy
so small a space.

In June

In town today
wind and sunlight
investigated together
the costumes of passers-by,
feeling and fluttering
the thin-spun stuffs
people put on in summer,
to find out whether they
belonged here or beyond, almost
painting them where they walked
or stood, constantly
reshaping with billowing
brush-strokes, with free-hand
fantasies of a preliminary
sketch – preliminary that is
to further alterations, as if
unwilling to leave them
and their things
as now winged and now
shrunk back
into unchanging normality
only to take fire there
and swell out once again
from man to angel

The Runners at San Benedetto

Two runners are crossing the shore by night:
   Their sound on sand, their lithe iambics gauge
The certainty of arrival and return
   Before the wide encroachment of the waters
Smoothes out their footprint frontier. Cloud
   Keeps dulling the cusps of a moon
Just risen. A steadier glow
   From the endless necklace of the lungomare,
A fitful one from the circling beam
   Of a lighthouse that dapples keels
Close-packed, rocking at anchor.
   For lovers crossing the shore by night,
None of this is their concern. They see
   In the unpaved pathway a chosen destiny:
They choose each other and this place,
   Place to return to and by night re-pace
In the twilit ritual that runs between
   The competing geometries of shore and sky
Where the first stars prick their courses.
   Lovers, how many years of light
Await you behind that sky I cannot say:
   Your compact with the dark will guide you where
Beneath time's leisurely eye, the common day
   Tests this accord that was confirmed by night.

July on the High Plain

Baled hay: the shaved land
   Where the cut crop grew and lay
Says that the multicoloured summer
   Is at an end. A pallid promontory
Extends between bare peaks,
   The roadside poplar rows
Crossing it at eccentric angles
   Beneath the bald crown of a mountain
Tonsured round by beeches. At noon

Each tree sheds a shadow,
A perfect, separate circle on the ground,
   A dark disc one might well lift
And take away. But one must be swift
   Before the atmosphere consolidates as mist
And extinguishes all outline to become
   The black rainstains on every stone
In the evening storm, the downpour
   Babbling on the roof its liquid glossolalia,
As lightning explores the sleeping face of nature.

The Journey: Pescocostanzo–Roma

The tunnel-mouth irises-in
   Encircling and then lets go
The heights we enter, free to grow
   Now beyond us, to fall away below
Repeating the story of their making,
   As shapes come flowing into solidity,
Ranges re-group and stand
   Firm for as long as it takes an eye
To grasp them and the car flash by
   Into a new configuration. The next
Mouth issues us out over cloud –
   We are not rising, we are coming down
Through all these petrine metamorphoses
   To where the mist hangs low above Sulmona
In the gradual descent – the serrated mountains
   Soon behind us, the ramparts raising
On stone hands walls, houses, towers
   Towards eventual snow – down
To the lesser slopes, the Roman seven,
   As slowly the vines climb back across the land.

Sulmona was the birthplace of Ovid.

Roma

I *Monte del Gallo*

The faintest breeze is stirring finger-fronds
Of the many-fingered hands that seem to stroke
The inaudible keyboard that is air:
The raised draped pine-boughs float on tides unseen
That lift then let them go, submerged
In the impersonality of trunks. Two cypresses
Grown close together, leaned on by the wind,
Seem to acknowledge one another's presence –
Human, would be moving to an embrace –
But they, too, like the sea-beast pines, submit
To the oceanic motion parting them,
Provoking us with their silences, their deep
Arboreal indifference to unsleeping Rome.

II *At Tivoli*

Did Hadrian bring Antinous his friend
To hear the nightingales beside this pool
On summer afternoons? They sing today
As though the centuries had done no harm
To one's authority and the other's charm
And we might find them here between these walls
Of what was once a palace and retreat
Built for the pleasure of the senses where
One naked headless athlete poses still
Reflected by the water. In the sun,
Drowning the crickets in the dusty grass,
The unquenchable loud nightingales flow on.

III *Liszt at the Villa d'Este*

How liquidly he matches cadences
Against suggestions that the lilt of water
Raises in his mind. The deliquescence
Still runs pure across the barlines of the score,

But under the centennial cypress trees
No shaping hand can purify this rush
Of currents you must neither touch nor taste
Laced with contaminations from a land turned waste.

IV   *In the Park*

In the park, a deserted carousel,
The *padrona* sits behind her newspaper.
Riderless the animals do not stir,
Then rock, half-restive, as traffic moves the air.

Two piebalds with a coach, an elephant,
A miniature house, a castle keep –
You could imagine them circling from their sleep
Awakened by wheezing music. I write it down

The childless silence, the animals of wood
Glittering, new-painted and unreal –
The prince's playthings left beneath the trees;
Quiet axle of the city's turning wheel.

But the woman's face rises above the pages:
Che fa, signore? She takes me for some spy
Inspecting the safety of her paradise.
Scrivo una poesia, I reply.

Half-convinced, she shifts from foot to foot
While she persuades herself. *Bene*, she says
At last, subsides once more beneath her sheets,
Invisible as the stanza's lock clicks shut.

Piazza Navona

The pigeons
make a moveable feast
for the leisured eye,
crowning the sculpture round the fountain: one
sits on the head of a cupid,
one on his wing,
another astride the back
of a petrified crab whose claws
steady it against the brow of a triton
mouthing a water jet
out of a seaweed-bearded
gap-toothed aperture
that grimaces pain: cupid
is indifferent to this
as he crawls towards the crab
but cannot take hold
because of the intervening pigeon
riding its carapace: his expression
– all interest and anxiety
to achieve his end – appears
to take in the unlooked-for
but now perceived obstruction,
and you might almost swear
a flash of infantile frustration
was dawning on his face: all this
in detail from a time
when architecture, too,
was one of the arts of decoration.

Farewell to Europa

Europa
carried away astride the back
of a motorcycle, horns
and handlebars make a fair match,
but this bride of the machine,

having lost her head,
shows no more now
than the disc of a breast,
an echo of the wheels,
hubbed by its nipple.
Speed has cancelled her out and she
is pleased to be no more
than this faceless rhyme in space
which cannot even see
the landscape of her future
rolling towards her
through the sodium glow
of dismantled towns.

Japanese Notebook

The falling blossom
I saw drift back to the branch
was a butterfly

Moritake

for Takashi Tsujii

The circular window
(unglazed)
in the shrine at Kamakura
borrows the landscape and transforms it
into a roundel on the wall

The rice grains
in the porcelain
of the teacup
let through light

Bridge of a spider's web
leaves resting on it
as on the telephone wires
above the bamboo grove

Legs of the spider
halfway between
the shambling of a crab
and the parrot's claw
scaling the wires of its cage
in laborious methodical ascent

Immense wooden temples
that look like celestial barns
full of invisible grain

Fat ropes of straw
embrace and sanctify
the trunks of the ancient pines
that climb so high
before their foliage begins

A tree mummified in bandages
it has been there seven hundred years
and must be fortified
against the diseases of old age

A bamboo pipe drips
dropping condensation
from rocks into a well
already overflowing

The falling leaf
that turns out not to be
Moritake's butterfly
has reached the ground

Bashō's cicada drills no rocks
but emerges from the dust
a tarnished link
in the foodchain of the ants
lifting it by its feelers

Clouds
that keep removing
the miniature mountains of Izu
have abolished Fuji

To Shizue

They tell me
'quiet bough'
is the meaning of your name.
Who now
will uncomplainingly accept
the given air? –
it was not this
they wanted, but the lurch
and wave-lash
of infinite variety:
too few will thank you
for the calm
your name contains
that, bearing fruit,
has no need
to greedily call out
for what is not here,
but lets the bough
ride the stir
on the scarcely
undulated atmosphere.

For Nōrikō

Seeing the blossoms on our cherry tree,
I thought of the strokes of your calligraphy
Riding on the air that was the page
Your brush was hovering over: stage by stage
A sudden blossoming of each character,
Of living letters, sprung from nowhere,
As though the sheet were both the bough and air.
If, in all this, your writing seemed a tree
Putting forth petals, what of your artistry,
How many centuries flowing through that arm?
One might have sworn each rapid touch was warm
With the life that was in you and others;

The brushwork at an end, the text still stirs
In this undecided light, this hesitating
English winter half-arrived at spring.

Macao

Banyans
spilling Spanish moss
shade a park. A fragment
of Catholic Europe – a church front:
the drift and perfume of joss
invade the missing nave
from the shrine beneath it. The library
vanished in fire like the nave itself,
neither to be restored. A cat
sits in the threshold dust
of the Pagoda da Barra, its kittens
asleep by the altar.
In the Protestant church
the basket-work pews
are painted brown
to resemble mahogany:
in its graveyard lies
the apprentice boy 'who died on board
of a fall into the hold'. It is four o'clock
in the world of time
through which pour
schoolchildren in blazers
past a bust of Da Gama
greening on its marble plinth.
Smouldering overhead,
feeding the temple haze,
hang the coils of joss
that soil with dropped ash
the stone bed
where bundles of dozing fur
do not stir below
those cigarettes of eternity.

On Lantau Island

A dog-pack circles the monastery grounds:
in the shade of its boundary wall
they take their rest, exuding an odour
like pungent tweed. The testier dogs
still snarl at one another. Leadership
or plain dislike puts them on edge
spikily vulnerable. Then they are off
and some collective impulse, subliminal sense of lack
steers them elsewhere: the ill-tempered
defer their resentments, mounted and unfulfilled
the copulatory lose balance, dragged
rolling apart into the spate of general will.
The tide washes on and subsides by the gate.
Heave and relapse, and the bickerings begin again.
Who reincarnated in them? They will be joined one day
by the nun reciting her scriptures *sotto voce*
who forfeits nirvana by periodically
baring her teeth and screaming
at the unbiddable tourists who insist
on photographing the gods of the temple annex:
in their lotus thrones the three gold buddhas
float weightlessly, buoyed up like the boats
that carried them here through the uncertain sea.

Waiting for John

The trains that day were running late.
    Near the station, swayed a stand of pines
Like a group of stranded travellers
    That had taken root. Suddenly
The wind passed through and drew from them
    A noise like a train arriving – though
After the windy onset, nothing occurred
    Except more such imitations. Bemused, I hailed the thought
Of a form of transport more than terrestrial
    In the alternation overhead of sound and silence,

In the battery of breeze among resonant treetops.
 But how quiet reality is, sliding into its berth,
And the twelve thirty-four arriving on earth
 Modestly filled up space under the roar of boughs.
I missed the hiss of doors opening, the clatter of feet.
 I had come merely to meet someone.
Had I been travelling, I would not have caught
 That stealthy arrival while staring at the trees.
But something caused me to turn and recognize
 An approaching face, good to see
After time's long gap. Let me take your case.
 What sounds were those that followed us from there?
Was it the rage of pines or a train's departure?

Bristol Night Walk

It is not far –
 Given the mind's propensity to travel
And not leave the spot. Morse
 From the Cabot Tower is signalling our existence
To Mars, and though there is no one there
 To appreciate the *clair de terre*, the pulse
Of light at the bottom of this well,
 You face all that emptiness overhead
With equanimity, the city spread before you –
 So much movement round fixed points,
Spire, tower and bridge. The dew
 Of this warm night will leave each statue
Drenched and shining. But not yet.
 They loom now in nocturnal gravity –
Burke advancing behind the gesture of his hand,
 And through the traffic fume the horse
Bearing royal William, stretches wide
 Nostrils that look as though they scent it.
The dew is gathering under darkness,
 Glistening in silence where the bridge
Leaps the vacancy of the abyss it spans:
 We hang here balanced between iron and stone

Under the equilibrium of such stars
    As prick the vault above us, our fragility
For the moment shielded in the palm of space.

Death of a Poet

i.m. Ted Hughes

It was a death that brought us south,
    Along a roadway that did not exist
When the friendship was beginning death has ended.
    How lightly, now, death leans
Above the counties and the goings-on
    Of loud arterial England. I see
A man emerge out of a tent,
    Pitched at a field's edge, his back
Towards the traffic, taking in
    The flat expanse of Sedgemoor, as if history
Had not occurred, the drumming tyres
    Creating one wide silence.
Oaks stand beside their early shadows.
    Sun makes of a man's two shadow-legs
Long blades for scissoring the way
    Across yet one more meadow, shortening it.
Hardy's rivers – Parrett, Yeo, Tone –
    Flash flood waters at us. Then,
As the flatlands cede to patchwork Devon,
    Again you cannot quite foretell the way
Dartmoor will rise up behind its mists,
    As solid as they are shifting. Sun,
Without warning, sets alight the fields,
    In anticipation of that other unison
As fire enters body, body fire,
    And every lineament gone, dissolves
The seal and simplification of human limits.
    Mourners drift out of the church,
Stand watching the slow cortège
    Of car and hearse wind through the street

To that last unmaking. The net of lanes
    Entangles our departure, hedges
Zapped spruce against the expectation
    Of another spring. Scarcely time
To recall the lanes we walked in or the coast
    That heard our midland and his northern voice
Against a wind that snatched their sounds.
    The small hawks caught the light
Below us, crossing the Hartland bays
    Over endless metamorphoses of water.
Voice-prints, like foot-prints, disappear
    But sooner; though more lingeringly
They go on fading in the ear.
    We join the highway that is England now.
The moon, a thin bronze mirror
    Reflecting nothing, a rush of cloud
Suddenly effaces. The line of oaks
    That at morning stood beside their shadows
Are shades themselves on our return.

For T.H.

I caught today something that you'd once said.
It re-formed in the echo-chambers of the head
Bringing with it the voice of its saying
(Your voice) and even the atmosphere of a morning
On Hartland's cliffs and the steady pace that we
Kept up beside the murmurings of that sea.
It was the music of speech you were describing
And the way such sounds must either die or sing,
The satisfactions of speech being musical
When we talk together: a man with no talent at all
For music in the matters of everyday
Stays tedious despite what he has to say –
Even on subjects that might wake one's fantasies,
For what we want is that exchange of melodies,
The stimulation of tunes that answer one another
In the salt and sway of the sea's own weather

As they did that day we faced into the wind there,
And now return in thought, so that I hear
The dance of the words, like verse itself, renew
The sounded lineaments of the world we move through.

Cotswold Journey

2001

A day before the war and driving east,
  We catch the rasp of ignited engines –
Planes practising combat above this shire
  Of Norman masonry, limestone walls.
In their quiet, they seemed so permanent
  Under the changing light. But the tower
We stand beneath is hacked by sound
  Out of the centuries it has inhabited
With such certainty. After the flash
  We stand once more on stable ground
Under chevroned arches, climb the stair
  Up to the dovecot where the priest
Once fetched the victims down that he would eat.
  The form remains, the victims have all gone
From nesting places squared in stone,
  Boxes of empty darkness now. The planes streak on
Returning out of the unsteady brightness,
  The blue that rain could smear away
But does not. Sun turns into silhouettes
  The gargoyles clinging to sheer surfaces
That rise above us. Sun travels beside us
  As we penetrate deeper in, lose track
Of the plane-ways that leave no vapour trails
  To decorate their passage through
In abstract fury. Courteous walls
  Rise out of stone-crowned summits,
Prelude and then surround a dwelling space
  With church and inn – for us the solace
Of a now twilit afternoon. We explore

Before we eat, the inn-yard and the street beyond,
Where Saxon masons, raising arch and jamb,
  Cut leaves of acanthus whose weathered surfaces
Hold onto fragile form. The night
  Slowly extinguishes their edges but bequeaths
To the mind the lasting glimmer still
  Of stone come to life. The inn
Recalls us through the village street
  And I remember how a friend once said,
Speaking with a Yorkshireman's conciseness,
  'A native gift for townscape, a parochialism
But of a Tuscan kind.' Our return
  Is silent although we travel by
Lanes tracing the outlines of the airbase
  And, there, all we manage to decipher
Is the gleam of wired restriction, barbs
  That bar us out from sterile acres
Awaiting the future in a moonless quiet.
  Rain, with the clink of the lifted latch
On our arrival, bursts from the darkness where
  East and west, preparing to unseam
The sleeping world below that height,
  Downpour drops its curtain on the past
And the cry of the muezzin infiltrates first light.

Spem in Alium

I have placed my hope in no other god but thee,
Transfiguring spirit of poetry,
And as the levels of the landscape rise
In roofline, tree and hill before my eyes,
Until the clouds themselves are earthed in light,
Their changes show the world is not complete
And never will be, as we read its book,
Transfiguration glancing with each look,

Spem in Alium: Tallis's motet for forty voices: 'I have never placed my hope in any other than thee...' (Spem in alium nunquam habui praeter in te...).

NEW COLLECTED POEMS

Whenever light (changing itself) descries
Another variation for the eyes,
All climbing like a counterpoint of voices,
And sight aware of what, unsighted, stays
Hidden behind a foreground and a meaning
Which cannot be restricted to the thing
Shorn of the spaces that surround its being.
Tallis, you tell the poet what is here
As if that arch of song which throngs the ear,
Shaping not only the invisible,
Rang like the currency of daylight, full
Of the nearby and the answering distances,
Outward and far to where the horizon lies:
And in the altered light there, you can weigh
The pull of the planet travelling its sky,
And one more journey to another day
Complete, and waiting on a dawn unseen,
Unhurriedly to let the changes re-begin.

Trout

A trout, facing upstream, hangs
    Balanced against the current he is riding:
Tail and fins countervail the force
    Which keeps compelling him into acquiescence:
The delicate blades of his resistance
    Outflicker the ceaseless pouring of its course:
He has taken his stand midstream
    And will stay suspended there as long
As the need lasts in this unhurried hunt
    For what will feed him. It is attention
Steadies him within this element where
    Nothing is still, toning his faculties
To penetrate the twilight of its depths,
    Holding him poised until a darker shade
Falls across the flow and could presage his end:
    As swift as he was still, he backs with the current,
Glides beneath the bank, waits there,

Meditates in the sliding gloom and lets
Death's trailing shadow slowly disappear
Into the summer growth of one more year.

Track

Out of the wood, into the wood beyond
Trails flatten the grass between, and tell
Of midnight passages. These signs for silence
Dwell within the mind's own silences
Breeding a mystery – mysterious, too,
Even when explanation has restored it
To a world not shaped by introspection
And to lives lived-out beside our own
Nocturnal and unseen. Tracing a track
Badger or fox had smoothed, our glances fell
With the slope it followed, with a certainty
That taught us too, to see – sheer as it was –
The sure line of what accuracy aimed it
Through tunnelled tussocks, out beneath a fence
And down once more, a slither across marl,
To vertically reach the brink and bank
Where water, telling a story of its own,
Quarrelling with the debris in its course,
Flashed with the light of early afternoon
That message, to be scented while we slept,
Of satisfaction to the ones who drink by night.

Slow Down

SLOW
DOWN
it has warned all winter
at the blind corner as if
yes all two syllables
were needed to impress

the speeding eye. The advance
of March grass and of weed
has overshot from D to N
the bottom line by now
to show that yes a single
syllable will do the work of two
with that succinct sign
springing up out of leaves
like a growing thing.

Newark Park: An Upward Glance

i.m. Robert Parsons, Texan

Low winter sun,
as accurate as a gunsight,
aims all of its light
at the façade glass
that blinds and blazes
from the hilltop.
The wood that comes between
our eyes and it –
a black phalanx of winter trees
puts out that brightness.
But among those trunks –
a hail of diamond,
comet train caught
through a drawn curtain.
Then the whole reflection
slides into sight once more.
'A lighthouse,' I say, and you:
'More like a ship
leaning into view.'
New ark, indeed,
ferrying toward the coast of evening
all those seeds of light,
all the energy futurity
cannot exhaust overnight.

The ship stands (it is darkening
along its decks)
in sight of the black coast
glimmering with frost –
cost of such clarity
as the January afternoon
brought to flare, higher and higher,
oxygen to that bonfire
now gone out.

Reflection

A reflection on the pane
has repositioned the chest of drawers
under the mahonia bush
on the lawn outside.
One drawer lies open to the rain
perfectly dry. Let the eye
follow that image
to where an interior door
cuts across the night,
as if there were many mansions to explore
under the gathered gloom,
room on room of them
in enfilade across the garden
left open to the coming generations
of this house already old.

In the Hallway

What I like in a house
is the room one cannot quite see –
the one with its door half-open,
showing a mere sliver of wall,
a picture sliced in half,

a mirror reflecting a window
that is invisible from outside
where you stand in the hallway
and the owner's lady
emerges from above, revealing
how intricate is the space up there
because of a landing which casts shadow
challenged from below by the clear
cut glass of a chandelier:
under this runs the hall,
drawing one deep into its recession
with a gleam on the floor-tiles,
and in the distance a flash
off conservatory windows
angled open to admit
a summer evening, the clip
of feet advancing, and a voice:
'I do not believe that you
have been here before,' she says,
and though one has
what she says is true.

A Riddle

The radial wheels of the season spiked with knives.
The hand which investigates such workmanship
Needs to go gauntleted, or leave it to the eyes:
Boudicca's bladed chariots rode like these,
Flesh flinching from them through the laid-waste field
That autumn has now invaded with this crop.

'A Riddle': autumn thistles.

The Even Numbers

for Richard Verrall

The even numbers, as beautiful as vowels
    Emerging from the consonantal clasp
Of sounds that contain and yet unbind
    The o, the hidden aria, the bud
Unsheathing itself to flower on ear, on air –
    What would they do without the impaired, the odd
That show them for what they are?

If Bach Had Been a Beekeeper

for Arvo Pärt

If Bach had been a beekeeper
he would have heard
all those notes
suspended above one another
in the air of his ear
as the differentiated swarm returning
to the exact hive
and place in the hive,
topping up the cells
with the honey of C major,
food for the listening generations,
key to their comfort
and solace of their distress
as they return and return
to those counterpointed levels
of hovering wings where
movement is dance
and the air itself
a scented garden

The Gift

A man stepped out of the field:
a hawk with both wings spread
rode at his wrist:
'She's still learning,' he said.

I heard her bells
clash in the winter air
and watched her stare
unfocused on any human thing.

'Not long since,
she hit out at me.'
'You mean beat you with her wings?'
'With her talons and feet I mean.

Since when she's behaved.' –
he let her
eat a morsel of game from his bag –
'Of course, she screams when I go to get her.

Someone offered me
real money – but we shall see:
I think I shall keep her –
four pheasants, a rabbit and a hare

this very week. Like one? –
a pheasant, I mean.' She began
to shift on the perch of his hand
while he dug from the bag his gift.

Then she eyed the bird
transferred to my keeping:
I was relieved she was jessed
firm to his hunter's wrist.

And so there passed this gift unforeseen
beneath her unblinking sight,
under the easterly chill
of a winter twilight.

Midwinter

Midwinter turning into twilight
  By the red farm: downpour drenches it,
A sore smear on a ground of green.
  A stream, surfeited with winter rain
Runs parallel to this hillside path
  As, far below, I sense suddenly
I am observed, sense before perception shows
  What eyes those are that follow me:
The stream is glancing skywards between trees
  That screen its banks, a thousand eye-whites
Divided by dark boles (their pupils),
  Each eye-white shared between two boles.
What I see's not real and yet is there –
  That endless stare goes on and on,
Eye after eye dogging my track.
  Turn back before darkness falls.
This I do, freed from that chain of eyes.
  The farm's owners have returned since I set out.
Their lights, extravagantly festive,
  Reveal the solidity of roughcast walls.
Twilight is kinder to their colour than the rain.
  The square flags of the barnyard are sleek with wet.
The new half-moon rides by with one straight side
  Cut out by shears.

The Transformation

A morning moon
caught in the tree
begins its slide
slowly from branch to branch
behind the web
and tangled spokes of winter,
its midnight brilliance
made pale by daylight:
it is like seeing a face
grown suddenly old
that one had known
in all its youthful luminosity.

Ode to Memory

'Bird-witted'
is unjust –
call them all
winged memories: food
stowed and stored
to them means
food to be recalled:
they can trace months later
the where and when,
and what we would leave
forgotten, they will retrieve
in order of preference,
i.e., that which tastes best,
or should, if rot
has not decayed it: respect
the despised intellect
of birds, and when a name
out of the hundred that you know
refuses to appear
wish yourself bird-gifted,
and then go airily outside,

and on lifted wings
re-train the sights
of unfocused recollection, and if you can
become bird-brained.

The Leaper

Going from pool
to pool the moon
leaps on ahead of us,
always arriving
before we do, always
discovering how many
hollows the rain
had found to fill
along the mudslick path
that clings at the hill foot
to the level land,
and winds beside this stream
where the moon
must also be if only we
were wading it east
away from the going sun:
then we should see
on its surface
the continuous rippled moonface
replace the athlete moon
but cease to see
this invention of foot and eye
that moves because we
move, to tantalize
and lead us on
though it has never
shifted from being
that mid-sky beacon.

Fire and Air

Silk scarves of flame
wind from the coals
liquidly leaping them to and fro,
uncircling whichever way aircurrents go.

They aim to join
the airstream flowing above the house,
disordering every tree,
that lures them upwards into nonentity.

Strange, that opposites
should reach for the same
unassailable altitude
as if air and fire were a single flame.

As they are
when a house burns down
and they race the stairway, lit
by the one desire to have done with it,

leaving a silhouette
blackened behind them,
cardboard cut-out where once was wall,
swaying unflamelike, tottering to downfall.

A truce on the hearth tonight
keeps all in peace, in place,
mingling fire and air beyond blame.
Do not cease to admire such a scene. Do not trust a flame.

Primal Fire

This iridescent chaos
that assails the sense
each day – number
will never sway it.
Why did Plato dream
this stream might be canalized
by calling it illusion?
Trust to surfaces –
these are profundities:
you can neither drown
in them, nor outgaze
the maze of their intricacy.
They tell you who you are
and where – which is here,
between the sunlight
wakening on the wall
these variegated shadows
and the sun itself,
through days uncounted, unaccountable
pouring primal fire.

Knowledge

The nicks in the panes of each window square
inflicted by spring rain:
the way things show themselves
is often in disguise – not lies,
but a way of stating what is there
despite appearances: what we perceive
is a kind of poetry,
no more illusion than
the black ripple of shadow
we drag at our back
and only others see. They
and we are fed by such incongruities,
such knitting and unroving of appearance,

arriving here which is where we are
behind the rain-nicked panes of each window square.

Watching Water

Why is it water, standing for itself,
    Runs to so many meanings? I watch
The flickerings, the flash, the out-and-through
    Past bridges, bankside, flank
Of sand that rains have thickened to obstruct
    Its progress and have failed. The stream
That was brown and dark all day
    At evening takes in the low light
Of yellow sundown and begins to brighten.
    The same stream where it flows through the wood
Seems to run over foil: its whisperings
    Fall then, splashing off the hillslope,
To tiny metallic crashes: it springs
    And bounds across the valley next,
Still swift, but fuller now, a bodied sound,
    Invitation to view the gathered present
Thing it is – watched water,
    Voicing a sinuous way near into far.

Along this Stream

Along this stream
catching the click and gurgle
of its water clock that does not try
to count the hours, I sense
long fingers letting go
the unseizable substance
that is time in steady flow,
feeling the cold shock
of this arrival, a chain

    multiplying links innumerable
    that instantly outgo the ear
    and then a new voice
    mouths its presence there
    from under a bridge – the sole
    punctuation to all this onrush
    as if it had entered
    (as it has) a barrel of brick
    unstoppered to endless contents
    that fill it and refill, then on
    in an insatiable search
    for ocean

Floodtime

A thick-piled mat of foam
    Laps at a fallen trunk and then
Floats off in fragments, instantly renewed
    By the chafing forces from below
And the whiplash blow on blow
    From a wind that suddenly will cease and then renew.
The millionaire looks to the lake he's made
    To show him himself as he would wish to be,
But it stretches today – all blind opacity –
    Across the grass it sucks at in frank greed,
As if licking it into life
    Not drowning out a separate existence.
Too full of itself, it pours off downhill
    To claim other acres, then joins the stream
That is river now and turns to watery morass
    Whatever it casts silt on,
The snakeshape current forcing a way inside
    The aperture of a bridge and getting through
By almost dragging the parapet after it,
    Repeating again and again this act
Of desolate possession, under a rain-choked sky,
    Waiting to end all here in blear not blaze,
In a world of water and as cold as stone.

The Martins

Like the particles of a bursting shell
　　That nevertheless stay suspended
Moving together, a flock of martins
　　Rising, prepare to ride the wind
Of their departure and their wings imagine
　　The pull of it, anticipate the veerings
Against its mastery they must make their own.
　　What they leave are eaves inhabited all summer
For the inhuman liberty of space:
　　This is the trial, tomorrow they must go,
And in the empty nests another year
　　Await its chances under clouds that steer
Rains across the mapped-out counties
　　Above the migrating trickle of traffic moving.

Tonight

Tonight the sky stands cleansed
　　Of all its trails save one that, slowly,
Before the dark comes on – dissolving
　　From wrack to wraith – lets through
A high transparency. I wait beneath
　　This no-man's territory to see
How far that fringe of vapour can prolong
　　Its fading signature against space –
Space spreading upwards above shadow
　　Whose steady seepage has now gained
The ground we are standing on. I grip
　　With the eye that last dissolution in the sky
And pace the isthmus of the darkness under
　　A solidity of trunks that wait to bear
The leaf-crowns of another year,
　　Penetrating earth, preparing to drink light,
Upright across their tilted hemisphere.

CRACKS IN THE UNIVERSE
2006

Above the City

It would be good
to pass the afternoon
under this lucid sky,
strolling at rooftop level
this city above the city,
all the tubular protruberances,
chimneys, triangular skylights,
sheds that have lost their gardens
spread before one. The details
are not delicate up here
among the pipes and stacks,
the solid immovables, and yet
each outcrop affords
a fresh vista
to the *promeneur solitaire* –
though only the pigeons
are properly equipped
to go on undeterred
by changes of level where
one of their flat-footed
number suddenly launches itself
off the cornice sideways
taking its shadow with it
and bursts into dowdy flower,
blossoms in feathery mid-air to become
all that we shall never be,
condemned to sit
watching from windows
the life of those airy acres
we shall never inherit.

New York

A View from the Shore

I woke this morning
to find Brooklyn Bridge
festooned with a fringe of vineleaves
along the entire length
of the frame of its steel harp
and beyond: an aquatic ivy
was clasping the stone piers and climbing
towards the topmost cables:
drivers could no doubt see
the flicker of leaves
ascending past them and – glancing down –
even sun picking out the spear tips
where shoreside reeds pressed on the eye
their foreground to a car-crammed vista: here
overnight a crisis in the environment
had found its vent
and out of the hemmed-in cornucopia
that was nature once, had started
unstoppably to pour itself back
through this crack in the universe
on this outflanked riverbank
where the triumph of suspended steel
and its aftermath
had first begun.

New Jersey–New York

The mergings of cars, the chains of light
Announcing bridges, intersections,
They would see it all differently
From apartment windows,
Not nervously alert to the swervings
As traffic swings out to fill the thoroughfare
That is feeding one in – between
Lights and lights, buildings and buildings –
With a million cars, each one

A travelling eye
Letting things occur, letting them appear
As they will, the city itself another nature
Cutting into the density of spaces
With its stepped-back panoramas, the place
As merciless and beautiful as the universe.

A Name on the Map

for Judith Saunders

I ask myself what Fishkill must be like.
There is a river pouring into town
Under its elegant bridge; I scan the house-fronts
For their carpentered rhythmic trim, baroque
Curlicues in a wilderness that was.
It is the name drives the imagination back
To when the fish were plentiful, the Indians
With wet, red arms spearing up shad on shad
Out of the falls. Next time I cross the state,
I shall investigate the curio shops,
And perhaps recover from the dust
Some modest sketch, composed – though left unsigned
By the hand of (could it be?) Church or Bierstadt –
One closing winter afternoon just when
The artist was not thinking about mountains:
'Fishkill in February', in whites and gold,
And let into the sky in bold relief,
The cross above the college towards sunset.

The Upstate Freeze

for Fred Busch

That spring the sap had risen when
The ice took hold. Under a sky
That was grey-black it lay
In packed particles that were the same colour.
Risen sap froze in trunks and branches
And tree limbs began to crack from within,
Whole trunks ripped open white
Though not with snow or ice: bare
Tree interiors unhusked themselves there
Smelling of secret places, an intoxication
Of sap filling each nostril. The tree
On which blue herons yearly nested
Lay tipped aside, a sanctuary smashed.
The world was lead and it had blown apart.

Apples

Across the orchards of abandoned farms,
Walking the hills above the town,
We found that fallen apples kept their flavour.
It had grown more various and precise,
A measure of varieties no longer sold.
What we lack is an archaeology of apples,
But apple is neither coin nor arrowhead.
Going back down our feet encountered
Among the grass the graves of apple growers
Buried beside their crop, hidden obstructions
Slowing our descent. I do not think
That Eve discovered evil in an apple,
As its sweeter knowledge filled her mouth.
Today, with Adirondack winter on us,
We watch the fire and scent the apple-wood,
Counting the trails we can no longer follow,
The hills around us one long sierra of snow.

Four for David Smith

to Paula

1   *Interior for Exterior*

They tried to bring the whole of the view
into the room. But the strain
of space four walls could not contain
forced them at last to see
you could let in the outlines only
of hill, house, tree
to compose a cosmos circling,
signs in supple flight that show
which way the winds blow,
angels about to alight on a pinpoint
but who keep on flowing.

2   *The Timeless Clock*

The circular ride was shaking it to pieces,
the same track, the same worn ratchets
slewed out of kilter
but pacing shakily on,
falling apart as it strained towards
the open air,
the crumbling clouds reshaping,
the continuity of rivers –
all that a circle cannot hold.

3   *Hudson River Landscape*

Not the sublime.
There is a time for that also,
but the present occasion
is more a question

David Smith: American sculptor (1906–65). He placed many of his works, their metallic surfaces reflecting the colours of nature, in the open air at Bolton Landing.

of how do you hold a conversation
and with whom. To make that clear
I have turned my house into a foundry:
Picasso, González, Miró
are all welcome here. Where are the trees?
These are the branches of the trees –
I have invited space in
to pick them clean. I have written them
on the air
like a letter that will arrive
by first post and the fable
of the first day turn fact,
the light equable.

4 *Bolton Landing*

The ballet
of steel
beneath
a winter sky:
it was a man
made these
bare boughs.

Recalling Orson Welles

When you brought the ceiling
into the picture –
prison and precision –
what it revealed
was that the space
silently clothing us
was not infinite
but contained
both the place and persons
in the case:
under the vague
ceiling of the years

you went on talking
with all the brio
of the twenty-five-year-old
and the tales you told
on the screen
lost their conviction
and the meaning
you had gathered once
into those interiors
sealed and solidified
by the fifth wall
overhead which said:
here you are what you are.

Providence

Morning shadows waiting to surprise us
Across the white façades under the jut of eaves,
Houses are accurate sundials in such light –
Though it is less the time on them one reads
Than intimations of the day's advance
From satin on the sun-greyed cedar fence
To porch and gable, roof-pitch, balcony,
All the invitations of geometry
To measure time by the rule of spaces
From the dawn coldness to the evening cool,
Sunpath of providential emphases.

Rhode Island

Thomas Jones in Naples, 1782

He preferred the unglazed windows of the houses,
The door left open onto dark inside,
That made the radiant stucco of the wall
Seem like a daily bread the eye might feed on.

A day like this, how little one has need of
To make that little much: the nondescript
Ochre paint that brings what light there is
Marked out by shade across a shut door's panels,
The stepped-up levels of the town beyond
Dustily receding, plane by plane,
Towards the background domes and spires – glories
Unaccounted where the skyline celebrates
The white shirt of a workman on the roof.

Stellar Friendship

after Nietzsche

We were friends: we have become
strangers to each other.
We were two ships
each with its course and aim –
ships that lay
in the same harbour,
under the one sun and on a day
they seemed to have reached their goal.
But then the force
of what it was we had to do
drove us apart and into
strange seas and zones
that must change our faces.
Even now, our paths
might intersect and we
celebrate that encounter
as before. But to become
strangers is the law
that governs us both,
and just by that
we shall measure
our meaning for each other,
where there is an immense
invisible track, an orbit
pinning the dark,

in which our ways
and ends, bending
beyond our lost beginnings,
can reconcile in a cosmic curve
friendship as separate as the stars.

The Pupil

Who painted these pictures that take in
    The whole curvature of the visual hemisphere,
Where the gables and the roofs appear
    As if they were the minims and the blocks
Of an entire universe that freezes, flows
    And then recomposes itself beneath
A different light? The humble and colossal
    Pissarro – the adjectives are Cézanne's,
Who painted side by side with this man
    Of humbler gifts, 'to learn from him'.

La Rochelle

The whiteness of the city and its towers
Recalls the trade in salt that made it rich.
Now time has soiled the limestone of façades,
And yet this light of spring can still retrieve
Their saline sharpness, as another evening
Ferries out the sun beyond a harbour
Bristling with the masts of anchored yachts:
Beneath their hulls the ballet of reflections
Ripples and twists in rhythm with the swell,
The jostled whiteness of disjointed spars
Gone gold already in the alchemic sun.

Monet's Giverny

A certain fierceness in the sky, a blaze
Cuts out the verticals of the poplar trees
Against its steepness, so that only they
(The wind is rising through their ruffled leaves)
Serve to record the bright pitch of a day
Whose brightness asks no more than this – to burn
To the answering scrutiny of an eye
Fed by the fresh resilience of trees,
A palisade against the climbing clouds
And all that is tugging out of shape
This pact with time, this urgent landscape.

Les Joueurs de Football

In the Douanier's picture
Les Joueurs de Football,
even I who
ever since the day
I was forced out onto
a cricket pitch
have detested all
forms of team sport,
can see that the ball
in this charming ballet
is a rugby ball, and that
the four players, two
to a side (each
provided with an identical
moustache) are Art's reply
to the banalities of Life.
Perhaps the smallness of the pitch
mirrors the ever smaller studio
Rousseau must move into

'Les Joueurs de Football': Henri Rousseau, known as the Douanier: French painter, 1844–1910.

each time he tried to retrench,
to find money for his paints
or for his *soirées familiales et artistiques*
at which he played his violin
and even sang. The wall
of remarkably small autumnal trees
that surrounds this scene
on three sides lies
open to a turquoise sky
across which clouds (one
like the snout of a beneficent
saurian) declare
a change in the air and season,
hinting at all that may yet occur
undreamt by any footballer –
even those who struggle
for possession of an egg-like
ball – as nature brews
overhead its unending future,
its heterogeneity we do not understand
of a field without obvious rules,
goal-posts or goals.

Bread and Stone

The fragment of a loaf, rejected, stale:
As beautiful as any stone, it bears
Seams, scars, a dust of flour and like a stone
If it could unfold its history,
Would speak of its time in darkness and of light
Drawing it towards the thing it is,
Hard to the hand, an obstacle to sight,
Out of an untold matrix. If a son
Ask bread of you, would stone be your reply?
Let the differentiating eye
Rest on this, and for the moment read
The seed of nourishment in it as the sun
Reveals this broken bread as textured stone,
Served out as a double feast for us
On the cloth of the commonplace miraculous.

Fantasia in Limestone

'A fox head', you say and I
'A limestone spatula,
ready for use, but what use?'
You might well think
stone could repel all metaphor,
a mere flake of bone
from the skeleton of this hill,
but there, too, in the act
of saying, metaphor looms:
no fact stands free
from its own reflection and we
with the proverbial milk
imbibe it, a glad ghost
dancing airily under the eye of reason:
this second creation,
as intricately unforeseen
as the first, and both
untwining in relation,
glance towards each other where they spin
on the needle-point of mind,
twin births, children of chance.

Choice

If I must choose
between stone and cloud
let me not refuse
either, imagining
that one or the other must be
foremost in hierarchy
of thing over thing:
nothing is king
in this weather-swept world –
years shaping stone,
cloud crowds amassed
in a single noon,

and each sight so various
whatever meets the eye
seems to stare back at us
in sharp mutuality.
I turn away
from the rising cloudscapes
and what do I see
at my feet but a pebble
as pocked and rounded as they,
like a minuscule cloud-copy,
but here for millennia
or as long as human hand
takes up such tokens of time
from the generous ground.

Pebble

Take it up between thumb and index:
A stone conundrum you might call
This pebble of limestone. Fragments
Of identities struggle here to be themselves,
Searching for certainty but preyed upon
By a dozen images. A circle
At the pebble's centre makes a roving pupil
That is content to blur and be merely
A vague stomachless navel, then
An unmistakable mouth wide open
To sing a silent top note,
Yet transforms itself even as you wait to hear that note
Into half a head with two eyes
And then decides to be only a snout
With nostrils. A single ear
Begins to sprout from the irresolute stone
And next ventures to appear
As proud, wind-tossed locks of hair
Distinct above the flock of petrine pretenders
Whose entire mass now marches towards,
Threatens to carry me away from what I am
And into their pebble desert of unending babble.

I must fling it far off towards anonymity
This multitudinous changeling and let it stay
With its fellows forever on their prosaic pathway.

Chinchón

Trees in this landscape
signal the presence of a river.
A side-road leads us on –
parched grass, a rock horizon –
and winds us towards
a town watched over by
the blind eyes of a ruined castle:
this is Chinchón.
December a week away,
the place is half deserted.
The square that can be converted
into a bullring or a theatre
awaits the arrival of actors
to perform the piece by Lope de Vega
promised on the playbills.
We sit in the bar of the parador
in the midst of a floral display
on blue tiles, over a drink
that creates a circle of warmth
in the growing chill
and is also called Chinchón.
Aniseed. Anise is
what these dry fields feed,
with its yellowish-white small flowers
and liquorish-flavoured seed:
we are drinking the distillation
of Spain – a certain pungency
which is not unsweet, like the heat
and tang in the Spanish aspirate.
The sky looks down on our departure
through each one of the blind eyes
of the castle. The car
is a lost beetle in the vast

spreading amplitude of Castile
expanding around us. Snowflakes
over the far Guadarrama
feel for the mountain spine
that reaches to the heights like a line
of surf suddenly breaking on the peaks. Below,
burning stubble in the fields
is turning the twilight blue
and losing the thread of the road we are on,
Chinchón lamplit behind us, Chinchón gone.

November in Aranjuez

for Ricardo Jesús Sola Buil

Trunks stand ankle-deep in leaves.
    Immense, each leaf has the proportions
Of a discarded broken fan. The court
    Came here in summer to escape the heat,
Did not stay long enough perhaps
    To greet the fallen foliage, their ears
Alert to the underfoot snap and splash,
    The crackle of autumn. The park is haunted
By the ghosts of their intentions. Colonnades,
    Paths, perspectives, squares, the palace
Is the place, its fountains still play on,
    And the season cannot cease flattering the statues
Radiant in the astonishment of an autumn sun.

Santiago de Compostela

Granite is the stone
in church and fishmarket –
except for the marble
where fish lie glittering:
the strong woman

who rules this place
wrestles a live conger
out of its tub:
we watch it snake
slippery in her grip –
she lets it writhe until
we have looked our fill,
then aims it back
waterwards and next draws out
(trawling a lower depth
on the scale of being)
a lamprey, all circular mouth
and inevitable eye:
it challenges her grasp,
seeing and seizing
a dead fish from her slab
in a single swoop
with that primordial sucker,
accurate as Iago
killer of Moors,
ancient as granite.

The Portuguese Ox

was led by a woman –
a hand on each horn:
she, stepping backwards,
encouraged its advance,
her man between plough shafts
setting the course
where the rye had failed
and maize must grow now:
they stopped to talk
to us strangers at the granite wall and
with a loquacious pride
told over their possessions –
two tractors, a car, the land:
the beast stood there
like an interested listener,

patiently translating
inside its ox's brain
what was being said –
rather like me, as I
tried to penetrate their sibilant Portuguese:
it loomed in a silhouette
that resembled the statue of an ox,
but not for long, and when
it must move on once again
took up the tenor of its advance
in contrary motion, a slow
music, step by step
fading across that field
whose half-light hid
a terrain of scattered stones
autumn would submerge in grain.

Lessons

1   On a Picture of Burslem by Leonard Brammer

He was that quiet man who taught us art –
Or rather left us to ourselves to learn.
I copied mannequins from Chirico
Hoping for recognition. Was it despair
Drove him to ignore his herd of boys?
'The self-taught man' – and that was us –
'Is taught by a very ignorant person.'
Constable said that. I saw it then,
As he issued sheets of paper, kept his peace.
There was no secret he would teach me
Although he knew them. Look at this thirties view.
It took me years to see that Stoke-on-Trent
Offered a theme for words. The waste, flat ground
Stretches behind roofs and bottle ovens,
And seems a lake beneath such pallid light,
All are on foot, the car not yet arrived.
He was a Lowry, not a Chirico man.
I'd traced the outlines and that didn't please him –

If only he had shown me how to draw.
This forgery of silhouettes was all he saw
And warned the class against, much to my shame,
Though being a decent, gentle sort of man
Blamed only 'someone', never spoke my name.

2   *The Fruits of Ignominy*

'An ignominious failure, Tomlinson.'
An ignominious teacher was my thought.
I bit it back and lowering my head
Accepted the rebuke, as I'd been taught.
If they could teach me that, why couldn't he
Teach me arithmetic? What he had said
He aimed from the doorway coming in,
An actor with a nervous audience:
Brandishing the sheets of their exam,
He trod the boards and taught me what I am:
Words were the sole abstractions I could use –
Words like *ignominious*, words and shapes
And what I could not grasp I might transfuse
Into lines and colours. I can now reclaim
Neither his cast of features nor his name.

3   *The Bicycle*

'You'll never ride a bike,' my father said.
He was the instructor – and at swimming too:
I never mastered that. A boy I knew
Took my cycling seriously in hand
And if my breast-stroke had been left to him
I have no doubt I would have learned to swim.
It was the bike that opened up those spaces
Beyond the smoking confines of the town,
Found me what swimming never would have shown –
George Eliot's Staffordshire and Wordsworth's north,
Though north was north of Leek, the Roaches there
(The rocks it meant), Rudyard was Windermere:
And if you could not make it to the spot,
You could relocate the place it was not:

I moved the Brontë parsonage further south
And Heathcliff roamed the moorlands far from Haworth.
Praise to the bicycle, transport of the muse:
It brought the only news that always stayed news.

4   In Memory of Agnes Beverley Burton

I did not learn to draw until that lady
(Not easy to please) saw my incompetence
At sketching trees and, 'Simplify,' she said,
'Follow only the leading lines of things,'
And commandeered my hand to imitate
A cluster of boughs, then sped it on
To face another jutting ganglion
Where both eye and trunk were made to feel
The presence of a directed force, taught me to see
The heaves of structure up the entire tree
And plot its course from roots to summit
In whatever season, where the branches
Hung simplified by winter, simplified by leaves.

5   To Nora Christabel Pennet

Benign aunt, sister to the above –
The idiom of epitaphs cannot catch
Her gentleness or her gentility:
She did not force my hand, but led me through
Landscapes of Ancient China, bound in silk:
A new space opened under a new light,
Though 'Pine Scent in the Clarity of Snow'
Taught me, not how to draw, but how to write.
Spent twenty years out East and then kept shop
In the provinces, painted when she could
Those curling roofs round courtyards and the fens
Of Lincolnshire. In *Modern German Art*,
A gift outright – her last – and not a loan,
Ernst's 'Bride of the Wind' distracted me
Back to the brush, the vagaries of chance:
She had hinted a new poise, a way to dance.

The boy on the sick-bed, now the man who writes,
Gazes – he lacks the strength to stare –
Out of the window through the rain-soaked air
Tinged by the smoke and by a fringe of fire
Where the steel-mills were and are no longer.
He asks his mother to draw what she can see,
She picks up the pencil he has thrown aside,
Narrows her eyes in taking steady hold
And draws the serried chimneys on the roofs,
Each with its jagged terracotta crown –
All the regality he will ever own
And lose before he finds the place again
And letting fall the pencil, takes up the pen.

The Photograph

in memoriam Edwin Albert Raybould

All these men are dead. One of them I knew.
From the silhouette of a blackened pithead
They eye the camera we cannot see –
Collar-and-tie men from the offices –
Brylcreemed hair, bunches of hands on laps –,
Miners in mufflers and with caps as flat
And comfortable as their Midland 'a's.
The one I knew? Sixth from the left and standing.
His history: Passchendaele, Ypres, the Mons Star,
The wounds he kept concealed to get the job
In a hard time – now fireman down this pit,
The one who lights the fuses and breaks through
Into untouched seams waiting for the pick.
Slagheaps, already greening-over, rise
Like a range of hills, faint figures there
Bend down to glean the fragments of those coals
Which, blown into a glimmer, then a glow,
Will feed their fires. It was the camera
And not the man behind it sought them out,

As unregarded as the shrapnel wounds
The fireman hid. He smiles and keeps his peace,
His good leg braced to move once poses cease.

Little Eve and the Miners

Little Eve looks through the slatted gate
To watch from her garden the miners pass.
They, leaning over and peering down in,
Offer her apples from their snappin' tin.

Returning apple-less at the end of shift,
In blackface and with startling eyes, they pass
The garden, abandoned by little Eve now,
To bath on their hearth before the coals' heaped glow.

In '35

There was that pub at Cobridge
whose landlord, a Blackshirt though a pleasant man,
followed the local usage
and allowed the children of his customers
to wait for them in the kitchen.
I remember the cheese on the table there.
I didn't touch it because of the mites
whose activity fascinated and repelled me.
Not once did I see the landlord in his uniform –
perhaps he owned none. Mosley
visited the place – the place not the pub –
but was never elected here. The populace
were soberer than that leader urging them
to put on their blackshirts, and to march in step
instead of downing their drinks at the bar,
their children warm before the backroom fire.

I Was a Child

when I played Tasmania
in the Empire Day pageant:
that was May twenty-fourth – Victoria's
birthday, another age in fact
and the old queen's head
still reigned on half the currency:
as I climbed up to the stage
robed and shoeless,
a splinter from the floor
penetrated my naked foot as keen
as a Tasmanian arrow.

Aubade

Those dawn flutes from *Daphnis and Chloë*
   Made me get up to see one day
Whether the dawn was like that and the way
   Hills above the city looked as smoke
Came drifting up through half-light,
   Meeting red embers from the lower sky:
Out there, far from Illyria,
   Cold dew, condensing on the grass,
Soon found me out, and sodden knees
   Woke me, a trousered boy, to where I was,
Above the steelworks and the dawning line
   Of the canal by Wedgwood's factory,
The spot the boy in him had called Etruria.

Seasons

      With the change of light
New forms of shade invade the house:
The window-frame, cut out in black,
   Lies beside the sun on surfaces

Not seen before – the walls that we had come
    To take for granted, as the unchanging shape
Of home. Why does this repetition
    Return out of the sky each year
As manna falling, dew upon the sense,
    Renewal of the place one finds it in?
The year is repeating itself afresh:
    It seems that we are nearing now
The roadstead of Cythera, and hear
    The music of our sailing and arrival
In a major key. We shall not harbour there,
    But take only time enough to breathe
The perfume of the lime-trees flowering where
    They meet the ocean odour in a mingled scent
Of home-coming and departure. What is that shade
    Spreading through the water – stain or shoal?
We feel the waves repeating themselves beneath us,
    Like the palpitation of light within that window
We left behind, before the spring went down
    Under oceanic summer, into tidal year.

In the Valley

Walking west, I could no longer find
    The spot the sun set only yesterday.
A cloud already shut the valley in,
    But darker than the cloud, its shadow
Spread across the valley floor
    In leisurely inundation. You could sense
Above the moving mass the solar force
    By the dark that went on rising
Round the sombre columns of the trunks
    Between sward and sky. My eye
Combed the shoreline of this flood
    But the shore fell sheer towards
The endlessly advancing tide. The trees,
    Already dense with summer, rooted
In that country of the blind, rose to where
    A light withheld that knew and yet

Would not reveal the secret of their green.
   Lethe rose beneath the layered leaves:
I thought of the murk of Dis, of lava-flow,
   But this was one of mercy's moments:
Lightly I trod between the shadowed earth
   And the unseen horizon, entering
A cool as of water. The drift
   Of a universe, rehearsing its own end,
Stood at a pause, in a present
   Brimmed with unexhausted time
Between the hidden sun and the awaiting dark.

Tree Talk

occurs when two
tortuous branches grind
one against the other and emit
as they rock in air
not cradling coos
but a lament of all you lose
in life's constrictions
like a wounded violin
a slow and comfortless
adagio scaling
higher and higher in a thin
scream of ultimate
rejection, of final
disaffection at
all that conspires
to plant thorn on thorn
in the yielding flesh
of innocence betrayed:
it goes on
penetrating bonewards
(where is the greensward now?)
in a way that only music can
as it quits all keys
and gasping in atonality
refuses to return

to the home note
or float dreamwards
on the drowsing stream of
a fawn's afternoon:
Venus is not here:
only the divine
marquis offering you the whip
as a hand-up on
the intersection of two
untuned almost twigs
that even in their twiggery know
that as the wind goes down they
must shut up.

Dragonflies

Dragonflies
flock to this garden
like swallows in autumn
(it is high summer):
such glamour
in predation, scissor-jawed
and single-minded,
they radar their way
past obstacles,
flying in formation,
pilots who are their own craft,
speed their sole stratagem:
cold that means death to them
makes them begin
to disappear just as the dark
comes cooling in.

Swifts

Swifts do not sing:
what they do well
is sleep on the wing
moving always higher and higher
in their almost entirely
aerial existence, alighting
only to nest, lay eggs,
rear their young and then
back to the airways
to teach them there
the art of high-speed darting
with narrow swept-back wings
and streamlined bodies:
when swifts descend
they cannot perch, they cling
by hook-shaped toes
to walls and so crawl
into sheltered cavities, into gaps
in eaves and church towers
where they can nest. Summer visitors
they seem always about to leave
and when they finally do
scream in their hundreds
that the time is now,
that the south awaits,
that he who procrastinates
has only the cold to explore
for those succulent insects
who are no longer there.

In Autumn

Moon rose, a clear
crescent. At dawn
a deer came down the slope
in fugitive distinctness

and the sun caught
the glimmer of gossamers
draping a wet bush. Where
is the hare bound
that parts the grasses? –
he is caution's creature
unlike the pheasant horde,
birds so tame
they must be kicked
off the ground into the air
to ignite the stone-
cold heart of the hunter
beside the artificial lake where
the passing moon
is pausing to inspect itself.

In January

After dark weeks of rain, the world
   Seems shut round on itself, itselves:
There is a secrecy, a veiling back that you
   Will never penetrate although you hear
A hundred voices tell it, far and near –
   Rain on the roof, wind in the leafless tree –
Or catch the sound that two streams make
   In moving across the territory
They divide between them before meeting.
   The slant rain, the receding light,
The closing-in of fields gone grey
   Beneath shadowless trees, refuse the blame
We would attach to them by robbing with a name
   The completeness of the nameless presence here:
'Miserable' – we try to make it fit,
   But weather washes our lament away
With a susurration that does not even scorn
   Our refusal of the encounter: our grain
Of misery waiting to sprout and spread
   Is not of the kin of twilight or the steady rain.

The Rain Is Over

The rain is over, the sky
has fallen in bright blue pieces:
you can no more pick them up
than before they fell
becoming sky-shards,
segments, a sliver
bisecting the road
with its shining chasm
which you straddle,
look into and see the way
the crowns of tree after leafless tree
have come down with it
crowding this narrow sky-pond
like underwater vegetation:
threads of what went on overhead
catch at the eye
wherever you gaze on ground,
each seam of light,
each bright stitch
a reminder of that perfection
before the heavens fell
which now – night coming on –
lie holding the stars.

Jaws

of cloud dispute
the sky of late afternoon,
the going sun suspended
before it drops behind the horizon
and leaves darkness to debate
whether these predatory shapes
are there still hanging in the black air
as the cold bright stars of Sagittarius
climb glittering and disclose
the prospect of their voyages, an invitation
to a freshly minted moon

to edge its way
towards the galaxy
until it stands mid-sky to show
the place where that unmappable murk
hung below and now not one
of those drifting saurians remains
beneath the high clear chart
stretched between earth and zenith.

Across the Dark

With so much sound below the silence, we
    Are left to make out what we cannot see –
That sonorous cavity between hollowed banks
    Where the current comes rushing through,
Advancing melodiously beneath the cry
    Of vigilant owls. They answer one another,
Deepening distance with their calls
    And – menace and music in a single note –
Fence round their little empires with the sound.
    Under it all, the tones of water tell
The distances that it has travelled through
    Where water, tonguing its song from stones,
Asks speech of us to measure and re-murmur
    Those fluid shapes that now besiege the ear
Sluicing past us, chiselling a way,
    To arrive, through limestone, time, palpable here.

Westminster Bridge from the Eye

written to be read in the Globe Theatre

What is a sonnet? 'Take these fourteen lines
Of *Paradise Lost*,' Wordsworth told a friend –
(A gathering music with no rhymes to end
Each line) 'The image of a sphere or dewdrop,
An orbicular body,' he went on.

This sonnet – globe within The Globe – is one
Way to double the sonnet circle. Take
The Eye also. From its orbicular cabins
You see Westminster Bridge extend as he
Never saw it – the same bridge with its view
Where ships, towers, domes, theatres lie below,
And now that clambering disparity –
Corbusier's children quarrelling for the sky –
In a paradise lost that Wordsworth did not know.

In the Wind

This animal hold,
bodily pull
against gravitation,
against the vertical, this
obstruction I lean into and swim,
this same force overhead
is unlayering with ease,
peeling apart
dark continents of cloud,
getting down to sun,
then letting it filter and flood
the sky I am wading towards,
out of which its vast breath
is prying apart the ties
in this middle place
of tiles, trees, chimneys
between the abyss above us
and the abyss below, the snapped boughs
barring my way as I crackle through.

Returning

My long-legged shadow
pointing east
measures out the sundown
across half a field:
I have become
a phantom giant and my home
as I approach it
seems unsure of me
and shrinks
as if to contain its threatened fire.
I turn
in the direction of the going sun –
it has suddenly gone
and the whole scene
grown dark and vast
in my wake, swallowing
the scale of my magnification
in a single quenching shade
that puts out all
including horizon
and my own tall shadow.
I turn again
to that glowing smallness
and I cross
the remainder of the field between us,
entering its jewel to become
my own right size
by the habitable light
inside the domestic diamond,
a Gulliver gratified.

In the Mirror

Angled towards the window,
the mirror sees things I cannot see –
even brings indoors to me
lost landscapes, vignettes
of cattle browsing beneath trees
that could have been painted.

'Why do you', she asks,
'keep looking at yourself?'
I am not 'looking at myself' I explain
'I am looking at a train
that has just entered the picture
in the silent distance.'

I can see time
through the mirror
by the town clock, but in reverse,
as if a curse
had been put on it
to travel only towards yesterday.

And now the train has disappeared.
Where have the cattle gone?
Of all the herd
only one to be seen –
a black shape in soliloquy
on a deserted green.

Gazing here,
Narcissus would have failed
to examine his own image,
letting his grimace stare
out of a dead centre –
margins are where true happenings are.

A Rose from Fronteira

Head of a rose:
above the vase
a gaze widening –
hardly a face, and yet
the warmth has brought it forth
out of itself,
with all its folds, flakes, layers
gathered towards the world
beyond the window,
as bright as features,
as directed as a look:
rose, reader
of the book
of light.

Return to Valestrieri

What draws the mind
back to that place must be
things like the courtesy
of the man who, eyeing us strangers,
said: Have you seen our Roman bridge?
We saw it, crossed it, climbed
the far hillside to where
before a solitary house
a woman hovered
craving conversation and
launched into a lament –
her son – a mariner – had left her here,
he loved the place, but she
had no one to gratify
her need for daily talk. In the town itself
a forgetful population
had left for years the declaration
painted on a wall
in tall neat capitals:
It is an honour to serve fascism.

Mandarinas

Ten hours on a bus
(four more to go) and then
orange sellers climb aboard,
their high feminine voices
bringing refreshment with the cry
Mandarinas, mandarinas –
voices of such a pitch
as you never hear elsewhere
cutting through the air,
more instrument than blade,
reaching their top C
with utmost ease. Cortez
travelled that way possessed
by one last ambition – to be
Marquis of Oaxaca. Who
would not settle without rank or rancour
just to hear voices of orange sellers
as now we retrace his ground and theirs
in memory, miles and years away
in a land where no orange trees
flower from the temperate green and no
oranges grow to be gathered into sound?

November

The freeze sets in:
frost is returning
at three in the afternoon:
a seam of ore
opens at the valley head
under a single cloud. Kenner is dead –
the man who knew, saw, told
and clarified our seeing
privileged by his own:
requiescat in pace.

Morning

When we open the curtains,
will it be white or wet?
Will it (remembered) blaze back at us,
or shall we then forget

the grey irresolution
of rain against frost,
the distances melted away
and the far view lost

to a closed-in glance
across sweating flagstones,
catching what little light there is,
what wine-dark tones?

The choice is not ours to make,
so we await the chance
of weather's looming, loosening
in its long advance

up the valley reaches
and straight at our panes,
not to be predicted, contradicted:
let us draw back the curtains.

Frost

The sky is blank with a single vapour trail
   Warmed by a sunset we cannot see:
The coming freeze is hurrying it away,
   But listen: owls are shaping out the spaces
With their map of sounds. Sparks of stars
   Pierce through where darkness deepens,
Sharp with an undiluted light. Tomorrow we shall wake
   At the crackle of first footsteps grinding white.

On Snow

Low light is raking the entire field
   This winter afternoon. Sundown soon
Will alter the tone of snow from violet
   Where the shadow crosses it, to a smoky blue:
As they lengthen out, running together,
   So feather-fine those shadows seem:
The snow-light, trapped beneath them,
   Turns their texture to a smouldering glow
That threatens flame which a thickened gloom
   Slowly extinguishes. Overhead, a moonbow
Shares sky with Venus, while below
   The eyes through half-dark can decipher –
Cut into the surface in keen line –
   The pheasant's foot as a perfect arrow.

Resemblances

Woodland creaks like the cordage of a ship,
Spar over spar, rigged with fraying ropes –
The stems of creepers tautening, as boughs
Dip and release themselves from the wind's grip.
Intersecting, grinding on one another,
They groan above us as they bring to birth
Yet more resemblances. But let them be.
Enough that those battle sounds arrive
Inland with the smell of sea that is the real sea.

In a Glass of Water

Cheap jewels flash
up from the inside of a glass
which I am draining –
the glints and splinters
of a room, the green
exit sign and the red
bandanna round a woman's head –
such a horde of pinpoints
the eye is left confused
by pulsating water that transmits
the hand's hesitations as
liquid disappearing towards one
leaves a glass that is drained.

Vessel

I place water
in a glass pitcher
on the evening table
at the centre of the meal:
the stream outside
flashes back
late afternoon light:
water within the pitcher
rocks a little, prisoner
of glass and restive perhaps
to be what it once was
in full flow and not
this filled roundness,
now shaped and stilled.
But summon no Ondine
to embellish the thought,
pour out and drink
the caught coolness
that breathes here. Beyond the window,
in the high perfection

of a February night sky,
a winter moon has risen,
summoner of waters, filler of pitchers.
Below its slim sickle
travel the tones of the stream
that fed this still vessel
reflecting wine, fruit and bread.

The Holy Man

In at the gate
A tramp comes sidling up:
'I called before,' – it's now eight –
'But you were still sleeping.' He smiles
Like an actor who is perfectly sure
His audience will approve of him, offers
To tell us his story in exchange
For provision (the word is his) and lists
Tea, milk, candles and ointment:
'I have been bitten by mosquitoes –
I bless them. They give only a love bite.
Did you see the moon last night? –
I blessed that too. Did you see its halo?'
I see the love bites on his wrists.
Beard, missing teeth, chapped hands.
'The Lord told me four years ago
To take up a wandering life. I made a vow
Of celibacy then, and I have broken it
Only once. That was in Limerick.
Now I am headed from Devon to the Hebrides.
The voice of the Lord is a strange sound
Both inside and out. I shall only know
When I arrive where it is he wishes me to go.'
He pauses, provision slung across one shoulder:
'I've blessed the stream that crosses your garden' –
With this elate sidelong affirmation,
Departing he leaves behind him an unshut gate.

Inheritance

What I was seeking was a mulberry tree,
    To draw the crinkled edges of its leaves
And catch the serpentine sprawled shape
    The trunk twists into through the years.
It was autumn – too late for berries now.
    And then that lady said to me –
I scarcely knew her – 'I have a mulberry tree.
    The gardener will show you where.' Her stretch
Of Gloucestershire I'd never visited. It lay
    Riverwards beyond the interminable highway,
Among farms and cottages, lost England
    Still communing with itself across the clay
That Saxon ploughs first broke. The house
    Stood on a hill, a buttressed church
Almost in its garden. Now I have been
    And seen, the first thing I recall
Is not the mulberry dome of yellow leaves,
    But the woodland walk beyond it:
When the house was at its height, the guests,
    Shaded by parasols and foliage, would climb
On a zig-zag pathway up the hill
    And in the summit summer-house confront
Over flatland fields that thrived
    Under the salt encroachment of the tide,
A foreshore of two hundred acres.
    The summer-house has gone, a single chair
Stares out at space. As you descend
    You see how that tide of woodland brought an end
To shape and form here, and the ornamental yews
    Must lose themselves to spindly neighbours,
Where a medlar grafted to a thorn
    May well outlast the mulberry tree
If once the undergrowth were cleared.
    Our gardener guide has more for us to see:
The superannuated ice-house, the pond
    Where once the carriages were driven in
To be cleansed of mud. A rootstore
    Remains there still, where root crops
Having been harvested, now lie

In the cool beneath a roof of earth
Packed tight above a roof of tile,
    And, all around, the half-kempt gardens
Once there were hands enough to tame.
    And, beyond these, the house itself
Stands where a house has always stood
    Throughout centuries. We reach
That chapel of the buttressed church
    Whose memorials confront us, slow our steps
And silently explain too much:
    Three stones, three sons, the war –
That duty done, another must be paid
    To parsimonious England craving coin:
Beyond inheritance, how should the dead
    Argue against a levy on that death
They did not grudge? Inside the walls,
    The mulberry tree has watched it all:
The generations tasting at that tree
    Could scarcely have foreseen this dereliction.
I draw the intricate foliage leaf by leaf
    Under the cloudy seashore in the sky
That echoes the tide beneath it, where
    The estuary waters slowly slide
Lacking all sea-like definition to the sea.

Nocturne

Midnight on lay-bys
and the great lorries, their drivers
like householders gone to bed –
doors locked, lights out
in a domestic darkness. Do they dream
of the road ahead, of route maps
to impassable towns whose medieval streets
narrowing, grip their sides and
grind them into stasis? They sleep sound
unconscious of our headlights
gone by, raking their windows, revealing
vast silent containers

freighted with cars
that, lodged on top of each other,
seem to have fallen asleep
copulating.

The Way Back

That night we returned late.
The high moon stood centre sky.
The traffic of the journey out
had disappeared to resurrect above the Marches
as the sparkle of stars.
We were no longer breathing
the chemical odour of congestion:
the way lay straight ahead
– until issuing at a turn
(was it the wrong one?) we
saw suddenly great yellow shapes
of construction lorries
moving beside us, accompanied
by men on foot with long brooms
with which to and fro
they smoothed the tarmac the vehicles
kept defecating. We were clearly trapped
between moving metal and falling filth and then
one of those foot soldiers
seemed to be bowing, indicating
a wooden obstruction, a fence
with an exit in it leading
once more along the route
we had been trusting to and eagerly
through we went, to rejoin mankind who
(though they had not yet re-emerged)
tomorrow would populate the entire highway.

And so they built it:
had it been water
you could have watched all day.
Its advantage is the ability
to flow uphill, filling supine valleys
and distant doorways
with voices they had refused to hear
that now bring them news of where they are –
not in place but time. Hill-top and valley
share the same locus now
brimming with identical sounds.
At the descent
the tarmac gives back an audible cataract
of tyre treads and changing gears
whose density vaporized, drifting
without limit you could not mistake
for water music. Though the present
has learned to flow without pause
it is no surface to contemplate all day
nor with headlight eyes through the dark.

A Ballad of Iole and Dryope

after Ovid

As we walked by the water, my sister and I,
We were plucking the flowers that grew in the way,
As fresh as the spring and the child that she fed
Whose wandering eyes their colours delighted.
A tree rose before us, close to the shore:
A lotus it seemed from the blossoms it bore,
And her hand was already stretched out to the stem
And snapping off stalks as she gathered them.
What I saw, and she did not, was blood from each wound
Drop from the blossoms and sully the ground,
And a tremor passed through that shook the whole tree

(So the tale may be true that taught us to see
Lotis the nymph flee Priapus's flame
And change to this plant that still carries her name).
Astonished, Dryope drew back from the blood,
Yet paused there to plead with the nymphs of the flood,
'Forgive my unknowing and cleanse me of sin',
Half-turned with her child, and yet could not begin
To break from the spot and to run to the wood:
Already her limbs, taking root where she stood,
Had started the changes that she must pass through
As she felt the encroachment of bark from below
Spread stealthily upwards, possess without haste
The freedom to move in her loins and her waist,
Until the sole motion her body still knows
Comes from above, but comes to confuse:
Trembling, her hands reach up to her hair –
Leaves rustle against her fingertips there.
In the mind of the child that was still at her breast
Came a sense of the hardness against which it pressed,
And loss of that moisture its mouth vainly sought
Brought a new lack into wakening thought.
We'd come here with garlands, and all for the sake
Of the powers that rule in the depths of the lake,
But fate has undone us and darkened their mood:
They lurk underwater in silent ingratitude.
What could I do, merely destined to see
The bole that was body transformed to a tree,
To rescue Dryope and set her limbs free?
I tried by embracing to hold back the growth
And longed for the bark to envelop us both.
Her husband and father, aroused by her cries,
Emerged to behold how her branches arise;
They printed their kisses against the harsh rind,
Embracing her roots as they knelt on the ground,
Repeated her name, as if that might still free
The woman not yet disappeared in the tree:
Until it was only her face that now kept
A human resemblance where bark had not crept.
With tears now bedewing the leaves she had grown
She struggled to speak before all words were gone.
'Before I am changed into merely a thing,
Let my innocence tell how my sufferings spring
From the gods' own indifference, not from my deed,

For my will was asleep in what my hands did.
If this be untrue, let all my leaves fade
And axes cut back all my boughs and their shade,
And fire crackle through the ruin they've made.
But take down my son from these branches my arms
And find him a nurse to soothe the child's qualms;
Let him often be brought where these branches are spread
And here let him play and here let him be fed.
Teach him, when words are beginning, to say
"It is my mother lies lost in this tree."
Let him master my name and pronounce it with tears,
Let him, when later in woods he appears,
Beware of the pools there and think that he sees
A goddess concealed in each one of the trees
And spare every blossom that grows from the bough.
Husband, sister and father, adieu to you now.
But if in your hearts there is love for me still,
Secure me from cattle, protect my boughs well
Against billhook and blade. Take my final adieu,
And since my stiff form cannot bend to kiss you,
Reach up to my lips and lift me my son,
To receive my last kiss, while kiss I still can.
But the bark as it spreads is sealing my lips,
And over my lily-white neck the rind creeps.
My head lost in shades, let none touch my eyes –
To close them the bark of itself will suffice.'
Then both speech and being the same moment cease.
On the trunk the glow of the human still warmed,
And so ends the Tale of Dryope Transformed.

An Ovidian Ballad

A woman sits beside the path –
you glimpse her half a field away –
swathed in sackcloth like the loose
entanglement of a grey burnous:
her hand is raised, her fingers spread
to hold up the weight of a brooding head
which though unseen is surely there
as proved by the tension of that hand

stretched to support or to withstand
the working of its hidden thought,
until you start to move and see
in the whole apparition a broken tree
as details falter and disappear:
this sudden metamorphosis
seems as stark as the seated figure
awaiting you like a fortune teller
bent at her crystal: level now
you watch her melt away as she
turns into that truncated tree
she always was and again must be.

Eden

There was no Eden
in the beginning:

the great beasts
taller than trees
stalked their prey through glades
where the pathos of distance
had no share in the life of vegetation:

there was no eye
to catch the rain-hung grass,
the elation of sky
or earth's incalculable invitation:

and when it came, that garden,
who was it raised the wall
enclosing it in the promise
of a place not to be lost,
guarded by winged sentries
taller than trees,
of an apple not to be eaten
and the cost if it were?

It was man
made Eden.

Index of Titles

708   NEW COLLECTED POEMS

Index of First Lines

NEW COLLECTED POEMS

NEW COLLECTED POEMS